D1391268

# Scottish Women

# Scottish Women

*A documentary history, 1780–1914*

Edited by

ESTHER BREITENBACH, LINDA FLEMING,
S. KARLY KEHOE AND LESLEY ORR

EDINBURGH
University Press

© editorial matter and organisation Esther Breitenbach, Linda Fleming,
S. Karly Kehoe and Lesley Orr, 2013

Edinburgh University Press Ltd
22 George Square, Edinburgh EH8 9LF
www.euppublishing.com

Typeset in 10.5/12.5 Adobe Garamond Pro by
Servis Filmsetting Ltd, Stockport, Cheshire, and
printed and bound in Great Britain by
CPI Group (UK) Ltd, Croydon CR0 4YY

A CIP record for this book is available from the British Library

ISBN 978 0 7486 4016 4 (hardback)
ISBN 978 0 7486 8340 6 (webready PDF)
ISBN 978 0 7486 8341 3 (epub)

# Contents

# Acknowledgements

We are very grateful to the following for permission to reproduce extracts from documents: Bishop Alexander Smith, 'A Notre Mère', by permission of Sr M. Anthony, Franciscan Sisters; Donald Maxwell Macdonald (Maxwell of Pollok Archive); Archibald Stirling (Stirling of Keir papers); 'Amhran Jaspar' by Janet MacKenzie, by permission of Maggie Smith, Kinloch Historical Society; Journal of Margaret Hinshelwood (NLS Acc. 12149), by kind permission of Ms Sally Harrower; Letter of Margaret McDonald (NLS Acc. 7024), by kind permission of Mrs Nancy B. Mackenzie; Medical journal of Lady Clementina Malcolm (NLS Acc. 9756), Memoir of Ann Anderson (NLS Acc. 11468), Letter from Christian Oliver (NLS Acc. 111000), Letters from Margaret Anderson (NLS Acc. 13107), Isabella Plumb papers (NLS Acc. 12680), by kind permission of the Trustees of the National Library of Scotland; Indictments against Annie Wilkie and Alice Robertson (Mu. Add. f50), by permission of University of Glasgow Library, Special Collections; Aberdeen City Libraries; Aberdeen University Library Special Collections; Birlinn; Duke University Press; Dundee University Archives; Edinburgh Labour; Edinburgh Museums; Edinburgh South Liberal Democrats; Glasgow City Archives; Glasgow University Library; Keeper of the Scottish Catholic Archives; NHS Greater Glasgow and Clyde Archives; St Andrews University Special Collections; Scottish Conservatives; Scottish Liberal Democrats; Shetland Archives and Angus Johnson for transcription of the manuscript from Bruce of Sumburgh papers (SA: D8/400/16).

The authors have made all reasonable efforts to trace the copyright holders for the following extracts to no avail, and therefore we include these for publication according to Fair Use under Copyright: letter from May McNicol, and journal of Jane Blackwood Mack.

We should like to thank the staff at the following libraries and archives for all the assistance they have given us: Aberdeen City Libraries, Aberdeen University Special Collections, City of Edinburgh Central Library, Dumfries Archives Centre, Dundee Public Libraries, Dundee University Archives, Edinburgh Museums, Edinburgh University (New College Library), Edinburgh University Library (Centre for Research Collections), Franciscan Sisters of the Immaculate

Conception, Glasgow City Archives, Glasgow University Archives Services, Glasgow Caledonian University Archives, Glasgow University Library Special Collections, Lothian Health Services Archive, Mitchell Library Glasgow Room, National Archives of Scotland, NHS Greater Glasgow and Clyde Archives, National Library of Scotland, Scottish Catholic Archives, and the Scottish Jewish Archives Centre.

In particular, we should like to thank the following: Sr M. Anthony, Kenneth Baxter, Maria Castrillo, Harvey Kaplan, Andrew Nicoll, Graham Roberts, Pat Whatley, and the Archive Team at Glasgow City Archives.

We would particularly like to thank Lynn Abrams, Rose Pipes and Siân Reynolds for all the advice, support and encouragement they offered as advisers to this project.

We should like also to thank the following for advice, support, suggestions on sources, reading drafts, and generally offering encouragement: Chrisma Bould, Catriona Burness, Tanya Cheadle, Aileen Christianson, Helen Clark, Gayle Davis, David Finkelstein, Elspeth King, Louise Jackson, Sue John, Caroline Lewis, Alison McCall, Cathlin McCaulay, Jane McDermid, Bill McLoughlin, Jim MacPherson, Eilidh Macrae, Donald Meek, Hazel Morrison, Stana Nenadic, Elizabeth Ritchie, Louise Settle, Domhnall Uilleam Siubhart, Fiona Skillen, Darren Tierney, and Ian Watson. Thanks are due also to Dr Norman Watson for giving us permission to reproduce as part of the cover design postcards from his personal collection, and to Rebecca Mackenzie of Edinburgh University Press for her work on the cover design.

Special thanks go to Anne Macleod Hill for her translations into English of 'Òran le Anna Ghobh air dhi dol chun fhògharaich Ghalld' and 'Òran 's i san sgoil am Peart'.

Thanks are also due to Women's History Scotland for financial support for costs of illustrations.

Many thanks also to John Watson at Edinburgh University Press for his advice, encouragement and patience.

# Abbreviations

| | |
|---|---|
| ALU | Aberdeen Ladies' Union |
| BWTA (SCU) | British Women's Temperance Association (Scottish Christian Union) |
| GCA | Glasgow City Archives |
| GCUA | Glasgow Caledonian University Archives |
| GUAS | Glasgow University Archives Services |
| GULSC | Glasgow University Library Special Collections |
| ILP | Independent Labour Party |
| NAS | National Archives of Scotland |
| NLS | National Library of Scotland |
| SA | Shetland Archives |
| SCWT | Scottish Council for Women's Trades |
| SJAC | Scottish Jewish Archives Centre |
| UFC | United Free Church |
| WLA | Women's Liberal Association |
| WSPU | Women's Social and Political Union |

# Readers' Guide

## 1. Authorship of extracts

Almost all the extracts in this book were authored by Scots, most of them by women. In our definition of 'Scottish' women, we have followed the practice adopted by the editors of the *Biographical Dictionary of Scottish Women*: 'to be included an individual should have been born in Scotland; *or* have lived in Scotland for an appreciable period; *or* have influenced some aspect of Scottish national life'. There is a small number of English authors quoted. Male authors have also been quoted where it has not been possible to identify women writing on particular subjects. Comments on authorship are included in introductions to extracts.

## 2. Biographical information about authors

It has not always been possible to find biographical information about authors but, where this is available, dates and some brief biographical details are included, usually on the first occasion an individual is mentioned. A significant number of women quoted or referred to in this volume have entries in the *Biographical Dictionary of Scottish Women*. An entry in the *BDSW* is indicated by the following symbol ‡.

## 3. Organisation of material

The thematic chapters each has a short introduction, and each thematic chapter is further divided into sections. Within each section sources are generally arranged chronologically, though are sometimes grouped thematically, with the mode of organisation being indicated in the introduction to the sources. Where the period referred to in the extract is earlier than the publication date of the text, in the listings at the beginning of each chapter this is indicated by placing dates in square brackets after the publication date.

## 4. Bibliographic information

Each source is introduced with full bibliographic details, and with information about authors and/or provenance. Where the sources are manuscripts or rare books before 1850, catalogue references have been given. Printed material published after 1850 may be found in several archives, and therefore specific information about the location of such material has not usually been given. Page references for extracts are in brackets after the publication details and should be read as referring sequentially to the extracts quoted from the source where applicable. At the end of each chapter is a select bibliography of secondary literature which readers may find useful to consult in conjunction with the primary sources.

There are listed below several resources which help to identify archival sources and secondary literature on Scottish women's history. Readers should note that there may be other resources than these, and that the list is intended to be illustrative only.

- *Women in Scotland: an Annotated Bibliography* (Open University, 1988) remains a useful resource for identifying secondary literature on women's history in Scotland up to 1988, and also lists some primary sources.
- The National Library of Scotland's Scottish Bibliographies Online provides a tool for searching by key words, author, and so on, for secondary literature published since 1988. See www.nls.uk/catalogues/scottish-bibliographies-online
- Dundee University Archive Services have created indexes for their collections by subject, and this includes 'Women'. See www.dundee.ac.uk/archives/sourcetop.htm
- The Women in Scottish History website at the University of Guelph provides an online bibliography of historical works concerning women. See www.womeninscottishhistory.org

## 5. Spelling and accents

All extracts have been transcribed with the aim of reflecting the originals as closely as possible. This includes idiosyncratic spellings, misspellings, typographical and printers' errors in originals. Given the frequency of these in some extracts, we have not included '[*sic*]' to indicate that we are following the original: readers should assume that the extract is faithful to the original even in reproducing errors. Similarly, we have followed original usage in the placing of accents in Gaelic texts; the originals varied in their practice, as do the texts here.

# Figures

# Chapter 1

# Introduction

The part played by women in Scottish political, economic, social and cultural life has been the focus of historical research for several decades, and the volume of work in this field continues to grow. As elsewhere in Britain, the women's movement, which emerged in the late 1960s and early 1970s, facilitated the emergence of feminist historical scholarship, with works on Scottish women's history beginning to appear from the 1980s onwards.[1] There were, of course, prior to this period historians who had demonstrated an interest in women's lives,[2] while various schools of historical writing have shed light on women's lives without necessarily having a primary focus on either women or gender relations as such. It is, however, the work inspired by late twentieth-century feminism that has shaped the key debates, definitions and terms of analysis of women's and gender history. This volume of extracts from primary source documents has arisen from our participation in Women's History Scotland,[3] and builds on our own work on women's and gender history. It complements *Gender in Scottish History* (2006) and the *Biographical Dictionary of Scottish Women* (2006),[4] and we hope that, as an additional tool for students and researchers, it will also stimulate further research. As others have noted, there is a distinction to be made between women's history and gender history:[5] the former may be broadly characterised as focusing on the nature of women's lives and role in society and aiming to put women 'in the picture'; the latter focuses on the negotiation of gender roles, the contested nature of gender relations, and the social construction of gendered identities. Despite controversies among feminist scholars on the relative value of these different approaches, they need not be seen as mutually exclusive, rather as forming complementary and overlapping areas of study. This volume, a 'documentary' history of Scottish women, perhaps falls more readily into the category of women's history than gender history, though the sources selected for inclusion permit many different usages by historians.

The period covered in this volume, the 'long nineteenth century', defined here as 1780 to 1914,[6] has perhaps been the most favoured by historians of women in Scotland, though there have also been developments in women's history in the medieval and early modern periods, and in the twentieth century.[7] The scholarship of recent decades has broken new ground in our understanding of the nature of women's lives in Scotland, and has challenged widely held assumptions about the nature of gender roles, their degree of rigidity and, in particular, the idea of women's confinement to domesticity and motherhood so beloved of the purveyors of Victorian domestic ideology. Indeed, the desire to challenge this ideological construction by demonstrating the presence of women in economic, political and public life was the fundamental impulse initially driving women's history in Scotland, and this is reflected in the variable attention that has been paid to other aspects of women's lives. The economic, social and cultural transformations of the long nineteenth century were all gendered in some way: for example, in the ways in which gender divisions of labour were shaped or the ways in which gender power relations manifested themselves in institutional and associational life. Women were active participants in these transformations, if not necessarily equal ones; as yet, our knowledge of the part they played remains incomplete.

### Women's bodies

Taking as our starting point women's experiences as embodied individuals, with physical and sexual lives, it is notable that this remains an under-researched area outside investigations with a medical focus. There is little research on how women approached the maintenance of their health, how they dealt with the typical events of female physiology – from menstruation to childbirth – or how they reacted to illness and treatments for physical and for mental conditions. In particular, finding women's own voices and testimonies in this sphere has often proved challenging. There are, of course, hospital and other institutional and statistical records that give information about typical patterns of infant and maternal mortality, life expectancy, incidence of diseases and so on. To date, much of what has been written on what might be broadly termed 'women's health' issues in nineteenth-century Scotland has tended to focus on health professions and the changing positions of women and men within these. New 'scientific' knowledge about women's bodies informing medical practice in obstetrics and gynaecology was very much a male preserve, and this 'science' itself served to construct ideas of female and male roles.[8] The consolidation of the professional status of male doctors marginalised female and working-class practitioners of traditional methods of healing and homeopathy. While men may have laid claim to scientific knowledge and progress in this period, women were not wholly absent from scientific study as Yeo has indicated, pointing out that this is an area in which further research is much needed. By the late nineteenth century, women had established themselves within medical and related professions, though their roles remained constrained and conditioned by gender inequalities and the ideology of woman as 'helpmeet' of man.

There were books on women's physiology and health, and books of guidance for married women. These, however, tended to be written by men, often doctors or professors of medicine.[9] Furthermore, there were certain aspects of physical experience, particularly those dealing with sex, that were not talked about in respectable society and where guidance given was often in euphemistic terms or in a language that contemporary historians must make an effort to decode. Within the sphere of sexual experience, it is particularly hard to come by any direct testimonies from women; one reason why the Madeleine Smith‡ case is so fascinating is the implication, albeit in euphemism, that the unmarried Madeleine had a sexual relationship with her doomed lover, Emile l'Angelier.[10]

For married women multiple pregnancies and frequent childbirth were the common experience. Furthermore, pregnancy among single women was also a common enough occurrence, though its incidence varied a great deal across Scotland.[11] Both the toll taken on married women by childbearing and the stigma of illegitimacy for unmarried mothers must have given incentives to women to seek remedies against pregnancy or methods of getting rid of the baby (and, indeed, kirk session records and court cases testify to this, albeit inevitably only in circumstances where the attempts were unsuccessful). This was likely to have involved a combination of methods communicated by midwives, folk remedies and treatments, and quack medicines that were widely advertised in newspapers. Demographers have noted declining fertility in the later nineteenth century, beginning among the middle classes and later being observable among the working classes. To what extent there was active practice of contraception has been, however, a matter of historical debate. Debbie Kemmer's study of declining fertility among the Edinburgh middle classes in the late nineteenth century has argued that abstinence from sexual intercourse is the most convincing explanation for this.[12]

Women's sexuality was often deemed to be threatening, a force that must be controlled whether by the activities of the kirk session, or by legal means. As Mitchison and Leneman have argued, 'The Scottish Church in the early modern period displayed extreme distaste for physical intimacy between the sexes', and this legacy continued to make itself felt in later centuries: 'In the nineteenth century the middle class held to a puritanical outlook on sexual matters, and regarded extra-marital sexual activity as the clearest indicator of the moral state of society'.[13] Such views underpinned various philanthropic endeavours, and informed discourses concerning responses to social change and social problems. Middle-class women do not appear to have been any more forgiving than their male counterparts of women who were 'debased' by their sexual appetites, and perhaps were less so, given that they had some sense of the male double standards at work, as is evidenced by debates around the regulation of prostitution.[14] Middle-class women did not always adhere to the moral standards in which they professed to believe, however. Cases where this might have come to light, such as Madeleine Smith's sexual liaison, appear few and were apt to provoke scandal. While it is impossible to get at the range of sexual practices that might have characterised nineteenth-century life, popular broadsides, scandal sheets and pornographic writing may be indicative both of different sexual orientations and diverse sexual practices.

### Women at home

It has been a central aim of feminist historians to challenge the view that Victorian 'domestic ideology' reflected the real lives and experiences of women. Thus, such public arenas as the world of waged work, politics, protest and associational life have been a dominant focus within their work. Indeed, reaction to the view that the study of women's history must lie in the scrutiny of family life has meant that, until recently, this area of investigation has been relatively neglected in Scottish women's history,[15] although studies of Scotland's changing demography have provided many insights about patterns of family formation, fertility and so on.[16] As Gordon has argued, despite the frequently articulated ideas about gender roles within the family, appropriate behaviour for wives, and so on, there was often a blurring of gender boundaries of authority and function, depending on particular family circumstances and the nature of economic contributions within the family.[17] In many parts of Scotland women made a contribution to the family economy through earning wages, household production and 'self-provisioning'. At the same time, there was not the complete separation of home and work that has often been assumed. This was true not just of subsistence farming communities but held for other classes, such as small retailers operating from their homes and professionals such as general practitioners and pharmacists. Nor was there a rigid division between work and family life for those engaged in business; entertaining business associates at home was part and parcel of Victorian life, and marriages often consolidated links between families that did business together, or facilitated the retention or accumulation of property and wealth. In working-class communities extended family networks often provided support in hard times, or help with childcare, as well as a focus for socialising. Strongly bonded communities and support networks were also characteristic of migrant and immigrant groups. In sum, the idea of the privatised nuclear family, with women at home and men at work, as the prevalent mode of household organisation does not stand up to scrutiny. Women did, however, have a major responsibility for nurturing and rearing children and for household duties. Men's role within the family has been neglected by historians; recent research has undermined the stereotype of the stern and remote Victorian paterfamilias.[18]

While the law reinforced patriarchal power within marriage, permitting marital violence to some degree, by the early nineteenth century brutal husbands were subject to greater censure. Wife-beating was still prevalent, however, and legal penalties sometimes very lenient although women were sometimes in a position to turn to their communities for support in the administration of 'rough justice'.[19] Divorce rates in Scotland were extremely low in the nineteenth century; women as well as men could have recourse to divorce. The divorce rate rose after the passage of the Married Women's Property Act in 1888, which suggests that economic factors had led some women to remain in marriages they would have preferred to escape. From the late eighteenth century the concept of companionate marriage gained ground and it has been argued that this idea changed women's expectations of marriage. There was, however, some variation in forms of marriage, according to class and perhaps locality, because in Scotland, unlike in England, 'irregular' marriage was still valid until 1939.

There were, of course, changing discourses of gender roles and of women's domestic role. Prescriptive literature on how to perform housewifely duties was an endemic feature of the nineteenth century. To what extent the prevalence of such literature was an indication of women's resistance to playing the expected role, or a reflection of how women lived, is not always easy to distinguish but many twentieth-century historians seem to have accepted nineteenth-century prescription as fact instead of the wishful thinking it often was. Women's public role was much more extensive than was previously believed, not just through participation in religious, philanthropic or public life but, as Gordon and Nair have shown, in their participation in social entertainments, in educational and leisure activities, and as consumers in the new urban environments of nineteenth-century Scotland.[20] Thus, even the classically domestic role of household management did not necessarily imply confinement in the home nor sheltered domesticity on which the outside world did not impinge.

One of the most dramatic transformations which took place in nineteenth-century Scotland was rapid urbanisation. As industrialisation shaped local economies in varying ways, it also generated new forms of distribution and consumption: in particular, in response to the growing purchasing power of the middle classes. Urban development and planning failed to develop in tune with the pace of migration to the cities by men and women in search of employment and a better life, resulting in concentrations of slum dwellings in city centres, sanitation problems, and endemic disease, eventually to be tackled by provision of better water supplies, public health regulations and attempts to improve housing conditions. By the mid-nineteenth century, middle-class suburbs of spacious housing were emerging in the larger towns and cities while some elite groups had town and country residences, and often also London residences (notable among aristocratic and political elites), not necessarily all owned but rented for the season.[21] Working-class housing was by contrast often inadequate to the needs of the families it sheltered. At its worst this constituted the multi-occupied single rooms of city-centre tenements where disease, squalor and abuse were rampant. The quality of such housing varied across Scotland, with Glasgow notoriously having the worst reputation. Rural housing was perhaps character-ised by an even greater variation of quality of living conditions, from the castles of the landed gentry to the 'blackhouses' of the Western Isles.

Habits of consumption in nineteenth-century Scotland have been a relatively neglected area of historical research,[22] and the status of women's consumerism in respect of the home merits more attention. The nineteenth century gave birth to a domestic consumerism that was very much a part of the wider economy and had a public profile.[23] This particular consumer culture configured the home as a female-managed space that was outside of the formal productive economy,[24] with a consequent loss of prestige to women's status as housewives and to domestic work itself.[25]

## Women's economic activity

Women and children's labour appears to have played a more important part in the industrial revolution in Scotland than it did in England.[26] Textiles com-prised the most significant sector in the earlier phase of rapid industrialisation of Scotland and became increasingly feminised in the nineteenth century. Until 1842 women and children worked underground in coal mines but, subsequently, heavy labour in the coal-mining, iron and steel industries was to become a male preserve. Until the middle of the nineteenth century, the majority of the Scottish population lived in rural areas and women's labour was as essential to agriculture as it was to fishing.[27] Women's role in agricultural labour was subject to much regional variation though, by the end of the nineteenth century, there was a generally debated problem of shortage of female labour in agriculture.[28] In the later nineteenth century, new forms of employment, including domestic service and shopwork, attracted women away from the land.[29] Indeed, domestic service was an important form of employment for women throughout the nineteenth century and well into the twentieth.

Typically, women were paid less than men and this provided an incentive for employers to use women's labour to undercut men's wages, a source of conten-tion among the working class. Demands for equal pay were articulated in the nineteenth century but were not widely supported by women workers whose circumstances might lead them to privilege family or community solidarity over gender equality or who may themselves have supported the idea of the 'family wage', a wage for the male breadwinner sufficient to support himself, his wife and family.[30] Certainly, this became an aspiration for certain sections of the working class, and a reality for some, if always a minority. It is likely, however, that many married women undertook paid work. Official census data tended to under-represent married women's paid work:[31] evidence concerning the sweated trades and homeworking has indicated that much of this type of work was undertaken by married women.[32]

The extent to which middle-class women were involved in earning a living or otherwise gaining an independent income through inheritance, investment, or renting out property, for example, has been little investigated apart from women's entry into professions. In Victorian Glasgow, for example, a considerable proportion of women, however, were heads of households earning an income by a variety of means.[33] Work on eighteenth-century Edinburgh has indicated the role of women in business and commerce,[34] and it is likely that there were continuities from this earlier period though there has been little research on women in business in the early to mid-nineteenth century. Stana Nenadic's study of small family firms and of garment trades demonstrated that, in the later nineteenth century, not only were women active within these business sectors but many had lifelong careers in business.[35] In 1891, women made up 10 per cent of all commercial employers in Edinburgh and 20 per cent in Glasgow.[36] Typically, women's businesses were in the food and accommodation trades, dress-making and millinery but women were also active in other sectors: for example, in Edinburgh, running lodging houses, stationers, booksellers, and private schools.

The growth of professional opportunities for middle-class women is a better-known story, especially in teaching.[37] For most of the nineteenth century, men comprised the majority of Scottish teachers but, throughout this period, there were also women teachers. The formation of teacher-training institutions in mid-century and regulation of elementary school education by the state from 1872 closed off opportunities for women without formal qualifications but greatly enhanced opportunities for women in teaching generally. This included opportunities for working-class girls through the pupil–teacher system, particularly in Catholic schools which were less well funded than board schools, while the foundation of the first Catholic teacher-training institute in Scotland in 1894, at Dowanhill in Glasgow, led to a better-qualified workforce and greater opportunities for women to enter a respected profession.[38]

Another important area in which women earned a living was that of medicine and health care: as midwives, nurses, doctors and health visitors. Women's traditional role as midwives was both displaced and modified by the encroachment of male doctors who had, by the mid-nineteenth century, consolidated their professional dominance within medical practice.[39] Nursing emerged as the first female profession,[40] while women campaigned to be admitted to medical schools. Edinburgh University was a particular focus of lobbying: Sophia Jex-Blake‡ and her colleagues' campaigns from 1869 onwards are well known, and women's fight for access to medical training has been well documented.[41] Health visiting and school medical inspections also developed around this time. Women's philanthropic efforts, whether concerned with women's health, women's poverty, or moral risks to girls and young women, paved the way for other areas of professional expertise. The deaconesses of the Church of Scotland were trained nurses or social workers, a significant part of the 'new professionalism of middle-class women'.[42]

## Women, discipline and the law

In earlier centuries the Church's influence was pervasive; the structure of Presbyterian institutions facilitated the surveillance and control of behaviour, particularly sexual behaviour. This was especially punitive in its attitudes towards women, as historians of witchcraft in Scotland have shown, and resulted in a criminalisation of women on a large scale for the first time.[43] Although the witchcraft statute was repealed in 1736, popular belief in witchcraft persisted far beyond this, and there were occasional prosecutions for the crime of pretended witchcraft until well into the twentieth century. While the criminalisation of women as witches largely entrapped older women, younger women were criminalised through prosecution for infanticide. The Church's attempts to control fornication led to a focus on illegitimacy and its censure by the kirk sessions, hence, in turn, a motivation for concealment of pregnancy and infanticide.[44] Child murder could incur a capital penalty until the change of statute in 1809 though, by the late eighteenth century, more lenient attitudes were being exhibited by the courts. After 1809, concealment of pregnancy and the death of the child incurred a maximum penalty of two years' imprisonment. Women accused of concealment and/or infanticide were usually unmarried and often domestic servants. Acts of infanticide could be extremely violent and, as Kilday has suggested, could constitute a type of temporary insanity.[45] Abrams's study of infanticide in Shetland has also focused on the distressed psychological condition of such women.[46]

Nineteenth-century urbanisation brought with it new patterns of crime, significantly gendered, as earlier and later, both in that there were some crimes specific to women and some to men, while crimes committed by either sex exhibited a gender imbalance in which men were far more likely to commit offences. Within cities the female crimes which engendered most debate were those associated with prostitution, about the extent and character of which there was a series of moral panics.[47] Despite Mahood's pioneering work, women's interaction with the law in nineteenth-century Scotland has remained relatively neglected. Ongoing research, however, is now addressing themes such as infanticide, prosecutions of women in local police courts, gender and murder, and prostitution in the late nineteenth and early twentieth centuries.[48] Work on the latter theme indicates the continuing attempts of police forces to restrain and control prostitution and the ways in which women exploited the changing nature of urban life to practise their trade.[49]

Urbanisation also facilitated opportunities for theft and robbery; women were both perpetrators of such crimes and accomplices of men.[50] The increased mobility fostered by industrialisation and urbanisation provoked concerns about vagrancy and about distribution of responsibility for the poor. Civic and political leaders responded by developing systems of policing, eventually put in place across Scotland.[51] They also legislated to regulate criminal behaviour, while new forms of penal institution were developed, as elsewhere in Britain.[52] Another emerging urban concern was juvenile delinquency, addressed by reformatories and industrial schools both for boys and for girls, the latter being established under the Industrial Schools Act 1854.[53] Further Acts on industrial schools and truancy extended the range of interventions designed to reform or protect working-class children. Conceptions of appropriate gender behaviours informed these interventions, managing girls' sexuality more closely than that of boys, although institutions also provided a place of safety for some girls at risk of abuse at home.

In the late eighteenth and early nineteenth centuries, penalties could be extremely harsh, even for minor crimes. In this period, one method of punishment applied throughout Britain was transportation.[54] The majority of women convicts were sentenced for theft, usually as persistent offenders. After serving out their sentences, some were able to overcome past misfortunes and find a family life and means of earning a living within the law.[55] Reform of the law and of the penal system ended transportation and reduced the severity of penalties overall. The Prison Acts of 1835 and 1839 created a new structure for the administration of prisons; new prisons were built, including a General Prison in Perth, housing women as well as men; all prisoners sentenced to nine months or more were taken there. Throughout the nineteenth century, women represented a substantial proportion of the Scottish prison population though the vast majority had short sentences for petty crimes.[56] Typical crimes were petty theft, prostitution-related offences, and offences against public order, such as drunkenness, obscene language, breach of the peace and causing a nuisance. A fundamental factor resulting in women's imprisonment was their poverty.

### Religious life

By the late eighteenth century kirk sessions no longer had the capacity to regulate moral behaviour throughout urban society. Many philanthropic organisations emerging at this time, however, were imbued with much the same belief in the necessity of policing morals and rescuing sinners.[57] The religious beliefs underpinning such philanthropic activity are well illustrated in Magdalene Asylum reports; descriptions of their institutional regimes also illustrate the importance attached to religion as a means of rescue and reform. For all their benevolent aims, these involved strict control and surveillance, and it is plausible to argue that the legacy of the kirk sessions was manifest in such institutional regulations.

Evangelical fervour made its mark in Scotland in the nineteenth century, a period riven with Presbyterian dissension, most notably the Disruption of 1843, over the right of congregations to call their own ministers, and larger questions of religious freedom from state interference. Around the same time, following Roman Catholic emancipation in 1829, there was an expansion of religious communities engaged in social mission and, in 1878, the Scottish Catholic hierarchy was restored. An increasingly complex religious landscape included a growing Catholic Church, three main Presbyterian denominations, many dissenting churches, the Scottish Episcopal Church, and various revivalist groupings and sects. Protestant sectarianism and Orangeism were also distinctive features of lowland urban communities. Jewish congregations were founded in Edinburgh and Glasgow in the early decades of the nineteenth century; as a result of immigration from Eastern Europe, the Jewish population in Scotland had grown to around eight thousand by 1905.

Callum Brown has noted that the sense of 'Christian belonging' in Scotland has been particularly important for women, the majority of church attenders throughout the nineteenth and twentieth centuries.[58] Despite this, much of the history of the nineteenth-century kirk has been gender blind, often focusing on Presbyterian factionalism. The history of religion in Scotland in this period has been dominated by Presbyterianism, the religion embraced by the majority; this volume reflects this tendency. In this period, however, the Roman Catholic Church was to experience a growing membership, largely through immigration from Ireland.[59] By the later nineteenth century, Catholic institutions for women, or involving women, became more common, in particular in the developing Catholic schools.[60] By the end of the century, other faiths, such as Jewish communities, were finding a place in Scotland while a small minority of Scots turned towards Eastern spiritual influences, represented by theosophy and the Baha'i movement. There was also a persistence of folk beliefs, especially perhaps in the Highlands and Islands, such as healing, customs surrounding childbirth, marriage and so on. Such religious affiliations and beliefs merit more research, as do the nature of individuals' private religious and devotional lives which have been overshadowed by institutional histories.

Religious conviction was for some the basis for their choices in life, such as becoming a nun, a missionary, a deaconess, or other form of dedication to a religious life.[61] Women's engagement in the institutional life of the churches was also significant, as members of congregations, Sunday school teachers, fundraisers for foreign and home missions, or as volunteers in outreach and philanthropic work. Their awareness of their role led them to contest the gendered power hierarchies of Church structures, seeking more formal recognition as, for example, the Church of Scotland's creation of deaconesses and the Woman's Guild indicates.[62] Within the Catholic Church sisters and nuns regularly asserted their authority in the realm of education when confronted by male clergy.[63]

## Politics and the public sphere

The idea that, in the nineteenth century, women were excluded from public life has been consistently challenged over several decades by work encompassing women and the Enlightenment, women workers and the labour movement, the women's suffrage movement, and the often parallel public lives of middle-class women and men in the Victorian period.[64] Feminist scholarship has led to reconsideration of what might be defined as 'political', extending this concept beyond the sphere of institutional and party politics, to forms of protest, and activities within the public sphere, such as membership of voluntary societies.[65] While using this broader concept of the political, it is worth noting that women were not wholly absent from political parties and movements even in earlier periods than the nineteenth century. For example, aristocratic women often had explicit political affiliations, and exercised their power of patronage in securing support for those they favoured. Many women were among the supporters of the Jacobite rebellions, and among those, with other members of their families, who suffered as a result. Women also participated in popular protests, as Kenneth Logue, an early adopter of a gender perspective, has shown.[66]

In the Enlightenment period, while there seem to have been no bluestocking circles or women's salons in Scotland, women participated in literary circles and social gatherings where events and ideas were debated. The anti-slavery movement, in which women's involvement became increasingly visible over time, was a feature of Scottish civic life from the late eighteenth century until the late 1860s, focusing firstly on abolition of the slave trade, then on the abolition of slavery in British possessions, and subsequently on the abolition of slavery in the United States.[67] As elsewhere, the anti-slavery movement prepared the ground for the development of the women's movement in Scotland. The temperance movement of the later nineteenth century also attracted much support from women.[68] The women's suffrage campaign, as such, emerged in the late 1860s at the time of the Reform Acts which extended the franchise further but which, despite John Stuart Mill's attempts, did not include women. By the end of the nineteenth century the campaign for women's suffrage had become a mass movement, predominantly middle class but with some working-class support. Earlier movements, such as Owenite socialism and Chartism, attracted working-class women but, generally, it was difficult for them to create durable organisations until the late nineteenth century. They did, however, take part in strikes and protests and joined trade unions, with women's union membership growing rapidly in the late nineteenth century when determined efforts were made across Britain to organise women workers.[69] By the late nineteenth century, too, women were increasingly joining political parties across the political spectrum.

## Emigration and empire

Migration from the country to the towns was one aspect of the mobility of Scots in the nineteenth century; there was also migration south of the border and, most notably, emigration to the United States and across the British Empire. Scottish emigration stands out as particularly high in proportion to its population, greater than for England or Wales, though smaller than for Ireland.[70] Thus, emigration must be counted as one of the major dimensions of nineteenth-century experience. Within this volume, emigration is considered in relation to the British Empire, and thus does not illustrate the American experience.[71] In the earlier part of the century, at least, women were often 'reluctant leavers', emigrating as part of family groups whether as mothers, wives, daughters or sisters,[72] but, by the late nineteenth century, many more unaccompanied women were emigrating to British colonies. This in part reflected the gender imbalance in the population, where there was a 'surplus' of women relative to men, and therefore emigration offered opportunities for employment, marriage, or both. McCarthy has commented that this topic merits more research which might shed light on the extent to which marriage or work was more salient as an explanatory factor in Scottish women's migration.[73]

India, the Caribbean, and dependent colonies in Africa were also destinations for Scots migrants. Among these, many more were likely to have been 'sojourners' rather than settlers, aiming to make a name or fortune abroad and then to return home to Scotland or elsewhere in Britain.[74] As yet there has been little investigation of the role of Scots women in such migrant communities, and the growing literature on Scotland and the British Empire has so far tended to focus on more typically male experiences and career patterns. Yet Scots men making their careers in Empire were often accompanied by wives and daughters, some of whom documented their experiences in letters and journals or published writings about these. A number of women also published accounts of their travels in the Empire (and elsewhere) and their observations on the peoples and cultures they encountered. These included women missionaries, journalists and those who made a name as 'travellers', as such, with accounts of this kind becoming more common in the later nineteenth century as technological changes in transport made long journeys both cheaper and easier.

As yet the burgeoning literature on gender and Empire has made little use of Scots experience or case studies. The sources illustrated in this volume indicate, however, that major themes which have dominated this literature are also relevant to an analysis of Scottish participation in Empire: how colonial rule structured gender relations for colonised peoples; the role of Western women within colonial societies in supporting the Imperial regime or as cultural imperialists; the interconnections between home and Empire.[75] As a group of Imperial 'actors', women missionaries have been a focus of interest for feminist historians;

some Scottish women have been included in this work.[76] It is undoubtedly the case that foreign missions captured the imagination of Scottish middle-class women, and to some extent also of working-class women as the examples of Euphemia Sutherland and Mary Slessor show.[77] Integral to the foreign mission movement was a discourse of women's higher status and equality at home compared to their degradation and subjection to men among colonised peoples. This facilitated the emergence of a racialised world-view which underpinned the rising imperialist enthusiasm of the late nineteenth century. Women in Scotland, as elsewhere in Britain, were among those who shared this enthusiasm, whether as supporters of women's emigration, or as members of the Primrose League or the Victoria League.[78]

### Education, arts, literature

This volume has no dedicated chapter on education, as such, but the theme of education surfaces in many places. It has a wider significance for the study of women and gender in Scotland than women's role in teaching referred to above, and is an area in which an important body of work has developed in Scotland. Early studies by Fewell and Paterson and Helen Corr have been developed greatly in the work of Jane McDermid and Lindy Moore, while leading commentators on Scottish education, such as Robert Anderson and Lindsay Paterson, have also addressed the gender dimension of the Scottish educational landscape.[79] This is not intended to imply that there is no further room for research, and indeed, Moore usefully points out where more work is needed while McDermid's comparative study also throws up further possibilities.[80]

Education is, of course, central to the construction of the current volume: the levels of education which girls and women attained were a key factor in their capacity to produce texts of whatever kind though their social and cultural milieux were also crucial in facilitating self-expression through writing. Class remains the most important determinant of the probability of women writing any form of text but the characteristics of their economic, domestic and cultural lives were also significant in shaping desire and opportunity. Indeed, writing itself was to become a means of earning a living for greater numbers of women as the century advanced. In the earlier part of the century, to earn money as a writer was not seen as entirely respectable for a woman but deemed permissible in certain circumstances: for example, where a widowed woman had little other recourse in order to support her family. Alternatively, women might write anonymously, as still happened in the later nineteenth century: writers such as Isabella Fyvie Mayo‡ and Annie S. Swann‡ published novels under male pseudonyms as well as works under their own names. Earlier in the nineteenth century, it was the convention that articles in periodicals, such as *Blackwood's Magazine* and the *Edinburgh Review*, be published anonymously, whether by male or female authors, and we owe a great debt to the scholarship of indexers of such publications which has enabled us to identify articles by women such as Christian Johnstone.‡[81] There is undoubtedly a lot more writing by women than we know of, some of which it may be possible to identify through further research but of much of which we will regrettably remain ignorant.

As with education, there is no dedicated chapter on women writers or artists. The work of women writers, however, tends to be more accessible than that of other women; they have often been the subject of memoirs, autobiographies, biographies, and critical literary appreciation and histories. Extracts from several well-known women writers are included in this volume but it is their role as social commentators that has determined this selection, and we have not attempted to encompass debates about their literary careers or status or how their work may be read from a gendered or feminist standpoint. With regard to women artists, Janice Helland and Siân Reynolds have already indicated women's involvement in this sphere, and that for some it was a means of earning a living.[82] It seems, however, that women artists writing about their work or art were few and far between. Furthermore, the work of painters, sculptors, jewellers and other craftswomen is best represented visually and understood through analytic tools that reveal artistic qualities and symbolism within the context of artistic production of the time.

## Locating and interpreting sources

This volume covers the 'long' nineteenth century from the late eighteenth century to World War I. The focus on this period is partly a reflection of our interests and expertise and partly a reflection of a period in which Scottish women's history has grown substantially over recent decades. Nonetheless, the work of historians of earlier and later periods suggests that there is plenty of scope for further documentary histories, and we hope that, in future, such collections will emerge. The long nineteenth century was a period in which Scottish society, the Scottish economy, the ways in which people lived and the built environment they inhabited underwent significant transformations. In the process, how women lived was also significantly changed, whether by rapid industrialisation and urbanisation, by the emergence of the professional middle classes, by large-scale migration, and by difficult social conditions. For a documentary source book, the period poses certain challenges, not only its length but also the changing nature of print publications and the press over the century. It has been our aim to provide a selection of source extracts that vary in chronology and therefore give some sense of changes over time. For many topics, however, the availability of sources is much better at the end of the nineteenth century than at the beginning. By the late nineteenth century there had been a massive expansion of newspaper, periodical and book publishing, corresponding with the rise in literacy, and many more women were writing for a public readership.

The thematic scope of the book similarly reflects our research interests though we also moved into areas of research that were new to us; and the ideas of others in Women's History Scotland helped decide its focus. We have aimed to cover areas of importance to the lives of many women, and to draw attention to some which have previously received little attention. Given the limits of a single volume, it is impossible to be comprehensive in coverage; certain aspects of women's lives and experiences have been given only a brief mention, such as their literary, cultural and artistic lives. Nor have we given much coverage to well-documented episodes of nineteenth-century Scotland, such as women's campaigns for entry into higher education and medicine. Rather, we have tried to avoid over-reliance on well-known historical figures because it is relatively easy for readers to find out about their lives. Where it has been hard to identify writing by women about particular issues, or where contributions to debates were crucial, we have quoted extracts from leading figures, such as feminist activists. It has been our aim, however, to illustrate as extensive a range of women's writings as possible, by women from diverse backgrounds, and to move beyond the articulate middle-class women who have already come to the attention of historians.

Our primary aim has been to give voice to women themselves, across the period, across the geography of Scotland, across class and social background, and across different types of sources. This is distinct from providing a range of sources about women: there are many other types of sources which women did not themselves produce but which provide rich insights into women's lives: for example, census data, statistical accounts, government reports, medical archives, court records, wills and testaments, newspaper advertising and articles, handbills, broadsides, ballads, poetry, and visual imagery of many kinds. We do not claim that women's voices are the only voices that offer deep insights into their lives but they add different dimensions and understandings, and are certainly vital as historical evidence. We would suggest, however, that women's voices, as represented in this volume, have not yet been fully incorporated into the writing of Scottish history. To focus on women's voices emphasises their agency, their reactions to events, and how they sought to shape their lives, from the domestic and private to the public and political. Furthermore, it illustrates their frequent interest in other women and how they lived.

The idea of 'women's voices' is, of course, not unproblematic. Indeed, we have not succeeded in making this a collection uniquely of women's voices: for certain themes we thought important to illustrate, we have been able to identify only male commentators while some texts, which purport to have women authors, may have been authored by men. The book contains extracts from many kinds of source material: letters, private papers, journals and diaries, poems, journal and newspaper articles, official records, court records, parliamentary papers, broadsides and ballads, autobiographies, travel accounts, annual reports of organisations, pamphlets and other ephemera. Most such sources were intended for public consumption though identifying what kind of public and how extensive is not necessarily easy, whether in terms of print runs or circulation figures or numbers of readers, nor is it possible often to say much about how publications were received. Some sources were probably completely private in character: personal letters intended for only one recipient, private notes or jottings concerned with household management, or private journals. But, even in the case of letters and journals, it can be hard to judge how wide a circulation was intended. Letters written by emigrants to family and friends at home were likely to have been circulated among a wider circle than their immediate recipients while, within organisational settings such as women's foreign mission societies, numerous copies of letters from women missionaries were often made and circulated to groups of supporters across Scotland. Similarly, diaries and journals may have been written purely as a private record, or have served as a place for meditation and reflection, or expression of spiritual and devotional life. Others were clearly written for a readership of one kind of another, whether as a family history to pass on to children or for publication in the press.

Where possible we have tried to find biographical information about authors of sources, and the *Biographical Dictionary of Scottish Women* has been an invaluable resource. But it has not always been possible to track down information about individuals. Sometimes texts are anonymous, and we have had to speculate about the sex of authors; sometimes texts are pseudonymous, and similarly the sex of the author is a matter for speculation. Furthermore, the widespread practice of anonymous publishing in the earlier decades of the nineteenth century has no doubt served to obscure women writers. While indexes to nineteenth-century periodicals have assisted in identifying articles written by women, there are probably many more articles by women that remain unidentified. By the late nineteenth century, women journalists were named as authors: for example, Marie Imandt and Bessie Maxwell who wrote for D. C. Thomson publications. It appears that D. C. Thomson were early employers of women journalists, and were well aware of their popularity with women readers. Women's contributions to nineteenth-century journalism is thus an area that merits more research.

Most of the texts quoted in this volume represent 'women's voices' either as directly authored texts or in the form of testimonies by women within official reports, such as parliamentary commissions, legal records such as precognitions, witness depositions, or reported speech in newspapers, extracts from letters or minutes quoted in organisational reports written by male authors, and so on. Each of these forms of text is governed by its own codes and conventions, whether the formal legal discourse of the courts, or the selection of quotations for presentational purposes for charitable organisations, or the aim of writing good journalistic copy, all factors that need to be taken into account in offering interpretations. Furthermore, most of the extracts we have quoted are in standard English. There are some divergences from this, such as the misspellings, or contractions, occurring in letters. More importantly, there are some examples of texts in Scots, and some in Gaelic, if regrettably few in number. This results partly from the fact that few literary and cultural sources have been included in this volume but also, with reference to Gaelic sources, from our own linguistic limitations. It is undoubtedly the case that scrutiny of local newspapers would bring to light many more examples of Scots dialect being spoken and written by women, as examples quoted from the *People's Journal* show.[83] But such speech was also sometimes rendered into standard English for the purposes of publication.

The nature of particular topics and women's class status influenced the likelihood of their writing about them. Social class has proved to be the great dividing line here, and it is often difficult to find the voices of working-class women unmediated by others. It is thus particularly working-class experiences that have been filtered through official investigations, criminal proceedings, reports by concerned observers, or writings by middle-class or male sympathisers or allies. Lower levels of literacy will have been one factor contributing to this but hierarchies of status and power were also at work in subduing women's voices. Testimonies of immigrant groups may also be hard to locate, though the voices of Irish women may be discovered in the archives of religious communities which ran parish schools for girls. Women of Scotland's immigrant Jewish community, already sizeable by the later decades of the nineteenth century, seem to have left little record of their own; first-generation migrants were Yiddish-speaking and, though many learned to speak English, very few could read or write in English.[84]

We have also attempted to bring to the attention of readers source material that is perhaps unfamiliar or not easily located. It has become clear in the process of preparing this book, however, that source material is increasingly becoming available in digitised form, and thus decisions based on ease of availability in libraries and archives are becoming less relevant. We have, however, been guided by the criterion that source material should be available to researchers in the United Kingdom, and in Scotland in particular. This has meant either documentary sources within Scottish archives or material available online; we have indicated in the text where sources are available online though we recognise this is not all public access but may require access through institutions that pay subscriptions to publishers. In the longer term, however, it is likely that more source material of this kind will be available in a digitised form for an increasingly wide public. Material from archives situated outside the United Kingdom has not been included but we recognise that there are many sources held in countries to which Scots emigrated, including the United States, Canada, Australia, New Zealand and South Africa, and that there will also be sources in southern Asia and Africa where formerly the British Empire held sway. We have aimed to include material that illustrates experience in different parts of Scotland, and this has included archives outwith the central belt. Inevitably, perhaps, the libraries and archives in Edinburgh and Glasgow were the most used in our research, given our own locations and the location of the National Library and National Archives. There is much to be discovered, however, within local libraries, archives and museums, as well as in privately held papers, and we regard further exploration of these as of great importance.

The process of searching for primary source material has been both challenging and rewarding. The research necessary to familiarise ourselves with the range of sources, and to make selections, has been carried out in our 'spare' time without any funding support. This has imposed limitations on which archives we were able to visit, as well as resulting in a lengthy period of gestation for the collection. The body of historical scholarship on women in Scotland that has emerged since the 1980s has been invaluable in directing our attention to many types of sources that are included here. The rich sources already drawn on in such studies deserve fuller exploitation while there are many more seams yet to be mined. As noted, the *Biographical Dictionary of Scottish Women* has been a much-used handbook in identifying women whose works have provided material for this collection. This project has been a process of continuous discovery and we have often found more source material than we anticipated. Many sources have been encountered by serendipity, turning up gems on one theme when looking for something else, and this has generated some lively correspondence between editors suggesting new sources to include. For some topics we have discovered reams of women's writing yet to be given consideration by historians. Yet, in other areas, the direct testimony of women appears practically non-existent: perhaps, despite our efforts to think of likely locations or forms of expression, we have not yet found the key to this, or perhaps such perspectives really have been lost to history.

The process has also revealed some significant gaps in the literature: some of these have had some coverage but deserve more, while others really stand out as needing investigation. In addressing these, it can be useful to look at what may have been written about other parts of Britain or other countries, as the case may be. While, on the one hand, the Scottish polity in the nineteenth century had distinctive features such as its legal system, religious institutions, and education system, the general trends at work in reconfiguring women's lives were observable elsewhere, whether industrialisation, urbanisation, advances in access to education, changing patterns of consumption, and dominant discourses of gender roles and femininity. The way scholars of English and Irish society, for example, have analysed aspects of women's experience, their thematic frameworks, and their use of sources can all provide models to adapt and also the stimulus to investigate the extent to which there were divergences in Scotland. But, perhaps above all, it is further exploration of evidence at a local level that will reveal most about the lives of women in Scotland in this period: in local archives, local organisations and societies, and local newspapers and publications.[85]

## Structure of the book

The introductory sections above have aimed to provide the historiographical context in which the selections of sources should be understood and to comment generally on the challenges and rewards of searching for women's writings in the archives. The remainder of this introductory chapter consists of brief outlines of each thematic chapter, discussing key themes that extracts address, as well as discussing the types and availability of sources relevant to that theme. As others have found, making selections for a collection of this nature is a challenge: many sources shed light on more than one of our thematic topics and could be placed just as well in one chapter as another. We have had to make decisions based on the overall balance between chapters but have indicated where appropriate that overlapping or related material is contained in another chapter. The order we have chosen for the chapters suggests a movement outwards from the embodied individual through family and work to public actions and their interface with the state and/or institutional life, and finally to the wider public world of politics, the British Empire and movement across international boundaries, but there are in reality no rigid divisions between the thematic areas which have many interconnections.

### Chapter 2: Bodies, Sexuality and Health

The focus of this chapter is on sources that tell us about women's everyday experiences as embodied individuals, about the relationship made between the physical appearance and behaviour of women and their social destinies, and about how the notion that women were prisoners of their reproductive functions affected female opportunities. Across these three themes, sources consist of private papers, letters, diaries, pamphlets, broadsides, periodical and newspaper articles, health records, an advertisement and an example of photography, as well as extracts from published books. These include accounts of women coping with physical and mental illness, advice given to women on issues such as menstruation, childbirth and the menopause, suggestions on sexual relations within marriage as well as warnings about sexual liaisons outside of marriage, discussion of the benefits or otherwise for women of physical and sporting activities, and some aspects of women's lives, such as contraception and abortion, that were deemed especially contentious. Finding women's testimonies and writings in this area has proved demanding, however; some male-authored sources are included where these illuminate typical gendered discourses on the experience of women. Moreover, some sources, which illustrate the rejection of accepted norms of sexual behaviour and which tend to be sensationalist, require careful interpretation.

Debates around appearance and fashion, and physical activities, illustrate dominant discourses of appropriate female behaviour according to social status and class, but also how these were subverted. The dangerous and threatening nature of women's sexuality is a theme also apparent in some sources. Ideas of what was appropriate sexual behaviour for women served to define boundaries between mental health and illness. Similarly, there were debates about whether, or what kinds of, physical exercise were appropriate for women. This was to become a particularly live issue in the late nineteenth century. There was an ongoing debate about whether women should ride bicycles,[86] while women's golfing also came under scrutiny.[87] There was also a Scottish women's football team in the 1880s.[88]

From the sources quoted, we also gain insight into the treatments that were commonly used for ailments, whether specifically female or otherwise. Folk remedies probably continued to be in widespread use and, while evidence is hard to find, there were, no doubt, common practices that were thought to prevent conception or to procure abortion. Certainly, the sale of such products was widely advertised, albeit in euphemistic language, and their efficacy may be doubted as they did not necessarily have a sound scientific basis. While issues around the body, sexuality, physical and mental health are interrelated, and may fruitfully be examined via medical records and writings of medical practitioners, such accounts are likely to reveal more about ill health and alleged malfunctioning of sexuality than about women's everyday lives. This chapter has extended its reach beyond medical discourse, identifying new perspectives in an area as yet little researched. To investigate issues affecting women's consciousness of their own bodies, sexuality and their well-being, and their continuing role in caring for this in respect of the home, a wide net has been cast; sources included intimate both change and continuity in common views of women's bodies, and suggest that this is a rich seam for further research.

### *Chapter 3: Hearth and Home*
This chapter focuses on women's experience within a variety of household roles and living conditions, examining their responsibilities in the home and advice on how these should be approached, the reality of housing conditions in which they lived, and housework and domestic consumption. The sources consist of letters and personal papers on domestic themes or household management and employment of servants, advice on household management, recipes, cleaning tips and so on, published in handbooks or newspapers, descriptions of how people lived in official documents or reports, court records, and poetry. The sources in this chapter include some authored by men: for example, statutory documents, such as poor relief records. Though these were usually written by male officials and produced with the aim of recording facts, the subjective, gendered views of writers undoubtedly emerged. As first-hand accounts, they often take us behind closed doors and provide intimate glimpses, albeit from particular points of view, of otherwise hidden features in everyday home life for many Scots. Some sources

that were created by women within the privacy of homes have survived, generally buried within family papers; unsurprisingly, the provenance of these tends to lie with women of powerful families whose household records have been deemed valuable to archives. Written sources created by working-class women are much rarer but they can be found, for example, in submissions to the popular press.

Fruitful genres for women's writing in this area are popular literature and manuals of household advice. Such texts had been in existence throughout the eighteenth century and even before but, though prescriptive literature does raise questions about the possible gulf that existed between ideology and practice, during the nineteenth century the gendered discourse of woman as homemaker became so pervasive that it hardly required didactic propaganda. Though, historically, instruction books on domesticity tended to include explicit ideological advice alongside household hints, in the nineteenth century they gradually changed to become more practical in orientation.[89] Such magazines were aimed at a female readership; it has been claimed that they rarely originated in 'provincial centres'.[90] Some periodicals, however, were certainly Scottish in their orientation and particularly attractive to a Scottish female readership, if part of a larger British one. The most enduring of such titles is the *People's Friend*, extracts from which are included.

The maintenance of the home was a task assigned primarily to women, varying in degree of difficulty according to economic circumstances. Housework could be hard and unrelenting for working-class women, whether making ends meet for their own families or in domestic service to the middle and upper classes. The household-management role of women responsible for a retinue of servants could also be demanding though such women would also have had control of their time and leisure activities, unlike those who worked under their command. Advice on how to run a home burgeoned with the expansion of print publications and newspapers while the evolving system of education, which came under state control in 1872, came to place greater emphasis on the acquisition of domestic skills for working-class girls.

The chapter also includes source material on servants. The domestic environment was a key site where class relationships between women were negotiated.[91] Discussions on servants were a perennial feature of the periodical and newspaper press: mistresses had difficulty finding servants or complained about their faults; servants voiced grievances over working conditions and mistresses' behaviour. Domestic service remained a major employment sector for Scottish women throughout the century. Among all formally employed women, the 1901 census gives the figure of 24.3 per cent as being employed specifically as domestic help.[92]

Though in this period there were only two major reforms to the law on marriage – on married women's property and on divorce – the ideology of companionate marriage masked a reality that might encompass dissatisfaction and discontent, an unsatisfactory sexual life, domestic violence and abuse. By their nature these experiences are difficult to research but a combination of court records, newspaper coverage of divorce cases, and advice given to women unhappy in their marriages is likely to prove revealing. Happy marriages did, no doubt, also exist though it is harder to find plausible representations of these: perhaps, as Tolstoy wrote, in the opening sentence of *Anna Karenina*, this is because happy families are all alike but unhappy families are each unhappy in their own way.

The sources quoted in this chapter are testament both to the pervasiveness of the discourse of Victorian domestic ideology, with its clear definition of gender roles and feminine duties and virtues in home-making, and to the diverse circumstances in which women actually lived which were often in stark contrast to such idealisations. This serves to confirm the disjuncture that often existed between ideal and reality, and noted by feminist historians. Given the dominance and prevalence of such discourses of female domesticity, however, it can be hard to gauge the extent to which ideal and reality differed: further studies reconstructing the everyday lives of women would perhaps conclusively scotch the myth.

### Chapter 4: Work and Working Conditions

This chapter focuses on women's waged work and business activity, their working conditions and reactions to these. The sources consist of: women workers' testimonies contained in official reports or reported in newspapers; women writing about the working lives of other women, whether in an official role such as factory inspector or as social observers; ephemeral literature on women workers' protests; popular satirical material; journal articles; reports of organisations; trade union publications; advertisements; and legal records. This is one thematic area in which there have been challenges in identifying sources written by women on certain topics. Class status is crucial here, with working-class women tending to be represented as witnesses to official enquiries, or in trade union literature which was sometimes authored by men. Furthermore, within the field of business operations, it is hard to find women writing about their experience as entrepreneurs or as partners in family firms but there is a range of sources that can be used to investigate this experience.[93]

This chapter illustrates the experience of working women across a range of sectors: in mining prior to 1842; textiles; agriculture; fishing; domestic service; middle-class professions; business; and commerce. Women and children were prohibited from working underground after the Act of 1842, and thereafter were excluded from heavier industries. Textiles, significant to the first phase of industrialisation in Scotland, remained an important source of employment for women in several parts of Scotland.[94] As Scotland's economy expanded so did demand for domestic servants, and this was to become increasingly important as a source of employment for working-class women. In rural and coastal areas, women continued to work in agriculture and fishing, as well as in domestic industries that contributed to the household economy. Urban patterns of employment varied across the major cities and included, as well as industrial employment, women's work in business, as entrepreneurs, running shops, boarding houses, and so on, as well as work in the 'sweated trades'.[95]

As far as middle-class women are concerned, it is likely that many more were economically active than has often been allowed, whether as governesses or teachers, earning a living from writing, arts and crafts, running businesses, or taking in lodgers. Certain business and retail sectors in the nineteenth century included significant numbers of women, in particular the clothing trades. Women's entry into the professions is a much better known story and, by the end of the nineteenth century, women had a presence within teaching, medicine and allied professions, and the emerging social work profession, though in some of these areas numbers would have been small. Demographic pressures were among the factors pushing women into employment but the demand for access to the professions was also integral to the campaign for women's political and social rights, as illustrated in Chapter 7. Middle-class women were vocal in demanding such rights and in urging other women to take up professional employment. As opportunities expanded, a place was also provided for middle-class women to take on the role of inspectors or commentators on working conditions more generally, as the examples of Mary Paterson's factory inspections and Margaret Irwin's‡ reports show. Irwin was a key figure here: a prolific producer of reports on the conditions of working women in several sectors; a leading light of the Scottish Council for Women's Trades: and one of the founders of the Scottish Trades Union Congress, and its first secretary.[96]

Trade unionism was, of course, a part of women's experience in the nineteenth century, and there is evidence of women beginning to organise from the 1830s. Gender was, however, a major fault line within the workforce, with employment typically being segregated into women's and men's jobs, and men resisting any encroachment by women into their areas of employment; this was often a tactic of employers to reduce their labour costs. Given women's lower wages, it was harder for them to find the means to organise unions on the friendly society model that prevailed in the earlier decades of the nineteenth century. Protests about wages and conditions or employers' behaviour were often more spontaneous and rumbustious among women workers than among skilled and organised men. By the end of the nineteenth century, expansion of certain types of employment was also accompanied by expansion of the numbers of women in trade unions, particularly following the creation of general, as distinct from craft, unions. Throughout this period, women's union organisation was often separate from men's, and indeed, bodies such as the National Federation of Women Workers played a key role in bringing women into trade unions in the late nineteenth century.

*Chapter 5: Crime and Punishment, Immorality and Reform*

The focus of this chapter is on four main areas: crime and punishment; women in prison; debates on female immorality; and institutionalisation and reform. It illustrates what were seen as typically 'female' crimes, such as infanticide, how women were penalised for their crimes and changing penal regimes, the idea of female immorality, and how philanthropists and the state sought to regulate and control the behaviour of women. The sources consist of court records, newspaper articles and letters to the press, broadsides and ballads, official reports, reports of philanthropic institutions, prison reports, and commentary by social observers. For this theme, it has proved difficult to come by testimonies of women unmediated by others. While women's voices may be heard in court records, such as precognitions or witness statements, they are presented by others and bound by the formal conventions of the law and systems of administration of justice. From a different perspective, accounts of women's crimes or women criminals were presented in newspaper articles and popular broadsides, similarly bound by their own conventions, such as the desire to titillate with sensational or dramatic accounts of women as murderers, their executions, and so on.

Women seldom committed serious crimes such as murder – then as now. Where women were convicted of murder, this appeared to attract much public attention and sensationalist accounts were circulated in popular broadsides. Mary Timney, an account of whose execution is quoted in this chapter, was in 1862 the last woman to be publicly executed in Scotland (the last public hangings of men in Scotland occurred in 1868). Earlier in the century, transportation had sometimes been the penalty for murder but, generally in the case of women, it was for persistent theft. Prison reform changed the nature of confinement, with separation of women from men, and separation of individual prisoners from one another. Labour regimes for women prisoners involved productive, rather than purely punitive, labour but it could be hard, involving long hours and constant surveillance. With the exception of suffragettes, imprisoned for their militant actions, women's testimonies of imprisonment may be impossible to find or may not exist. It has not been easy either to locate testimonies of women as prison visitors or advocates of reform though some sources commenting on women undertaking these roles are quoted.

There is some evidence of the legacy of earlier times in the treatment of women's crimes: for example, the persistence of the influence of kirk sessions in some areas, especially small communities, and the persistence of belief in witchcraft and occasional prosecution of women for 'pretended' witchcraft. Infanticide and crimes associated with prostitution (which was not in itself illegal) remained the main specifically female crimes. While attitudes towards women who committed infanticide became more sympathetic and legal penalties less heavy, the stigma of illegitimacy remained strong within certain social groups and communities, and levels of illegitimacy were regarded by some as a measure of women's morality, though not of men's. Concerns about prostitution were a recurrent theme in public debates in the course of the nineteenth century, with various commentators attempting to quantify it, explain the factors giving rise to increased prostitution, and putting forward proposals for its regulation. These debates included consideration of the economic conditions that led to the rise of prostitution in the nineteenth century; it is apparent that prostitution was often resorted to as a temporary expedient by women in low-waged and insecure employment.

The situation of girls and young women who had infringed the dominant sexual morality of the Church and middle classes became the focus for philanthropic activity from the late eighteenth century onwards, as the establishment of the Edinburgh Magdalene Asylum in 1797 indicates. Institutions of this kind were to become common in nineteenth-century Scotland and persisted throughout the course of the century. A further mode of philanthropic intervention was the development of reformatories designed to deal with juvenile delinquency: these became common after the mid-nineteenth century and included provision for girls as well as boys. Problems of public drunkenness had become a matter of much debate by the late nineteenth century, resulting both in legislation inflicting harsher penalties and the establishment of homes for inebriates, including those for women. Thus, regimes of confinement, which aimed to reform the behaviour of certain categories of women and girls, became more extensive over time.

### *Chapter 6: Religion*

Women's religious life, widely defined, is the focus of this chapter, including religious experiences and devotional life, the place of religion in daily life, women's ministry and mission as expressed in charity, philanthropy, and support for foreign missions, and women's attitudes to church governance. The sources consist of letters, diaries, meditations, memoirs, reminiscences, blessings, hymns and poetry, pamphlets, church periodicals, and newspaper articles. They focus largely on the experience of Presbyterian women but also include sources on Catholic women and other religious faiths and beliefs.

In nineteenth-century Scotland, religion occupied an important place in the lives of many women, particularly those in the upper and middle classes. Regular church attendance was central to the achievement of respectability while many aspects of church activities had an important social function. For some, religious observance was a matter of duty, related to the display of social status, and may not have been accompanied by any deep religious feeling or commitment. For others, however, religious belief underpinned their sense of self and shaped their involvement in charitable, philanthropic and even political causes. Within this chapter, the contribution of religious belief and discipline to the regulation of women's behaviour is less emphasised than in Chapter 5, which indicates how middle-class women believed it was their Christian duty to intervene in and to oversee the lives of working-class women and girls deemed to have strayed from the straight and narrow. Nonetheless, a morality of self-sacrifice and sexual purity is often apparent within both individual and collective expressions of women's religiosity, whatever the context in which it was articulated. This can be seen both as a system of internalised values governing individual behaviour and as a means of policing the behaviour of others.

This is an area in which there is a great volume of relevant source material, given the high levels of church membership throughout the nineteenth century and the pervasiveness of religious discourses both in private and in public writings. Religious periodical literature provides an extensive record of women's interests and activities related to church membership. As with other forms of literature, it may be hard to identify women's authorship of articles in the earlier decades of the century, and it is notable that causes which were run and supported almost entirely by women may have had male office bearers on their committees or leading ministers as their spokespersons. By the later nineteenth century, however, such periodicals came to be edited by women, to have many articles attributed to women, and to contain letters by women missionaries, and so on. They thus provide a commentary on the emergence of women into more public arenas, a parallel process taking place both in religious and in secular life. As well as the more reflective and spiritual dimension of women's religious life represented by the sources quoted in this chapter, female challenges to male authority are also illustrated, from women's preaching to assertion of a more formally recognised role as deaconesses and the strengthening of women's organisations within church structures. By 1914, women were able to celebrate the first ordination, by a Pentecostalist church, of a woman in Scotland.

### *Chapter 7: Protest and Politics*

This chapter focuses on protests and campaigns in which women participated, the claims of right they put forward and the arguments they advanced for these, and their activity within political and public life. The sources consist of official records, newspaper reports, women's writings published in journals and pamphlets, poetry, autobiographical writings, organisational reports, and political party papers. Most sources in this chapter were authored by women; inevitably this privileges the voices of middle-class women though working-class women were clearly participants in protests, and in social and political movements, from the popular protests of the late eighteenth century to Chartism, trade unionism, left-wing political organisations, and the emerging co-operative women's guilds of the late nineteenth century. The sources quoted in this chapter illustrate the range of women's public and political activities, broadly defined, and the diversity of their beliefs. They also illustrate the kinds of activities out of which feminist discourses emerged in the latter half of the nineteenth century, and indicate links over time and to other forms of action and discourse.

For the earlier part of the nineteenth century it has been harder to find women writing about politics or about their involvement in associational life than has been the case later in the century. Women are relatively invisible in associational life in the early decades of the 1800s though they were clearly involved in a range of philanthropic societies within the public sphere. Indeed, as sources such as the Magdalene Asylum reports (see Chapter 5) indicate, women were involved in hands-on management of such institutions and their inmates. Political opinions were perhaps more likely to be expressed in private papers or letters, as Jane Rendall's work has shown.[97] The anti-slavery movement, arising in the late eighteenth century, over time attracted many female supporters with female associations first being formed in Scotland around 1830. In this, Scots women were very much like their English sisters, likewise active in anti-slavery campaigns and missionary societies. The anti-slavery movement was closely interconnected with the women's suffrage movement and wider women's movement of the later nineteenth century, as illustrated by various sources in this chapter. Another dimension of women's involvement in public life was their membership of organisations such as the British Women's Temperance Association (Scottish Christian Union). The temperance movement was not only a popular movement, with both middle- and working-class supporters, but it was also closely linked in Scotland to the women's suffrage movement and the Scottish Women's Liberal Federation.[98]

The emergence of the women's suffrage and wider women's movement in Scotland generated a far broader range of source material. This subject has tended to dominate interest in women's political lives, fuelled perhaps by the desire to establish the precursors of late twentieth-century feminism, and to look for exemplars of women's political agency. This has not only left working-class women's actions in the background but has also neglected women's engagement with party politics and the political debates of their times other than those concerning women's rights. As the sources quoted in this chapter indicate, by the late nineteenth century, women were joining political parties or affiliated organisations across the political spectrum. This was facilitated by changes in party organisation and structures that were responding to the extension of the franchise to some sections of working-class men and also to the women's suffrage movement, even if not all parties were yet committed to women's enfranchisement. After the 1872 Education Act, women could stand for school boards; while they remained a small proportion of the total membership of boards across Scotland, some individual women were prominent board members as well as well-known public figures.[99] Also by the late nineteenth century, while still remaining without the parliamentary franchise, women had the vote at municipal elections and could stand for election to parish councils, as indicated by sources illustrating the careers of women such as Lavinia Malcolm‡ and Agnes Husband.‡

*Chapter 8: Empire Experiences and Perspectives*

The final chapter focuses on several aspects of the experience of Scots women in the British Empire: Scots women as emigrants; accounts of colonial life; women's accounts of travelling in various parts of the empire; and varying perspectives on empire and imperial administration. The sources consist of personal letters, papers and journals, memoirs and autobiographical writings, reports of organisations, travel writing published in the form of books, pamphlets, and newspaper articles, and works commenting on various aspects of colonial societies. Emigration apart, it is only relatively recently that historians of Scotland have turned their attention to Scotland's participation in the British Empire, the experience of Scots abroad and the impact of empire at home.[100] Insofar as this work has been gendered, it is has tended to concentrate more on male careers and masculinity,[101] and it thus offers much scope for research on women's history.

Historians of emigration have noted the greater difficulty in identifying women's testimony about their experiences or their role in decision-making concerning emigration,[102] and this is borne out, for example, by the small number of letters or other texts by women emigrants in comparison to the substantial volume of material by men, whether letters, papers, pamphlets, or handbooks. The extracts from emigrants' letters and journals quoted in this chapter highlight a number of aspects of the emigrant experience. Emigrants' journeys could be long and hazardous, and even though technological change had significantly reduced journey times by the later nineteenth century, voyages to Australia, for example, could still take weeks and entail risks such as illness and death to which young children were particularly vulnerable. Women emigrants were among the pioneers who built the new colonial societies, with a number of the sources quoted providing accounts of how they did so, the kind of houses they lived in, and how their families earned their livelihoods. This included commenting on agricultural work as well as domestic life, the cost of living and the costs of livestock, the differences in climate and farming practices, and so on. Women's role in contributing to the economic management of the household is clearly in evidence here, and this extended to requesting materials from Scotland if they were not easily or cheaply available in the new homelands. Promotion of women's emigration, in which some Scottish organisations or Scottish branches of British organisations participated, had two primary aims: on the one hand, the placing of poor girls and young women in domestic service; and on the other, the maintenance of good British stock in settler colonies, this being aimed at middle-class women. Most women's migration, however, was like that of men, voluntary and supported by individuals themselves or by family networks.

It is perhaps surprising that, in the texts quoted in Chapter 8, women settlers in Canada, Australia and New Zealand made little reference to the indigenous peoples they encountered, often only passing references if at all. Where they do occur, they tend to reflect both racial stereotyping and a certain amount of anxiety and fear. In contrast, commentary about the nature of other peoples was prominent in the accounts of women travellers, women missionaries and women resident in the Caribbean, India and Africa. Several of the texts quoted in this chapter articulate racialised discourses that implied the superiority of the Imperial power and its 'civilising' mission, though there is a spectrum of views, from a liberal and benevolent Christian standpoint to a more explicit racism. As has been argued elsewhere, the continuous circulation of such tropes as the 'degradation' of women in India, or the 'primitive' and 'savage' nature of African societies, in particular through missionary literature of various kinds which became more voluminous and popular in the course of the nineteenth century, contributed to the development of the 'scientific racism' that was central to the age of high Imperialism.[103] It is notable, however, that supporters of foreign missions from the early decades of the nineteenth century placed great emphasis on the benefits of female education, insisting that this was essential to improving women's status. The anti-slavery movement, too, was the site of benevolent but racialised discourses. Writings about the position of enslaved women also spoke of their 'degradation', and women activists denounced plantation slavery for denying family life to women. Nonetheless, it tended to be only in the context of anti-slavery writings or writings about women in India that critiques of Imperial governance were voiced.

The accounts of travels quoted in this chapter were published in a variety of forms, and intended for different readerships with different aims. The women whose writings are quoted were mostly resident in colonial territories for part of their lives, sometimes accompanying their husbands, or working there, as in the case of missionary Isabella Plumb, while one of the journals quoted was written by a woman accompanying her sea captain husband on a voyage. The women journalists' 'Round the World Tour' funded by D. C. Thomson of Dundee appears to have been unique as a Scottish journalistic enterprise, and is of particular interest, not just in its depictions of the peoples and societies encountered but in its stress on connections between Dundee, Scotland and Empire, and its offering of practical advice to would-be emigrants.[104] Indeed, what these sources testify to, as do emigrants' letters and journals, missionary letters and literature, is the degree of mobility which characterised the lives of many women in the nineteenth century, their maintenance of connections with the homeland, and their place in networks stretching across and beyond the Empire.

## Notes

1. For example, Glasgow Women's Studies Group, *Uncharted Lives: Extracts from Scottish Women's Experiences, 1850–1982* (Glasgow: Pressgang, 1983); Siân Reynolds, *Britannica's Typesetters: Women Compositors in Edwardian Edinburgh* (Edinburgh: Edinburgh University Press, 1989); Eleanor Gordon and Esther

Breitenbach (eds), *The World is Ill-Divided: Women's Work in Scotland in the Nineteenth and Early Twentieth Centuries* (Edinburgh: Edinburgh University Press, 1990); Linda Mahood, *The Magdalenes: Prostitution in the Nineteenth Century* (London: Routledge, 1990); Eleanor Gordon, *Women and the Labour Movement in Scotland, 1850–1914* (Oxford: Clarendon Press, 1991); Esther Breitenbach and Eleanor Gordon (eds), *Out of Bounds: Women in Scottish Society 1800–1945* (Edinburgh: Edinburgh University Press, 1992).

2. See Catriona Macdonald, 'Gender and Nationhood in Modern Scottish Historiography', in T. M. Devine and Jenny Wormald (eds), *The Oxford Handbook of Modern Scottish History* (Oxford: Oxford University Press, 2012), pp. 602–19.

3. Women's History Scotland was founded as the Scottish Women's History Network in 1995 and became Women's History Scotland in 2004. WHS is a membership organisation which, among other things, promotes research into all areas of women's history. See www.womenshistoryscotland.org/

4. Lynn Abrams, Eleanor Gordon, Deborah Simonton and Eileen Janes Yeo (eds), *Gender in Scottish History since 1700* (Edinburgh: Edinburgh University Press, 2006); Elizabeth Ewan, Sue Innes, Siân Reynolds and Rose Pipes (eds), *The Biographical Dictionary of Scottish Women* (Edinburgh: Edinburgh University Press, 2006).

5. See, for example, discussion by Lynn Abrams, 'Introduction: Gendering the Agenda', in Abrams et al, *Gender in Scottish History*, pp. 1–16.

6. We have included three sources that lie outside our period of 1780–1914: one from the 1760s, one from the 1770s, and one from 1915–16.

7. See, for example, Elizabeth Ewan and Maureen M. Meikle (eds), *Women in Scotland: c.1100–c.1750* (East Linton: Tuckwell Press, 1999) for the earlier period. There are numerous articles and books that cover some parts of the twentieth century but, as yet, no general overview of Scottish women's history in the twentieth century.

8. Eileen Janes Yeo, 'Medicine, Science and the Body', in Abrams et al., *Gender and Scottish History*, pp. 140–69.

9. Debbie Kemmer, 'Occupational Expansion, Fertility Decline and Recruitment to the Professions in Scotland 1850–1914' (unpublished PhD thesis, University of Edinburgh, 1989).

10. Eleanor Gordon and Gwyneth Nair, *Murder and Morality in Victorian Britain: the story of Madeleine Smith* (Manchester: Manchester University Press, 2009).

11. Michael Anderson and D. J. Morse, 'The People', in W. Hamish Fraser and R. J. Morris (eds), *People and Society in Scotland*, Vol. 2, pp. 8–45.

12. Kemmer, 'Occupational Expansion'.

13. Rosalind Mitchison and Leah Leneman, *Sexuality and Social Control: Scotland, 1660–1780* (Oxford: Basil Blackwell, 1989), p. 9.

14. Mahood, *The Magdalenes*.

15. Eleanor Gordon, 'The Family', in Abrams et al., *Gender in Scottish History*, pp. 235–67.

16. See, for example, Michael Anderson, 'Population and Family Life', in A. Dickson and J. H. Treble (eds), *People and Society in Scotland*, Vol. 3 (Edinburgh: John Donald, 1992), pp. 12-47.

17. Gordon, 'The Family'.
18. Lynn Abrams, '"There was nobody like my Daddy": fathers, the family and the marginalisation of men in modern Scotland', in *Scottish Historical Review*, 78: 2 (1999), pp. 219–42.
19. Anna Clark, *The Struggle for the Breeches: Gender and the Making of the British Working Class* (London: Rivers Oram Press, 1995); Annmarie Hughes, 'The "Non-Criminal" Class: Wife-beating in Scotland (*c.*1800–1949), *Crime, Histoire & Societies/Crime, History & Societies*, Vol. 14, No. 2 (2010), pp. 31–54.
20. Eleanor Gordon and Gwyneth Nair, *Public Lives: Women, Family and Society in Victorian Britain* (New Haven, CT and London: Yale University Press, 2003).
21. See, for example, Gordon and Nair's depiction of the frequent changes of residence and mix of rented and owned accommodation in use by the Smith family, in *Murder and Morality*.
22. See W. Hamish Fraser, 'Necessities in the Nineteenth Century', in Trevor Griffiths and Graeme Morton (eds), *A History of Everyday Life in Scotland, 1800 to 1900* (Edinburgh: Edinburgh University Press, 2010), pp. 60–88.
23. Judy Giles, *The Parlour and the Suburb: Domestic Identities, Class, Femininity and Modernity* (Oxford: Berg, 2004).
24. Lynn Abrams, *The Making of Modern Woman: Europe 1789–1918* (London: Longman, 2002), pp. 128–37; Deborah Simonton, *A History of European Women's Work: 1700 to the Present* (London: Routledge, 1998).
25. See, for example, Ann Oakley, *Housewife* (London: Allen and Unwin, 1974) and *The Sociology of Housework* (London: Robertson, 1974).
26. Christopher Whatley, *The Industrial Revolution in Scotland* (Cambridge: Cambridge University Press, 1997).
27. Deborah Simonton, 'Work, Trade and Commerce', in Abrams et al., *Gender in Scottish History*, pp. 199–234. See also, for an example of a community dependent on fishing, Lynn Abrams, *Myth and Materiality in a Woman's World: Shetland 1800–2000* (Manchester: Manchester University Press, 2004).
28. T. M. Devine, 'Women workers, 1850–1914', in T. M. Devine (ed.), *Farm Servants and Labour in Lowland Scotland 1770–1914* (Edinburgh: John Donald, 1984), pp. 98–123.
29. Lynn Jamieson, 'Rural and Urban Women in Domestic Service', in Gordon and Breitenbach, *The World is Ill-Divided*, pp. 136–57.
30. See, for example, Gordon, *Women and the Labour Movement*; Reynolds, *Britannica's Typesetters*.
31. Gordon, *Women and the Labour Movement*.
32. Alice Albert, 'Fit Work for Women: Sweated Home-workers in Glasgow, c. 1875–1914', in Gordon and Breitenbach, *The World is Ill-Divided*, pp. 158–77.
33. Gordon and Nair, *Public Lives*.
34. Elizabeth Sanderson, *Women and Work in Eighteenth Century Edinburgh* (London: Macmillan Press, 1996).
35. Stana Nenadic, 'The Small Family Firm in Victorian Britain', in *Business History*, Vol. 35, Issue 4 (1993), pp. 86–114; and 'The Social Shaping of Business Behaviour

in the Nineteenth-Century Women's Garment Trades', in *Journal of Social History*, Vol. 31, No. 3 (spring, 1998), pp. 625–45.

36. Nenadic, 'Social Shaping of Business Behaviour'.

37. Lindy Moore, 'Education and Learning', in Abrams et al., *Gender in Scottish History*, pp. 111–39; Jane McDermid, *The Schooling of Girls in Britain and Ireland, 1800–1900* (Abingdon: Routledge, 2012).

38. McDermid, *Schooling of Girls*; S. Karly Kehoe, *Creating a Scottish Church: Catholicism, Gender and Ethnicity in Nineteenth-century Scotland* (Manchester: Manchester University Press, 2010).

39. Yeo, 'Medicine, Science and the Body'; Lindsay Reid, *Midwifery in Scotland: A History* (Erskine: Scottish History Press, 2011).

40. Olive Checkland, *Philanthropy in Victorian Scotland: Social Welfare and the Voluntary Principle* (Edinburgh: John Donald, 1980).

41. See Yeo, 'Medicine, Science and the Body', and the citations on this topic listed by Yeo on p. 164, fn. 35.

42. Checkland, *Philanthropy in Victorian Scotland*, p. 88.

43. Christina Larner, *Enemies of God: The Witch-hunt in Scotland* (Baltimore: Johns Hopkins University Press, 1981); Julian Goodare (ed.), *The Scottish Witch-hunt in Context* (Manchester: Manchester University Press, 2002).

44. See Mitchison and Leneman, *Sexuality and Social Control*; Anne-Marie Kilday, 'Maternal Monsters: Murdering Mothers in South-West Scotland, 1715–1815', in Yvonne Brown and Rona Ferguson (eds), *Twisted Sisters: Women, Crime and Deviance in Scotland since 1400* (East Linton: Tuckwell Press, 2002), pp. 156–79.

45. Kilday, 'Maternal Monsters'.

46. Lynn Abrams, 'From Demon to Victim: The Infanticidal Mother in Shetland, 1699–1899', in Brown and Ferguson, *Twisted Sisters*, pp. 180–203.

47. Mahood, *The Magdalenes*.

48. We are grateful to Louise Jackson for drawing our attention to this research. See also the Institute of Historical Research 'Theses online' at www.history.ac.uk/history-online/theses/thesis/in-progress

49. Louise Settle, 'The Geography of Prostitution in Edinburgh, 1900–1939', *Journal of Scottish Historical Studies* (forthcoming, 2013); doctoral research on 'Controlling the Social Evil: Prostitution in Glasgow and Edinburgh, 1892–1939'.

50. Deborah Symonds, *Notorious Murders, Black Lanterns, and Moveable Goods: Transformation of Edinburgh's Underworld in the Early Nineteenth Century* (Akron, Ohio: University of Akron Press, 2006).

51. Kit Carson and Hilary Idzikowska, 'The Social Production of Scottish Policing 1795–1900', in Douglas Hay and Francis Snyder (eds), *Policing and Prosecution in Britain 1750–1850* (Oxford: Clarendon Press, 1989), pp. 267–97.

52. Russell P. Dobash and Pat McLaughlin, 'The Punishment of Women in Nineteenth-Century Scotland: Prisons and Inebriate Institutions', in Breitenbach and Gordon, *Out of Bounds*, pp. 65–94.

53. Linda Mahood, *Policing Gender, Class and Family in Britain, 1850–1940* (London: Routledge, 1995).

54. Ian Donnachie, 'Scottish Criminals and Transportation to Australia, 1786–1852', in *Scottish Economic and Social History*, Vol. 4 (1984), pp. 21–38.

55. In her study, *Abandoned Women: Scottish Convicts Exiled Beyond the Seas* (Sydney: Allen and Unwin, 2012), Lucy Frost tracked the lives of Scottish women convicts shipped on the *Atwick* in 1837. Using archives both in Scotland and in Tasmania, she has been able to construct narratives of the lives of convict women, and to investigate what happened after they had served their sentences.

56. Dobash and McLaughlin, 'The Punishment of Women'.

57. Checkland, *Philanthropy in Victorian Scotland*.

58. Callum G. Brown, 'Religion', in Abrams et al., *Gender in Scottish History*, pp. 84–110.

59. S. Karly Kehoe, 'Unionism, Nationalism and the Scottish Catholic Periphery', *Britain and the World*, 4:1 (2011), pp. 65-83.

60. See Kehoe, *Creating a Scottish Church*; Jane McDermid, *The Schooling of Working-Class Girls in Victorian Scotland: Gender, Education and Identity* (London: Routledge, 2005).

61. Lesley Orr Macdonald, *A Unique and Glorious Mission: Women and Presbyterianism in Scotland* (Edinburgh: John Donald, 2000); Kehoe, *Creating a Scottish Church*.

62. Orr Macdonald, *Unique and Glorious Mission*.

63. S. Karly Kehoe, 'Irish Migrants and Recruitment of Catholic Sisters to Glasgow, 1847–1878', in Frank Ferguson and James McConnell (eds), *Ireland and Scotland in the Nineteenth Century* (Dublin: Four Courts, 2009), pp. 35–47.

64. Gordon, *Women and the Labour Movement*; Gordon and Nair, *Public Lives*; Reynolds, *Britannica's Typesetters*; Jane Rendall, '"Women that would plague me with rational conversation": aspiring women and Scottish Whigs, c.1790–1830', in S Knott and B Taylor (eds), *Feminism and the Enlightenment* (London: Palgrave, 2005), pp. 326–47; Elspeth King, *Scottish Women's Suffrage Movement* (Glasgow: People's Palace Museum, 1978; Elspeth King, 'The Scottish Women's Suffrage Movement', in Breitenbach and Gordon, *Out of Bounds*, pp. 121–50; Leah Leneman, *A Guid Cause: The Women's Suffrage Movement in Scotland* (Edinburgh: Mercat Press, 1995).

65. Sue Innes and Jane Rendall, 'Women, Gender and Politics', in Abrams et al., *Gender in Scottish History*, pp. 43–83.

66. Kenneth J. Logue, *Popular Disturbances in Scotland, 1780–1815* (Edinburgh: John Donald, 1979).

67. C. Duncan Rice, *The Scots Abolitionists* (Louisiana: Louisiana State University Press, 1981); Iain Whyte, *Scotland and the Abolition of Black Slavery, 1756–1838* (Edinburgh: Edinburgh University Press, 2006); Clare Midgley, *Women Against Slavery: the British Campaign, 1780–1870* (London: Routledge, 1992).

68. Megan Smitley, *The Feminine Public Sphere: Middle-class Women in Civic Life in Scotland, c.1870–1914* (Manchester: Manchester University Press, 2009); Mahood, *The Magdalenes*; Kenneth Boyd, *Scottish Church Attitudes to Sex, Marriage and the Family* (Edinburgh: John Donald, 1980).

69. Gordon, *Women and the Labour Movement*.

70. For patterns of emigration see, for example, T. M. Devine (ed.), *Scottish Emigration and Scottish Society: Proceedings of the Scottish Historical Studies Seminar* (Edinburgh:

John Donald, 1992); T. M. Devine, *To the Ends of the Earth: Scotland's Global Diaspora, 1750–2010* (London: Allen Lane, 2011); Marjory Harper, *Adventurers and Exiles: The Great Scottish Exodus* (London: Profile Books, 2003); Angela McCarthy, 'The Scottish Diaspora since 1815', in Devine and Wormald (eds), *Oxford Handbook of Modern Scottish History*, pp. 510–32.

71. For sources on emigrants to the United States, see Allan Macinnes, Marjory Harper and Linda Fryer, *Scotland and the Americas, c.1650–c.1939: A Documentary Source Book* (Edinburgh: Scottish History Society, 2002).

72. Rosalind McClean, 'Reluctant Leavers? Scottish women and emigration in the mid nineteenth century', in Tom Brooking and Jennie Coleman (eds), *The Heather and the Fern: Scottish Migration and New Zealand Settlement* (Dunedin: University of Otago Press 2003), pp. 103–16.

73. McCarthy, 'The Scottish Diaspora since 1815'.

74. For a discussion of 'sojourners' see, for example, Harper, *Adventurers and Exiles*.

75. See, for example, Antoinette Burton, *Burdens of History: British Feminists, Indian Women, and Imperial Culture, 1865–1915* (Chapel Hill: University of North Carolina Press, 1994); Clare Midgley (ed.), *Gender and Imperialism* (Manchester: Manchester University Press, 1998), and *Feminism and Empire: Women Activists in Imperial Britain, 1790–1865* (London: Routledge, 2007); Catherine Hall, *Civilising Subjects: Metropole and Colony in the English Imagination 1830–1867* (Cambridge: Polity Press, 2002); Phillipa Levine (ed.), *Gender and Empire* (Oxford: Oxford University Press, 2004); Catherine Hall and Sonya Rose (eds), *At Home with the Empire* (Cambridge: Cambridge University Press, 2006).

76. Cheryl McEwan, '"The Mother of all the Peoples": geographical knowledge and the empowering of Mary Slessor', in Morag Bell, Robin Butlin, and Michael Heffernan (eds), *Geography and Imperialism: 1820–1940* (Manchester: Manchester University Press, 1995), pp. 125–50; Natasha Erlank, '"Civilising the African": the Scottish mission to the Xhosa, 1821–1864', in Brian Stanley (ed.), *Christian Missions and the Enlightenment* (London: Curzon, 2001); Rhonda Anne Semple, *Missionary Women: Gender, Professionalism and the Victorian Idea of Christian Mission* (Woodbridge and Rochester: The Boydell Press, 2003); Deborah Gaitskell, 'Re-thinking Gender Roles: the Field Experience of Missionaries in South Africa', in Andrew Porter (ed.), *The Imperial Horizons of British Protestant Missions, 1880–1914* (Grand Rapids, MI: William B. Eerdmans, 2003), pp. 131–57.

77. See Orr Macdonald, *A Unique and Glorious Mission*, and Esther Breitenbach, *Empire and Scottish Society: the Impact of Foreign Missions at Home c.1780–c.1914* (Edinburgh: Edinburgh University Press, 2009).

78. Catriona Burness, 'The Long Slow March: Scottish Women MPs, 1918–45', in Breitenbach and Gordon, *Out of Bounds*, pp. 151–73; Eliza Riedi, 'Women, Gender and the Promotion of Empire: the Victoria League, 1901–1914', in *The Historical Journal*, 45 (3) (200), pp. 569–99; Breitenbach, *Empire and Scottish Society*.

79. Judith Fewell and Fiona Paterson, *Girls in their Prime: Scottish Education Revisited* (Edinburgh: Scottish Academic Press, 1990); Helen Corr, 'The schoolgirls' curriculum and the ideology of the home, 1870–1914', in Glasgow Women's Studies

Group, *Uncharted Lives* (Glasgow: Pressgang, 1983); R. D. Anderson, *Education and the Scottish People: 1750–1918* (Oxford: Clarendon Press, 1995); Lindsay Paterson, *Scottish Education in the Twentieth Century* (Edinburgh: Edinburgh University Press, 2003).

80. Moore, 'Education and Learning'; McDermid, *The Schooling of Girls*.
81. For example, Walter E. Houghton (ed.), *The Wellesley Index to Victorian Periodicals, 1824–1900* (Toronto: University of Toronto Press, and London: Routledge and Kegan Paul, 1966); David Finkelstein, *An Index to Blackwood's Magazine, 1901–1980* (Aldershot: Scolar, 1995).
82. Janice Helland, *Professional Women Painters in Nineteenth Century Scotland* (Aldershot: Ashgate, 2000); Siân Reynolds, 'Gender, the Arts and Culture', in Abrams et al., *Gender in Scottish History*, pp. 170–98.
83. See also William Donaldson, *Popular Literature in Victorian Scotland: Language, Fiction and the Press* (Aberdeen: Aberdeen University Press, 1986) for evidence of writing in the vernacular.
84. Linda Fleming, 'Jewish women in Glasgow c.1880–1950: gender, ethnicity and the immigrant experience' (unpublished PhD thesis, University of Glasgow, 2005).
85. Local histories, such as Elspeth King, *The Hidden History of Glasgow's Women: The Thenew Factor* (Edinburgh: Mainstream, 1993); Norman Watson, *Daughters of Dundee* (Dundee: Linda McGill, 1997); Lillian King, *Famous Women of Fife* (Windfall Books, 1999); Mary Henderson, *Dundee Women's Trail* (Dundee, 2008), see also the Dundee Women's Trail website at www.dundeewomenstrail.org.uk/; Susan Bennett, Mary Byatt, Jenny Main, Anne Oliver and Janet Trythall, *Women of Moray* (Edinburgh: Luath Press, 2012), see also the Women of Moray website at www.womenofmoray.org.uk/, indicate the possibilities here, while the availability of nineteenth-century newspapers in a digitised form provides enormous scope for researchers. The recently launched NLS website of Post Office Directories is also a valuable resource for identifying local organisations, businesses, and so on.
86. The Primrose League had cycle corps in which women participated. See Primrose League Scottish Branch Manual (no date but probably 1890s): NLS: Acc. 10424/1.
87. 'The Spread of Golf', *Scots Observer*, 24 November 1888; 'Golf for Women', *Scots Observer*, 19 January 1889.
88. See www. swns.com/the-tarty-army-never-before-seen-pictures-of-scottish-suffra gettes-football-team-081656.html
89. Margaret Ponsonby, 'Ideals, Reality and Meaning: Homemaking in England in the First Half of the Nineteenth Century', *Journal of Design History* 16: 3 (2003), pp. 201–3.
90. Margaret Beetham, *A Magazine of her Own, Domesticity and Female Desire in the Woman's Magazine 1800–1914* (London: Routledge, 1996), p. 7.
91. Giles, *The Parlour and the Suburb*, p. 65; Jan Merchant, '"An Insurrection of Maids": domestic servants and the agitation of 1872', in Louise Miskell, Christopher A. Whatley and Bob Harris, *Victorian Dundee: Image and Realities* (East Linton: Tuckwell Press, 2000), pp. 104–21.
92. See Jamieson, 'Rural and Urban Women in Domestic Service'.
93. See Nenadic, 'Social Shaping of Business Behaviour'.

94. Gordon, *Women and the Labour Movement*; W. W. Knox, *Hanging by a Thread: the Scottish Cotton Industry*, c.*1850–1914* (Preston: Carnegie, 1994).

95. Gordon, *Women and the Labour Movement*; Alice Albert, 'Fit Work for Women'; Nenadic, 'Social Shaping of Business Behaviour', 'The Small Family Firm'.

96. See Gordon, *Women and the Labour Movement*.

97. Jane Rendall, '"Women that would plague me"'.

98. Smitley, *Feminine Public Sphere*.

99. Moore, 'Education and Learning'; Jane McDermid, 'School Board Women and active citizenship in Scotland, 1873–1919', in *History of Education*, 38 (3) (2009), pp. 333–47; 'Blurring the Boundaries: School Board Women in Scotland, 1873–1919', in *Women's History Review*, Vol. 19, No. 3 (July, 2010), pp. 357–73; 'Place the Book in their Hands: Grace Paterson's Contribution to the Health and Welfare Policies of the School Board of Glasgow, 1885–1906', in *History of Education*, Vol. 36, No. 6 (November, 2007), pp. 697–713.

100. See, for example, Michael Fry, *The Scottish Empire* (East Linton: Tuckwell Press, and Edinburgh: Birlinn, 2001); T. M. Devine, *Scotland's Empire* (London: Allen Lane, 2003); Breitenbach, *Empire and Scottish Society*; T. M. Devine and John MacKenzie (eds), *Scotland and the British Empire* (Oxford: Oxford University Press, 2011).

101. See, for example, Andrew Mackillop, 'Locality, Nation and Empire: Scots and the Empire in Asia, *c.*1695–*c.*1813', in Devine and MacKenzie, *Scotland and the British Empire*; Edward Spiers, *The Scottish Soldier and Empire* (Edinburgh: Edinburgh University Press, 2006).

102. McClean, 'Reluctant Leavers'; McCarthy, 'Scottish Diaspora since 1815'.

103. Esther Breitenbach, 'Religious Literature and Discourses of Empire: The Scottish Presbyterian Foreign Mission Movement', in Hilary Carey (ed.), *Empires of Religion* (Basingstoke: Palgrave Macmillan, 2008), pp. 84–113; Breitenbach, *Empire and Scottish Society*.

104. See Susan Keracher, *Dundee's Two Intrepid Ladies: A Tour Round the World by D. C. Thomson's Female Journalists in 1894* (Dundee: Abertay Historical Society, 2012).

# Chapter 2

# Bodies, Sexuality and Health

*Linda Fleming*

## Introduction

This chapter looks at aspects of Scottish women's experiences of their bodies in terms of three, often interrelated themes: physical appearance, sexuality and health. The chapter is ordered in three sections: within each, the extracts *predominantly* address one of these themes. Sources are presented chronologically indicating change and continuity in ideas that circulated in this period affecting women's everyday understanding of their bodies.

The first section includes sources that are mostly concerned with women's appearance. How women looked was fundamental not only as a display of their femininity but also for social status: a middle-class woman would have been as easily identifiable by her clothing as a domestic servant was by her uniform. Gendered expectations about the female body and social conventions in respect of dress and cosmetics also affected women's activities and provoked lengthy debates about appropriate manners and conduct for women.

The second section illustrates aspects of women's lives commonly configured around behaviour related to sexuality and sexual relations, whether consensual or forced. The nineteenth century is often characterised as an era of ignorance about the physiology of sex, particularly among women; to some extent this is unfair, because sexual difference and the biology of reproduction were then the subjects of lengthy and serious scientific study. Nonetheless, scientific interest did not necessarily equate with progress in changing views about supposed inherent weaknesses in the female body and mind as compared with men. Characteristics of health and sickness are dealt with in the final section where sources explore how these two sides of the corporeal coin were approached within discourses of female experience, most particularly, in respect of the supposed medical implications of the ordinary functions of the female body.

## Section 1: Looking the part

This section contains sources addressing various aspects of women's appearance and some of the means used to achieve this. Corsets, discussion of which is illustrated here, were an iconic example of a form of apparel much debated throughout the nineteenth century. Fundamentals of everyday life such as clothing can easily be overlooked in historical examination but we can clearly see how changes in opportunities for women were facilitated by dress and vice versa. Women's physical activities, whether for leisure or for work, served as a focus for moral and medical discussion about the female body, and how women looked was often used as a barometer to measure perceived assaults on the status quo of gender relations.

Most of the extracts come from literary texts, including traditional broadsides and newer journalism. Though most ideas about women's appearance were governed by local custom and practice, and the written word likely operated in tandem with oral custom to influence women's awareness of their bodies, the power of new forms of commercial writing should not be underestimated because they reached an increasingly wide readership across the country. The messages delivered by magazines were sometimes the antithesis of those embedded in custom and practice, being all about the fickleness of fashion and embracing new ideas. Though they did not reflect everyday reality, articles in women's magazines expressed a great deal about changes within popular consciousness of common ideals of attractiveness. Social class, however, cut across the immediate power of such gendered discourses. The servant girl may have been just as interested in reading about new cosmetics, fashionable clothing, sporting activities, and the latest cure-all potions for female maladies as her middle-class employer but it is not at all likely that she would have had access to even a fraction of the latter's purchasing power. Also included in this section is an example of photographic evidence. The rapid development of photography in this period has provided abundant evidence of the physical appearance of Scottish women, the kinds of clothing worn by them, and changes that came about in dress. Such images can be compared with the largely unattainable ideals that were promoted in the press.

Tight lacing in pursuit of an exaggerated female form became an increasingly common feature of fashionable dressing. Corsets were aptly called 'stays', operating as an everyday physical control over women's bodies. They restricted extravagant movement and helped enforce ideas about graceful feminine demeanour. Simultaneously, however, they also carried erotic signals through embellishing sexualised characteristics of the female body and were undoubtedly embroiled in a particular type of masochistic thinking about disciplining the female form. From the early nineteenth century, a variety of commentators fulminated against corsets; this debate involved the male medical profession and ordinary women who were expected to submit to corsets themselves and ensure that their daughters conformed. Corsets also had their apologists, both female and male, and their enduring popularity, despite changing fashions, continued to be debated within the context of discussion of larger-scale social and cultural changes affecting women. Though most closely associated with middle-class dress and the work of specialist corsetières, working-class women also wore corsets which might be purchased ready-made in small drapers' stores or second-hand. The two sources quoted below display antagonism to the corset: though written by different authors (quite possibly of different genders) the influence of medical discourse is clear. This pattern was set to increase as the power of medical opinion made ingress into multiple aspects of women's everyday lives. Nevertheless, female tastes in dress as well as commercial interests appear to have won this battle, and corsets did not go out of fashion.

### 1.1 Articles, *The Scotsman*, 1829

'On the Compression of the Waist in Females, By the Use of Corsets', *Scotsman*, 20 May 1829

> 'He spak and he praised my sma' waist,
> My bonnie waist, my jimp waist,'
> *Aiken Drum*

We have been favoured with the perusal of an interesting essay on this subject by a medical gentleman, which has more fully opened our eyes to the mischiefs resulting from the compressed waists now in fashion – mischiefs which, in the paper before us, are exposed with a clearness and weight of evidence that must carry conviction to the mind of the most incredulous. The paper is ably written and conclusive, that we should have been happy to print it entire had its scientific form not rendered it too learned for the readers of Newspapers. In the abstract of its contents which we shall submit, the author's statements must lose something of the precision and force which the introduction of anatomical details, and a frequent reference to plates, enable him to bestow upon them; but we think we shall be able in a general way, to shew young ladies what injury to health their compliance with the present unnatural fashion, if persevered in, is certain to entail upon them.

Fashion lives on novelty, and we have on this account much charity for its wanderings and eccentricities, bonnets with a snout as long as an elephant's proboscis, or a margin as broad as a Winchester bushel, are merely ridiculous. Shoulders that look like wings, and sleeves as wide as a petticoat we think are not particularly graceful; but they have at least the merit of being airy, and we take no offence. We cannot, however, extend our indulgence to the compressed waist which is the rage at present. We know that as often as the waist is extended to its natural limits, this tendency to abridge its diameter appears; and we confess that we are puzzled to account for the fact; for surely it is strange, that a permanent prepossession should exist in favour of a mode of dress which is at once ugly, unnatural, and pernicious. Were fashion under the guidance of taste, the principles of drapery and sculpture would never be lost sight of in its changes. The clothes that cover us may be disposed in an infinite variety of forms without violating those rules which the artist is careful to observe. The true form of the body ought to be disclosed to the eye, without the shape being exhibited in all its minutiae as in the dress of a harlequin; but in no case should the natural proportions (supposing the figure to be good) be changed. Ask the sculptor what he thinks of the fashionable waist, pinched till it rivals the lady's neck in tenuity; and he will tell you it is monstrous. Consult the physician, and you will learn that this is one of those follies in which no female can long indulge with impunity; for health and even life are often sacrificed to it . . .

'Letter to the Editor', *Scotsman*, 23 May 1829

SIR, – Your paper of Wednesday last contained, in my opinion, a most important piece of information, in regard to the dangerous tendency of the use of corsets, stays, or stiff jackets. As a parent I am obliged to you. I request that you will give room in your paper to the following quotation on the same subject, from Dr Faust's catechism of health, revised and recommended by the late eminent Dr James Gregory. I am &c A.S.

"Stays and stiff jackets are inventions of the most pernicious nature; they disfigure a beautiful and upright shape, and instead of rendering a woman straight, as erroneously supposed they make her crook-backed; they injure the breast and bowels; obstruct the breathing and digestion; hurt the breasts and nipples; many hence get cancers, and lose both health and life. In short they in general destroy health; they render parturition difficult to both mother and child. It is therefore the duty of parents, and especially mothers, to banish from their houses and families stays and jackets. Those girdles or sashes which press or constrain the lower part of the body, are almost equally injurious."

In the example below of a sensationalist news story, it is claimed that restrictions on women's employment encouraged cross-dressing subterfuge and, indeed, cross-dressing may not have been so unusual, or only confined to tall tales and stage performances in the Victorian music hall. This is a difficult area to research because there was no law prohibiting sexual relations between women although prosecutions might enter the courts under other forms of jurisdiction such as slander or libel. Individual women undoubtedly had their own complex reasons for adopting the guise of a man but, in nineteenth-century Scotland, beyond the most avant-garde of Scottish society, female same-sex relations were probably 'beyond belief'.[1] This broadside is available on the NLS Word on the Street website at: http://digital.nls.uk/broadsides/

### 1.2 'The Life and Strange Adventures of Margaret M'Donald the Female Foot Boy' (*c*.1870–80) [NLS, Shelfmark: L.C. Fol. 178 A.2 (085)]

Margaret M'Donald, the subject of the following narrative, was born in 1842, of poor, but respectable parents in this town. When she was but 13 years of age, her parents died & left her & an older brother, totally unprovided for. Her brother though 5 years older, was but an apprentice tailor, and his scanty wages went but a short way in supporting them; and having no relations to assist them, poor Margaret was obliged to try and earn an honest penny, by running errands, washing out houses, or doing any little service the neighbours might require her to do. She at length obtained a situation with Mrs Walker to take charge of her child, but Margaret being of a gay & thoughtless disposition, she neglected the child for play, and was in consequence soon discharged. Her brother gave her a good thrashing, & told her he would not encourage her idleness any longer. The next morning she rose early; and when her brother went to his work, she dressed herself in a suit of his Sunday clothes, thinking by assuming male attire, she would be more fortunate in obtaining employment. With a heavy heart and a light purse she took the road. But she had not proceeded far, when she was engaged to assist in taking a drove of sheep to the Market. With the few shillings she received from the drover, she next proceeded to Edinburgh; and, on the day after her arrival in that City, while walking along George's Street, she had the good fortune to pick up a young lady's purse, which she had just dropped. She ran after the lady and returned to her the purse, which contained a considerable sum of money. Miss Gordon of Rock-Vale Terrace was the ladys' name, who was so well pleased at the honest action, that she told the supposed young man to call upon her the next day, which she did. The plain and simple story she told of herself, the prepossessing features, the good address, and the honesty of returning the purse, all tended to gain the favour of Miss Gordon and friends, who at once took her into her service, and under the name of John M'Donald, acted as footman, to the entire satisfaction of the whole family. However, amongst the female portion of the domestics, frequent quarrels occurred through jealousy of the footman . . . It was at length discovered, that M'Donald was paying his addresses to Miss Wilson, the daughter of a respectable Grocer and Provision Merchant, in the neighbourhood . . . For upwards of 3 years they kept a correspondence with each other . . . until it became known to Mr Wilson, that his daughter was keeping company with Miss Gordon's footman . . . Her father called on Miss Gordon, who gave her servant such an excellent character . . . [he] could find little or no objections to their union. Matters being thus arranged, then were duly proclaimed and the happy couple were at length joined in matrimony, for better or worse The wedding party returned, and partook of the good things that were provided by Miss Gordon; for the wedding was solely at that lady's expense. After supper, drink went round, and healths were freely drank, to the welfare of the happy couple; the music struck up, and dancing commenced, in which the bride and groom freely entered. All went happily on, until by some accident M'Donald slipped, and fell heavily on the floor in a swoon. The usual restoratives were applied, with little effect. They next opened his vest, to give him air, when to the great astonishment of all present, the handsome young footman was discovered to be a female. On being restored to consciousness, she related the history of her past life, to the great mirth of the whole wedding party; but as may be expected, it was a great disappointment to the newly made wife, Miss Wilson, who could scarcely believe what had occured. M'Donald assumed her proper character, and wishes to join in wedlock with a suitable young man, with a £100, One about to go to Australia would be preferred.

The following pseudonymously written verse inspired a reply by the feminist poet Marion Bernstein‡ (1846–1906),[2] whose poems are quoted in Chapters 3 and 6. What is striking in comparing the two poems is that in her reply, Bernstein makes no mention of the appearance of an ideal husband but comments only on his required talents and virtues; but for 'Eleve' there are clear connections between a woman's appearance, underlying virtues and marriageable prospects. There were numerous publications like the *Mail*, taking over, as literacy increased, many of the previous functions of broadsides. Women were active in engaging with this medium and used it to air their views. Bernstein was a regular sparring partner of male and female poets within the Scottish popular press throughout the 1870s and, fired by feminist ideals, took pleasure in contradicting male opinions.

1.3 'Eleve', 'Wanted', *The Glasgow Weekly Mail*, 12 December 1874

WANTED

Wanted a maiden to be my good wife,
A lover of justice, a hater of strife.
One about twenty, and not very small–
Say five feet six inches is nothing too tall.
Handsome in person, and fresh as the dew.
With fresh dimpled cheeks 'neath a bright rosy hue:
Blue eyes that bespeak true virtue within,
'Neath an unclouded brow, true wisdom akin.
Her hair medium length, the darkest in hue,
I like the dark ringlets, but all must be true:
False hair and false colours can only fools please,
Their beauties are full of deceit and disease.
Tho' beauty of form I've sought and defined,
I prize something higher – 'tis beauty of mind.
'Bove all that can charm in form and in face,
True beauty of mind holds the loftiest place.

Now there are duties that I can discern
Devolving on housewives and these she must learn –
To sew, wash, and weave, and darn a stocking,
Abilities rare you'll find I'm not joking:
Baking and cooking, scrubbing and dressing –
Accomplishments grand, well worth the possessing:
Economy too, with wisdom discreet,
My wife must practise to make all ends meet.
A Christian too must be my good wife,
To love and serve God, the sustainer of life.

ELEVE

The five extracts below are from articles written by unknown authors giving advice on appearance, an ongoing feature of *Woman at Home*, which was one of the journalistic vehicles of the prolific Annie S. Swan (1859–1943).‡[3] Though the attempt to improve on nature with cosmetics was nothing new, the beauty industry began to grow in this period. Then, as now, youth, or the illusion of youth, as well as socially constructed views about what constituted physical beauty, all contributed to idealised notions of feminine attractiveness that required a great deal of energy to resist. Such advice traded on female insecurities alternating between supportive guidance and stern admonitions about the perils of neglecting personal appearance.

Two of the extracts concern corsets, the debate around which heightened with the arrival of the 'New Woman' in the last decade of the nineteenth century. Some advice given may seem preposterous to the modern eye but the types of clothing worn by women, whether ready-made or handmade to order, were designed to fit the corseted shape; and, as exhibits of Victorian couture in museums often demonstrate, fashionable waists were extremely small. Fashions in women's clothing changed radically across the century from the tightly laced corsets and extravagant crinolines of the early to mid-Victorian period, which would have made any kind of physical exertion extremely difficult, to the incorporation of aspects of 'rational dress' as women took up sport. Yet across all such change, the corset, in one form or another, persisted. Women's consumption of magazines and the beauty practices promoted within them has not been explored in Scotland; as one example, virtually nothing is known about when hairdressing salons started to become a feature of every provincial high street.[4]

### 1.4 *Woman at Home*, Vol. 1 (1893–94); Vol. III (October–March 1894–5)

Advice on ageing, Vol. I. (74)

> It is not given to every woman to be beautiful, but until thirty it is not difficult to most women to seem attractive, given pleasant ways and easy manners; youth has a charm of its own, and beauty lies to a great extent in the eye of the beholder. Indeed until forty many women could be spoken of as pretty, and prettiness, be it remembered, is an attitude that implies the appearance of youth. From forty to sixty an attractive appearance demands more study; a shady hat tossed anglewise on a touzled head is no longer picturesque when the eyes beneath it are sorrowful and the cheek growing thin, nor do exuberant proportions retain their dignity if clothed in white to multiply them, or in tawdry snippets to render them grotesque. A middle-aged woman requires careful dressing, not because she is middle-aged, but because in middle age her own particular style asserts itself, and can no longer be ignored. Dressing as befits one's age conveys nothing, because there is no style of toilet adapted to any particular period of life, but there is a style in which each woman looks best, and the middle-aged woman who intends that her appearance shall continue to count will not wear black habitually if she has grown sallow, nor tailor-made gowns of thick material when she tends to *embonpoint* . . .

Advice on hairdressing, Vol. I (74–5)

> Some years ago, when fair hair was the fashion, hair was often washed with an alkaline solution of soda or potash, until a considerable portion of the colouring matter

was removed, and with it much of the silky beauty of the hair, which when thus blanched seemed dead. In the present day, by the aid of chemistry, the hair artist moves further, and adds a dye to the outside of the hair to replace the subtracted inner colouring. But the effect is never good or natural, and such unworthy aids to beauty are never advisable. Some harmless preparation to darken hair that is turning grey is much more desirable, as few people can contemplate with equanimity the fast descending snows of years on heads that but yesterday were glowing with the sun of youth. There comes a time when dark hair is unnatural, and even when undyed is unbecoming, when the worn face seems to ask for a silver frame; but when hair turns grey in youth it is a hardship, more especially in a woman's case. The following wash will be serviceable and altogether harmless: – Scald two ounces of black tea in one gallon of boiling water. Strain and add three ounces of glycerine, half an ounce tincture of Spanish flies, and one quart bay rum. Digest the mixture for two or three days, and perfume with essence of rose or bergamot. This mixture may be rubbed daily into the roots and brushed through the hair, and will, while darkening, also serve to strengthen it . . .

## Advice in reply to a letter on freckles, Vol. III (316)

A Scotch lassie is in trouble about the freckles on her complexion. Cheer up Scotch Lassie; people are beginning to own to admiring them now; but as a matter of fact, artistic folks always did. Freckles on a fair skin, harmonising with red hair and red-brown eyes, make a delicious harmony of colour. People used to *call* it ugly, but a freckled girl is never short of partners at a ball, or admirers anywhere else. Moreover, freckles nearly always go with a lissom figure, splendid health, and a bright disposition, and from her letter "Scotch Lassie" seems no exception to the general rule. Still the freckles, if they really annoy her, can be removed by the following application: the juice of one lemon, as much powdered borax as will lie on a sixpence and the same quantity of powdered sugar; apply this frequently.

## Advice on waist size to 'an affectionate but misjudging mother', Vol. III (315)

To begin with measurements. The natural size of the waist is exactly double that of the throat. You do not give the throat measurement, but it is generally double that of the wrist; that in your elder daughter's case would be 14 inches, which would make her natural waist 28 inches. Modern taste and modern habits demand waists slightly smaller than is natural. Your daughter might safely and without discomfort reduce her waist to double the size of her upper arm, which would be 22 inches. The smallest size at which a waist looks well is the size of the head at the largest part; in your daughter's case that will be 21 inches. An 18 inch waist with a 38 inch bust cannot but look ungraceful and coarse in the extreme.

## From 'Dress and Fashion', Vol. III (390)

Athletic women are still on the increase; it has become an established fact that "our girls" vie with "our boys" on the golf links as well as on the dangerously attractive cycle! It is essential that golf gowns should be as light as possible, and that they should clear the ground by, at least, six inches. Quite an ideal costume, which was destined to be worn at St Andrews links, was of fine black serge with a broad band of scarlet leather on the hem of the skirt. The scarlet blouse, with full bishop's sleeves, was arranged in soft folds which would in no way interfere with the movements of the wearer, who is said to be the best golfer in the St Andrews district, and a most bewitching little black Tam O' Shanter, with a bright red wing at one side, completed the "red upon black" harmony. Black cloth knickerbockers were to be worn with this costume, and dainty little black gaiters faintly outlined with scarlet leather.

The extract below, from a longer review article, deals with themes often subsumed under the titles 'The Modern Marriage Market' and the 'New Woman Movement'. These *fin de siècle* issues were pored over in print and involved Scottish feminists. This source, however, was written by a man: T.P.W. was the pen name of Thomas Pilkington Whyte (b.1837). An ex-army officer, he wrote for *Blackwood's Magazine* on the subject of women and politics.[5] The extract illustrates the growing anxiety, not to say panic, about the emergence of women who wanted more control over their own bodies and their social destiny. The spectre of an excess of middle-class women seemed to promote discussion of the behaviour of women enjoying new physical activities. The appeal to women to stop behaving like men has, of course, been an enduring one whenever women breach a former male prerogative. The spread of articles like this was in response to the increased visibility of women using bicycles, playing tennis, golf, and even football! The tide could not be turned, however, and women's sport persisted; such activities may be seen as one yardstick of women embracing greater freedoms. Surviving documentary sources which address these and other outdoor activities specifically for Scotland are in diverse places, such as small notices and articles in local newspapers and in photographic evidence. In respect of cycling, the Glasgow-based publication, *The Scottish Cyclist*, carried a 'woman's page' during the late 1890s.[6]

### 1.5 T. P. W , 'The Redundancy of Spinster Gentlewomen', *Scottish Review* No. 36 (1900: July), pp. 88–112 (102, 111–12)

. . . The outburst of athletics among the middle and gentlefolk circles, is scarcely over a dozen years old. But meantime it has so bitten these classes that apart from the present war troubles, little is talked, little is done, little has a chance of being cared for, among them, save muscular sports of one kind or another. Boisterous bodily exertion is enshrined in the modern young lady's creed and ambitions, as at once 'the correct thing' and the chief thing in life worth living for . . .

At present, the ordinary man regards the Amazonian woman of epicene tendencies rather as one views a freak of nature, only that the freak in this case is not Nature's, but an artificial social product. He looks at her critically, sorrowfully, while in the matter of matrimonial leanings towards her he too often holds his peace and goes his way. It may be, could he get behind her mannish mask, the starved modicum of genuine woman within her might reveal itself, and be weaned back to tread the dear old paths of enchantment. But she cannot have her bread buttered on both sides. She cannot expect to go in for the role of the male, and yet exact his deference or win his devotion . . .

I say our girls of the social midlands and higher levels must reconsider their position and their ways, if they would check one of the contributory causes of the augmenting bachelorhood and spinsterhood within their ranks. The frantic pursuit of mere outdoor personal amusement must be abandoned. The delights of hockey, with its occasional incidents of bandaged heads, broken teeth and bruises, must be left to the virile sex which has to do for the most part the rough-and-tumble work of the world. The feebleness of adult girls' cricket, their farcical attempts at football, the overstrain of their bicycling (not its moderate use), with all the diverse forms of sport and muscular exertion unsuited to the female, and so constantly overdone, must be discarded. And still there will remain for the sex healthful recreation in plenty. Manners must be mended. The use of men's slang; sporting and stable talk; the growing habit of ladies' smoking; the mannish stride, the swagger and knock-you-down demeanour, the strident self-assertive voice tones—all must go. The sweetness and refinements, the sympathetic atmosphere, the graciousness and grace, of women's genuine nature—after our mother's pattern—must return into favour. That this will come about before our new century is half over I firmly believe. The swing of the social pendulum will by that time have done its work. Woman travestying as athlete, like the New Woman of evolution, and of bygone revolutions, has not come to stay. She will pass; and her sisters of the future will look back and marvel what bad dream it was which for a while possessed so many of the sex . . .

T. P. W.

## 1.6  Photograph of a woman and children, *c.*1900–10

Photographs of working-class women showing them going about their work or involved in what were perceived to be quaint aspects of local customs were often taken by Victorian enthusiasts of folk culture as well as of photographic art. Portraits such as this item, however, were usually taken for a family reason; typically, they commemorated special occasions. Until the advent of inexpensive box cameras in the early part of the twentieth century, and even for decades after this, photography was usually the province of professionals, took place in a studio, and was expensive to commission; therefore, in this sort of photography, images of affluent women by far outweigh those from the poorer classes. This image is perhaps unusual because not only does it depict a working-class woman and, we must presume, her own children, but, additionally, it was taken on the street rather than in a studio despite it clearly being posed. It demonstrates that a woman's social class was easily identifiable through her clothing: the shawl and apron were standard garments for this period in Lowland Scotland because, for most women, clothing had to be practical and hardwearing rather than fashionable. Yet other aspects of her appearance, and that of the children, suggest that, within her class, she was likely reasonably well off. It is not known why this

**Figure 2.1** Woman and children, Newton-on-Ayr, *c.*1900–10. From a private collection of
family photographs with the permission of James and Christina Law.

image was taken; the woman came from a family in Newton-on-Ayr, however, where the menfolk frequently went to sea as fishermen or merchant sailors. This was also a period of large-scale migration and it is known that within this family many emigrated. Perhaps the photo was taken as a memento for a husband who was away for one of these reasons.

## Section 2: Behaving and misbehaving

This section looks at women's sexuality which was often related to under-standings of the reproductive functions of the female body. Lessons on the body increasingly became couched in new science-led doctrines about public health and the preservation of national vigour as well as public morals. Deeply embroiled in all this were questions about women's abilities to withstand the rigours of repeated pregnancy, bear healthy children and set the moral tone by performing all such duties of much-vaunted authentic womanhood within the sanctity of marriage. In the context of such thinking, the second issue, para-doxically, concerns the ways in which female sexual behaviour was construed as problematic and required control.

The first extract is from a report of the Glasgow Lock Hospital which was founded in 1805 and survived until 1940 (information about the surviving records of the hospital is available at www.hospitalsdatabase.lshtm.ac.uk/hospi-tal.php?hospno=885). This institution had combined aims to cure, contain and, if possible, reform women who were suffering from venereal diseases. The notion of the supposed dangerous sexuality of women is most clearly seen in nineteenth-century attitudes towards prostitution. Many of the social problems brought about by urbanisation in Scotland served both to force women into selling sex and increased the visibility of the trade. The Lock Hospital was an independent institution that operated as a charity, though it may have had trouble in attract-ing philanthropic generosity. The 'Magdalen Institution' referred to was estab-lished in 1812 but had an earlier counterpart in Edinburgh (1797), as illustrated in Chapter 5. The Contagious Diseases Acts of the 1860s were never adopted in Scotland where local measures were preferred; the Lock Hospital, together with the later Magdalene Institution, were partners in tackling what they referred to as the 'social evil'. The term 'prostitute' was, however, a loose one which might be applied to any woman who challenged sexual mores. The medical treatment of venereal disease changed with greater medical understanding by the end of the nineteenth century, though there was no reliable cure.[7]

---

2.1 *Report of the Glasgow Lock Hospital*, 1810 [GULSC: BG33–g. 14] (np)

Of the Patients admitted during this year, a considerable proportion has consisted of those who, though reduced by their own misconduct to the lowest state of abject poverty and disease, have not appeared to be so completely abandoned as the inmates of this House are generally supposed to be. Patients of this description are in general completely thrown off by their relations and former connections; they are with the greatest propriety refused admission into other Hospitals; but at the same time, though criminal, they are certainly proper objects for commiseration and charity; and many of them have perhaps some principles remaining, which, with proper care, might even be rendered virtuous.

It has been the object of the Medical Attendants, as much as possible, to separate those Patients who had still some appearance of decency from those whose morals seemed to be hopeless; and there is reason to believe these means have occasionally been beneficial. At the same time, the Managers have still to regret the total want of a Magdalen Institution, or of some fund, to prevent the necessity of some females returning to their former irregularities, after they have been dismissed from the Hospital . . . They beg that the Subscribers would also reflect, that in these times of mercantile distress, many females may, through poverty, be driven to courses which in times of prosperity they would, in all probability, never have descended to . . .

Using the pseudonym of T. Bell, the author of the text quoted below was John Roberton (1776–1840), a Scottish physician who specialised in the treatment of venereal disease.[8] This book fuses elementary anatomy with references to classical and Enlightenment scholarship, all in order to talk about sex. The discussion is almost as much concerned with men's bodies and natures as women's so it has to be concluded that the title was a means to sell the book more successfully or disguise the fact of its central subject matter which may have been considered pornographic. The notion of nature versus nurture in determining sexual instinct was a continuous one in this period. The views of Rousseau were commonly invoked but, by the end of the century, those promoting debate were no longer moral philosophers and physicians – they had been joined by the new disciplines of sexology and psychoanalysis. It remains a matter of contention whether very much had changed for women, however, given the sexologists' view that men's biological drives were essentially aggressive and women's responsive.

> 2.2  T. Bell, MD, *Kalogynomia Or the Laws of Female Beauty: Being the Elementary Principles Of That Science* (London: J. J. Stockdale, 1821) (65, 66–7, 67–8, 128–9, 133)

'Of the Model of Female Beauty'
The influence of the organs which distinguish the two sexes, and the actions of those organs, is evidently the primary cause of their *peculiar* beauty. This influence is incontestable. The appearance and the manners of eunuchs approach to those of a woman. Women in whom these organs remain in a state of inertia during life, acquire the appearance and the manners of men . . .

The particular circumstances which contribute to female beauty, independently of that original happy organization which in general these only modify, but which in a series of generations, they may totally change, are a mild climate, a fertile soil, a generous but temperate diet, a regular mode of life, the guidance and suppression of passions, and even cosmetic attentions. The more also that a people is advanced in social, moral and political institutions, the more (other causes being proportional) does it advance, as to the nobleness, the elegance and the grace of the individuals who compose it.

Female beauty differs among the various races of mankind . . . The negro, who widely in a hot clime, prefers for his mate a woman of colour, always awards the superiority in beauty to the white . . . Everywhere throughout the universe a young and beautiful woman of the European race commands the admiration and receives the homage of men.

'Of the Economy of Love'
To accomplish the purposes of love, as Rousseau has well remarked, man ought to attack, women to defend. Man ought to choose those moments when the want of the attack is evident, and when that very want ensures its success: woman ought to choose those in which the surrender may be most advantageous to her; she ought to know how to yield in due time to the violence of the aggressor, after having softened his character even by her resistance, – how to give the greatest possible value to her defeat, – how to make a merit of that which she herself has desired not less ardently, perhaps, to grant, than he to obtain, – and how, in time, to discover in the prudent and mild guidance of their mutual pleasures, a supporter, a defender.

The sentiment which allows woman thus to act, is shame. This sentiment, however, is, in a state of nature, unknown both to man and animals. Why should they be ashamed to appear as nature has produced them? Why should they be ashamed to procreate their race? . . .

Since shame is thus an object of social agreement, we cannot determine its limits: they vary among every people. In our European societies, they change once a month. One day fashion demands all women to cover the bosom; – on the following, on the contrary, she bids them display it without reserve; . . .

The policing of women's sexual behaviour by the kirk sessions was a well-worn path in Scotland but one which had begun to decline in influence by mid-century, though regional differences certainly existed. The movement of women into positions of responsibility in churches and philanthropic agencies, however, meant that this was an area of interest to female religious activists and, it seems, sometimes with no less fire-and-brimstone admonitions. Certainly, the 'double standard' in sexual conduct did not disappear with this development.

2.3 *Kind Words to the Young Women of England and Scotland on a very serious subject by A Lady* (Lancaster and Edinburgh Religious Book and Tract Society, 1858)

When a woman gives willingly into danger, a man certainly will be no shield or prop to her virtue. Though, at times, innocence may have been betrayed by lying pretences, yet, without any doubt too many women who have fallen from purity have fully shared with their partners in the known and wilful sin, and some have even been the first to tempt, and by forward advances have plainly given the invitation to loose intentions which would have otherwise have found no opening.

It is a sure blot indeed on women that she should ever take the tempter's part, and, to her own injury study to be man's hindrance rather than his help in the right path. A flauntiness of manner and look – often only too common – always tends to this. That sort of free jeering talk which some people fancy as smart, romping actions, giddy laughter, finery in dress, and other such like baits for notice, always mislead young men to over free and loose thoughts, always lower a woman's character, always tend to evil. Avoid all such errors as in themselves bad, and the almost sure leadings to worse.

The wish to please is a natural wish, and not in itself wrong. But be persuaded that you may more truly please at a just and proper distance, by being quietly civil, and avoiding offence, than by coming forward to break down the barrier of respect which should always stand between the sexes . . . It is generally within a woman's powers to check too great a familiarity with little difficulty, by shewing a real dislike to it, and by preserving a civil distance . . .

Woman may rise high or she may fall very low. Purity and piety make her a guide to heaven, a friend and comforter in every vexation of life – the want of these may cast her to a depth of infamy the vilest and most degrading to which any of God's creatures can sink. There cannot be found on this earth an object at once more revolting and saddening than a woman brutalised by vice, and shameless. The downward path is slippery . . .

No: look steadily at the truth, and believe and confess that this sin of fornication is a sin indeed . . .

Alice Ker‡ (1853–1943) was born in Banffshire and was as a young woman involved with the campaign for women's entry into medical education. She also became a suffrage campaigner; as a member of the Women's Social and Political Union (WSPU) she spent two months in Holloway prison during 1912 for window smashing. It was more usual for men to write this type of text, dealing with aspects of women's bodies and with sex but it is clear that Ker wished to promote the services of female medics to women by making advice as practical as possible, Victorian sensibility notwithstanding. The first extract below deals with sexual relations within marriage and touches on contraception and women's rights in the arena of sexual relations. Ker's views on sexual relations, like those of many nineteenth-century feminists, were in opposition to much male medical opinion. In a review of her book in a medical journal, issue was taken with her views on sex within marriage which were stated to be giving the wife control 'over the husband's person'.[9] Ker's views were certainly at odds with what would later emerge from the sexology movement which enshrined men's unbridled need to be sexually aggressive. The second extract concerns what Ker calls, 'advanced womanhood'.

## 2.4 Dr Alice Ker (Mrs Stewart Ker), *Motherhood: A Book for Every Woman* (Manchester and London: John Heywood, 1891) (28, 29, 30–1, 122–3, 123–4, 124–5)

Extract concerning matrimony:

It [is] important to prepare a girl's mind for the duties of matrimony, by teaching her its dignity and beauty. And here I would emphasise . . . the evil that is done by encouraging the habit of jesting and laughing about love-making. The minds of both young men and maidens should be kept sedulously free from this vulgar habit . . .

Every young woman, before entering on the duties of matrimony, should have them fully explained to her, either by her mother, or by someone standing in a similar relation to her. To act otherwise is to be guilty of a great cruelty, and cases have been known where ignorance has caused the greatest misery and distress . . . In doing so the girl must be taught that her body is her own, subject only to her Maker, and that she has no right to make the undue ownership of it over to her husband. This is the great law that needs to be fully understood and acted upon, if the next generation is to be better and purer than this one. Let no one look upon such plain speaking as unnecessary, for it is impossible to give the help to our sex which I wish to afford without saying very distinctly what I consider to be the essential laws of Nature in this matter. In the marriage relation, the choice of time and frequency is the right of the woman, by reason of the periodicity which characterises her being, and the violation of this law injures not only herself, physically and morally, but also her husband and her children . . . If a wife has not got the control of her own person, in what respect is she better than those most unhappy members of our sisterhood who are pathetically defined as "unfortunates"? . . .

. . . I must make it plain that I am speaking in the interests, not of women only, but of men as well. The best and truest-hearted men will be the first to acknowledge that this is, indeed the true law; and who can tell how far the great problem of our civilised life, which is known as the Social Evil, might be remedied by the adoption of a higher standard of continence even in matrimony . . . I must take this opportunity of saying a word – which I fear, is only too much needed – in emphatic condemnation of all artificial checks to conception. Their employment is contrary to all sacredness and spirituality in love and marriage, and there is not one of them which is not liable to injure the health of either husband or wife. Besides, they are often ineffectual in compassing the end for which they are employed, and, on that case, the effect upon the child must be anything but beneficial. There is no legitimate means of limiting offspring except by continence, and, if this were more practised in married life, we should have fewer and much healthier children, begotten in the most favourable circumstances, and developed under the influences of joyful anticipation and loving welcome.

Extract concerning the menopause:

Strange and uneasy sensations may affect even the purest minded of women at this time of their lives, resulting entirely from the physical effects of the change in their circumstances, caused by the cessation of the monthly discharge. The mind should be diverted from these feelings as much as possible, but if a careful attention . . . does not succeed in removing them, professional advice should be sought, and this may now be done without embarrassment, seeing that few women are entirely beyond the reach of a qualified doctor of their own sex . . .

. . . Loss of memory is very common, and is generally very distressing to the patient, who must be encouraged to look upon it as only a temporary inconvenience, caused by her condition of health, and likely to pass away with the increased strength which will come when the change is completed; and not as a sign of old age . . . Change in the disposition is sometimes seen, a sweet-tempered woman becoming hasty or peevish, and a bright and energetic spirit being exchanged for dulness and despondency, whilst jealousy and suspicion are very frequent signs of the unsettled mental health. Habits of drinking may be acquired, and kleptomania, or even worse forms of insanity, have been known to supervene, all of which may pass off with the disturbances which have caused them, but none of which can safely be left to sure themselves without treatment . . . [I]t is often beneficial when strangeness of disposition is noticed, to remove the patient from her friends, and to let her be treated in the house of a physician, or in some such retreat with regular hours, plain food, and constant though unobtrusive supervision. This often results in a speedy cure, and the patient must not, by any means, be considered to have been insane, any more than dizziness is to be regarded as a fit of apoplexy . . . The knowledge that such a condition of mind is possible may save some of us from being unjust to a fellow sister, and from suffering disappointment ourselves, when we see signs of what looks like carelessness and indifference in the performance of work; and we may comfort ourselves by remembering that, after this tumultuous period is over, the old disposition and the conscientiousness that we valued will probably return as vigorous as ever . . .

Marriage about this time is not advisable, and it may even be dangerous, as it has a tendency to bring on inflammation, if nothing worse. Even after the first appearances of the change have begun pregnancy may occur, and may prove very injurious, so that the risk of it should always be avoided . . . [N]o suffering whatever need attend this epoch in a woman's history if the laws of health have been faithfully followed in the past years, and that the period need not be dreaded for any reason whatever. On the contrary it will sometimes be found that some slight ailments which previously existed have entirely disappeared, and that the health has become more firmly established than ever, a supposition which is borne out by the fact that hardly any of the special diseases of old age are described as affecting women, and that they are generally more long-lived than men. There is no greater fallacy, either, than to imagine that old age, in a mental or spiritual sense, supervenes as soon as the physical characteristics of womanhood cease. Those who think so must be singularly unfortunate in their elderly acquaintances, and must ignore or forget the vast amount of work, social, philanthropic, and public, which is daily performed by women on the heavenly side of fifty, whom no one would think of referring to as "old women" . . .

Jane Hume Clapperton (1832–1914) was a writer on social reform who associated with many well-known figures of her day. She published articles in literary journals; the book from which this extract comes was her best-known work, however. It covers an array of subjects from a social evolutionary point of view. She subsequently wrote novels that critiqued marriage and the domestic role of women. It is clear that Clapperton had radical opinions: for example, on contraception; and she appears to have been in the vanguard of socialist and eugenicist views that later gained greater currency.[10] Her work also provides interesting parallels in utopian thinking with that of her better-known contemporary, Patrick Geddes, who published *The Evolution of Sex* in 1889.

2.5 Jane Hume Clapperton, *Scientific Meliorism and the Evolution of Happiness* (London: Kegan, Paul, Trench and Co., 1885)[11] (172–3, 174–5, 176–7)

Next in order to the animal instinct or appetite of eating and drinking comes that of the sex instinct or feeling. Of equal importance to life – that is the life of the *race* – this latter differs in its essential nature from the former. Mr G. H. Lewes, in his important work "The Problems of Life and Mind," makes clear to us, that whilst the individual functions of man (alimentation being one of these functions) arise in relation to the cosmos, his general functions, including sex-appetite, arise in relation to the social medium; and "animal impulses" he says "become blended with human emotions," till "in the process of evolution, starting from the merely animal appetite of sexuality, we arrive at the purest and most far-reaching tenderness." . . .

This appetite, then, holds in reality a higher position . . . It is not purely egoistic, it has a wider range; and when exercised under moral conditions it calls into play emotions that are of the highest, most purifying order . . .

. . . [I]n the present day, the strength of this inherited instinct differs in the sexes, although the appetite is common alike to both. The difference varies of course in individual cases; but as a rule, the instinct is in all men keen and strong, whereas in many women who have tenderness and all the sympathetic qualities largely developed, the appetite from which these latter have arisen is in itself extremely weak, and sociality in them entirely dominates animality . . .

. . . I must say a word regarding artificial checks to reproduction. There are many parents in the middle classes, who, aware that they have brought up their children luxuriously, and that their personal requirements are therefore great, dread early marriage for them on account of the expense and cares that an establishment and a young family would bring. On the other hand they plainly see the dangers to sons and daughters of a dissatisfied and restless youth, and they know that in many cases, although not in all, the true meaning of giving equipoise, *i.e.* a healthy balance of mind and body, would be by entrance into married life. To such parents the thought of obtaining for their children the advantages, without the drawbacks, of early marriage would be hailed as an inestimable boon but for ideal scruples which confuse the judgement and perplex the mind. It has been said that artificial checks do not suffice, and that if they did, to use them is improper and contrary to nature. Now, my reader will easily perceive, that in a work of this kind it is the abstract aspect of this question *only* with which I have to deal; but when we look at France, a nation quite as civilized as our own, and see that her population is all but stationary, and that the small birth-rate is not confined to cities (where licentiousness might be suspected as a partial factor), but extends to country districts, where the industrious peasantry lead a pure, domestic life, it becomes evident that there is *no* practical and insurmountable obstacle to be overcome . . . To reverence human nature is to give it freedom for the exercise of every pleasurable function . . .

And now one other point . . . Where animalism is strong and instinctive, and love of offspring deficient, the tender joys, the anxious cares of parentage are not desired, and will be, by means of artificial checks, easily and intentionally avoided. Not animalism alone, but animalism combined with philoprogenitiveness will be the complex force to bring into the world the coming generations, and two results will follow. The inestimable blessing of parental love and parental responsibility, assumed by choice, will be the outward heritage of all, and inwardly, the new race will by inheritance partake of natures that are broader and fuller than the type of man in whom the pure and tender love of children has no existence, and animality dominates sociability.

The following extract comes from a text originating in North America but it also received a Scottish imprint through a well-known Edinburgh publisher. Its author styled himself a lecturer on 'sanitary science'. The book was a companion volume to others in a series, including *Confidential Talks with Young Men* (1893) and *Confidential Talks with Young Women* (1894). All received a Scottish imprint and were advertised in newspapers such as *The Christian Leader* and *The Scotsman*. Sperry's work engages with the issue of female desire, though only when sanctioned by marriage and initiated by a husband.

> 2.6 Lyman Beecher Sperry, *Confidential Talks with Husband and Wife: A Book of Information and Advice for the Married and Marriageable* (Edinburgh: Oliphant Anderson and Ferrier, 1900) (121, 122, 124, 125, 126)

All well informed men know that normal, adult males, almost without exception, have strong sexual appetites . . . Comparatively few women appreciate this fact regarding men until a knowledge of it is forced upon them – after wedlock . . .

In a general way, and for the purposes of approximation in this matter, we may divide women into three classes, with a probability that the numbers in each class will be not far from equal.

1. Those who are naturally as amorous and as responsive in sexual passion as the average man.
2. Those who, while less passionate than men, still have positive desire for, and take actual pleasure in, sexual congress, – especially just preceding menstruation and immediately following its periodical cessation.

3. Those who experience no physical passion or pleasurable sexual sensations, and submit to copulation only from a sense of duty, or for the purpose of bearing children, or simply for the pleasure of gratifying the husband.

It is probable that class 2 is somewhat the largest . . . Doubtless most women who notice this classification and estimate will feel inclined to question its correctness, for nearly every woman believes that, in the matter of sexuality and the impulses springing from it, she herself represents a very large percentage of her sex . . . One reason why women entertain false ideas on this subject is because so many of their sex think it derogatory and shameful to admit the possession of sexual passion. Not a few women think it a cause for congratulation that they have a positive distaste for all sexual activity . . .

While nearly every woman enjoys the kissing, caressing and all the evidence of affection and pleasure that is so universally exhibited by a husband immediately preceding and during the gratification of his sexual desires, there are many who experience absolutely no pleasant local sensation, no real amative delight . . .

It is important to know that many women who, at the beginning of married life, belong in one of the above classes, gradually undergo changes of desire so marked as to transfer them to another class . . . Those who start in the first class are perhaps least likely to undergo a change; and yet, hard work, grievous hardships, child-bearing and an increasing want of respect for a brutal husband may result in reducing a woman's amorousness till she will seem to belong in the second class; or possibly, she may settle down even into the third grade, and come to loathe all sexual demonstration. On the other hand, many of those who naturally belong in the third class may, by such cultivation as an amorous, but clean, kind, affectionate, considerate and ingenious husband can bring to bear, be developed into representatives of the second class . . . [and] be brought into full sympathy with his desires . . .

A wife of good sense is quite apt, in due time, to become practically about what her husband appreciates in the matter of sexual activity and responsiveness, – provided the husband be a man of intelligence and conscience, and makes only healthful and reasonable demands . . .

The Glasgow parish council report quoted below aimed to attract public attention and encourage changes in the law, as well as a more rigorous approach to the application of existing laws. While Church discipline may have declined, the Scottish churches continued to perceive sexual immorality as a widespread menace. In this period, understandings of its causes were often tainted by xenophobia. Over this century, Scotland was a country of net emigration but this did not prevent prejudice against immigrant groups, such as the Irish, Italians and eastern European Jews, becoming embroiled in discussions of alleged moral dissipation in Scottish society. Moreover, though religious groups did wish to combat the very real problems of incest and child abuse, near hysteria about the 'evil' of prostitution tended to get more publicity. The behaviour of mothers and young girls was especially targeted as a way to remedy female behaviour generally; to deal with this issue, parish mission sisters were appointed to work in working-class communities. Reports by several of these female workers are included in the memorandum. Extracts from different parts of this memorandum are presented here, including part of the general discussion, an extract from a female parish worker's report, and extracts from an appendix containing evidence about the abuse of young girls (Appendix 11 is a return of a conviction against ice cream shop proprietors between 1908 and 1910; and Appendix 111 concerns children found in brothels). The council published a further similar report, *Glasgow Parish Council Immoral House and Venereal Diseases Minute of Joint Conference* (1911) (GRML: Shelfmark: GCf351.76GLA).

> 2.7 *Memorandum on a Social Evil in Glasgow and the State of the Law for Dealing With Certain Forms of Immorality, Glasgow Parish Council* (October 1911) [Glasgow Room, Mitchell Library. Shelfmark: GCCDf.351.764PAR] (11–12, 60, App. 1, 18–19)

Extract from the memorandum's general discussion:

> By far the worst case was one where the uncle and aunt, guardians of a girl of 14, were charged with encouraging her prostitution by allowing her to consort with another prostitute a girl of the same age, the aunt being sentenced to 3 months imprisonment, and the uncle bound over. The second girl stated in evidence that she had been "on the streets" since before she was 13. Her mother was a widow, and she led her to believe that she was out working after school hours. She had intercourse with all sorts of men, in closes, lanes, and in sublet houses, and the other girl watched for the police while she was in the close with men, until she too took up the same mode of life, and thereafter they watched time about. They had certain ice cream shops to which they went by appointment at stated periods, and one or two offices as well. Some months before we got charge of her, she contracted venereal disease, but notwithstanding continued to have intercourse nightly with all sorts of men. The Italians, finding out her condition then resorted to other horrible practices which cannot be described, and these outrages were regularly committed on the companion as well. It was only when she was apprehended by the police for disorderly conduct while under the influence of drink – a girl of 14, be it remembered – that her disease was discovered and she was sent to the Lock Hospital. After the conviction we got both girls committed to the care of the Parish, and placed them in separate R. C. Institutions. The second girl was sent to one on the Borders, but escaped the second night after her admission, in a semi-nude state, taking another girl with her . . .

Extract from a report by a female Parish worker:

> . . . I should think that the following are some of the principal causes of this condition of affairs:
> 1st. Condition of Home life. When the house consists of one or two apartments, and the family is large, or there are younger children, the elder ones prefer to go out on the streets. Here they mix with companions of both sexes, they hear obscene

language and stories, and meet with suggestive advances, ultimately leading to temptation (dancing halls, ice cream saloons, etc., are much frequented by this class). Once they have started this, the next step is that of receiving money, and finding they get it easily they continue the life.

2nd. There are those who are brought up amongst vice, see it and hear it spoken of, and naturally drift into it.

3rd. There are some who start the life, with the definite object of making money, having a weakness for "finery," and a desire for pocket money.

4th. There are some who appear to have no control over their passions and to whom money making is a secondary consideration.

5th. There are a few who have previously lived a moral life but have been led astray by the man with whom they have been keeping company and finally left to their fate.

6th. The promiscuous housing of the sexes.

Once a girl has started on this life she soon loses all self respect and has no desire to go back to what she considers a monotonous life, especially when she finds she can make money more easily this way than by honest labour.

Information included in Appendix 1: *Return Showing the Number of Girls Under 16 Years of Age Reported As Defiled During The Past 12 Months.* The Appendix lists twenty-five cases including the following which have been extracted:

| Date | Name | Age | By whom reported | Nature of defilement | How case disposed of |
|---|---|---|---|---|---|
| 1-8-10 | A | 9 | A medical practitioner | Rape (communicating venereal disease) | Robert Fisher (19), sentenced to 3 years' penal servitude at High Court on 18th October, 1910. |
| 1-10-10 | B | 8 | The Secy., Lock Hospital | Venereal Disease | Reported to Procurator Fiscal. Not taken up. No evidence except statement of the child. |
| 14-10-10 | C | 13 | Do. | Do. | Reported to Procurator-Fiscal. Not taken up. No evidence except statement of the child. |
| 29-10-10 | D | 5 | Do. | Do. | Reported to Procurator-Fiscal. Not taken up. No evidence except statement of the child. |
| 8-11-10 | E | 3 | Do. | Do. | The child could not give information. |
| 9-1-11 | F | 13 | Mother of the girl | Carnally known | A man reported to Procurator-Fiscal. Not taken up. Girl examined by doctor. No appearance of interference. |
| 10-1-12 | G | 15 | The Secy., Lock Hospital | Venereal disease | Girl had been a prostitute for 12 months, and had the disease 4 months prior to admission to hospital. |

| Date | Name | Age | By whom reported | Nature of defilement | How case disposed of |
|------|------|-----|------------------|----------------------|----------------------|
| 13-1-11 | H | 6 | Do. | Do. | The girl stated she had been tampered with by a man in a court at 237 Bernard Street, and also at a watchman's fire at Marlborough Street. A watchman was shown to her, but she could not identify him. |
| 11-2-11 | I | 3 | Do. | Do. | Child's mother a prostitute. Disease supposed contracted from another prostitute with whom the child slept. |
| 14-2-11 | J | 5 | Do. | Gonorrhoea | Refused to give information to parents or nurse. |

The list continues until 'case Y', which is presented as follows:

Case Y., at present a patient in the Lock Hospital, 41 Rottenrow, Glasgow, says: "I am 15 years of age on 27th October, 1910. I reside with my grandmother at — Street, Govan. My father and mother are in Birkenhead, but I do not know their address. I have not seen them for three years. I was employed in —laundry in — Street, Govan, before being admitted to the Hospital. About a year ago, in an ice-cream shop in Govan Road, near — Street, I made the acquaintance of A. B. (18), an apprentice caulker in Elder's shipbuilding yard, and who resides at — Street, Govan, and within the last two months he has had carnal connection with me six times in closes in the vicinity of — Street. C. D. (21), a painter in Fairfield shipbuilding yard, who resides at — Street, had connection with me three times within the past two months in a close in Govan Road, Govan; and also during same time, a young man whom I only know by name of E.F., had connection with me once in a close in Govan Road. I do not know where he resides, but he runs about the corner of — Street with A. B. and C. D. I am sure it was A. B. I got the trouble from, as he had connection with me on a Thursday night, and on the following night, he had connection with my chum, — (16), of — Street, Govan. A week afterwards, we both felt something wrong. We both bathed ourselves with Condy's fluid. She got better but I got worse and was not able to walk. I would not tell my grandmother what was wrong. She got the doctor to examine me, and he sent me to the Lock Hospital. I never importuned on the streets, and did not get money from any of the lads."

The following extract from a report on a conference held in Edinburgh demonstrates that public discussion was taking place of what was by then the undeniable reality of family limitation by the middle classes.

### THE DECLINING BIRTH RATE IN EDINBURGH

Dr Ballantyne, who opened the discussion, said that in Edinburgh in 1881 there were 7360 babies born. In 1912 there were something like 6600, nearly 700 fewer babies born in Edinburgh, with roughly 100,000 more of a population . . . [H]e said it seemed to him as if they must conclude that in late years the civilised part of the human race was beginning to experiment with its reproduction very much in the same sort of way as the human race had experimented in other directions, with, if he might say so, its mode of locomotion, and in many other ways. By the falling birth rate they were face to face with what one might call in commercial language the appreciation of infant life . . . The Chairman said that the remedy must be a moral remedy, a quickening of the conscience of the population, and that quickening founded on scientific and social facts . . .

## Section 3: In sickness and in health

As well as being responsible for child rearing and housework, women performed a further key role of giving advice and assistance in the care of the body. Indeed, many aspects of domestic labour were themselves aimed at ensuring the good health of women and their families: this might be cooking nutritious food, cleaning, balancing the household budget to ensure sufficient clothing and heat were available, or tending to the needs of sick family members. In pre-industrial times, such female duties involved women in being the keepers of knowledge about health-giving tonics, remedies and procedures for dealing with life events that impinged on the female body, such as menstruation, pregnancy, childbirth and old age. Despite the upheavals of the century, this important role was largely maintained and women continued to be the primary givers of health care and advice. Medical treatments were expensive, sometimes difficult to access for any but the wealthy and, even in this scientific age, still unreliable. Such factors ensured that, despite the growing investment in scientific understanding of the body and the gradual movement of women into the medical profession, interventions in women's health were uneven in their effects. Indeed, the majority of Scottish women would rarely consult a doctor during their lifetime but depended on either home-made remedies or those purveyed by largely unlicensed healers. At the beginning of the century and for many decades beyond this, most women learned about caring for their bodies either at home or within their immediate communities, and coped with major life events, such as childbirth, outside of institutions and with the aid of other women. Gradually, however, this aspect of women's experience altered, and the increased professionalisation of medicine has often been seen as working to deprive and demote the status of women who earned an income from midwifery and healing. On the other hand, philanthropy played a large part in the institutionalisation of health care, and this often involved middle- and upper-class women. The spread of hospitals, however, was not simply an outcome of concern and altruism because such places also provided much-needed medical, nursing and midwifery training; a further feature of the period was the increased requirement by professionals for certification and accredited practice.

The extract below is from a report of the Edinburgh Lying-In Institution, founded in 1813 and surviving until 1933. It mostly provided care in women's own homes; in doing so, it supplied obstetric experience for doctors and later for trainee midwives. It was the earliest and longest surviving of eight such women's facilities in Edinburgh, the most famous being that founded by Elsie Inglis (1864–1917)‡.[12] Married women only 'who may be recommended either by the Subscribers, by the Clergymen, or by the Elders of the different Parishes or Congregations to which the Applicants belong' were able to use its services, the clear implication being that only the respectable poor were eligible. Similar facilities were opened in all of Scotland's cities during the century; many records of these institutions survive in local health board archives, and advertisements for them can easily be found in Post Office Directories and almanacs.

3.1  *Edinburgh Lying-In Institution for delivering Poor Married Women at Their Own Houses* (Edinburgh: printed by Murray and Mitchell, 1824) (6–7)

The Objects of this Institution are, to afford every requisite attendance, either by a Medical Gentleman, or a Midwife, (as circumstances may require) to Poor Married Women lying-in at their own habitations; to furnish them with the necessary Medicines; to supply the most needy of them with the temporary use of Childbed Linen, Flannels, Blankets, &c., and with any other addition to the means of comfort and health that may be essentially necessary.

At present there is not any Public Institution of the same kind established in this City, embracing such manifold advantages to the Industrious Poor at such a period of anxiety, when all the evils of Poverty are felt in an accumulated degree.

In furtherance of the object in view, it is proposed to form a Committee of Ladies, to superintend the Clothing, or Wardrobe Department: The Committee to consist of Twelve Ladies, Two of whom (to be selected by themselves) are to undertake the Charitable Office of Visitors. The two Visitors are, in rotation, to be succeeded in that duty by two other Ladies, at such periods as their own convenience may render practicable.

... [T]here is every reason to hope and believe, that the benevolent feelings of the Ladies of the City of Edinburgh will very much contribute to the measure of affording relief to the deserving Poor who may require the assistance of this Charity.

The source below reveals the attempts of so-called 'man-midwives' to share knowledge about new treatments and practices. Attending to women in labour could be a very lucrative trade, and medical men who obtained a reputation for safe deliveries were assured a good livelihood as family doctors. Journals, such as that quoted, proliferated during the century, serving to promote the advancement of knowledge and securing the professional standing of the authors. Scottish physicians regularly featured as leading contributors. The extract typifies the knowledge-sharing that took place in medical periodicals. Armour outlines in detail five cases, which had variable results, and discusses the published findings of others on the use of a drug. The dangers of childbirth to women and infants made obstetrical practice into an increasingly contested field, fought between ongoing and unregulated traditional practices and doctors who were becoming more interventionist. This led to the demise of the traditional, uncertificated midwife or *howdie*, as she was known in some parts of Scotland, and, though the vast majority of women continued to give birth at home, the medicalisation of childbirth took off in this period. The drug discussed below was far from new: *Secale cornatum*, or ergot of rye, is a fungus that grows on rye, the use of which as a remedy had been established in Europe since the sixteenth century.[13] Accidental ingestion of ergot causes poisoning but it also has therapeutic properties when prepared and given correctly. Midwives and physicians had long used ergot to induce labour pains and to prevent or to treat haemorrhage; this preparation could also work to procure abortion in the early months of pregnancy. At the beginning of the century, many doctors began to publish on their use of the drug in obstetric practice, but many also contested its efficacy. This resulted in a century-long heated debate that was disseminated through medical publishing. Such articles exploring the use of medicines and instruments such as forceps often involved vivid descriptions of childbirth.

3.2 James Armour, MD, Andersonian Professor of Midwifery, 'On the Uses of the Secale Cornatum, particularly in Parturition', *The Glasgow Medical Journal*, 3: 12 (Glasgow: Griffin and Co., 1830), pp. 351–72 (352–3).

. . . I proceed, first, to detail the cases in which I have either given, or advised the administration of this medicine, in labour. Case 1st. Mrs. C, aged 25, was seized with the symptoms of genuine labour, on a Thursday, in July, 1825. On examination, it was reported, by the gentleman in attendance, that the os uteri was found to be high, and very much turned backwards. He did not perceive any evidence of malformation of the pelvis. The bowels were opened by castor oil, and afterwards an opiate was given, which produced a few hours of restless sleep. He did not see her again till Friday, at 10 a.m., when he was sent for. The head of the child could be distinctly felt through the membranes, and he entertained hopes of a speedy termination to the process; but the labour continued till Saturday, at 10 a.m., before the head distinctly entered the brim. The uterine action was now, for a time, nearly suspended. The bowels were opened by an injection. She dozed a good deal, till Sunday morning, about 8 o'clock, when the pains again recurred with vigour . . . The woman laboured on till Tuesday evening, during which time several fruitless attempts had been made by another surgeon, who had been called in, to extract the child by the forceps. It was at this period that I first saw her. The head was now pretty well advanced in the cavity of the pelvis. Her strength was greatly exhausted; the pains extremely weak, and perfectly inefficient; and I thought there was no possibility of their ever expelling the child. The vagina was in a very disagreeable condition; and I imagined there was considerable risk in applying the forceps, from the injury which, in this state of the passage, they might very readily occasion. Perhaps, the best thing I could have done, would have been to have opened the child's head, as, from the history of the case, and from every concomitant circumstance, there was reason to believe that it was dead. It is an unpleasant thing, however, to introduce the perforator into a child's head, unless we are quite sure of its death, or perfectly convinced that there is great danger to the woman, from any other mode of proceeding. It occurred to me to recommend the ergot of rye, which, however, I had not previously used, nor seen used. Exactly at half-past 6 o'clock in the evening, the infusion of 3ss. of this medicine was given. Eight minutes afterwards the pulse had fallen from 90 to 74, and had become, I thought, rather fuller. The labour, at the end of that time, became more brisk, more uninterrupted, and continued so for about 15 minutes, when the same dose of the medicine was repeated. The pains, in the course of other 10 minutes, became extremely severe and continuous, or, to use the words of the gentleman in attendance, who afterwards sent me a note of the case – "It would be vain to attempt describing the uterine efforts which followed; they exceeded, in violence, any thing I ever saw, either before or since." The child was born exactly 40 minutes from the time of the exhibition of the first dose of the medicine, dead and soft . . .

Lady Malcolm (1785–1830), whose diary is quoted below, was married to a naval commander who had charge of Napoleon's exile in St Helena, and she is known for her posthumously published *Diary of St Helena*.[14] These excerpts are from a journal she kept in the weeks leading up to her death in Scotland, and are transcribed as faithfully as possible from the original handwritten manuscript. For most of the century, even the most serious illness was dealt with at home, as hospitals were often situated within poorhouses and were a last resort for those destitute through illness. A doctor might be in attendance but, because advances in medical science took time to be reflected in clinical practice, traditional remedies were still commonly used alongside medically prescribed treatments. Before the development of anaesthesia and antiseptic procedures later in the century, surgery for this kind of tumour would not have been an option. Some of Lady Malcolm's remedies had a very long history. Her descriptions are no doubt understated but it is clear she suffered greatly. Even so, she had assistance from servants and access to bathing which would have not been available to poor women whose distress in similar medical circumstances can only be imagined.

### 3.3 Lady Clementina Malcolm's Diary of her Breast Cancer (*c*.1830) [NLS. Acc. 9756]

Monday May 3rd    went into the bath took the medicine at night and applied a plaster to draw the tumours, did not sleep well having considerable pain . . .

| | |
|---|---|
| Tuesday | removed the plaster, took the medicine, Dr W said the increased discharge was what he wished, at night besides the medicine took a rhubarb pill, not a very good night and considerable pain. |
| Wednesday | removed the plaster and took the medicine. Dr W . . . left me a sort of bark to make a Poultice he said I sh' find very soothing. I had a better night but not free from pain. |
| Thursday | continued the Poultice and medicine morn and even . . . was free from pain in the night . . . |
| Friday | considerable pain in the tumours after breakfast and uncomfortable all day . . . Dr W said the discharge was what he wished and the appearance what he expected . . . |
| Saturday | had a better night continued the poultice and medicine and was more comfortable all day, took meat and vegetables at luncheon time, and fish and pudding at dinner. In the even the pain returned and besides the medicine took half a rhubarb pill. |
| Sunday | had a good night though some pain in the tumours, besides the poultice on the tumours I covered my back and shoulder when I felt pain with the plaster and kept it on in the morn. The rhubarb had more effect than I wished, my skin felt sore (as formerly over my back and chest) the tumours smarted, and the back ached, altogether I felt very uncomfortable . . . the discharge from the tumour smelt offensive and so it continued after the Poultice has been on some hours . . . on the whole I can perceive no change I can call much better. |
| Monday May 10th | Felt easier in the morn – had the bath and was more comfortable than usual in the even, no pain in the night a new medicine instead of that I had before, and an addition to the poultice. |
| Tuesday | The bad smell returned but not [helped?] by the addition to the poultice, the tumour uncomfortable after I was up . . . took the rhubarb pill in addition to the medicine. |
| Wednesday | A good night, but much pain after I was up, and for a short time after. |

Jane Welsh Carlyle‡ (1801–66)[15] grew up in Scotland and later married the essayist and historian, Thomas Carlyle, spending most of her married life in London where the couple were part of a metropolitan intelligentsia. Jane was something of a martyr to health problems and regularly complained in her letters of headaches, colds, and a variety of aches and pains in a highly dramatic fashion. Yet she seems also to have resented the effects of illness in her otherwise busy life. Though she had recourse to medical opinion, the services of local retail pharmacists and self-medication with patent remedies for everyday complaints were quite usual. Such freely available pharmaceutical remedies, however, included substances that were undoubtedly toxic. The 'blue pills' referred to in this extract were taken for digestive symptoms and contained mercury; they operated as a laxative. Other letters describe Jane taking regular doses of morphia for persistent insomnia. She also favoured quinine for a variety of symptoms. Of course, it is highly likely that such remedies served only to further undermine health. Carlyle's letters are available at *The Carlyle Letters Online* [*CLO*] (2007) http://carlyleletters.org

> ### 3.4 Letter from Jane Welsh Carlyle to her Cousin Jeannie Welsh (mid-April 1845) in Vol. 19 of the *Collected Letters* (January–September 1845) (58, 59)

Dearest Babbie

I said that I would write yesterday *god willing* but god was *not willing* and the manner of it was thus – on the preceding night I had *five grains of mercury* (!) introduced into my interior *by mistake* – instead of *one half grain* the quantity I am in the habit of taking at one time – and which is quite *enough "for anything"* – So much for my husbands *false refinement!* I had been wretchedly bilious for some days and sent him to Alsop's for *my* blue pills – *he* also being in the practise of getting pills there – of *five grains* – which he swallows from time to time "in werra desperation" (as you know) and in fellowship with an ocean of Castor oil – the pills came and I swallowed one; merely wondering why they had sent me only *three* instead of my customary *dozen* – but ten minutes after when I became deadly sick I understood at once how it was Carlyle frankly admitted it was quite likely there had been a mistake – "when he went into the shop a gentleman was with Alsop and he *did not like* to say *send the blue pills for Mrs Carlyle* but said instead send the blue pills *for our house* – Alsop of course had prefered the *masculine gender* as grammatically bound to do – and so was *delicacy* another person's 'own reward' All yesterday I was sick enough you may fancy – for I felt too weak to deliver myself from the confounded stuff thro a great doze of physic – I thought it safest to let it work away there in the unfortunate *interior* of me until it had its humour out – Carlyle comforted himself and tried to comfort *me*, by suggesting that "it might possibly do me *a great deal of good* in the long run"! It may be "strongly doubted" (as they say in Edin*r*) – anyhow it has not begun to do me good *yet* – for today I am still passably *sick* . . .

Lady Susan Lucy Leslie-Melville (*c.*1838–1910) was the unmarried aunt of Sir William Stirling Maxwell, and Lady of the Bedchamber to HRH the Princess Christian between 1868 and 1883. Her household papers include a handwritten recipe book. This type of notebook kept by women often contained remedies alongside cooking and cleaning instructions (the Wellcome Library has digitised a number of such books, mostly originating in England in the seventeenth and eighteenth centuries: http://archives.wellcome.ac.uk). Such recipes may have been passed on orally for centuries and, as can be seen, might be known to women of all ranks. Despite the growth of commercial pharmaceuticals, traditional herbal remedies did not disappear; violet, a plant-derived remedy, was and continues to be used in the treatment of tumours. In 1906, its properties as a cure for cancer were discussed by no less than the Royal Society for Medicine.[16]

### 3.5 Memorandum books of Lady Susan Lucy Leslie-Melville: 'Recipe Book' (no date *c.*1880s?) [Papers of the Maxwell Family (Diaries, Household Account Books): GCA ref.: T-PM 121/42]

Recipe for Infusion of Violet Leaves For use in cases of Cancer.
Take a handful of fresh green violet leaves and pour about a pint of boiling water on them. Let them stand about 12 hours until the water is green, then strain off the liquid.

Dip a piece of lint into the infusion of which sufficient quantity must [be] warmed. Put on the wet lint wherever the malady is, cover the lint with oilsilk or thin mackintosh, change it when cold or dry.

The infusion should be made fresh about every alternate day.

This treatment relieves the pain and sometimes cures.

The type of health advice illustrated below often appeared in household manuals, providing a good example of how traditional remedies made the transition from oral to print culture. Where women's role as household healer is concerned, these items also demonstrate continuity; indeed, the widespread nature of such texts suggests prescriptive attempts to reinforce this role as another means to improve the general health of the population.

### 3.6 *Cookery for Working Men's Wives Being Recipes by Martha H Gordon as Taught in Mrs John Elder's Domestic Classes, Govan* (Paisley: Alexander Gardner, 1888) (57, 61)

#### Useful Homely Recipe for a Cold or Cough

1 oz Spanish juice, 2 oz honey, ½ lb treacle, 1d worth of Laudanum, 1d worth of Oil of Peppermint, 1 Pint of Water.

Boil down 1 pint of water with the Spanish Juice, honey, and treacle in it to a gill; let it get cold and add laudanum and oil of peppermint. Bottle tight; and shake the bottle before using. Dose for an adult a tablespoonful at night and morning.

#### Mustard Poultices

Dry Mustard, cold water.

Mix enough cold water with the mustard, to make it into a thick paste. When quite smooth spread it upon a piece of thin old linen, or cotton; sew it round, so as to form a bag. Be careful not to make the poultice larger than required. Hold it to the fire for a few minutes, so as not to chill your patient. Time from fifteen to thirty minutes. Have ready a piece of clean soft cotton, or a piece of clean wadding, and when you take of the mustard poultice, put on the cotton or wadding.

Bread and Milk Poultice

Stale bread, cold milk.

Boil bread with enough milk to make a thick pulp. Spread it on a piece of soft cotton, and apply it very hot. This poultice is often applied without a cloth, between it and the affected part; but poultices put in a bag are cleaner and easier pre-warmed. Bread poultices are cleansing and soothing.

As we have seen in source 2.6 above, Sperry's stock-in-trade was to be forthright on issues that contemporaries may have found difficult and indelicate to discuss but, generally, his views uphold the notion that women were prisoners, all too literally, of reproductive biology.

### 3.7  Lyman Beecher Sperry, MD, *Confidential Talks with Young Women* (Edinburgh: Oliphant Anderson and Ferrier, 1894) (71, 72)

. . . All girls or women whose nerves are especially sensitive and easily disturbed during menstruation, should at such times exercise great caution about attending parties, picnics, sleigh rides and excursions; and if possible to avoid it, should not start on journeys during the earlier days of the menstrual period, for the reason that the excitement, fatigue and exposure incident to such efforts and pleasures are quite apt to arrest, or in some way to derange, this function. Many times, of course, it is very annoying to be obliged to stay at home while others are off having a "jolly good time;" but often it is the safest, and hence the *best* thing to do . . . Be particularly careful to keep the feet dry and warm, and always take with you extra wraps, ready for sudden changes in the weather, or for sitting in the shade . . . Avoid lingering in cool draughts, standing on cold or damp ground, sitting on cold stone steps or on cold, damp seats. Many of these precautions seem trivial to young and inexperienced persons; but disregard of them has brought upon many a beautiful girl a life of misery and regret . . .

If any exposure or influence during menstruation arrests it, or even threatens to interfere with its progress, the wise thing to do is promptly to get into a warm bed and take a hot drink of some kind . . .

### 3.8  Advertisement for Towle's Pennyroyal Pills (*c*.1890s)

This product was advertised widely in the Scottish press (as well as elsewhere in the United Kingdom and overseas) and was only one of a variety of marketed solutions for menstrual dysfunction. Its herbal base was well known in folklore and traditionally used to regulate menstruation as well as to induce miscarriage. It is doubtful if any such commercial preparations were effective in either procuring abortion or regulating fertility; nonetheless, many were huge commercial successes. This particular image was identified in the Glasgow-based weekly newspaper, *The Christian Leader*.

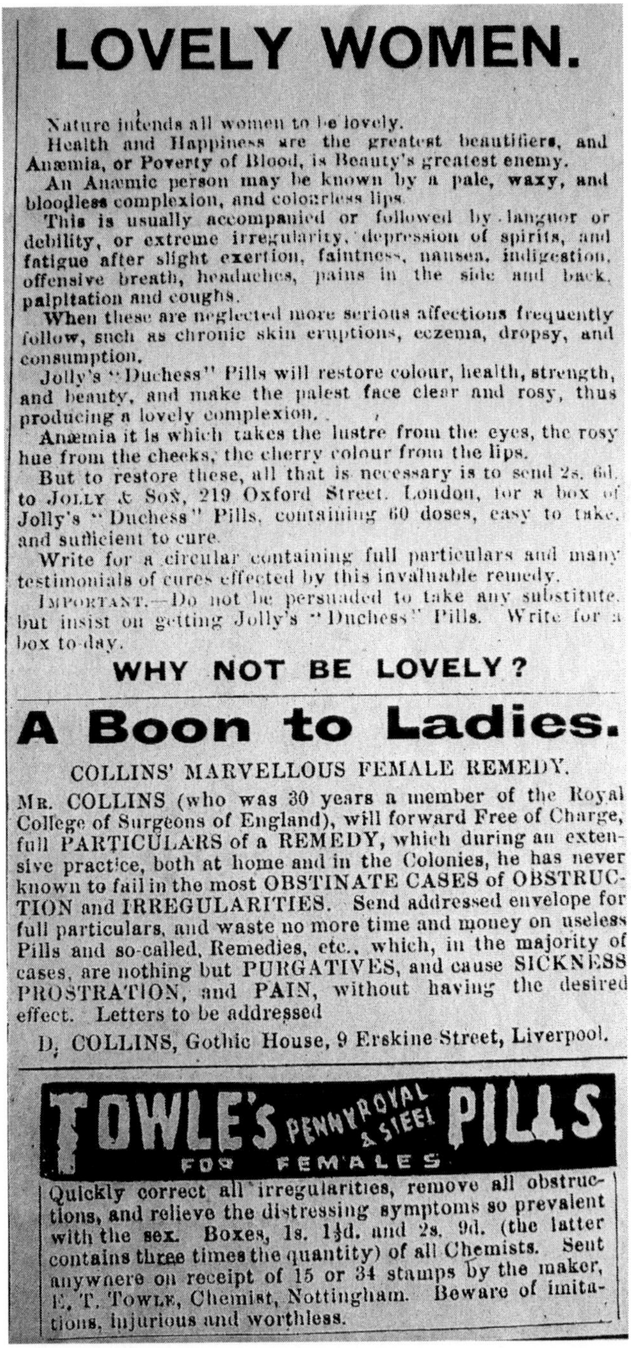

# LOVELY WOMEN.

Nature intends all women to be lovely.

Health and Happiness are the greatest beautifiers, and Anæmia, or Poverty of Blood, is Beauty's greatest enemy.

An Anæmic person may be known by a pale, waxy, and bloodless complexion, and colourless lips.

This is usually accompanied or followed by languor or debility, or extreme irregularity, depression of spirits, and fatigue after slight exertion, faintness, nausea, indigestion, offensive breath, headaches, pains in the side and back, palpitation and coughs.

When these are neglected more serious affections frequently follow, such as chronic skin eruptions, eczema, dropsy, and consumption.

Jolly's "Duchess" Pills will restore colour, health, strength, and beauty, and make the palest face clear and rosy, thus producing a lovely complexion.

Anæmia it is which takes the lustre from the eyes, the rosy hue from the cheeks, the cherry colour from the lips.

But to restore these, all that is necessary is to send 2s. 6d. to JOLLY & SON, 219 Oxford Street. London, for a box of Jolly's "Duchess" Pills, containing 60 doses, easy to take, and sufficient to cure.

Write for a circular containing full particulars and many testimonials of cures effected by this invaluable remedy.

IMPORTANT.—Do not be persuaded to take any substitute, but insist on getting Jolly's "Duchess" Pills. Write for a box to-day.

## WHY NOT BE LOVELY?

# A Boon to Ladies.

### COLLINS' MARVELLOUS FEMALE REMEDY.

MR. COLLINS (who was 30 years a member of the Royal College of Surgeons of England), will forward Free of Charge, full PARTICULARS of a REMEDY, which during an extensive practice, both at home and in the Colonies, he has never known to fail in the most OBSTINATE CASES of OBSTRUCTION and IRREGULARITIES. Send addressed envelope for full particulars, and waste no more time and money on useless Pills and so-called, Remedies, etc., which, in the majority of cases, are nothing but PURGATIVES, and cause SICKNESS PROSTRATION, and PAIN, without having the desired effect. Letters to be addressed

D. COLLINS, Gothic House, 9 Erskine Street, Liverpool.

# TOWLE'S PENNYROYAL & STEEL PILLS FOR FEMALES

Quickly correct all irregularities, remove all obstructions, and relieve the distressing symptoms so prevalent with the sex. Boxes, 1s. 1½d. and 2s. 9d. (the latter contains three times the quantity) of all Chemists. Sent anywhere on receipt of 15 or 34 stamps by the maker, E. T. TOWLE, Chemist, Nottingham. Beware of imitations, injurious and worthless.

**Figure 2.2** Advertisement for Towle's Pennyroyal Pills, *c.*1890s, *The Christian Leader*.

Tuberculosis was a scourge of the nineteenth century and not confined to urban slums though it was in such homes that the disease was most endemic. Membership of friendly societies and the growth of charitable institutions helped provide medical care for many workers. This was hindered, however, by the survival of the Scottish parochial system which had no facility to give financial aid to those unable to work. In the extract below, William Leslie Mackenzie (Chief Medical Officer for Scotland from 1904) describes a familiar chain of events using an equally well-known gendered focus.

### 3.9 William Leslie Mackenzie, *Health and Disease* (London: Williams and Norgate, 1911) (215, 216)

Let us follow a case. Here is a workman earning £2 a week. He has a wife and five or six children, and keeps them in comfort. His wife develops tuberculosis of the lungs. She was, perhaps, infected in early youth, and overworked and underfed, rapidly becomes unfit for her duty. What is a husband to do? He goes to his private doctor who advises sanatorium treatment. But he finds sanatorium treatment beyond his means. He goes to a voluntary hospital in the locality, seeking admission for his wife; but he finds either that they do not admit cases of the kind or that no beds are available. For a time, he keeps his wife at home, procuring the best treatment that his means afford. But with no extra food, no fresh air, no constant medical direction, she grows no better and tends to grow worse. She may, at the same time, infect the children. The husband occupies the same room with her, possibly the same bed. He, too, may take the infection. At last he comes to the end of his resources . . . he applies to the Inspector of Poor. In Scotland, he would not be entitled to relief for his wife, because, by law, he is able-bodied, and no able-bodied person is entitled to relief. Legally therefore he cannot have his wife removed to the sick wards of the poorhouse; but if the Poor Inspector and the Parish Council are generous, they may, as they sometimes do, admit such a case to the poorhouse, and take the risk. The Public Health Authority is under legal obligation to take charge of the case; but, in many localities, the transfer from poor law to public health has hardly begun, and the poorhouse may be the most convenient destination, even if the health authority pay.

   . . . [D]riven by the cares of a sick consort and himself overworked, he gradually loses condition and ultimately shows signs of tuberculosis himself . . . then he goes through the same weary round as his wife, and ultimately joins her in the poorhouse, or in the health authority's hospital. The children are boarded out . . .

The surviving documents of Gartnavel Royal Hospital, which dates from 1814, are voluminous and form a very rich source on mental illness.[17] They also provide valuable insights into all kinds of social and cultural attitudes concerning women's behaviour which, in turn, informed medical thinking. A real prize of these particular records is the correspondence they occasionally contain, sometimes written by patients themselves and revealing intimate details of their lives. 'Self-abuse', as masturbation was known, received widespread medical condemnation, popularised in medical advice books such as that by Sperry, quoted in sources 2.6 and 3.7 above. That this patient was influenced by a book on eugenics indicates that such publications had a popular readership.

### 3.10 Gartnavel Royal Hospital, Glasgow, *Case Book Series Female*, Vol. XXIII (*c.*1915–18): in-patient notes and personal memoir of RF, pp. 468–74 and 573–4 [NHS Greater Glasgow and Clyde Archives: Ref: HB13/5/171]

Extracts from handwritten medical case-notes:

Admitted; 2nd Nov. 1916; Voluntary Patient; aged 36. Teacher; protestant; unmarried; first attack; duration probably about six weeks; not epileptic; is suicidal; not dangerous to others.

Family History: (Obtained from the patient): the patient's father is dead, he was a stern parent & the children were always alarmed at his passionate temper; her mother is alive and is over 70 years of age; the patient is the 7th child of a family of 12 children of whom two died in infancy & 1 was drowned when bathing, the remaining 3 brothers and six sisters are all alive & except the patient, apparently all well. An uncle was insane.

Previous History: The patient speaks of an unhappy childhood due to her father's stern temperament & passionate temper & to the restrictions under which they were all brought up; they were not allowed to mix with other children, did not go to parties or have any of the usual normal outlets for the high-spirits & vivaciousness of their youth. Amongst themselves apparently the young people did not get on well & there was a great deal of quarrelling. Miss RF became a pupil teacher at 14 and then went steadily on through the normal schools with her teaching & training & did very well in this part of her career but says that she was never fond of teaching. In 1911 Miss RF went to Canada & had a school post in Vancouver for 3½ years & liked her life & work & friends very much, a younger sister, a medical woman, is married in Vancouver. In 1915 Miss RF came home & spent a year moving about visiting relations and friends & then returned to Canada in January 1916. She kept pretty well till the end of August when she became sleepless & the doctor advised complete change of work & scene & she went to Calgary feeling very queer. The day after her arrival she was in church with her friends and seems to have had a more or less hysterical attack, thought her brain was going to burst & had to clutch hold of those about her. Three days were spent in hospital & then about three weeks were spent with her friends during which time she only slept when heavily drugged. Finally Miss RF came home reaching Liverpool about 23rd Oct. She travelled alone but had sedative powder and a bottle which the doctor at Calgary gave her. On arriving home Miss RF seems to have been extremely depressed & on the Wednesday before coming to the institution went to the reservoir with the intention of drowning herself.

Physical Condition: Miss RF is a well-nourished young woman with a depressed somewhat shamefaced expression & manner . . .

6th Nov    On the Friday afternoon (4th) Miss RF was very agitated, strung up, very apprehensive lest she should do any harm to herself & so upset

that a 15/20 chloral bromide draught was given early in the afternoon
. . . During a recent conversation this patient stated that she had been
addicted to the habit of masturbation since she was about 14 years of age
& that a year ago she read a book on eugenics that talked of this matter
& that only since then had she ceased to practice the habit. All along
she was aware it was wrong but the true significance & real wickedness
of it had not completely dawned on her until after reading this book &
since then she had been utterly overwhelmed with shame & self-disgust.
Her idea of committing suicide had not been impulsive in nature but
quite deliberate as being a less shameful end for her both for herself &
her family's sake that becoming insane & an inmate of an asylum as she
now realised she must become owing to her former bad habits. At the
same time she reproached herself for a bitter & unhappy letter that she
had written to her mother when she first went to Canada casting up the
unhappy life she had had as a child & the difficulties under which they
had all suffered. Miss RF says this is the only letter she has written her
mother & that she has never had a reply to it . . . It is curious to note how
firmly fixed the idea is that because masturbation was practised insanity
& more especially imbecility must follow; evidently an unnecessarily
literal interpretation of the attempted teaching of personal hygiene in
the particular book that was read . . .

10th Jan     In a conversation last night the patient gave an impression of a very
marked degree of depression, she harped back on the question of having
disgraced herself and her family, of being utterly incapable of returning
to live with her people in Cambuslang; she said she still felt convinced
she was going to become feebleminded because she found it impossible
to concentrate on anything, that she felt "dead" emotionally unable to
care about what affected others, but chiefly & always Miss RF spoke
about the "disgrace" of having been here, said she was an "outcast" now
from her family but that she quite acknowledged she deserved it . . . It
is rather difficult to disentangle the threads of this lady's real trouble,
when she speaks of "disgrace" for having been here she as a matter of fact
usually means the "disgrace" of having been a masturbator that finally
conduced to bring about this mental breakdown; also at times one gets
a very definite impression that the distress & emotion displayed about
having "disgraced" her family etc, cloaks a much deeper bitter feeling of
having erected a gulf between herself & some particular individual by
her conduct . . .

10th Feb     . . . Miss RF on the 6th handed the writer a bulky epistle consisting of
a letter of thanks for her kind treatment here etc. & of farewell as she
intended to take her own life once she could get clear of the asylum. The
rest of the document consisted of an extremely fluent & well-written
account of the writer's intimate life almost wholly from the sexual side,
a most tragic document if accepted in its entirety but probably largely to

be discounted. This manuscript had been completed on the 28th when Miss RF had had deliberate intention of committing suicide intending to escape from her sister when in town with her some day, going to Gourock & then drowning herself, on the way posting back the two documents referred to Dr Robertson. The plan was frustrated by the doctor's distrust of Miss RF's condition and with the sudden reversion of feeling etc. that came with the elated state . . .

19th Feb  Miss RF was beginning to improve after last note, becoming less restless & showing more general control & sleeping better & more easily at night but on the morning of this 16th Feb she received the appended curt document from her sister which naturally affected her very much & in this afternoon she left the asylum on her own & her brother's responsibility to attend her mother's death bed. As no further information has been received from Miss RF or her relations & as the lady was a voluntary patient she is discharged today.

Discharged 19th Feb. 1917
Relieved.

Text of note delivered to the patient:

Dear B
Mother arrived yesterday morning in her own house. She came in an ambulance from London where she has been ill for a month. She was conscious yesterday <u>but very, very weak</u> & we think it is her last illness on this earth. She has been in great pain and still suffers much. With love
Jeannie

Extracts from a handwritten personal account entitled, 'Story of a Ruined Life' (dated 24 January 1917) enclosed in the case record of RF:

I was one of a large family born in the country & brought up on father's large farm. My father, a very clever man, strictly just, with many good qualities & of a strict moral character, belonged to a large family of brothers, noted for their quick tempers, quarrelsome and passionate natures & as children we feared rather than loved him. Our young life was one of stern repression & owing to the many scenes of quarrelling between father & mother – very often over one of the family – we had a very unhappy childhood. Family worship was taken up spasmodically & we never knew when it was going to be brought to an abrupt close with an exhibition of temper over something, perhaps of a trivial nature. Mother seemed always to be too harassed & busy to bother much talking to us & we were pretty much left to our own devices. Our grandparents (on mother's side) lived near us and my sister, then 10½ yrs – she was like a twin to me and we were inseparable – and I, a child of 9 yrs, spent a lot of time with them. We were then as innocent as babes & of evil knew nothing. We used to delight in climbing up to Grandpa's knee as he always kept a stock of sweets & pennies in his pockets. At these tender years we were both corrupted by him for he it was who began an evil practice. I think now, that we must have been born with the low animal life strongly developed in us, for though we knew we were doing something wrong, some force of nature of which we knew nothing, led us back again & again to him. That continued for nearly a year, when our innocence was further destroyed one day. We were both so thoroughly disgusted and frightened that we made a compact – even at the risk of forfeiting sweets and pennies – not to go near him again when he was alone, which agreement we strictly kept but alas! For the knowledge gained! Oh if parents & especially mothers only realized how important it is to gain their children's confidence when young – what a difference it would make in after lives. Far be it from me to reproach mother for I have much to regret in my own conduct towards my parents but looking back on my childhood from my experience of life now, I cannot help from seeing certain things. I was naturally a shy, reserved and super-sensitive child, but we could never tell mother anything nor ask questions of her . . .

To continue the degrading story, when I was 12 years & still ignorant if no longer innocent, an indecent assault was attempted twice on me, by another relative – then a youth of 20 years, & though badly frightened & longing to confide in someone, somehow I could not go to mother.

Educated at the village school, I began teaching as a Monitor Pupil-Teacher at the age of 13½ years & served an apprenticeship of 5 years under a schoolmaster noted for his brilliant scholarship & at the same time, his immoral character, though a married man with a wife and family . . .

During the first 4 yrs as a P.T. I had lessons with the other P.T.s – one of them my sister – from our master after school hours. But during the last year I was left alone, the others having left. Instinctively I feared that man & used to dread these private lessons. On different occasions I ran away from the lessons to escape his hateful embraces & caresses. Still at home I kept silence . . .

When 18 years I had another fright from a gentleman of 35 yrs who was spending the evening at our home. He was looked up to by all for his high morals and principles & was a lot in the public life of the district. Taking advantage when I happened to be a few minutes alone with him, he again showed me the brutal side of human nature & it was only by a fierce struggle that I escaped . . .

Is it any wonder that I grew shy of men & looked on every man as a kind of wild animal?

During these years, the evil habit learned in childhood, was indulged in by my sister & me until we became veritable slaves to it. Again & again we vowed to help each other & tried valiantly, but our lower nature conquered & we would fall.

We rose to hold good positions in schools near home after the family moved to Cambuslang. Our home life was still one of repression of social life, such as other girls enjoyed, we knew little. All the time the sexual instinct was becoming stronger & for our super-abundant animal life – we had no healthy outlet in the way of Dancing, Skating, Tennis (later on I learned Golf & Swimming, but was reproved for doing so). As I grew older the woman's natural craving for love & attention came to me and I began to take an interest in men & enjoyed their company, while losing the fear of former years . . .

During my past years, I had a few love affairs like the most of girls & though never engaged, I had two offers of marriage, one from a good man who, I believe, was genuine in his regard for me, but unfortunately I did not care for him . . .

During varied experiences in the past years, I was often exposed to strong temptations – every woman is who goes abroad – yet in that respect I always kept pure. What I told you about having finally cured myself of the sin before 1916, was true & for a number of years previous to that, a lapse only took place a few times a year – when I always loathed myself for being so weak-willed. This breakdown, I believe, is nature's revenge for the sin in earlier years & that have begun nearly 2 years ago with great fits of depression, & worrying – all the time I did not know or realize what was wrong with me. God & nature gifted me with a fine brain & excellent constitution to begin life with, but oh! what a failure I have made of it! . . .

You will perhaps wonder what my object is in writing all this revolting tale & in soiling so much good paper with such a record, but if you have occasion, as a doctor, to lecture to mothers to talk to them, I would plead with you, from the wreck of my life, to use your influence as a doctor to impress upon them how vitally important it is that children, at a certain age, should be told something of the physiological laws governing their own bodies. And <u>more important</u>, should they be <u>encouraged</u> to bring their childhood's troubles to their mother's knee for it is in childhood very often, that the foundations of character, for good or evil, are laid & I would like my awful lesson to be a warning to others . . .

In deepest shame, remorse, and sorrow

I sign it

R. F.

## Select bibliography

Lynn Abrams, *The Making of Modern Woman: Europe 1789–1918* (London: Pearson, 2002); chapter on 'Sex and Sexuality', pp. 149–74.

Michael Anderson and D. J. Morse, 'The People', in W. Hamish Fraser and R. J. Morris (eds), *People and Society in Scotland 1830–1914* (Edinburgh: John Donald, 1990), pp. 8–45.

Andrew Blaikie, 'Rituals, Transitions and Life Courses in an Era of Social Transformation', in Trevor Griffiths and Graeme Morton (eds), *A History of Everyday Life in Scotland, 1800 to 1900* (Edinburgh: Edinburgh University Press, 2010), pp. 89–115.

Mary Orr Johnson, 'The Insane in Nineteenth-Century Britain: A Statistical Analysis of a Scottish Insane Asylum', *Historical Social Research*, Vol. 17 No. 3 (1992), pp. 3–20.

Linda Mahood, *The Magdalenes: Prostitution in the Nineteenth Century* (London: Routledge, 1990).

Alison Nuttall, '"Because of Poverty brought into Hospital": A Casenote-Based Analysis of the Changing Role of the Edinburgh Royal Maternity Hospital, 1850–1912', *Social History of Medicine*, 20 (2), (2007), pp. 263–80.

—, 'Maternity Charities, the Edinburgh Maternity Scheme and the Medicalisation of Childbirth, 1900–1925', *Social History of Medicine*, 24 (2) (2011), pp. 370–88.

Lindsay Reid, *Midwifery in Scotland: A History* (Erskine: Scottish History Press, 2011).

T. C. Smout, *A Century of the Scottish People 1830–1950* (London: Fontana, 1987 edition), includes a chapter on 'Sex, Love and getting Married', pp. 159–80.

Eileen Janes Yeo, 'Medicine, Science and the Body', in Lynn Abrams et al. (eds), *Gender in Scottish History since 1700* (Edinburgh: Edinburgh University Press, 2006), pp. 140–69.

## Notes

1. Lynn Abrams, *Making of Modern Woman*, p. 169.
2. In the *Biographical Dictionary of Scottish Women* Bernstein's birth year is given as 1847; subsequent research showed it to be 1846.
3. Margaret Beetham, *A Magazine of her Own, Domesticity and Female Desire in the Woman's Magazine 1800–1914* (London: Routledge, 1996).
4. Susan Storrier, 'Toilette' in Storrier (ed.) *Scottish Life and Society: A Compendium of Scottish Ethnology* (Edinburgh: John Donald, 2006).
5. I am indebted to David Finkelstein for this information.
6. I am indebted to Fiona Skillen for advice on women's sport; and to Eilidh Macrae for allowing access to her unpublished essay: 'The Scottish Cyclist and the New Woman: Representations of Female Cyclists in Scotland, 1890–1914'.
7. See Roger Davidson, *Dangerous Liaisons: A Social History of Venereal Disease in Twentieth Century Scotland* (Amsterdam: Rodopi, 2000).
8. Brenda M. Whyte, 'Medical Police, Politics and Police: The Fate of John Roberton', in *Medical History*, No. 27 (1983), pp. 407–22.
9. *Dublin Journal of Medical Science*, Vol. 93, No. 3 (1892), pp. 203–12.
10. S. M. den Otter, 'Clapperton, Jane Hume', *Oxford Dictionary of National Biography* (Oxford: Oxford University Press, 2004).
11. I am grateful to Tanya Cheadle for alerting me to this text.
12. See Alison Nuttall, 'Maternity Charities, the Edinburgh Maternity Scheme and the Medicalisation of Childbirth, 1900–1925', *Social History of Medicine*, August, 24(2) (2011), pp. 370–88.
13. C. E . C. den Hertog, A. N. J. A. de Groot, P. W. J. van Dongen. 'History and use of oxytocics', *European Journal of Obstetrics and Gynacology and Reproductive Biology*, 94: 1 (2001), pp. 8–12.
14. *A Diary of St Helena (1816, 1817): the Journal of Lady Malcolm: Containing Conversations of Napoleon with Sir Pulteney Malcolm* was published in 1899, long after the author's death. Lady Malcolm encountered Napoleon through her husband, then naval commander of the Mediterranean fleet. Much of the journal records Sir Malcolm's recollections of meetings at which his wife was not present.
15. We are grateful to Aileen Christianson for her extremely knowledgeable and generous assistance in selecting suitable extracts from Jane Welsh Carlyle's writing.
16. See William Gordon, 'The Effects of Violet Infusion on Malignant Growths', *Medical Chirurgical Transactions* 89 (1906), pp. 355–94.
17. See Jonathan Andrews and Ian Smith (eds), *'Let There Be Light Again': A history of Gartnavel Royal Hospital from its beginnings to the present day* (Glasgow, 1993).

# Chapter 3

# Hearth and Home

*Linda Fleming*

## Introduction

This chapter explores an area of experience that underscored most women's lives in the period, across the female life course, and within a variety of household roles. For running the home and organising family life involved responsibilities that were nearly always devolved to women, whether as daughters, wives, widows or as paid servants. The sources presented are arranged thematically in three sections. This arrangement reflects some of the most important and insightful themes for exploring domestic life.

Sources in the first section deal with widespread ideals regarding the management of the home and nurture of family that affected women; domestic ideals were also often reflected in attitudes towards paid domestic help, and this section includes some sources concerning servants. All demonstrate, among other things, that, during this century, skill in domestic management came to underpin a particular version of feminine identity that, while focused intensively on the private activities of the home, was just as surely aimed at a very public demonstration of respectability. The second section includes sources that deal less with home and private life as an ideology that shaped women's lives and more as a physical space wherein household relations were played out. Though prescriptions about the feminine sphere applied across the social spectrum, class structures and varying degrees of poverty, affluence and individual family dynamics also intersected strongly with women's lived experience. The final section uses sources that describe an unavoidable element in domestic life for women – housework. This labour was not simply a matter of undertaking cleaning and cooking but made women responsible for the fundamental physical and emotional needs of members of the household for shelter, food and comfort.

An effort has been made to reflect the diversity of Scottish domestic life in the selection of the sources but these cannot be exhaustive. In addition to the documentary record, paintings, illustrations and photographs of interiors can provide rich sources for understanding domestic life and the relationships contained within this. Anyone interested in further researching home life in nineteenth-century Scotland will be able to spread a wide net and use an eclectic mix of material. While this presents challenges, it also offers opportunities to review the ways in which images of domesticity and family life, as well as the gendered ideologies that underpin these social institutions, have been made and remade in many areas of Scottish cultural and social life over time.

## Section 1: Advice and assistance

Though prescriptive literature does raise valid questions about the gulf that existed between ideology and practice, during the nineteenth century this type of writing grew and diversified to appeal to a wider range of readers; and much of it became chatty and light-hearted in tone in contrast to the rather worthy tenor of earlier domestic advice. While the messages being delivered did not always go unchallenged, they had a pervasive quality which rendered them difficult to ignore entirely; and not all was aimed at middle-class wives. Domestic ideology was promoted to working-class women through widespread employment in service; but, in addition, by the end of the century, it was also being delivered within the formal schooling of young girls. Some of the sources deal specifically with paid servants. The high standards expected of women in terms of domesticity created a greater need for assistance with housekeeping. Live-in servants, though, were not the preserve only of the very rich. Census documents for Scotland reveal that female servants could be found in quite humble homes as the middle classes expanded. Indeed, having 'help' in the home was a marker of both social rank and increased respectability in nineteenth-century Scotland.[1] Since the 'perfecting of home life' was a female responsibility, and the numbers of women in paid domestic service massively outnumbered men, it is clear that the relationship between servant and mistress had implications for both and, in turn, for the general atmosphere of the home.

Jane Carlyle's‡ lively and witty writing provides an exceptional resource for exploring all kinds of domestic details. Like many women of her class, she mostly managed with the help of one servant and often took on domestic labour herself, thus belying the popular image of the indolent middle-class woman of Victorian times. 'Kirkcaldy Helen', referred to in the first of these letters, and described in more detail in the second, was clearly a memorable maid! She appears as a character in many of Jane's letters, and descriptions of her indicate how intimately live-in domestics were viewed as part of the household. There were plenty of other servants in the Carlyle household, however: over the thirty-two years Jane spent living in London, she had no fewer than thirty-four general housemaids, discounting numerous other occasional and temporary domestics.[2] 'Old Mary', Mary Mills, referred to in the second text, was a servant in Jane's mother's household, and it is clear from this and other correspondence that Jane paid some kind of pension to Mary until the latter's death in 1854.[3]

The extracts below are from *The Collected Letters of Thomas and Jane Welsh*

*Carlyle*, Vol. 21 (September 1846–June 1847) pp. 143–44, and Vol. 23 (April 1848–March 1849), pp. 239–40 (Durham: Duke University Press, 1970–continuing), edited by Aileen Christianson (and many others). The letters are also available at *The Carlyle Letters Online* [*CLO*] (2007) http://carlyleletters.org

### 1.1  Letters from Jane Welsh Carlyle, 1847 and 1849

Letter from Jane Welsh Carlyle, Bay House, Hampshire to her uncle's widow, Margaret Welsh, a governess in Cullen, Tipperary, 22 January 1847

MY DEAR MRS. WELSH, – Your letter found me just recovering from a long and serious illness . . . I had a great domestic calamity some two months ago which was indeed the immediate occasion of my illness – a maid who had been with me eleven years and took entire charge of my house and self was invited to Dublin by a prosperous brother to keep house for him – He is making very rich as a manufacturer of coach-fringe and had suddenly bethought him of having this sister to be his servant – I fancy – not his 'Mistress' as she flattered herself. And it was too much to expect that her human nature could resist such tempting offer. So off she went not without tears to leave me – and I entered into possession of a young woman selected for me in Edinr by our old Haddington Betty. Betty has taken into the Free Church and I fear has lost her once excellent judgment in it for the creature she sent me turned out to have nothing earthly but 'free grace' plenty of *that* – but no '*works*' nor disposition to acquire any. She informed me to my horror that she had been partly educated at religious meetings held by my Aunt Anne! Had I known *that* at first she should never have sailed to London at *my* expense. In trying to get her to do her work – and doing it for her when she could not or would not; I caught the dreadful cold which confined me nearly a month to bed and from which I am only now emerging – Just a fortnight after her arrival – whilst I was lying at death's door – a doctor seeing me every day – she sent me word by my cousin one night that if I did not let her go away she 'would *take fits* – and *keep her bed for a year* as she had done once before in a place she did not like'!! *One* in bed was enough at a time and so next morning a *Sunday morning* (Oh my Aunt Anne!) she went her ways dressed out like a street walker – in the finest spirits – leaving me as I have said in bed – no servant in the house – a visitor who had to turn herself into a servant – and so full was she of free grace that it never once seemed to cross her mind that there was no reason in justice that I should have paid two guineas – to afford *her* an opportunity of paying a visit to some cousins she had in London! –Defend me from servants educated by religious Ladies they are all alike – I have now got a little English woman who promises to do well enough – and whom I think none the worse of that she cleans her grate and washes her dishes on Sunday all the same as on other days of the week!

From Jane Welsh Carlyle from her London address to her friend Mary Russell in Dumfriesshire (22 February 1849):

Dearest Mrs Russell

I snatch two minutes from confusion worse confounded to send old Mary's money, which I fear is already past time – It has been in my mind for the last three weeks;

but I could not come at the needful in the country place where we had gone for a short visit, and since our return to London I have been "troubled about many things" – with a vengeance!

On Monday last we drew up at our own door, in Capt Sterlings carriage (the gentleman with whom we had been staying) meaning to drive on to *his* town house to settle some concern of a Governess for him, when I should have deposited my Husband and luggage at home – We rapped and rung – a long time without being opened to at last the door opened and an apparition presented itself which I shall certainly never forget as long as I live! – *There* stood Helen – her mouth covered with blood, her brow, cheek and dark dress whitened with the chalk of the kitchen floor, like a very ill got up stage-ghost, her hair streaming wildly from under a crushed cap – and her face wearing a smile of idiotic self-complacency! My first thought was that thieves had been *murdering* her (at least one in the forenoon!) but the truth came fast enough: "she is mortal drunk"! Mr C had to *drag* her down into the kitchen – for she was very insubordinate and refused to budge from the door – Capt St & his coachman looking on! Of course I remained in my own house for the rest of the day – A woman who lives close by came to help me – and take care of the drunk creature who so soon as she got her legs again – rushed out for more drink! She had had *half a pint* of gin in the morning in the afternoon *half a pint* of rum and some ale!! that is what one would call good drinking! between nine and ten she returned – and lay *locked up* all night insensible then we had a fit of delirium tremens, then twenty four hours of weeping and wailing and trying to take me by compassion as she had done so often before – but it would not do – I have never liked her ways since she returned to me – the fact has been, tho I did not know it, that she was always partially drunk – So I felt thankful for this *decided* outbreak to put an end to my cowardly offputting in seeking myself a new servant –The very day this horror happened, a very promising servant was sent to me quite providentially to *look at*, by a Lady who has been a good while urging me to be done with Helen, and who thought it a pity I should not have the refusal of this one – So I "went after her character" and engaged her the following day, but could not have her home till the wretched being was removed and the horribly dirty house cleaned up – in which process I am now over head and ears – I wished Helen to go back to her Sister in Kircaldy and offered to pay her expenses but she *wont* – She was *determined to stay here!* – but I put her into a carriage yesterday, whether she would or no and carried her off to a woman she has been long intimate with and established her in a room of her house – for a fortnight – to look after a place – but who will take her without a character for *sobriety?* and *I* certainly will not be criminal enough to conceal her drinking propensity *if I am asked.* God knows what is to come of her! – I told her yesterday she would be better *dead!* – if she were not so old and ugly of course she would go on the streets – for all morality is broken down in her – I find now that she has not been even *honest* since she returned from Dublin – a pretty mess that Brother of her's has made of his own flesh and blood – but I must not scribble any more here –having a hundred and fifty things to do.

The source quoted below, penned by an author using the name 'Shirley', reveals that domestic ideology was publicly questioned; Shirley's plea may have struck a chord with many of the educated, middle-class women readers of this popular periodical. Demographic shifts, including an excess of migration and an earlier age of death among men, created an imbalance in the population. In Scotland specifically this meant that in 1861, for example, there were 'only 77 men for every hundred women.'[4] Numerous articles in literary magazines worried over this issue, perceived as being an acute problem, especially for women of the middle classes. Yet it may have provided something of an impetus to feminists who were able to make the case for improved education and employment prospects that would benefit women who were excluded from the marriage market or, indeed, who opted out of this.

> 1.2 'The Sad Position of Single Women' in *Chambers's Edinburgh Journal*, 315, 12 January 1850 (32)
>
> Look at the numerous families of girls in this neighbourhood – the Armitages, the Birtwhistles, the Sykes. The brothers of these girls are every one in business, or in the professions; they have something to do; their sisters have no earthly employment but household work and sewing; no earthly pleasure but unprofitable visiting; and no hope in all their life to come of anything better. This stagnant state of things makes them decline in health; they are never well; their minds and views shrink to wondrous narrowness. The great wish, the sole aim of every One of them is to be married, but the majority of them will never marry; they will die as they now live. They scheme, they plot, they dress to ensnare husbands. The gentlemen turn them into ridicule; they do not want them; they hold them very cheap; they say – I have heard them say it with sneering laughs many a time – the matrimonial market is overstocked. Fathers say so likewise, and are angry with their daughters when they observe their manoeuvres; they order them to stay at home. What do they expect them to do at home? If you ask, they would answer, sew and cook. They expect them to do this, and this only, contentedly, regularly, and uncomplainingly, all their lives long, as if they had no germs of faculties for anything else; a doctrine as reasonable to hold as it would be that the fathers have no faculties but for eating what their daughters cook, or for wearing what they sew. Could men live so themselves? Would they not be very weary? And when there came no relief to their weariness, but only reproaches at its slightest manifestation, would not their weariness ferment in time to frenzy. – Shirley.

Though within the privacy of homes ideals of womanly perfection were probably always negotiable, in mid-Victorian Scotland few women were publicly hostile to the opinion that housework was women's work. The poet Marion Bernstein‡, whose poems are also quoted in Chapter 6, often used humour to make serious points about inequalities between women and men, and her radical ideas were well ahead of more mainstream feminism. This is part of a verse which was a reply to an earlier poem submitted to the *Mail* by a male author. Bernstein was twenty-eight years old when she wrote this and evidently preferred to remain unmarried, which was the case for many middle-class women in Victorian Scotland where demographic trends alone do not fully account for the proportion of single women. This verse is also in Bernstein's only published volume of poetry, *Mirren's Musings* (Glasgow: McGeachy, 1876); and in Tom Leonard (ed.) *Radical Renfrew: Poetry from the French Revolution to the First World War* (Edinburgh: Polygon, 1990) p. 299. Detail about Bernstein's life, together with the full collection of her surviving verse which includes many poems on feminist themes, can be found in, Edward H. Cohen, Anne R. Fertig and Linda Fleming (eds), *'A Song of Glasgow Town': the Collected Verse of Marion Bernstein* (Glasgow: ASLS, 2013).

---

1.3 Marion Bernstein, 'Wanted a Husband', *Glasgow Weekly Mail*, 19 December 1874

Wanted a husband who doesn't suppose,
That all earthly employments one feminine knows, –
That she'll scrub, do the cleaning, and cooking, and baking,
And plain needlework, hats and caps, and dressmaking.
Do the family washing, yet always look neat,
Mind the bairns, with a temper unchangeably sweet,
Be a cheerful companion, whenever desired,
And contentedly toil day and night, if required.
Men expecting as much, one may easily see,
But they're not what is wanted, at least, not by me.

---

First published in 1882, Margaret Black's (1830–1903) book went through several editions. It was published by Collins of Glasgow as part of its well-known 'School Series' and was stated to be 'suitable for Junior and Senior Classes'. The international reach of this publisher meant, however, that it almost certainly achieved an even wider readership far beyond the United Kingdom.[5] Its author's status reflects the increasing professionalisation of domestic management which, ironically, provided a career path for many women who wished to work outside the home, including married women such as Black. A teacher, Black was also a temperance advocate and member of the School Board for Barony Parish in Glasgow. She founded the West End School in 1878; it eventually became a teacher-training centre and the founding institution of what was to become Queen's College. The good of all society was held to be at stake in the proper domestic education of young girls, not only in tasks associated with housekeeping but also in managing the home as a place of ordered and prudent consumption. This fine distinction is important for it underscores the notion that however integral the home was to society it was still configured as standing outside the supposed productive world of commerce and politics. Yet it also illustrates that this relationship was not so much one of division and opposition but of mutuality. Archival holdings for the West End Cookery School are held at Glasgow Caledonian University Archives, see www.gcu.ac.uk/archives/wsc/index.html

### 1.4 Margaret Black, Head Mistress of the West End Training School of Cookery, Glasgow, *Household Cookery and Laundry Work* (London and Glasgow: Collins, 1882) (7–8)

A great deal more of a country's prosperity depends upon comfortable homes than philosophers might be willing to acknowledge; for people cannot prosecute business with great energy, or study with much enjoyment or profit, if there are worries at home, or muddle and discomfort there. This is quite apparent to all, and though it seems a matter of minor importance compared with the great interests and objects that have to be carried on out of doors, yet if the household machinery is out of order, or not moving smoothly, the derangement may be carried forward till very important interests are disturbed.

The home is the nursery of the present and future inhabitants of a country, and the care of the home devolves generally upon woman – in our country, at all events, it does so universally; and by the manner in which she performs her most important duties, not only the present comfort, but it may be the future destinies of the inmates may be influenced, if not moulded. Incapacity on her part leads to many certain evils – disorder, waste, and muddle; and may have still worse effects on the health and tempers of the family. Whatever other duties a woman may have, she must either manage her house herself or devolve the care of it upon some other woman; consequently, all women should be carefully trained for this, their occupation.

Parents would never think of setting a young man up in business unless he had been trained, probably by a long apprenticeship; and yet it has been practically decided by many people that a young woman instinctively knows all about house-keeping: that she can cook without being taught, and can manage a house, and instruct servants without ever having studied the subject of domestic management; that if she has received a liberal education and some knowledge of needlework, everything else necessary to set her up as a mistress of the house comes naturally. Good mothers do and have always done great things in training their daughters, but many girls do not have that advantage; and even mothers may see the necessity of their best instructions being supplemented.

Happily most people are now alive to the necessity of training girls of all classes for their natural and certain occupation – the care of the home; and domestic economy and cookery . . . few girls of any rank finish their education without these branches being studied.

The ideal that married women should not be part of the labour market was an improbable one for many working-class women; yet, even for the middle classes, it is important to note that economic dependence did not imply social dependence, and in not a few cases, married women could possess both financial independence and marital security. Annie S. Swan‡ was one such woman: a prolific, commercially successful, and hugely popular author. Swan wrote Kailyard novels, but also wrote for a number of periodicals, most notably the Dundee-based publication, *The People's Friend*, to which she contributed for many decades from the 1880s onwards and to which she owed a great deal of her early fame.[6] Swan also turned her pen to non-fiction. This source reveals that for her intended readership the world was beginning to change. Though marriage and homemaking were still deemed a woman's primary destiny, Swan is keen to show that it need not be her sole role in life.

> 1.5 Annie S. Swan, *Courtship and Marriage and the Gentle Art of Home Making* (London: Hutchinson & Co., 1894) (64, 65, 127)

Ignorance of the prosaic details of housekeeping is the primary cause of much of the domestic worry and discomfort that exist, to say nothing of the more serious discords that may arise from such a defect in the fitness of the woman supposed to be the home-maker . . .

Some blame careless, indifferent mothers, who do not seem to have profited by their own experience, but allow their daughters to grow up in idleness, and launch them on the sea of matrimony with a very faint idea of what is required of them in their new sphere.

It is very reprehensible conduct on the part of such mothers, and if in a short time the bright sky of their daughters' happiness begins to cloud a little, they need not wonder or feel aggrieved. A man is quite justified in expecting and exacting a moderate degree of comfort at least in his own house, and if it is not forthcoming may be forgiven a complaint. He is to be pitied, but his unhappy wife much more deserves our pity, since she finds herself amid a sea of troubles, at the mercy of her servants, if she possesses them; and if moderate circumstances necessitate the performance of the bulk of household duties, then her predicament is melancholy indeed . . .

'What shall we do with our daughters?' is one of the great questions of the day. Formerly marriage was their only destiny; if they missed that, they were supposed to have missed all that was worth the winning here. But that old fallacy is exploded. While still holding that in happy marriage is to be found the fullest and most soul-satisfying life for women, no open-eyed person will deny that a single, independent, and self-respecting life is far preferable to the miserable, starved, inadequate wifehood to which many women are bound . . . The wise mother will rear her daughters to be independent, self-respecting, and, if possible, self-supporting; not hiding from them that she considers a real marriage . . . the highest destiny for them, but at the same time impressing on them that there are other spheres in which women may be as happy and comfortable, and where they will certainly have less anxiety and care.

Lady Aberdeen‡ [Ishbel Gordon] (1857–1939), a well-known and influential Scottish aristocrat, was the founder of the Onward and Upward Association and its magazine, *Onward and Upward*. The magazine purveyed domestic ideals in an unambiguous and, occasionally, heavy-handed way, and was intended to appeal to single and to married women. Among the magazine's aims was that of improving relations between middle-class women and the female servants they employed.

> **1.6 Address by Lady Aberdeen to the annual meeting of the Onward and Upward Association at Haddo House, recorded in *Onward and Upward* magazine, Vol. 4, No. 9 (August 1894) (213)**
>
> It is a high and dignified thing to be a servant. We want to get this idea of domestic service into the heads of our girls, and into the heads of our Mothers, who are bringing up the girls; we want them to realise that it is a position of great dignity and honour, and for which they must use their best powers; and there is a great deal of training required; that they must put their best thoughts into all the common things of life if they are to be good, trained servants. And then let them realise, too, that there is no reason why, as servants, they should not be cultivated and educated people. We want to lay stress upon [how] much we need to give our best mental powers to the perfecting of home life and domestic duties. If we can succeed in getting them to understand this idea of domestic service, we shall find much less unwillingness amongst our young girls to go into that profession.

Mamie Smith (*c.*1860–1941) married a Glasgow MP and government minister.[7] She had three children and was involved with a variety of philanthropic works; she could only have managed her households in Glasgow and London with the aid of many servants. The preservation of letters from servants underlines the domestic management role played by women like Mamie. Hours in service were long, the work itself was arduous, and servants could be subject to a variety of tyrannies. Nevertheless, as the Dundee Domestic Maidservants strike, illustrated in Chapter 4, shows, female servants were willing to be militant. By the late nineteenth century, the balance of power between mistress and servant had begun to shift. Even so, while trusted servants with ability might be valued and have a secure place to live, as well as care during illness, perceived infringements could result in an individual losing everything in an instant. In addition to sources such as these, which can be difficult to find, many works of fiction dealt with the life of servants, albeit in a romanticised fashion. A notable example is Isabella Fyvie Mayo‡ (1843–1914)(written under the pseudonym Edward Garrett), *Her Day of Service* (Edinburgh, 1892).

Letter from Nettie Alexander to Mrs Parker Smith:

130 Buccleuch Street,
Edinburgh
27th March 07.

Mrs Parker Smith,

Dear Madam,

I have just received your letter & write to say I have had a few replies to my advertisement but they are all further away so I will consider yours. I will come & see you this morning between now and 11.30.

Yours Respectfully
Nettie Alexander

Nettie Alexander's two letters of recommendation, given to Mamie Smith in support of her application for a position in the Smith household and preserved in the Smith Papers:

1, Queen Anne Street
Cavendish Square, W.
12th May 1905

Madam,

I can give nettie alexander a good character, she is honest, sober, clean and pleasant in manner. She cooks well and sends up her dinners nicely served. I much regret her leaving as I consider her a satisfactory servant, quiet and conscientious. The cook spoke highly of her rising early and doing her work well. It is unfortunate that disagreement arose. Nettie Alexander could not stay at Balgreen under the cook – she wrote to me from 130 Buccleuch St. Edinburgh. If you find her recommendation satisfactory, I fancy she could go to you when you wished her. I cannot think nettie alexander in fault in being obliged to give up her situation at Balgreen and am glad to help her. Believe me.

Yours Faithfully

Susan Brodie

59 Green Street
Grosvenor Square
May 12th 1905
Madam

In reply to Mrs Crum's letter received today.

I can recommend Nettie Alexander as being very suitable for Mrs Crum's situation as cook.

I taught her more than I generally teach those under me. Nettie was quick to learn and very clean both in herself & her work. During last London season I have often left her dinners for six & six courses to do by herself & the help of the scul-larymaid, they were always satisfactory.

I never had a complaint of servants' food & Nettie always cooked for them. I gave her over the key of my store cupboards when I went for a holiday & found everything as it should be when I came back.

I remain
    Madam
Yours Obediently
Kitty Hassett

Letter to Mrs Parker Smith:

Sconser Portree 16. 3. 07

Dear Madam,
    You will be pleased to hear that I am getting on so well. I feel quite strong again. I have a good appetite and can take anything without causing the least pain. About getting my teeth out, there is a dentist coming to Portree in May so by that time I think I shall be quite strong to have them taken out. I was thinking of taking a light place near home for the summer months so as to help me get a new set. I hope Miss Kathleen* is keeping well. We have very cold weather in Skye.
    Thanking Mrs Parker Smith for her great kindness to me during my illness.
    I remain,
        Yrs. Respectfully
            Robina Fraser

*Kathleen was Mamie's daughter.

Handwritten note marked 'copy', included within Mrs Parker Smith's corre-spondence and probably written by her:

I am sorry for you.
I give you one last chance to go out of the house in three quarters of an hour – with wages paid in full & out of pocket expenses. Otherwise you will regret it – but you can decide for yourself which is best to do.

### Section 2: Havens and hardships

Private life is a notoriously difficult area to research, and documentary sources for this can be more than usually challenging to interpret. Several of the extracts in this section are from statutory documents. This type of source can produce a bleak picture of home life, because they were often written with the agenda of documenting poverty, dirt and dysfunction. Moreover, such official accounts and reports were more usually written by men and produced with the aim of recording facts although, however dispassionately recorded, the subjective, gen-dered views of their authors undoubtedly emerge between the lines. Yet, because these are often first-hand accounts, they do admit us behind otherwise closed doors and provide intimate glimpses, though from particular points of view, of features in everyday home life that are all too easily hidden from historical scrutiny. It was rarer for women to author such documents, but source 2.9 provides a good example in the form of extracts from a scientific report. Further items in this section (and Section 3) come from creative genres, including an example of domestic crafts. Reflecting popular views about the importance of home in this period, domestic poetry, novels, and journalism were fashionable, and for some women writers this could be commercially successful. Writing of this nature indicates a complementary growth of a literate female readership who had both disposable income and leisure time. Yet these, too, require careful scrutiny to understand how they may have been read in their contemporary setting. Sources include descriptions of some of the commonest domestic difficulties experienced by women as well as narratives that reveal the contentedness and security that many women found within their domestic roles.

The notion that marriage was more than just an economic arrangement, and the growth of the companionate ideal, are usually viewed as developments that gathered pace during the nineteenth century because of changes in the nature of the wider industrial economy and society. This extract shows that this supposed transition was far from seamless, and that unhappy matches were the business of the Scottish courts long before more contemporary developments in matrimonial law. This type of source demonstrates that, even at the outset of industrialisation in Scotland, civil society at least recognised that marriage was a legal as well as a religious and social arrangement, and one that could go awry if one or both parties failed in their obligations. Though divorce itself was restricted to certain conditions, such as adultery or desertion, unlike elsewhere in the UK, legal separation sanctioned by the courts was possible. These comprise a very rich source for understanding changing expectations of marriage from the point of view of women. The full transcript of this and many other similar cases is a legacy of the work of the historian Leah Leneman. The original document can be consulted in the NAS (Ref: CC8/5/34); the source reproduced here, however, consists of selected extracts taken from the transcription made of the original manuscript by Leneman.[8] The transcripts are in the Qualidata archive at: http://www.esds. ac.uk/findingData/snDescription.asp?sn=3628&key= (Ref.: SN 3628 – Marital Breakdown in Scotland, 1684–1832).

## 2.1 Register of Consistorial Decreets; selected extracts from case AD74 – 2 and 23 June and 7 July 1815: Margaret Rae, daughter of farmer in Moffat, agt John Aitken

Margaret Rae, daughter of farmer in Moffat, against John Aitken. Married Dec 1813.

Soon after that he began to act as a 'tyrant and tormentor' and in a variety of instances both in words and deeds he so insulted and abused her as to deprive her of all comfort and happiness and to make her perfectly miserable and her life almost a burden to her. That while suffering under this state of misery in her husbands house it was proposed & agreed in the month of June last that the private Pursuer should go for a short time and reside in the house of her father in Moffat, which she was induced to agree to, under the expectation that a little sober reflection in her absence would bring the said John Aitken to a due sense of his unbecoming and unfeeling conduct and induce him to conduct himself thereafter as became a husband towards his wife . . .

But from the subsequent unjustifiable conduct of the said John Aitken it appeared that in place of intending this as only a temporary, he meant the same as the commencement of a permanent separation 'twixt him and her, for although the Pursuer had repeatedly offered to return to the house . . . and that from her being in a state of pregnancy and most solicitous to return to her husbands house before her confinement should take place, she most pressingly wrote him on the subject . . . even promising to forget & forgive all his past misconduct towards her if he would receive her back', but he refused, insisting that 'she should continue to live separate from him without assigning a single reason or ground for his unaccountable conduct further than that he was not happy in his married state and chose to live separate from her, and with this view he had produced and sent her the Draft of a Contract of Separation betwixt them, containing provisions altogether inadequate and unsuitable to the Pursuers support and that of a son of whom she was delivered . . . November last . . . and greatly under and inconsistent with the provision stipulated by the contract of marriage . . . whereby he engaged to provide her in an annuity of one hundred and twenty pounds sterling per annum and in the sum of Five hundred pounds sterling for furnishing a dwelling house'. If he fails to adhere she asks for this sum for her aliment as well as 50 per annum for the child and expenses of the process.

## Extracts from The Husband's Defences:

Denies maltreating her in any way and that her motive for going to her father was misrepresented. Says that 'from the day of his unhappy marriage with her until the day of their separation her conduct was such as to disappoint entirely the expectations of domestic comfort in her society which he had formed . . . The misconduct was all on her side, and as such a kind as not to admit of even the supposition of her being again under the same roof with him.' It was not true that he gave no reason for refusing to have her back. 'Neither party was silent. There was enough of recrimination. But that circumstance was at present of no consequence.' In his offer of a contract of voluntary separation he was willing to make concessions and 'forget her demerits', but now that she had brought this case to court he was no longer willing to do so. When he signed the marriage contract it was in expectation of domestic happiness, but his wife 'instead of contributing to his domestic comfort was to him the source of incessant misery . . . '.

## Extracts from the Wife's Answers to her Husband's Defences:

[The] tone of defences was 'preposterous and absurd. The Pursuer was the married wife of the Defender. She was not only his equal in point of rank but more than his equal in other circumstances. Her education was liberal and at eighteen years of age she married the Defender about fifty. She had since become the Mother of a Son to him. Notwithstanding these circumstances the Defender thought proper to declare his intention not to live with the Pursuer and when he was sued for an aliment he put a defence upon record offering the Pursuer about one third part of the aliment which he became bound to pay her by his contract of marriage in case of his death. Her position was "deplorable"' . . . The Pursuer expected that she would find a guide and adviser in the Defender. Instead of that she had not lived many weeks with him when she found that his temper was peevish and his disposition so mean, narrow & sordid as would have been almost incompatible with the comfort of the humblest female servant . . . Produces a letter which she wrote to him after they had been living apart for 3 months, expressing surprise at not hearing from him. 'By reflecting seriously upon all that has passed I think neither your own situation nor mine is very respectable at present, and can only say it is my anxious wish to forget every thing disagreeable that has taken place between us and to return to your house and live on the best and most affectionate terms with you, provided you behave to me as becomes a husband to a wife, and allow me the privileges of other married women. I make no doubt we were both much to blame in not conforming a little to one anothers temper; by doing so we might have been more comfortable than we are now.' . . . Also produces a letter from the pursuer to her agent with regard to the defender's defences: 'From the very commencement of my most unfortunate marriage, Mr Aitken rendered his house extremely uncomfortable to me; – he found fault with everything I did complained of extravagance when every thing was done in the most economical manner. I had a number of most respectable acquaintances both in Edinburgh & Leith who were willing on my account to pay Mr Aitken every attention and who of course called upon me on my first going there and as was customary on such occasions to offer wine & ale; This was counted extravagance I also received our friends in the dining room, the breakfast parlour being too small and there being a fire in the two rooms was also much complained of – and I was no sooner arrived at home than he began to complain excessively of the expense of his marriage . . . Mr Aitken had lived so long a bachelor and contracted so many peculiar habits, that he ought to have remained as he was, and not have come to destroy the peace of any young woman, and made so many promises which he never intended to fulfill I was led to expect very different treatment from what I received. There never was any thing like his narrowness. He grumbled at every thing that was got into the house, even the very coals & many other things too trifling to mention. He gave me a book of house expenses in which I marked down every penny I laid out but he did not approve of the way in which I kept it and therefore gave it to the servant a circumstance which very few women would have put up with . . . '

## 2.2 A sampler by Jessie Mercer aged 8 years (1841)

The sampler has become something of an emblem of idyllic domesticity and, indeed, often depicts a physical house. Such needlework invites discussion of the balance between continuity and change within the domestic role of women.

**Figure 3.1** A sampler by Jessie Mercer, aged 8, 1841. Courtesy of Smith Museum
and Art Gallery, Stirling.

The change from a labour-intensive, productive role in households to a largely decorous one has often been seen as the lot of middle-class wives and daughters during the transition from agrarian to industrialised societies. The domestic sampler was ostensibly a means of teaching different stitches and sewing techniques, yet the appearance of most samplers is highly decorative and appears to symbolise in a particularly vivid way the economic devaluing of women's household production that accompanied the emergence of the middle classes. There can be no doubt that samplers became more than a means of simply teaching sewing, and did develop into a recreational pursuit that often required a high degree of skill. As such, they have been re-evaluated and reclaimed by many feminists as expressions of women's artistry. The story told in this sampler is a typically romantic tale of a forbidden love match between a girl and a shepherd. Within the stitched text, we see recorded that the child who produced this work did so within one of a plethora of small girls' schools that were emerging. The education provided was probably quite genteel and domestic in orientation; nevertheless, such schools played a role in increasing female literacy and, as we see, writing was certainly on the curriculum, reflecting widespread approval for the educated homemaker.

Poor relief documents provide good evidence of the bleak conditions many women lived in; they also show how itinerant some women needed to be in pursuit of employment, so that the notion of a secure home, never mind a place where domesticity could be exercised, was certainly a chimera for significant numbers of women and families. In documents like this, officers, including medical doctors who worked for the parish, often make brusque comments that suggest little sympathy for those seen as feckless poor. In this record, however, Dr Harvey clearly feels the need to comment candidly on dreadful living conditions. The only means of relieving this plight was by removal to the local poorhouse.

### 2.3 Poor Relief Records for Barony Parish, Glasgow [GCA ref.: D-HEW 10/4/23/24 (1851), record no.: 4/9855] (380)

21st May 1851. Mary Gilmour Aged 18 born in Glasgow presently residing in 41 New Vennel first Corr door on right – with Isabella Leonard Milligan.

Applies with a swelling in the Groin – Dr Harvey

This is the worst of all the bad habitations I ever saw – A Cellar – earth floor, joist roof – unfit for pigs – neither stool nor aught else. – Landlady stuffing skins of dolls with Sawdust – a blind son about 8 years of age as naked as when born helping his mother. – Clothes sold for their breakfast. – Applicant, huddled amongst straw in a recess between the jam and wall scarcely long enough for a child to lay in. – Her clothes also gone for food – she is naked. – Admits that for a long time past she had been associating with a young man who was to marry her, but he has deserted her. She wrought in Port Eglinton Wool Mill till within the last 4 weeks & was compelled to give up her situation on acct. of ill health. – has sold all to pay for medical advice and to support herself before making application to Parish. Applicant's father is John Gilmour a labourer at Barrhead, her mother Mary Collins died 2 years ago. – Has resided in present house 3 weeks – prior Back Wynd 4 weeks – 41 New Vennel 2 months – Bridgegate 4 mths, 80 Main St Gorbals 6 months – Bridgegate 2 mo: Main Street Cameron's Land Govan Parish 3 years – Molly Stuffers Close Main Street Gorbals 2 years – Scoullers Close Main Street Gorbals 2 years – 80 Main St Gorbals Royle Close 18 months – Edinburgh & Musselburgh 10 months.
1/6 –
Admitted to House to be treated.

Jessie Russell‡ (1850–after 1881) was a Scottish working-class poet. Written in vernacular Scots, *The Blinkin' o' the Fire* is the title poem from her only published volume. It hints at a well-known trope in Victorian domestic poetry that often carried a sentimental strain; that of hearth and home. This juxtaposition was, and perhaps remains, shorthand for the closeness and security associated with a family home. Russell, however, cleverly combines sentimentality with a seam of realism by including other common features of family life, such as infant mortality.[9]

2.4  Jessie Russell, *The Blinkin' o' the Fire* (Glasgow: Cossar, Fotheringham & Co., 1877) (9–10)

The Blinkin' o' the Fire
WHEN gloamin' shrouds in gloom the couch, the couch o' dying day,
And ilka busy worldly sound seems unco far away,
Then memories flood aroond my heart in tides which never tire,
When a' is dark an' lonely save the blinkin' o' the fire.

The noo the blink is bleezin' bricht, an' shows a happy wean,
Jist toddlin' in the race o' life an' kennin' ne'er a pain
But what my mother's hand could soothe, an' a' my heart's desire,
Tae cuddle in her bosom by the blinkin' o' the fire.

But when thae twa wee ither lives, my sister an' my brither –
Wha shared wi' me parental love – had followed ane anither,
And faither tae was ta'en away tae swell the heavenly choir,
My wee hands tried tae dicht her tears, by the blinkin' o' the fire.

I see mysel' at ten years auld, I feel that mony a pang
I maun hae cost my mother's heart, wha has been ailin' lang;
Again that sufferer's holy thoughts her dying lips inspire –
An' fancy hears her angel voice in the blinkin' o' the fire,

The blink grows dim an' feeble noo, an' dark the swelling wave
That surges through the achin' heart which shrines her early grave;
Still darker grows the crimson spark, its last faint beams expire,
An' I read the orphan's fitful fate in the blinkin' o' the fire.

They ca'ed me dour an' stubborn, sae few can understa'
The throbbing o' the wild heart's stilled at touch o' tender han',
When ither means are vainly tried; an' then I fee'd for hire, –
Fareweel tae idle moping by the blinkin' o' the fire.

I see mysel' at seventeen; my thochts hae played a jink,
Indeed the years the mind recalls are only jist a blink;
My bosom's beatin' lichter noo, an' dowie thochts retire
While I poker tae a cheery lowe, the blinkin' o' the fire.

I feel the thrill through every vein young love's first vows awoke,
The orphan lassie had her dream as weel as ither folk,
That first attuned the strains to which I strung my rustic lyre,
In the glow o' love's aurora, jist the blinkin' o' the fire.

Anither twa three years glide by, it's hard tae ha'e tae tell,
Coortship has mony oots and ins which seem tae break the spell;
Wi' ither thochts and ither cares, I plied the stocking wire,
Instead o' fancy's weaving by the blinkin' o' the fire.

But, hark! the whistle lood an' shrill, that brings me nearer hame,
In haste I pit the kettle on an' blaw the coal to flame,
And noo I greet my kind guidman in his auld wark attire,
While he draws oor bairnies on his knee, by the blinkin' o' the fire.

Helen McFarlan's posthumously published book, quoted below, and also in
Chapter 6, is a rather lovely evocation of everyday life in a rural part of Scotland.
McFarlan was raised in Edinburgh; following her marriage to a minister in
1871, she moved to a village parish in Dumfriesshire. She spent almost twenty
years there and raised six children. Before her death, she instructed a friend, the
Reverend Ballingal, to compile a selection from her correspondence and journals
for publication. As a historical source, it alerts us to the need for careful interpretation of this kind of personal testimony. Though some intimation of the challenges McFarlan faced as a wife and mother do emerge in these selections, such
as her struggle with the bleakness of winter in this relatively isolated place and
the death of her oldest child (Christian) from whooping cough, these trials are
virtually eclipsed by the more positive tone of the extracts selected by Ballingal.
Moreover, it must be assumed that McFarlan always had some kind of public
legacy in mind for her writings because she retained copies of letters that she sent
and seems to have been assiduous in keeping a journal. The following consists of
short excerpts from the writings, chosen to illustrate McFarlan's evident talents
for domestic life in a rural manse and for motherhood.

2.5 Helen McFarlan, *Selections From Letters and Journals of Ruthwell Manse
Life*, with an introduction by the Reverend J. Ballingal, DD (Edinburgh:
privately printed, 1914) (6, 20, 29, 41, 72–3)

Journal entries

October 1871.
On Saturday, the day after we arrived, the minister was busy writing his sermon
in the study. Suddenly the pig began to squeal, and made so much noise that he
could not write. He asked me to go out and see what was the matter. So out I went,
and spoke kindly to the beast. There did not seem to be anything wrong with it
. . . No words of kindness, however, had any effect. I appealed to the servant. She
made a despairing gesture, and said that she had never lived near a pig in her life
before. The advice of experience had to be sought, and at the glebe cottage I found
it. A gentle, courteous old man respectfully assured me that, 'The beast's just fair
hunger, mem; it wants meat.' Humbly I begged to be instructed as to the feeding
of a pig . . . I have indeed much to learn!

November 2nd 1871.
We are settling down now, and it is really a nice place . . . I am going to send
my mother the Annan paper with an account of the 'welcome to Ruthwell of Mr

McFarlan and his amiable bride.' We enjoy all our furniture and things very much. I felt very strange at first, did not like seeing people and being called 'Mrs McFarlan,' but I am quite getting used to it now, and this quaint old house with its fine trees begins to feel like home.

November 6th 1871.

My way here is not free from difficulties. The servant I found here tells me she cannot stay; even with the help of the girl Mary she finds the work too much. She is not strong. I must get a woman who knows how to feed hens and pigs . . .

April 22nd 1873.

With a spring cleaning going on, and a baby to keep, (born in February) you may imagine that I have plenty to do. Thank you for your sympathy. I did get very depressed and dispirited, you would have been disgusted with me. However, that's all by and I am very well now . . . I wash and dress the boy, and feed him during the night. Today he is eight weeks old. He lies on the floor kicking and perfectly happy if he can find any shining object to fix his eyes on. But his bath is his great delight, and very difficult it is to hold him, he kicks and splashes so . . .

Our place is looking very tidy and pretty, all ablaze with daffodils and cowslips. I have got a nice little maid from the village who keeps Baby and helps . . .

December 24th 1873.

I am sitting under our first Xmas tree. And hoping we may have many more. It is very wee, and we had nothing but candles and oranges to put on it till last night, when a box arrived from our fairy godmother at 22 Lynedoch Place, filled with bun and shortbread, jam apples, and many other delights . . . [The Glasgow address of Mrs Archibald Campbell].

August 6th 1875.

Yesterday I sent the twins to visit the two old Misses Thomson at Greenhill. They were pleased to see the babies and sent them home each with an egg and some salt rolled up in his pinny for luck.

. . . We are all rather languid, but we must see our plum jam made and the harvest over . . . I have just been out for a little walk with my three sons. Jane wanted to iron and Mary was washing. So Christian wheeled Willy in the pram and I carried Allan. We took them to see the trains.

July 9th 1881.

I hope that mine is the over-anxiety of a mother, but I am very anxious about Christian. This is the seventh day of fever, both pulse and temperature very high . . . His cough is very sore and exhausting.

July 11th 1881.

The doctor found Christian rather better to-day . . . We are thankful and a little more hopeful . . . All the parish is most kind and concerned.

Undated entry.

Christian died on July 16th; and soon after that, kind Aunt Jane took us away to Moffat for a little change.

July 26th Moffat.

We are getting rest here after all the strain of 'bearing up'. We talk about our dear little man, remembering things that make us laugh, and then we fall a-weeping . . .

*Woman At Home* was subtitled the *Magazine of Annie S. Swan*. In fact, Swan was not its editor but her influence upon it is very clear and her popularity was a vehicle for its success.[10] It was published in London but it was well known that Swan was a Scot and so, as well as having phenomenal national appeal, it often also displayed something of a Scottish provincial bent through much of her writing. 'Over the Teacups' was one of Swan's regular columns, and it was probably the first 'agony aunt' feature in the modern sense.

### 2.6 Annie S. Swan, 'Over the Teacups', *Woman at Home*, Vol. 111 (1893) (145)

"J.B.M.," writing from the West of Scotland, is another whose letter is of so private and painful a nature that it ought to be answered privately, but since she gives no address, she leaves me no alternative but to deal with it here.

Her sad story adds another to the long list of ill-assorted unions which ought never to have taken place. The mistake was hers from the beginning in marrying a man to whom she had not given her whole heart. The little trials of temper and patience, which seem great to her, every married woman has to go through, and where love is they are trifles too small to mention, but of course where love wanes and indifference takes its place, these little frets, the turns of daily life, become intolerable. Her husband is now an invalid and requiring her constant care, which she gives dutifully, but feeling it a burden all the while. It is truly a sad case.

She asks my advice on a very delicate theme, whether she would be justified in urging him to go into a home where he would be cared for, so that she might have time to devote to the children.

This is a very hard question to answer. Sympathising as I must and do with the peculiar nature of "J.B.M."'s position, I yet cannot see it as my duty to advise her to the course she suggests. She married "for better or worse" – and that it has proved to be for worse is no reason why she should shirk her duty. Seeing her husband is, on her own showing, a good and upright man, though a little hard, she has not the shadow of an excuse for deserting her post. That it tries her nerves and her heart I can well believe, but let her think of the heaviness of his cross as compared to hers. She is dwelling too much upon herself and her own personal worries; let her take the wider view. Very specifically I must warn her against dwelling morbidly on any "what might have been". Her duty as wife and Christian woman is plain. Let her do it as to God and he will reward her when she least expects it with a gleam of joy, which will glorify all service, and make the rough places smooth. She has my very heartfelt sympathy.

The two short extracts quoted below provide good examples of gendered con-tradictions which abounded in Scottish society and which posed challenges to Victorian ideas about the sanctity of the home as a place of retreat, and the

Christian family as the most effective social means for instilling morality. While Poor Law Inspectors had complete impunity to enter the homes of the poor and direct the fortunes of beleaguered households, simultaneous notions about the inviolable privacy of family life had drastic repercussions for many women. In the first extract from this record, Mary Ann's condition is deemed 'partially' disabled due to being 'near confinement'. She already had two of her children at the time: John aged six and William who was two and suffering from measles. As we see, some years later, her plight is even more wretched: this time she is described as 'wholly', meaning totally disabled, by her injuries, dependent children and sheer poverty. Women like Mary Ann often relied on neighbours or family and, in the last resort, shelter within the public poorhouse; many such documents are available in local record offices across Scotland.

> 2.7 Poor Relief Records for Glasgow City Parish: (1897–1903). Application for relief by Mary Ann Gillespie Bryce, entries for 29 December 1897 and 7 December (1903) [GCA: ref.: D–HEW 10/5/97 record no. D89843] (80)

Application made on 27th December 1897, as her husband 'sent to prison on 20th inst for a month for assaulting applicant' who was at the time of application 'near confinement'.

   Granted Medical Relief: but on visiting found she had not been with Certificate and Order to Dr Orr, as directed, though her younger child was lying ill. Lives in a Single apartment, moderately clean, rent 9/- mo [per month]. Husband has been in jail before for beating her – he is an old soldier and not well behaved. She is stated not to be always sober herself & to have a wicked tongue when under the influence of drink.

Additional note made for 7 December 1903

William Bryce's wife Mary Ann Gillespie, 8 Church Place 1 up 3rd door. Husband gave her a severe hammering on Saturday night and has now bolted as the Police are on his track; he worked in the Elmbank Foundry. Family:– John 13 years; Mary 4 years; James 1 year 8 mths all at above . . .

   Application made by Mrs Cairns, same address for her removal to Poorhouse as she is in a bad state and requires medical attention. Certd wholly "Injury to ribs – right side" – 3 chn – "privation". 7/12/03: Self and 2 chn John & James removed to City Poorhouse. 8/12/03: Order sent up. Her sister who resides at same address, top flat is keeping Mary.

   I called at husband's mother, who is on roll, at 13 Sawmillfield Street but she could give me no information regarding him. 16/12/03:– Poorhouse and apprehend husband.

Reports such as the above were often the outcome of enquiries into living and working conditions that sought to find solutions to combined problems of overcrowding, disease and mortality within the poorer classes. The application of sanitary science was a feature of nineteenth-century British life, and the problems it addressed were even more profound in Scotland than in other parts of the United Kingdom. The tradition of tenements promoted high-density living and served to compound levels of overcrowding. Yet officials, such as this house factor, were still inclined to blame the poor, and especially poor women, for the problems of slums. By this point, the rhetoric of blameworthiness included immigrant women. The infamous Gorbals district south of the River Clyde was truly cosmopolitan by the end of the nineteenth century: home to Italians, central and eastern European Jews as well as in-migrants from the Scottish Highlands, England and especially, Ireland. Though Gilmour does not specify in this part of his testimony which aliens are referred to, he means Jews, and Jewish women in particular who were held responsible for the upkeep of slum homes.[11]

> 2.8 *Minutes of Evidence taken before Glasgow Municipal Commission on the Housing of the Poor,* Vol. 1 (1903) [GULSC ref.: Sp Coll Mu24-x.1, 2; paras 7399–764, pp. 346–60] (paras 7401, 7442)

Evidence of Mathew Gilmour.
It is the lowest of the slum class which causes what problem there may be. The slums in Glasgow are simply the dwelling quarters of this class . . . The condition of the houses and surroundings of these people have really nothing to do with their social and domestic condition. They would turn the finest buildings that ever were built into slums in a few months . . . In my opinion most of the trouble and misery which exist are due to intemperance, gambling, betting and the inordinate love of sport, and by the want of a proper domestic training education and training for the women. Great numbers of the women know little or nothing of cooking or sewing, and are miserably ignorant of house management or domestic economy – hence discomfort, ill-health, expenditure in excess of income, and poverty.

The slum class is also recruited by aliens, of whom there are now a great many in Glasgow. They have a baneful influence wherever they dwell; sanitation and cleanliness are to most of them things absolutely unknown, and to be strenuously resisted . . . [O]n the south side, where my work is principally situated, their number is very great, and increasing considerably year by year, especially in the Gorbals and Hutchesontown districts . . . These parties will neither clean their stairs nor their houses, nor empty their refuse where they ought to, nor do anything of that nature. It is utterly impossible to get them to recognise the desirability of cleanliness and air.

The Glasgow study quoted below was one of a rash of works undertaken in Britain and North America, looking at the relationship between diet and health; a similar project in Edinburgh in 1902, was co-authored by Elsie Inglis‡ (1864–1917). Lindsay's report is rare, if not unique, as solely authored by a woman. She attended the Park School in Glasgow which promoted a scientific education for girls and encouraged their movement into higher education, and she later graduated from Glasgow University and became a factory inspector. In 1913, the magazine of Lindsay's former school, *The Park School Chronicles,* cited a *Glasgow Herald* report, published on 3 March 1913, on the work and career of its former pupil, and stated that her report currently was 'on sale at the Sweated Industries Exhibition for the modest sum of threepence'.[12] Lindsay's work was reviewed in the *British Medical Journal* (29 March 1913, pp. 674–5) where, in a typical example of paternalism towards woman scientists, it was described as being under the supervision of Dr Noel Paton. This locally well-known figure certainly wrote an introduction for the book but the manager of the research appears to have been Lindsay. Acknowledgments to her team reveal that she had nine fieldwork assistants, seven of whom were women. Most of the text is given over to statistics of data concerning calories and nutritional content of the diets among sixty households; as these extracts show, however, commentary on the lifestyles and home styles of the families, and particularly of the women in them, was thought necessary to gain an accurate picture of their diets. These comments provide fascinating insights into how educated women like Lindsay viewed the plight of the poor and took an almost anthropological interest in the domestic tastes and habits of such families. Life in one or two rooms for families such as these was arduous, with many bodies in a confined space creating constant labour to maintain even minimally hygienic standards in which cooking and eating could take place. Lindsay ends her comments by stating:

> [it] is to be feared that in the face of old established dietary habits, of ignorance, and of the stultifying influence of the surroundings, any reform in the mode of feeding which might set free a greater proportion of the income will only be slowly achieved as the result of proper teaching and training in the schools.

This type of teaching was destined to be aimed at girls for much of the twentieth century, and it is appropriate to note that often it was forward-thinking, well-educated women like Lindsay who promoted this.

> 2.9 Dorothy E. Lindsay BSc, *Report Upon a Study of the Diet of the Labouring Classes in the City of Glasgow carried out during 1911–1912* (Glasgow: 1913) (11, 12, 13, 14, 15, 16, 17, 19, 20, 21, 22, 23, 25)

. . . Studies were made in altogether 60 houses selected from various of the poorest districts in the city of Glasgow – Cowcaddens, Anderston, Bridgeton, Gorbals, Woodside . . . The earnings varied from 13s. a week to nearly £3. In some cases the wages were regular and steady; in others they fluctuated enormously, and could not be depended on for two weeks in succession . . . For convenience of description these sixty households have been arranged in 10 groups . . .

FAMILIES WITH A REGULAR INCOME
GROUP A.
*Wages regular: children earning: average income, 39s*
In these seven households the wage of the head of the house is supplemented by that of the children . . . This is the period of family life among the poor when

circumstances are most favourable, as the children have taken their places among the wage-earners and have not yet left the home. It is only when enquiry is made, however, that one realises how much money is actually coming into the house. The houses themselves show few signs of it in increased comfort. These families nearly all have a good show of china and "the other room" may be well furnished. In [family] XIII., for instance, the second room boasted a horse-hair sofa and chairs, a clock, photographs, &c. This however is not always the case, and study XXXIX. shows the reverse – a very bare house up a dark stair in one of the worst streets in the district, in which there was little attempt at comfort, though the house was fairly clean and well kept . . .

### GROUP B.
*Wage regular: lodgers kept: average income including amount paid by lodgers, 43s.*

In these eight households to the wages of the head of the house the amount paid by lodgers falls to be added . . . I. and IV. are Irish families; one consists of adults, in the other are eight children . . . There is an absolute lack of any appearance of care in these two houses, and things are left to manage themselves as they best can. The inmates are happy and cheery, however, and do not seem to mind the perpetual muddle . . .

### GROUP C.
*Wage regular, from 27s. to 31s.*

In these three households there is a distinctly higher standard of comfort. LIV. is a superior family. The husband is a carpenter, and the appearance of the house and their manner of living belong rather to the artisan than to the labouring class. The family, almost the only one of the series, has a church connection . . . The other two families live more on the standard of the households of the labouring classes, but the houses have a more comfortable, prosperous look about them . . .

### GROUP D.
*Wage regular, from 20s. to 25s.*

These [families] represent the average poorer working-class family. The income is steady but not large, the children not very numerous – 4 to 5 on an average – and the life on the whole is reasonably comfortable. The appearance of the houses varies according to the ideas of the housewife . . . In II. the housewife is most careful and the best manager of all the houses visited. Sometimes she got the most extraordinary bargains – for instance, one day she bought four pounds of halibut for 2d., and the fish was in good condition in spite of its price . . . These studies show what can be done with care and economy . . .

### GROUP E.
*Wage regular, under 20s.*

In these five households we have a sad state of affairs – poor houses and inadequate diet . . . All these houses are dark, and one very damp. In XXV. the gas is needed in winter, even at mid-day. The room however is clean and comfortable, and in the gaslight has quite a cheerful appearance. There are five children, and the income is only 18s a week, so that after paying rent, coal, gas, and societies, which together amount to nearly 6s. a week, the surplus left for food is very small . . . In these houses one notices that there is much less crockery on the shelves, *e.g., china dogs and jugs*, and the houses are barer than where the weekly income is more than 20s., but they are nearly all clean and well kept . . .

### FAMILIES WITH IRREGULAR INCOME.
### GROUP F.
#### *Wage irregular, over 20s.*

In these seven households the life is very irregular. The fluctuations in the work lead to days of hard work followed by days of idleness, days of plenty followed by days of starvation. The houses are clean and comfortable or the reverse according to the capacity and ideas of the housewife. The funeral societies are, as a rule, paid regularly, and are considered the first charge, coming almost before the food. When the housewife has any idea of management at all she lays past 1s. now and then towards the rent . . . XI. is a house where everything is spotlessly clean. It is one of the best kept of the whole sixty visited. XXI. is an extraordinary contrast. It is the only case where the mother worked at home. She fringed shawls and every day was found working at these. She got 1s. 4½d. a dozen for them, and could manage to earn 5s 6d. a week if working steadily at them. The husband was also earning but most irregularly. The seven children, none of whom were earning, managed as best they could. The family was the reverse of healthy – one child was mentally defective, two were off school through illness, and one or more were rickety. The house was up a bad stair in a bad neighbourhood, and was the third they had been in since the first visit paid to see if they would allow such a study to be made – a period of three months. The girls were learning to sew at a girls' club, and did most of the house work. Once a week or so the mother cleaned the house. This was usually done when the shawls given out to be fringed were especially delicate in colour and easily soiled . . .

### GROUP G.
#### *Wage irregular, under 20s.*

In these eight households . . . [a] hand to mouth existence is the rule . . . The houses are very poor, some very damp or dark, but often wonderfully well kept. [In LV.] weekly income was one of the lowest recorded . . . There were three children, all small, one of school age. The mother was small and ill developed, but the children were fairly healthy. The house contained one apartment, and was very damp and airless. Through ventilation was only possible when the neighbour opposite combined, and even then was not very satisfactory . . .

### GROUP H.
#### *Wage irregular, father heavy drinker.*

In the families just considered very few of the parents were abstainers, and in several they drank when they had the money, but these four families have been singled out specially, because in each the father was a habitual drinker, and the amount of money available for food, &c., was only what could be wrung from him . . . In study XIV. the mother was a melancholy woman, whose heart was nearly broken with the struggle. The daughter was in fairly steady work, and this helped matters, but only by constant visits to the pawnshop could they manage to get along. Of the 20s. which came into the house during the week of the study, 7s. 6d. was contributed by the father, 7. 3d. by the daughter, and 5. 3d was got by pawning things. The factor was pressing for his rent, which was much overdue. XV. presented a great contrast. The housewife was a bright cheery woman. Two of the children were earning, and the mother went out occasionally for a day's cleaning. She was a most enterprising woman, and painted and papered the house herself, making it most comfortable and cheerful . . . [t]he husband rarely worked more than two or three days at a time, and unless the wife met him just after he had received his pay she got very little from him . . .

### GROUP K.
#### *Jewish Families.*

The five Jewish families studied are on the whole better off than most of the British families visited. The average weekly wage is 35s . . . In V. the father earns 17s a week, and this is supplemented by the earnings of the wife and son. The appearance of the house and the style of living are much the same as in the British houses, but the mother is more grandly dressed. A lodger sleeps in the house, which has three apartments . . . There are ten children, all small and delicate looking; one of them with rickets was attending the invalid school. The Jewish houses are all larger than the British, and had at least three apartments . . . The kitchen is as usual used as a living-room . . . The parlours are wonderful rooms, with full suites of furniture, photographs, crystal or china ornaments, antimacassars, &c . . .

### GROUP L.
#### *Italian Families.*

Only three Italian families were visited. It was found difficult to carry on these studies as the women had no idea of accuracy. These three families presented marked differences in their mode of life. XX., where there was one child, and that a baby, had a more than ample diet . . . They lived in a two-roomed house, but only used one room. The mother said the house was really too large for them, as they could not use a second room . . . Study XI. is in a household in receipt of Parish relief. This is their sole source of income, unless occasionally when the wife gets a day's washing, or goes out with an organ and a bird. The husband is incurably ill, and the wife is not strong. Of their seventeen children only three, all young, are at home. The house is fairly clean, but has a cheerless look, and there is not much appearance of comfort . . .

## Section 3: Housework and homemaking

All the sources in this section look at housework in its various guises, many of them displaying a concern with thrift. This was a pervasive motif of Victorian society, most famously written about by Samuel Smiles in several works including one simply called *Thrift* (1875). For the likes of Smiles, women were even more responsible than men for inculcating the habit of thrift. Multiple aspects of cooking, cleaning and domestic consumption can be seen throughout these texts. Clearly, the labour of the home differed for poor women compared with better-off households with paid help; nonetheless, homemaking was considered the province of all women.

Hannah Ann Stirling (1816–43) was the eldest daughter of the Stirling of Keir family, landed gentry whose ancestral home was near Dunblane in Perthshire. She was also the niece of Sir John Maxwell of Pollok (1791–1865). The male lineage of the Maxwell and Stirling families is quite fully documented in a variety of dictionaries of the British peerage but very little is known about the families' women. Hannah's papers reveal that she was involved with housekeeping at Keir. She did not marry and died at the spa town of Carlsbad a month before her twenty-seventh birthday.[13] The source gives an indication of the size of this household, as well as an insight into what may have concerned women of Hannah's status and education in terms of budgeting.

---

3.1  Personal and Household Accounts of Hannah Ann Stirling, *c*.1830s
[GCA. File T-SK/27/25/1–8, item ref.: T-SK/27/25/8]

---

*Memorandum of Butchermeat*

*Abstract of butchermeat used in Keir House from 1st Nov. 1837 to the end of October 1838*

|  | St | lbs | Rate | Cost |
|---|---|---|---|---|
| *Beef in Stones of 14lbs &16oz per lb* | 231 | 9 at | 7/-st | £81,, 1,,6 |
| *Mutton ------ Do --------- Do ----------* | 192,, | 2 | Do | £67,, 5,, |
| *Suet ---------- Do --------- Do ----------* | 10,, |  | Do | £3,, 10,, |
| *Pork ---------- Do --------- Do ----------* | 49,, | 10,, | Do4/1 | £10,, 3 |
| *Beef from Alex Buchanan----------------* | 58,, | 9,, | at7/-p/st | £20,,10,,6 |
| *Beef Veal and Tongue from Sundries* | 12--- |  | Do | £4 4 |
|  | 554,, | 2,, | Cost | £186 14 |

*or 443 Stones 5½ lbs at 16 0z p lb & 1½ lb per Stew = 7758 lbs which allowing the family & servants always to be 24 in numbers would give 323¼ lb to each.*

The extract below is from the autobiography of prolific novelist, Henrietta Keddie‡ (1827–1914), who wrote under the pen name Sarah Tytler. In this memoir, Keddie reflected on the experience of her grandparents, parents and finally, that of her own generation. She recollects the domestic social life of her parents' home in Cupar in Fife when she was growing up during the 1830s and 1840s; though much of women's social life within the Scottish middle classes was centred on home and family, domestic social occasions could be used as a means to cement local business and political alliances. Conspicuous consumption might mean that this class often struggled to keep up appearances though the Scottish middle classes may well have mixed pragmatism with ambitions to display their social status through domestic culture.[14] Elsewhere in her narrative, Keddie described tasks performed by the wives and daughters of middling households. By this period, families such as Keddie's could draw on the likes of Margaret Dod's (pseudonym of Christian Johnstone‡) *Cook and Housewife's Manual*, which had many reprints from 1826 onwards.

### 3.2 Henrietta Keddie, *Three Generations: the Story of a Middle-Class Scottish Family* (London: John Murray, 1911) (80–2)

The family life of the town's middle class was not unlike that of the country, except that the hours of the three meals – breakfast, dinner, and supper – were not the same. Tea was a fourth meal – a regular meal, not an afternoon refreshment – but, as a rule, it was only the women and children who sat round the central table, with its prominent tea-tray and its array of plates, bearing its variety of tea-bread, butter, and preserves. The breakfast and the dinner, both early, were the substantial meals; the supper was a light and simple affair. Even in houses of good standing it frequently consisted solely of a bowl of porridge or "sowens," served in soup plates and supped with milk; or of a dish of herrings, fresh, salt, or red (cured), to be eaten with new potatoes when in season; or of "bread and cheese and radishes" . . . Luncheon did not exist. One is tempted to think the cost of living in professional classes must be about doubled by our modern practice.

Even at social gatherings the entertainments were reasonably free from extravagance. Dinner-parties were comparatively rare, and the guests were mostly confined to men, when sherry and port were the only wines drunk, and that very moderately. With cheese and dessert there was Edinburgh strong ale or porter. If excess followed it was in the shape of whisky toddy.

The prevailing form of gaiety was what was styled "tea and supper," the invitation to which often included the words "in an easy way." The company did not often exceed five or six couples. The gentlemen not infrequently omitted the first part of the programme, but they came in time for the amusement provided – whist at sixpenny points. If any young people drifted in to what was essentially a party for married couples, they had a separate table with round games of cards. The supper was modest enough, limited to such dishes as are now banished from our tables, or only figure as breakfast-dishes or dinner entrees – such were tripe, kidneys, "minced collops" (the Scotch dish was made from fresh meat, not rechauffe from meat already cooked), crab-pies served in the crab-shells, etc. On this light fare the merriment and the wit, which represented the feast of reason and the flow of soul, played freely: more freely than at the more formal and more substantial dinners – banquets which, when married women were present, marked "house-heatings," marriages, etc.

Such rivalry as existed was chiefly in connection with the menu furnished by the presiding matron, as it was an affair for which the mistress of the house did not disdain to hold herself accountable. Even if she relegated the dinner to her cook, she was understood to be in possession of sufficient superior knowledge to qualify her in guiding and superintending the cook . . . There were dishes with which a house-mother's special gift was associated . . . One lady had a reputation for home-cured rounds of beef, which were near to bearing her name; another was known for her pigeon-pies, another for her tipsy-cake. My mother pinned her faith in her hare-soup.

There was private and personal honour for individual dishes, as there was private and personal honour for after-supper music, given by the singer, unaccompanied, in the seat which he or she occupied for hours at table. Each tuneful lady or gentleman had her or his particular song as an acknowledged right. To have misappropriated the right established by long usage would have been a distinct act of rudeness. There was no craving for novelty in the songs; rather a cordial welcome for old favourites: "Scots Wha Hae," "Ye Mariners of England," "Ye Banks and Braes," or "Allan Water," were sure to be received with acclaim.

The Scottish domestic environment was often differentiated from that of its near neighbours, the English, but not always in a positive light. Negative stereotypes of Scottish hospitality characterised by dour Presbyterianism, extreme miserliness and austere discomfort, as well alternative caricatures of free-and-easy slovenliness, can be found in many literary descriptions. A good example of the latter is contained in Elizabeth Hamilton's‡ (1758–1816) *Cottagers of Glenburnie* (1808) where the domestic habits of Highlanders are subject to a 'civilising mission'. In the following extract from Jane Carlyle's correspondence to her Scottish mother-in-law, however, and in many other possible examples, it is evident that Jane incorporated a positive view of Scottish domestic pragmatism into her own self-image as a homemaker, and did so with more than a little satisfaction. This extract is from the *Collected Letters*, Vol. 7, pp. 287–8.

### 3.3 A letter from Jane Welsh Carlyle from her London address to her mother-in-law, Margaret A Carlyle, in Scotland, 1 September 1834

My dear Mother,

. . . Our little household has been set up again, at a quite moderate expence of money and trouble (wherein I cannot help thinking with a *chastened vanity*, that the superior shiftiness and thriftiness of the Scotch character has strikingly manifested itself). The English women turn up the whites of their eyes and call on the "good Heavens["] at the bare idea of enterprises which seem to me in the most ordinary course of human affairs – I told M*rs* Hunt one day I had been very busy painting: "What?" she asked is it a portrait? "O No," I told her "something of more importance; a large wardrobe" – She could not imagine she said "how I could have patience for such things" – And so having no patience for them herself what is the result? she is every other day reduced to borrow my tumbler's, my teacups, even – a cupful of porridge, a few spoonfuls of tea are begged of me, because "Missus has got company and happens to be out of the article" – in plain unadorned English because "Missus is the most wretched of Managers and is often at the point of having not a copper in her purse" – To see how they live and waste here it is a wonder the whole City does not bankrape and go out o sight – flinging platefuls of what they are pleased to denominate "*crusts*" (that is, what I consider all the best of the bread), into the ash-pits – I often say with honest self congratulation in Scotland we have no such thing as "*crusts*." On the whole, tho' the English Ladies seem to have their wits more at their finger ends, and have a great advantage over me in that respect I never cease to be glad that I was born on the other side the Tweed, and that those who are nearest and Dearest to me are Scotch.

Like the title verse from Russell's volume (see 2.4), the following reveals intimate details of family life but avoids sentimentality. In this instance, Russell couples humour with the necessary practicality required of the 'wives o' working men' in managing their households on a tight budget.

> 3.4 Jessie Russell, 'Domestic Dirge', in *The Blinkin' o' the Fire* (Glasgow: Cossar, Fotheringham & Co., 1877) (20)

A Domestic Dirge
I'VE little need tae joke in rhyme,
For wi' the stormy weather,
There's been sae muckle broken time,
An' ae thing an' anither.

Wi' rent an' taxes a' tae find,
An' mind ye, wi' "expenses,"
The verb "tae plan" I hae declined
In a' its moods an' tenses.

At my guidman I tak the "huff,"
For tho' he's no a "snuffer,"
He whiles keeps something kent as "snuff,"
The "pinch" I gar him suffer.

He's lang intended for tae get
New claes. The mischief wi' i'm!
I doot it wull be langer yet,
We eat sae much per diem.

The wean has been tae get a frock
An' me a Sunday bonnet,
But if I jaunt, frae ither folk
I'll ha'e tae crave the loan o 't.

In summer time we'll surely "fen"
When "broken pay" is "seckit,"
Uphaud me, wives o' working men,
We'll "strike" tae git the feck o 't.

The extract below is taken from a handwritten manuscript of instructions evidently aimed at housemaids; it is possible, however, that it may have been copied from a published text, the original provenance is unclear. It possibly formed instructions to staff employed at Sandlodge or Sumburgh House in the Shetland Isles *c.*1880. Many such texts circulated in this period; this is of particular interest, having been recovered from the papers of an upper-class family in Scotland's most remote and northerly location. The manuscript lengthily describes the detail of housework and reveals the long hours and back-breaking labour entailed in domestic service. The source alerts us to aspects of the domestic environment that, even in grand houses, created constant work, such as coal fires and mechanical sweeping. Nevertheless, for many women, particularly in rural areas, there was little choice in the matter where choosing employment was concerned. In Shetland, despite competition from other locally available employment, this type of work might still have appealed to young women who wished to make a career in service. This extract covers only the first few hours of work in the morning but continues in this same manner to describe all a servant's waking hours of unremitting labour.

---

**3.5 'Duties of a Chambermaid', in Bruce of Sumburgh Papers (Bruce family correspondence, 1816–87) [SA ref.: D8/400/16, no date but probably *c.*1880]**

To keep every part of the house and furniture always clean and in order, for which purpose she must rise by six o' clock at least every morning and first kindle a fire in the children's room and then the dining room. She must every morning regularly, sweep down the soot as far as she can reach up the chimney and then take off the ashes carefully, leaving not the least dust of them behind. She must then every morning scour the ribs and apron of the grate before she puts on the fire, and after it is on, brush every part of the grate, fender and hearth, till they shine very well . . . When she has done her dirty work about the fireside, she should wash her hands before she touches anything else in the room. Before she begins to brush the carpet she should dust the cornice of the room and put everything in its place and never brush the carpet without first sprinkling tea leaves on it, to prevent the dust from rising, and she must sweep carefully out of every corner, and from below every chair, and every table, every morning. When done with sweeping she must with a clean cloth rub off the dust off every part of the room the looking glasses, tables, chairs and windows, and she must give all the mahogany a brush every morning and rub the breakfast table and children's table every morning with a little milk, beer or water and give them both a brush after it. The kindling should be out to the dining room fire just in time to be well taken before breakfast and neither so soon as to be burnt away before breakfast, nor so late as not to be taken at breakfast time. When she has finished everything in the dining room she should open a bit off one of the windows whenever the weather is dry to air the room and should then shut the door and put everything in the lobby, stairs and passages in their own places and carry everything that she finds there which ought not to be there to its own proper place.

She must shake the lobby carpet every morning and then sweep carefully every part and corner of the lobby, stairs and passages, from the top of the house down to the bottom first sweeping down the cobwebs from the roof and walls and sprinkling sawdust to keep down the dust. She should then gather all the dirt she has swept out of the dining room, stairs, passages, lobby carefully in a bucket and carry it immediately to the house meant for it to be put in and empty it there, and then put the bucket in its own place where she knows to find it again.

All that has been mentioned already should be done every morning by eight o' clock when the maid should clean herself and then put down the breakfast things taking care that everything that will be needed at breakfast is in the tray before she carries it in, that the knives and everything is bright and perfectly clean. She should then get her own breakfast . . .

### 3.6 'A Highland Washing', Valentine's Postcards, *c*.1878

Differences in washing traditions between Scotland and England rested upon the practice of tramping laundry in the open air, often called 'Scotch Washing'. In some Victorian pictures of this activity, the fact that women's legs are exposed to view undoubtedly had lascivious associations. This commercial image capitalises on picturesque associations with the Highlands; it is certainly tame but the participants who have been posed for the photograph do not look to be enjoying the experience.

Contrary to stereotypes, by the late nineteenth century, outdoor laundry

**Figure 3.2** Balquhidder. A Highland Washing, *c*.1878. J. Valentine & Co. Courtesy of the University of St Andrews Photographic Collections.

would have been confined to remote places in Scotland, and washing had been raised to an activity that required expert instruction. Indeed, the perfection of laundry involved a sheer palaver that was the scourge of many women. The extracts below are from a much longer set of directives about how to launder different household items and clothes. In middle-class households, washing was done by a servant or by a washerwoman hired for the task. Skill with laundry could provide an income for wives and widows unable to take live-in positions provided they had stamina! Most working-class households, even if they had any form of indoor plumbing, lacked the facilities of space or appliances for heating the large amounts of water needed to undertake this arduous operation; consequently, public washhouses or 'steamies', as they were aptly named in Scotland, became a feature of urban localities. These provided boilers, sinks and wringers but, of course, washing still had to be transported to and from home. By the late century, some tenements were built with outdoor, shared wash houses but these, too, could be a source of friction between women as such facilities depended on co-operation over allocation of their use.[15] Many women took a pride in being able to master laundry because this was a skill very much demonstrated in public. 'Dirty' washing denoted the slovenly housewife.

### 3.7 Margaret Black, *Household Cookery and Laundry Work* (1882) (129, 130, 131)

The day before washing, look out all the articles that require to be washed, and arrange them in lots; mend what requires to be mended, and soak what requires to be soaked . . . Begin work early on the washing day. The best part of the day is the forenoon, and an hour gained in the morning is worth two later in the day . . .

Fill up the boiler with cold water; put into it a quarter of an inch of soap to each gallon of water, and a dessert spoonful of washing powder (soda is not nearly so nice, as it gives linen a greyish colour); wring the clothes roughly out of the cold water, and put them in the boiler; cover with the lid, and let them boil gently for about ten or fifteen minutes. The rinsing in cold water before they are boiled has the great advantage of removing all the dirty water from the clothes, otherwise it gets boiled into them, and injures the colour.

When boiled enough, take them out of the boiler; add more water and soap, and put in the next quantity ready, always remembering the finest are done first. Now pour some cold water on the boiled clothes, wash them out, and rinse them once or twice . . . let them be well wrung out of the last rinsing. They must now be blued [a common household product made of iron agents which created the optical illusion of greater whiteness] . . . Put in a tub a small quantity of water, and tinge it well with blue. Dip each article in and wring it out; shake fold and set aside. Never allow clothes to lie in blue water, or put more than one in at a time; but just dip once or twice, and wring out, repeating till all are finished. Add a little blue from time to time to keep up the shade. Repeat this process with the bed and table linen till all are finished, then hang them out to dry. Use up the soapy water in the tubs to wash kitchen towels, dusters, etc . . . The clothes already hung out to dry must be attended to. Remember to have them folded before they are hung out, to remove the creases of the wringing, and they will dry much better . . .

The extract below comes from a cheaply produced manual, the outcome of a school of domestic economy, begun in 1885, which ran classes and arranged incursions by teachers into the homes of women in the shipbuilding district of Govan. Its benefactress, Isabella Elder‡ (1828–1905), was known for a variety of philanthropic initiatives; Martha Gordon was one of a small army of domestic science teachers who made a career out of promoting domestic economy. This pamphlet was given further scientific authority through an introduction by Dr James Russell, the well-known Medical Superintendent for Glasgow who stated that a 'good cook is sure to be cleanly – sweet and wholesome in person, neat and tidy in dress'. Gordon's remit was to inculcate thrift along with teaching on nutrition. The recipes give 'proportions suitable for a family of four to six in number, and the prices given are averages'; they were 'intended for the ordinary kitchen utensils and open fires'. These two extracts provide examples perhaps at opposite ends of the culinary spectrum: the first is for 'Sheep's Heid' broth. The writer Elizabeth Haldane‡ (1862–1937) claimed in her popular history, *From One Century to Another* (1937), that, in rural Scotland, this was a typical Sunday dish as it needed long cooking and could be set on the fire while the family was at church. The following recipe for Christmas pies would have been relatively expensive to make and, in this instance, no costs were included by Gordon, nor indeed was any alcohol! Other parts of the text indicate that the school was one which advocated temperance.

3.8 *Cookery for Working Men's Wives Being Recipes by Martha H. Gordon as Taught in Mrs John Elder's Domestic Classes, Govan* (Paisley; Alexander Gardner, 1888) (29, 43–4)

### SHEEP'S HEAD BROTH

| Head and Trotters | 6d; | Barley and Peas | 1d |
|---|---|---|---|
| Mixed Vegetables | 1½d | Total | 8½d |

Get head and trotters singed. Have the head split, take out the brains, wash every part well. Pierce the eyes, and wash the skin well with the liquor that flows out. Scrape out the eye cavities with a knife, then put the head and trotters in a pail of clean water, with a little salt and soda. Let them steep all night. Take them out and scrape them well. Put them in a pot with one gallon of water, and a teacupful of peas, and ¾ of a teacupful of barley. Boil for three-quarters of an hour. Add half a turnip cut in slices, the other half with carrot, parsnip, and cabbage cut very small. Boil for an hour. Add leeks, celery, and parsley cut small and boil for another hour. Dish the broth, and serve head and trotters with slices of turnip for garnish. Sheep's Head Broth requires longer boiling than other broths.

CHRISTMAS PIES (SIMPLE)

½ lb apples, ¼ lb figs, ¼ lb currants, ¼ lb raisins, ¼ lb sugar, ½ oz cinnamon, ½ oz ginger, 1 lb flour, ¼ lb lard, 1 teaspoon baking powder.

Peel and core the apples, and cut them into small dice, put them in a basin with the sugar; mince the figs fine; stone and mince the raisins (or use Sultana raisins); pick and rub the currants very carefully with a cloth. Put all into a basin with the apples and sugar, add the cinnamon and ginger (and any other flavourings that is liked). Mix all *well* together (the mince is all the better of being prepared some time before it is wanted).

For the crust, mix the flour, lard a teaspoon of baking powder, and a pinch of salt, well together, then add enough cold water to make a stiff paste; rollout to about a quarter of an inch thick. The pies can either be made in small tins or soup plates. Rub the tins or plates well with lard, cut the pastes to the right size, put the mince meat in carefully, wet around the edges, and cover the top with paste and bake in a not too quick oven.

*The People's Friend* originated in Dundee; its popularity quickly spread. Initially subtitled 'A Scottish National Literary Miscellany', as its fame increased, the description 'Scottish National' was dropped. It purveyed a particular brand of homespun 'Scottishness' in its choice of articles and stories. The core readership of the *Friend* was female and middle class although popular but respectable periodicals like this were often handed on to servants, or passed among less affluent family members, so its overall readership almost certainly had a wider social base. The first extract is typical of the kind of household hints and tips that appeared regularly. The second is from a much longer article describing kitchen equipment in detail. Hand in hand with increased consumerism for the home was a shift in how domestic tasks could be managed as the middle classes expanded. In 1900, the majority of working-class homes still consisted of, at most, three rooms with many families continuing to live in one-roomed apartments. Kitchens were living space and all social life took place in them – cooking, eating, talking, reading, sleeping, giving birth and dying. The advice in this article is clearly aimed at the lower middle classes with smaller families, separate kitchens and, increasingly, no live-in servants. In households like this, women did have to turn their hands to all and, with its popular approach, the *Friend* provided advice. Accompanying this turn was the rise of formal domestic education; for example, from the 1890s women could undertake a 'Housewife's Diploma' at the Edinburgh School of Cookery and other similar establishments that sprang up.[16]

### 3.9 Two articles from *The People's Friend* (1890 and 1900)

'Workmen's Dinner Recipes', Kate Turnbull, Vol. XXII, 6 January 1890

Suppose, a working man with a wife and four of a family, earning 28s per week, the following might be taken as a list of their dinners for a week :

DAYS DISHES

*Sunday* – Stewed meat, potatoes, turnips; grated bread pudding.
*Monday* – Rice soup; bread and meat; cornflour.
*Tuesday* – Tripe, potatoes; boiled rice and milk.
*Wednesday* – Baked fish, potatoes; stewed apples.
*Thursday* – Mutton broth, potatoes; semolina.
*Friday* – Mince meat, boiled rice; fig pudding.
*Saturday* – Pea soup, bread; ground rice pudding.

. . . Total cost for the above seven dinners would be 7s 3d, but a little less might be sufficient if a stone of potatoes is purchased . . .

## 'A Well-Furnished Kitchen: To Those Who Intend Starting Housekeeping', no author, Vol. XXXII, 23 July 1900)

"A bad workman never gets good tools" is a common saying, and it may be too true that an incompetent person is apt to blame everything but his own want of skill. At the same time it is equally true that a workman who respects himself at all will not work with blunt inferior tools . . . How is it, then, that in the majority of houses – I speak advisedly – every room is better furnished than the kitchen? This seems to be the case alike in the middle-class and working-people's houses. In the former the cook is left to struggle away with a meagre supply of badly chosen articles – she herself may be unaware of the existence of better – and expected to send in up-to-date dishes without any of the up-to-date "labour savers". Then mistresses bemoan the scarcity of good servants, and wonder like Dickens's "Waiter," why cooking and incompatibility generally go together. In working-class kitchens again bright cooking utensils are too often relegated to the kitchen wall, where they are for all time simply regarded as "scoorin' things". It is not so much my object to recommend those

UP-TO-DATE LABOUR SAVERS,

as many of them are but cheap flimsy " catch-pennies," but to advocate the use of standard articles which have always been considered by those who deserve to be called authorities on the subject as necessary to the comfort and regularity of the household generally. For the most ordinary kitchen a clock is required. Be accurate in timing your dishes, and insist upon your domestic doing the same . . . Weights and scales are no less important. Do not trust to "your eye" as some people talk about, nor any rule of thumb . . .

SIEVES, KNIFES, &c.

In the matter of sieves most kitchens are deficient. One hair sieve, through which you will rub all acid substances, such as tomato soup &c., indeed all soups which you want to be soft and smooth . . . One large wire sieve [and] two small smaller ones . . . Lots of people content themselves with one wooden spoon . . . there should be half a dozen at least. Two or three of those knives called "cook's knifes" will be found invaluable . . . The bread knife is extra . . . Then you will require a chopper, or a little mincing machine. The latter will repay itself over and over again. A cleaver has a murderous sound, but it is indispensable for breaking up bones for stock, jointing rabbits &c., while a small saw comes in very handy occasionally. One or two large, strong metal spoons for stirring soup and stews will save your good ones, and your fingers many a burning. A colander, a fish-slice, a skimmer, an egg whisk, a spiral egg-beater, a set of skewers, a couple of moulds, a toaster or Dutch oven, a grid-iron, a pair of steak tongs, all these are necessary to keep the domestic temper even. Have two fish pans, large and small, and it is advisable to have one very small one entirely devoted to the homely herring . . .

By the end of the century, home-making had become an aesthetic, as well as a practical, pursuit for many women. This is clearly seen in Christmas preparations. It is often asserted that, unlike in other parts of the United Kingdom, until relatively recently Christmas was little celebrated in Scotland, being shunned by Presbyterians as idolatrous. Christmas was perhaps a much lesser festivity than New Year's Eve among the working classes but this does not preclude some forms of celebration. And it is necessary to query whether the Scottish middle classes who had the means also eschewed celebrating Christmas. Was the condemnation of Christmas revelries by Scottish churches powerful enough to trump the power of Scottish female consumers by the end of the nineteenth century? This seems unlikely, though many overburdened housewives might have wished this was so! Indeed, we have already seen in source 2.5 that the minister's wife, Helen McFarlan, rejoiced in a Christmas tree. In articles such as this we can clearly see that commercialisation was advanced and the burden of providing entertainment was shouldered by women.

> ### 3.10 'Christmas Dinner', in *Woman at Home*, Vol. 1 (1893) (228, 230)

A CHRISTMAS DINNER
Hare Soup.
Boiled Turbot.
Roast Beef. Boiled Turkey.
Mashed Potatoes. Broccoli.
Plum Pudding. Mince Pies.
Raspberry Trifle.
Biscuits. Cheese. Walnuts.
Dessert Biscuits.
French Sweets. Chocolate

If some of our readers think we are giving a menu far beyond what a small income can afford, to such we say, "Christmas comes but once a year, and when it comes it brings good cheer." But a very good dinner can be got by omitting some of the items. For instance, those who have only one servant might leave out the fish and the trifle. But it is wonderful what a few hours of patient, skilful work can accomplish . . .

TABLE DECORATION
Now that the flower gardens are nearly desolate, we must go to the shrubbery, the woods, or the conservatory for leaves to embellish our table, and as our dinner is a

Christmas one, the place of honour must be given to the holly, which with an abundance of its red berries might be put in a round or oval dish in the centre of the table. To take off the rather hard metallic look of the leaves put mistletoes along with it. Half way down the table place a plant of white camellia or azalea with maidenhair fern on both sides, and if it can be procured, a poinsettia might be placed near the top of the table, that is, if the table is a large one . . . Fold the table-napkins in the mitre shape, and put a tiny piece of holly with berries on each . . .

### Select bibliography

Annette Carruthers (ed.), *The Scottish Home* (Edinburgh: National Museums of Scotland, 1996).

W. Hamish Fraser, 'Necessities in the Nineteenth Century', in Trevor Griffiths and Graeme Morton (eds), *A History of Everyday Life in Scotland, 1800 to 1900* (Edinburgh: Edinburgh University Press, 2010), pp. 60–88.

Eleanor Gordon, 'The Family', in Lynn Abrams et al. *Gender and Scottish History Since 1700* (Edinburgh: Edinburgh University Press, 2006), pp. 235–61.

Eleanor Gordon and Gwyneth Nair, *Public Lives: Women, Family and Society in Victorian Britain* (New Haven and London: Yale University Press, 2003).

Stana Nenadic, 'Middle-Rank Consumers and Domestic Culture in Edinburgh and Glasgow 1720–1840', in *Past and Present*, No. 145 (1994), pp. 122–56.

T. C. Smout, 'The Tenement City', in *A Century of the Scottish People 1830–1950* (London: Collins, 1986, Fontana imprint 1987), pp. 32–57.

Susan Storrier (ed.), *Scottish Life and Society: Scotland's Domestic Life*, Vol. 6, *A Compendium of Scottish Ethnology* (Edinburgh: John Donald, 2006).

### Notes

1. Stana Nenadic, 'The Victorian Middle Classes', in W. Hamish Fraser and Irene Maver (eds), *Glasgow*, Vol. 2, *1830–1914* (Manchester: Manchester Uuniversity Press, 1996), pp. 265–99.

2. Jane Roberts, 'The Carlyles and Their Servants', in *The Carlyle Society Papers – Session 2005–2006*, New Series No. 18, p.39.

3. For discussion of Jane's relationship with servants, see Thea Holme, *The Carlyles At Home* (Oxford: Oxford University Press, 1979).

4. Michael Anderson and D. J. Morse, 'The People', in W. Hamish Fraser and R. J. Morris (eds), *People and Society in Scotland*, Vol. 2 (Edinburgh: John Donald, 1997), pp. 8–45, 31.

5. See Sarah Pedersen, 'Educational, Academic and Legal Publishing', in David Finkelstein and Alistair McCleery (eds), *Edinburgh History of the Book,* Vol. 4 (Edinburgh: Edinburgh Uuniversity Press, 2007), pp. 311–29.

6. For Swan's publishing life see Andrew Nash, 'Annie S. Swan', in Finkelstein and McCleery, *Edinburgh History of the Book*, pp. 294–5, and Edmund F. Gardiner, 'Annie S. Swan – forerunner of modern popular fiction', in *Library Review*, Vol. 24: 6 (1974), p. 251.

7.  See George Eyre-Todd, *Who's Who in Glasgow 1909* (Glasgow: Gowans & Gray), at Glasgow Digital Library: http://gdl.cdlr.strath.ac.uk/eyrwho/eyrwho1619.htm

8.  See also Leah Leneman, *Alienated Affections: The Scottish Experience of Divorce and Separation, 1684–1830* (Edinburgh: Edinburgh University Press, 1998).

9.  For discussion of Russell and examples of her verse see Florence Boos, *Working Class Women Poets in Victorian Britain: An Anthology* (Peterborough, ON: Broadview Press, 2008), pp. 321–7.

10. See Margaret Beetham, *A Magazine of her Own, Domesticity and Female Desire in the Woman's Magazine 1800–1914* (London: Routledge, 1996).

11. See Linda Fleming, *Jewish Women in Glasgow: Gender, Ethnicity and the Immigrant Experience c.1870-1950* (unpublished thesis: University of Glasgow, 2005).

12. For archival material on the Park School, see MLGR ref.: TD 1665/1/7/1.

13. Charles Rogers, *Monuments and Monumental Inscriptions in Scotland* (London: Charles Griffin & Co., 1871), p. 172.

14. See Stana Nenadic, 'Middle-Rank consumers and Domestic culture in Edinburgh and Glasgow 1720–1840', *Past and Present*, No. 145 (1994), pp. 122–56.

15. Lynn Abrams and Linda Fleming, 'From Scullery to Conservatory: Everyday Life in the Scottish Home', in Lynn Abrams and Callum G. Brown (eds), *A History of Everyday Life in Twentieth-Century Scotland* (Edinburgh: Edinburgh University Press, 2010) pp. 61; T. C. Smout and Sydney Wood, *Scottish Voices* (London: Collins, 1990), pp. 25–8.

16. Tom Begg, *The Excellent Women* (Edinburgh: John Donald, 1994).

# Chapter 4

# Work and Working Conditions

*Esther Breitenbach*

## Introduction

The first phase of industrialisation in Scotland was dominated by the textile industry in which many women were employed. Textiles remained an important source of employment for women in several parts of Scotland though, by the end of the nineteenth century, this sector had much declined in significance. In rural and coastal areas, women continued to work in agriculture and fishing, though rapid urbanisation was accompanied by rural depopulation. By the late nineteenth century, fishing was providing seasonal employment for large numbers of women and girls from the north-east coast to the Highlands and Islands. In such areas, women's labour in weaving, tweed and lace-making also contributed to the household economy. As Scotland's economy expanded, alongside the rise of the middle classes, demand grew for domestic servants, and this became increasingly important as a source of employment for working-class women. Urban patterns of employment varied across the major cities and included, as well as industrial employment, women's work in business, as entrepreneurs, running shops, boarding houses, and so on, as well as work in the 'sweated trades', whether in small workshops or at home. While there had always been some middle- and upper-class women earning a living throughout the period, from the 1870s, middle-class women actively demanded both the right to work and access to higher education, and subsequently the numbers of women in professional employment increased.

This chapter provides extracts illustrating the experience of women workers in industry, agriculture, fishing, business, professions and crafts, and also illustrates trade union organisation and regulation of working conditions. With respect to working-class and rural women workers, it is a challenge to find texts authored by such women themselves. Thus, some of the extracts are commentary by middle-class women about working-class or rural workers, and there are also some by male authors, whether as sympathisers or in an official capacity. On occasion, this includes men writing pseudonymously as women.

## Section 1: Industrial work

Textile manufacturing took place in many locations across Scotland, such as the larger centres of Aberdeen, Dundee and Paisley, and also in many smaller towns, such as Brechin and Forfar in Angus and Galashiels in the Borders. Dissatisfaction about working conditions led to a strike in Aberdeen in 1834. The extract below gives an insight into working conditions: a further extract in the trade union section [6.1] illustrates women's efforts to form a union. It is likely that the pamphlet was written by a male trade unionist.

1.1 Aberdeen Female Operative Union, *Detailed Report of the Proceedings of the Operatives, since the turn-out, at the Broadford Mill, on Friday, the 7th Instant, containing the speeches delivered at the GREAT MEETING, held in Robert's Hall, Queen Street, on Saturday evening together with the Rules and Regulations of the Union, which was then organized, &c.* (Aberdeen, 1834) (10–11)

A great many of the female spinners and others connected with Factories explained the nature of those grievances for which they now seek redress. Some of their complaints were indeed calculated to keep up the spirit of discontent which at present exists against the manufacturers, and it was certainly obvious from what they stated that there must have been something radically defective in the manner in which the Factory Commission conducted its investigations, when such abuses as those complained of could be allowed for a moment to continue.

A girl from the Bannermill stated that she had been fined 6d. for singing in the Mill. Another, who had the misfortune to force a splinter of wood into her foot, was fined 6d. for sitting down to get it extracted; and other two girls were also fined 6d. each, for endeavouring to assist her in taking it out. A female at the same Mill, was mulcted of a sixpence, because the glue on the end of a bobbin at which she attended, loosened while she was working; and she was thus compelled to pay for the time which was required in replacing it. About 50 persons from this Mill, and some other one, called out at the same time, that they were compelled twice-a-day to pay a fine of a penny, for changing their clothes after going into the Mill, although only occupying them for less than five minutes at a time. Other Mill Girls confirmed these statements, and added, that it was customary to pay 6d. for being a quarter of an hour behind "time" in the morning or afternoon. Some were fined a penny for turning their backs to a frame; a penny for speaking to their neighbour, and twopence for reading a book! On one occasion the person who paid the wages at the Bannermill had made a mistake, by paying wrong wages to the females; and while they were engaged in rectifying this blunder amongst themselves, by returning to each other the proper wages, *they were fined 6d. each for a fault that was not their own!!*

The fact that women and children worked in coal mines, often in atrocious conditions, was a major area of concern in the early decades of the nineteenth century. Following the Royal Commission of 1842, the Mines and Colleries Act (1842) prohibited the employment of women and children underground. In some mining areas this had the consequence of depriving women of any source of income, and the provisions of the Act were not always respected in the years following its passage.

Reports of the Children's Employment Commission were published on the three major mining areas of Scotland: East Scotland, Lanark and Dumfries, and West Scotland. Of the three reports, that on East Scotland appears to reflect in the most direct manner the testimony of women and girls about their working conditions, as well as having many striking illustrations of women working underground. The extracts below are from the East Scotland report.[1] A facsimile edition was published in 1968 by the Irish University Press, and is held at the NLS. The reports are available at House of Commons Parliamentary Papers online accessible via the National Library of Scotland and university libraries.

1.2 *Children's Employment Commission* (1842) REPORT by ROBERT HUGH FRANKS, ESQ., on the Employment of Children and Young Persons in the Collieries and iron works of the East of Scotland, and the State, Condition, and Treatment of such Children and Young Persons (383, 479, 436, 458)

From the introduction to Section II. Places of work:

6. Many of the mines in the East of Scotland are conducted, as to the above and underground arrangements, in the most primitive manner: the one-horse gin to draw up the basket, no separation in the shaft, the ventilation carried on in many places by means of old shafts left open, &c., the negligence of the under-ground

workings corresponds with that above, the roads being carelessly attended to, and the workings very irregularly carried on, so that the oppression of the labour is as much increased by the want of good superintendence as by the irregularity of the workpeople themselves.

7. The roads are most commonly wet, but in some places so much so as to come up to the ancles; and where the roofs are soft, the drippy and slushy state of the entire chamber, is such that none can be said to work in it in a dry condition, and the coarse apparel the labour requires absorbs so much of the drainage of water as to keep workmen as thoroughly saturated as if they were working continually in water.

8. The workings in the narrow seams are sometimes 100 to 200 yards from the main roads; so that the females have to crawl backwards and forwards with their small carts in seams in many cases not exceeding 22 to 28 inches in height. This will be found illustrated in the statement of Margaret Hipps, coal putter, . . .

No. 233 – Margaret Hipps, 17 years old, putter:

'On short shifts I work from eight in the morning till six at night; on long ones until 10 at night: occasionally we work all night. When at night-work, from six at night till eight and ten in the morning. Only bread is taken below; and the only rests we have are those we have to wait upon the men for while picking the coal. My employment, after reaching the wall-face, is to fill a bagie, or slype, with 2½ to 3 cwt. coal. I then hook it on to my chain and drag it through the seam, which is 26 to 28 inches high, till I get to the main-road – a good distance, probably 200 to 400 yards. The pavement I drag over is wet and I am obliged at all times to crawl on hands and feet with my bagie hung to the chain and ropes. I turn the contents of the bagies into the carts till they are filled; and then run them upon the ironrails to the shaft a distance of 400 to 500 yards. It is sad sweating and sore fatiguing work and frequently maims the women. My left hand is short of a finger, which laid me idle four months.'

Janet Cumming and Jane Peacock Watson, whose testimonies are quoted below, worked at Prestongrange, in the 'coal property in the parish of Dalkeith' of the Duke of Buccleuch and Queensferry.

Janet Cumming (No. 1), 11 years bears coals:

Works with father; has done so for two years. Father gangs at two in the morning; I gang with the women at five and come up at five at night; work all night on Fridays, and come away at twelve in the day. I carry the large bits of coal from the wall face to the pit bottom, and the small pieces called chows in a creel; the weight is usually a hundred weight; does not know how many pounds there are in a hundred weight but it is some work to carry. It takes three journeys to fill a tub of 4 cwt. The distance varies as the work is not always on the same wall, sometimes 150 fathom, whiles 250. The roof is very low; I have to bend my back and legs and the water comes frequently up to the calves of my legs; has no likening for the work, father makes me like it; mother did carry coal, she is not needed now, as sisters and brothers work on father's and uncle's account. Never got hurt, but often obliged to scramble out when bad air was in the pit.

The evidence of Jane Peacock Watson, aged 40, coal bearer (No. 117), shows yet more painfully the suffering of women following this laborious employment:

> I have wrought in the bowels of the earth 33 years. Have been married 23 years, and had nine children; six are alive, three died of typhus a few years since and have had two dead born; thinks they were so from the oppressive work: a vast of women have dead children and false births which are worse, as they are no able to work after the latter.
>
> I have always been obliged to work below till forced to go home to bear the bairn, and so have all the other women. We return as soon as able, never longer than 10 or 12 days, many less, if they are much needed. It is only horse-work, and ruins the women. It crushes their haunches, bends their ankles, and makes them old women at 40.

One woman factory worker who gave an account of her life was Ellen Johnston‡ (1835–73), a poet known as the 'Factory Girl'. In her autobiography Johnston states that she was the granddaughter of a canvas-weaver from Lochee, that she went to work in a textile factory in Glasgow at the age of eleven, and subsequently worked at the Verdant Works and other factories in Dundee. Her poems and songs were popular with a working-class audience. The poem below does not describe her working life, however, but rather is a panegyric to the mill-owning Baxter family for their beneficence in endowing the city's population with a new park.

1.3  Ellen Johnston, the 'Factory Girl', *Autobiography, Poems and Songs*
(Glasgow: William Love, 1867) (102–4)

The Opening of the Baxter Park
The ninth day of September
The sun arose in splendour,
His glory to surrender
    To Sir David of Dundee.
The Trades came forth in grandeur,
Each led by its commander,
Bold as an Alexander
    Of eighteen sixty-three.

Rosettes and ribbons flowing,
A radiant hue bestowing
On bosoms warmly glowing,
    Where freedom's fire ran through;
Their banners gaily swelling
Hailed from each hall and dwelling,
Their mottoes proudly telling,
    'Give honour where it's due.'

They, with their drums a-beating,
The Barrack Park did meet in,
Hailed with a hearty greeting,
        Saluted with three cheers;
With eyes like star-lights dancing,
With drawn swords brightly glancing,
So warlike and entrancing
        Were our brave Volunteers.

God bless our gallant sailors,
Our shoemakers and tailors,
Our engineers and nailers,
        With all their kith and kin!
May our gardeners gather honey,
Our bakers still have money,
Our autumn still be sunny
        Till our crops are gathered in.

Our Queen, peace rest upon her!
Her Noble Lord of honour
Came here to greet the Donor
        Of *our* Park, and get the key
To open for our pleasure
That lovely flower-gemmed treasure,
Where we may sport at leisure,
        When from our toil set free.

May the brightest boon of Heaven
To the Baxter race be given!
When from us they are riven
        Their loss we will deplore.
The statue of their glory,
Immortalised in story,
Shall stand through ages hoary,
        Till time shall be no more.

The extract below comes from John Campbell's history of power-loom weaving, published in 1878. He notes that the 'whole of the matter' contained in 'this little book' had been previously published in newspapers, *The Glasgow Herald*, *Rutherglen Reformer*, *Paisley and Renfrewshire Gazette*, and *North British Advertiser and Ladies' Journal*. The extract below, signed Jessie Campbell, purports to be the views of an older woman with many years of factory experience. The tone and style, however, are similar to those of Campbell's other writings on factory life while he was also the author of humorous stories also sometimes written under women's names. It seems likely that 'Jessie Campbell' was one of his pseudonyms.

1.4  John Campbell, *History of the Rise and Progress of Power-Loom Weaving; Vindication of the Character of Female Power-Loom Workers; also notes from Pollokshaws, Barrhead, Calton of Glasgow, and West Highlands* (Rutherglen, 1878) (14–15)

POWER-LOOM WEAVING IN THE WEST OF SCOTLAND

Glasgow, March 13, 1874

SIR, – Will you be kind enough to allow space for a few remarks on the above subject by an old maid who has had the misfortune to be toiling constant and hard at the power-loom for the last forty years, and will have to do so, I doubt, to my end? I commenced factory work in the once flourishing village of Duntocher, which belonged to the late William Dunn, whose demise scattered the happy inhabitants like mice at the pulling down of a corn stack, and caused them to seek work and homes elsewhere. Before the Factory Acts came into existence I was at a very tender age placed in the mill to learn the power-looms, consequently my school days were but very few. I therefore beg to be excused for my imperfect way in writing a letter to the *Mail*. Having been so many years now working at the old and new styles of work and machinery, and having wrought in some of the worst and many of the best factories in Glasgow, I consequently must know something of the matter in question – viz., how does it come that there are so many looms standing in the different factories, both in town and country, for want of weavers, and some of the more inferior weaving flats totally deserted at present. It would seem, from the numerous bills posted up in all our thorough-fares and elsewhere in town and country, by several parties, soliciting weavers to call at their works, where good wages will be given, that the power-loom cloth manufacturing is more brisk at present than what it has been in Scotland for many years past. The only drawback, it appears, is just the want of weavers, and masters and managers wonder and ask how they cannot be had as in former times. Well, there are several causes for that, and the chief one is this – There are more power-looms in operation at present in Glasgow than ever there were at any time before, and there are not weavers anent them all. Consequently those parties who pay worst are worst off for want of hands at present. I am glad to say that there are still employers in the West of Scotland who have always a sufficient supply of weavers, for the very good reason that they go wherever they are best paid and used well; and if some of the masters in town would look better after how some of their unjust cloth-passers in the warehouses act with the weavers there would not be so many of their looms standing. The reason that the weavers are generally scarce at present is this, but few young girls have gone to learn the looms some years past, for it will now take months to learn instead of weeks, as in former times, for the style of work and machinery now are quite different from what they were in my younger days. It was plain white work with one shuttle box, but now-a-days it is all fancy work, such as lappets, flush boards, and various kinds of coloured checks – the looms with from two to six boxes, and some upwards. The work is so difficult that weavers will have nothing to do with learners, as they would only spoil the patterns and do other damage. On the other hand, again, it takes so long to learn the looms now that parents are sending their young daughters to the sewing machines, where they can get wages sooner. Then there is always some old weaver dropping into her grave, some younger ones getting married, and many going every summer to the Far West, where they get a fair day's wage for a fair day's work, which they do not get at home. There is a large mill in Manchester, New Hampshire, America, which is at present almost filled with check power-loom weavers from Glasgow; and the fact of it is, if the weaving masters in the West of Scotland do not do something to encourage the learning of weavers, some of them may in a short time lock up their works altogether. Let them take the hint in time. – I am, &c.,

JESSIE CAMPBELL

In 1881 a series of articles entitled 'Sketches of Life in a Jute Mill' was published in the Dundee-based *People's Journal*. Written by an unidentified male author, whose family of hand-loom weavers had moved to Dundee from Fife when he was a small boy, the articles provide a graphic account of working conditions in the Dundee jute mills. Children were employed in the mills along with women, as the extract below illustrates.

## 1.5 'Sketches of Life in a Jute Mill', *People's Journal*, 28 May 1881

### Chapter III – The Spinning Flat.

My ear would be suddenly greeted with a shrill whistle, heard above the constant rush of the machinery, and I noted the woman who had used it hurrying her troop of young girls and boys into their places in one of the passages, one loiterer who comes last perhaps getting a clip with the light strap or *tawse* hanging by her side. When all were forward they would stand at regular intervals in front of the spinning frame. It was stopped, and in an instant all the little hands were busy. The thread of half-spun yarn above the flyer was broken off, the flyer unscrewed, the bobbins slipped off the spindles, tossed into a skip, and empty ones – which they took out of the bags hanging about their waist – set in their places; the flyers screwed on again, the broken ends drawn down and twisted through them, and all again ready for action. Those young people are the "Shifters," who, as a rule, are half-timers. The mistress shifter has to keep her eyes about her, and find the time when her active band are required at another place. One of those shifts is effected in less time than it takes to describe it, and here also the special movements and exigencies are soon understood so well that the agile workers do their duty infallibly by habit. In the intervals between the shifts, the youngsters may be seen lying about or sitting in the broad passages, playing or talking, or reading, or dressing their hair, ready at the signal of the mistress for another two minutes' brush of work. I see in my mind just now one of those shifter mistresses. She was quite a handsome young woman disguised in a plain and almost dirty garb, and a few flecks of caddis might be on her black hair, and her bare arms stained with oil in one or two places, but her form was erect, her step graceful, her eye sharp and intelligent. This work of hers had a tendency to cultivate not only quickness of perception and promptitude of action, but a spirit of mastery which encouraged ease and self-confidence when the apparent bewilderment of so many frames to look after and so many young people to manage were matters of no extra anxiety, and her duties and responsibilities fitted together like clockwork . . .

## Section 2: Agriculture, fishing and rural home industries

In the earlier part of the nineteenth century a still substantial proportion of the population lived in rural areas and small towns. Many women were engaged in agricultural work alongside their menfolk although gender roles in such labour were often rigidly defined. The size of farm, type of farming, changing agricultural technology, wage levels, and existence of other employment opportunities all had an impact on the ways in which women's and girls' labour was employed in agriculture. In Scotland, women's participation in agricultural work was extensive, if regionally varied, but, by the end of the century, shortages of female labour were being widely debated. Because much agricultural labour was seasonal, women also engaged in other forms of economic activity, such as weaving or other craft production, or in the expanding herring fisheries of the later nineteenth century.

Janet Bathgate was born near Selkirk in 1806 to poor parents, and went into service with other families in the Borders around the age of eight. She later became a nursemaid to the children of Susan Scott-Moncrieff of Dalkeith, retiring from service on her marriage. Her memoir, full of Christian homilies informed by her devout Cameronian background, is primarily about her life in domestic service. She was eighty-eight years old when her memoir was published. The extract below describes the farming work that her service involved when she was around ten years of age.

2.1 Janet Bathgate, *Aunt Janet's Legacy: Recollections of Humble Life in Yarrow at the Beginning of the Century* (Selkirk: George Lewis & Son, 1894) (121–2)

To the shepherds in those quarters, the lambing time is the most anxious of the year, especially if the season should be a wet one. Janet has her share both in the anxiety and toil. We see her up in a cold, wet, spring morning, her petticoats tucked up with her garters, her plaid around her shoulders, climbing the hill appointed to her by Willie [a son of her mistress]. She carries a pitcher of warm milk, and lays hold upon any little trembling lamb that lies in her way. Having been taught the art of feeding such feeble ones by Willie, she pours from her own mouth the warm milk into the mouth of the little helpless creature. It may be that she finds the mother ewe dead; in that case she takes off her plaid, ties the little orphan lamb in it, and gets it on her back. After hours of such wearying toil, she returns home wet and worn out, with sometimes two lambs on her back and one in her arms. Then she lays them around the good peat fire, and rubs them gently, giving them more warm milk. When they are sufficiently revived, she takes them to the byre, where accommodation has been provided in anticipation of these events. Here Janet attends to their wants; she gives to each a name by which she calls them; and long after they have been sent out to the green hill-side to shift for themselves, when she calls them by name they will run to her and share in her forenoon "piece;" and sometimes they will follow her into the house, which, however, is now felt to be an annoyance to the inmates.

Anna Gobh [Anna Gow] was the daughter of poet Mairiread Ghriogarach [Margaret MacGregor ][see 3.1 below], and herself a poet.[2] The poem below reflects on her search for work in the Lowlands in the 1820s, and her intention to return to her work of weaving at home. Gobh was to become famous as a weaver, commissioned by the local aristocracy to produce fine tartans for formal and military dress uniforms.

2.2 Anna Gobh, 'Òran le Anna Ghobh air dhi dol chun fhògharaich Ghalld' 'sa bhliadhna 1827', in Margaret MacGregor, *Co-chruinneach dh'Òrain Thaghta Ghaeleach nach robh riamh ann an clò-buala*, Les an ughdar Donncha Mac Intoisich, ed. by Duncan MacKintosh (Edinburgh: John Elder, 1831)

| Luineag | Chorus |
|---|---|
| B' fheàrr nach tighinn san àm, | I wish I had never come to the Lowlands, |
| A dh' ionnsaigh machair nan Gall, | without comfort, without a bed, without |
| Gun àird gun leaba gun fhodar, | straw, |
| Ag iarraidh obair 's gach àit'. | searching everywhere for work. |

1

Ràinig mi an leitir an toiseach,
'S mi an dùil ri cosnadh a b' fheàrr,
Gun dèanainn airgid is òr ann,

Nuair rachainn an òrdugh mar b' àbhaist,
Labhair na fìor ghillean còir,
'S e am bròn gun d' thàin' thu cho tràth,
Chan eil againn gràine coirc no eòrn',
Bhios abaich gu leòr gu Di-mairt.
B' fheàrr nach tighinn san àm &c.

1

I came to this country at first
hoping for better wages,
thinking that I would make gold and
    silver
when I got myself established.
These fine respectable fellows say
that it's a pity that I have come so early,
that they have neither oats nor corn
that will be ripe enough until the Fair.
I wish I had never come. &c.

2

Nam bi fios aig Clann Donnachaidh,
An t-uisig tha orms' an drast',

Luighe gun aodach gun fhodar,
Air gràine de shliseagan chlàr,
Chuire' iad each agus gille,
Gu h-eallamh gam shire' a-bhàn,
Chan fhàg iad mise na b' fhaide
A' fritheil' air obair nan Gall.

2

If Clan Donald knew
of the treatment that I am getting just
    now,
lying without bedclothes, without straw,
on a handful of wood-shavings,
they would send a horse and a boy
quickly to search me out,
they wouldn't leave me any longer
searching for work in the Lowlands.

3

Ma bhios mi maireann,
'S gum pill mi Bhràigh Athol gun dàil,
Ag innse do m' chairdean 's luchd eòlais,
Gach dìth-fhortan chòmhlaich mi an
    dràst',
Le botal is gloinne air bòrd
Ag òl deoch slàinte nan Gàidheal
An caisteal toilichte glan òrdail,
Gun chùram ri m-bheò orm bonn màl.

4

Nuair ruigeas mi dhachaigh
Thèid sùrd air an tartan gun dàil
Deise do Chòirneal Mac Dhòmhnuill,
Do Mhac Coinnich Mhòir a Cinntàile,
Nì mi suidh nam sheòmar,
Le m' choinneal air bòrd mar a b' àbhaist,
Gun dèan mi cada is clòthlain
'S chan fhaicear rim bheò mi 'measg Gall.

3

If I survive
and get back to Bràigh Athol soon,
I'll tell my friends and family,
of each misfortune surrounding me just
    now,
with a bottle and a glass on the table,
drinking the health of the Gaels
in a cheerful, clean, orderly castle,
with no worries over rent as long as I live.

4

When I get home
a tartan will be started upon immediately,
a suit of clothes for Colonel MacDonald,
for Great MacKenzie of Kintail.
I will sit in my room
with my candle on the table as usual,
I will make tartan and cloth
and will never be seen in the Lowlands
    again as long as I live.

Translation by Anne Macleod Hill.

Christian Watt‡ (1833–1923), was born and brought up in Broadsea, a fishing community near Fraserburgh. Afflicted by the loss of family members, several of her children and her husband, she experienced a breakdown and spent time in the Aberdeen Royal Mental Asylum, Cornhill. During her time there she wrote an account of her life. Her papers were published by David Fraser in 1983. Here she describes the work of women and girls in the 1840s.

> 2.3 *The Christian Watt Papers*, edited and with an introduction by David Fraser (Edinburgh: Paul Harris Publishing, 1983) (27, 28, 29)

I had learned to gut when I was 10; curing had started in a big way. In 1844 during the summer, most Broadsea fishers went to the west coast and the Hebrides. We as lassies went to cook for the men. We lived in sodbuilt bothies on the shore, I shared one with Annie Rogie and Suffie Noble, at Loch Eishort in Skye.

The work was hard for children, but we had a lot of fun. I enjoyed the long sail round the north of Scotland hugging the coast, I was with my father, and had faith in his skeelie seamanship. The scenery was really bonnie. For some reason the Highland folk didn't trust us. You could not make friends with them easily, but a few I did, those who could speak a little English. Kate McLeod, a quinie who brought milk from Susnish, gave us all the clake. We gutted the herring, and packed them in barrels and ships from Glasgow took them away.

. . .

We went again and again to Skye. The coastline was dotted with the bothies of girls; it was hard work to bake wash and cook to 27 men. The catches were not big; at this time the fishermen did most of the gutting, it had not yet become wholly a female job.

. . .

I liked August best. Then the whole coast of fishwives went into the Grampian Mountains to dispose of their summer cure of dried fish, barns were cleared out and wifies and their bairns moved in. My mother, my two youngest brothers and I always went to the barn at Corrybeg; young Charlie Forbes's wife was connected with us in some way. We paid a small rent for the barn where we slept, and our food was cooked on a fire outside. We had a lot of orders to deliver on our way out. Mistress Gordon at Crathes always gave us an order to deliver at Craigievar Castle. The change was so health giving, for the Highland air and the sun built you up to face the winter. We stayed two weeks till all our cure was sold. McGrigor, the horse hirer at Strichen, took about 10 tons of fish inland for us: I shall aye regard this as the happiest days of my life.

Songs and ballads were an important part of the culture of farming communities across Scotland. According to tradition, this harvest song, the 'Lothian Hairst', was written by a 'Highland lassie' around 1860. At that time it was common for Deeside harvesters to work in the Lothians in the summer, where the grain cutting began earlier than in the north-east. As Ord noted:

The contractor, or maister as he was called by the workers, engaged a foreman, who was held responsible by the contractor for carrying out the various contracts. The foreman was in every case expected to act like "Logan" in the song, and to see that the male reapers visiting their female co-workers at their bothies terminated their visits at a given hour.[3]

2.4 John Ord, *The Bothy Songs and Ballads of Aberdeen, Banff and Moray, Angus and the Mearns* (Edinburgh: John Donald, 1974) (264)

The Lothian Hairst
On August twelfth from Aberdeen
   We sailed upon the *Prince*,
And landed safe at Clifford's fields,
   Our harvest to commence.

For six lang weeks the country roun'
   Frae toon to toon we went,
And I took richt weel wi' the Lothian fare,
   An' aye was weel content.

Our master, William Mathieson,
   From sweet Deeside he came;
Our foreman came from the same place,
   An' Logan was his name.

I followed Logan on the point,
    Sae weel's he laid it down,
And sae boldly as he's led our squad
    O'er mony's the thistley toon.

My mate and I could get nae chance
    For Logan's watchful eye,
And wi' the lads we got nae sport,
    For Logan was sae sly.

He cleared our bothy every night
    Before he went to sleep,
And never left behind him one,
    But strict the rules did keep.

And when we come to Aberdeen
    He weel deserves a spree,
For the herding o' us a' sae weel
    From the Lothian lads we're free.

Farewell M'Kenzie, Reid and Rose,
    And all your joyful crew,
An' Logan, Jock, and Chapman, Pratt,
    And Royal Stuart too.

We'll fill a glass and drink it round
    Before the boat will start
And may we safely reach the shore,
    And all in friendship part.

In the absence of women's direct testimonies, reports of Royal Commissions are an important and rich source of descriptions of working practices, and variations across Scotland. The extract below, from the commission of 1867, quotes the report by Mr R. F. Boyle on the counties of Lanark, Renfrew, and Argyll, and describes the organisation of women's labour on a large cropping farm. A more recent account of women's farming work has been provided in oral testimonies recorded by Ian MacDougall, some from the beginning of the twentieth century; these indicate the continuities in women's agricultural role.[4] The report is available at House of Commons Parliamentary Papers online.

> 2.5 *Commission on the employment of children, young persons, and women in*
> *agriculture (1867). Fourth report of the commissioners, with appendix part I*
> (1870) (Great Britain. Parliament. House of Commons) (108)

14. Mr. Scott, of Rhindmuir, who owns one of the largest cropping farms near Glasgow, employs as regular hands, a foreman, four ploughmen, and two women-servants: in the summer he takes on two or three extra men, and the number of extra

women employed varies according to the work required; in the winter there will only be a few about the thrashing machine, or perhaps putting the potatoes in sacks; but for turnip-pulling in the spring or potato-digging in the autumn, he sometimes has as many as 80 out. These are mostly miners' wives and daughters, the married women preponderating; sometimes a labourer's wife or widow, and sometimes in harvest even the wife or daughter of a small tradesman. Mr. Scott and his neighbour, Mr. Wilson, of Glendufhill, both consider that the mineral class make the best workers. The following is a brief statement of the work done by women, compiled chiefly from the evidence of these two gentlemen: – the first spring work is the potato-planting in April, which employs about 20 or 25 women: for this purpose the manure-cart is usually filled by men in the yard, but sometimes the women do it if men are scarce: they seem to prefer it to the spreading, as not being such constant work. In the field two men usually go with the cart, the foreman and one other man, the rest of the work being done by women. The foreman throws the manure out into the centre drill, and one woman divides it out into three drills; three other women break it out and spread it, and three more follow with the seed. "Sometimes a woman goes with the cart, a strong girl of 25 or so: a young woman will lead a horse as well as a lad; they like doing it." The next work consists in stone-picking, turnip-planting, and weeding rough land: for stone-picking the hands take baskets, and a cart goes with them; each fills her basket, and empties it into the cart, but if the ground is soft the cart goes down the side of the field, and two of the workers carry the baskets to it. Hoeing potatoes begins about the end of May. This work employs 40 to 50 hands, and the same are generally kept on for the turnip-singling which immediately follows. For these employments the women are put to work in a row, the foreman accompanying them; he generally puts one of the best workers among the women at the end of the line, and a few other good workers next to her; the foreman helps on those who fall behind, for those who fall behind easily get disheartened, so a great deal depends on having a good foreman, who can humour them. "As a rule," says Mr. Scott, "the hoeing is easy work, and we never let one go too fast in front, so as to get it well done." An Avondale farmer told me that at hoeing a woman can do fully as much as a man. Turnip-singling follows, and this is generally done with the hand, for the soil is cloddy, and a hoe is liable to bring up the manure or the wrong plant with the clod; some farmers allow them to hoe, if they like, and they generally prefer it. This turnip-singling is the work that is generally considered the hardest. In Renfrewshire I saw rows of women all down on their knees working away with their hands. "They try all ways of working," says Mr. Wilson, "when the back gets tired with stooping; it is not hard work, but sometimes one hand is down, sometimes both, sometimes they stoop". They have to go down on their knees to ease their backs. But the difficulty of the work is naturally much greater in a wet season than in a dry. The long hoe too undoubtedly makes the work much easier; the short hoe is as bad as none at all. Mr. Wilson's foreman once attempted to introduce short hoes, but all the hands threatened to go. A girl can use a long hoe fairly well at 15 or 16 years of age. Most of the large farmers expect them when they came to know how to work, and they usually learn on some smaller farm: but the learning does not take long, if the hands be willing.

It was commonly the case in rural and fishing communities that there were other forms of economic activity besides farming and fishing. Such 'home industries' were undertaken by women in many places, as Anna Gobh's poem above illustrates, and as the extract from the Highlands and Islands Home Industries report below also illustrates [2.10]. The extract below describes the Shetland knitting industry, as represented in a brochure for the Edinburgh International Exhibition of 1886. The whales' jawbones, forming the entrance to Jawbone Walk on the Meadows, were part of the Shetland and Fair Isle knitters' stand.

### 2.6 *Women's Industries, Edinburgh 1886 International Exhibition of Industry Science and Art* (11–13)

Knitting (Zetland Islands).

The Zetland Islands are upwards of 100 in number, varying in size from the Mainland, which is about 70 miles in length and 30 at its greatest breadth, to two small rocks not even affording pasturage to sheep. The population in 1881 was 17,049 females, and 12,656 males. The female population thus outnumbers the male, and this state of matters, existing from an early period, has most probably led to the development of the special Zetland industry of knitting by the females, and the fineness of the wool of the small native Zetland sheep also gave a very early impetus to it.

It is recorded that in the 17th century a great fair for the sale of hosiery was held each year, on the occasion of the visit of the Dutch Fishing Fleet to Bressay Sound. The finer articles now known as Zetland shawls, veils, etc., were not manufactured till a much more recent date. Dr. Edmonstone, one of the best historians of the islands, speaks of stockings as if they were the only product of the Zetland knitters' industry, and stockings and gloves are the only articles of woollen manufacture specified as made in Zetland by the writers of the *Statistical Account* in 1841. Originally the trade was entirely carried on by persons knitting the wool grown by their own flocks, or procured from their neighbours; and they bartered, as they still do, the articles so made to merchants in Lerwick or elsewhere for goods of every kind.

A much older industry is exhibited (for the dyes and patterns were romantically introduced in 1588, nearly 300 years ago) from one of the small islands of the Zetland group, viz. the Fair Island. One of the ships of the Spanish Armada was wrecked on the shores of Fair Island, and the Spaniards who were saved taught the islanders the art of dyeing and knitting the variegated hosiery of the beautiful Moorish patterns for which the island is now famous. The trade has very much grown of late years.

All the families in the islands, above mere children, are engaged more or less in knitting, but their wages are an unknown quantity as regards commercial value, because the custom of barter in kind is prevalent. In Lerwick or Scalloway the women combine, some supplying and spinning the wool, and one the knitting, in preparing one of the fine lace shawls, for which the yachtsman or other visitor

**Figure 4.1** Front cover, *Women's Industries*. International Exhibition of Industry Science and Art, Edinburgh, 1886. Reproduced by permission of the Trustees of the National Library of Scotland.

may give them £2 in cash, or even more. Veils are also sold for cash, say at 2s. 6d. or so, to similar customers; but these are only occasional instances of good fortune, which unhappily prevent knitters recognising the truth and value of the trade secret, "Small profits and quick returns."

The fishing communities in north-east Scotland became the focus of women's home mission work in the later decades of the nineteenth century. In the extract below, Mrs Watt, a home mission volunteer, described the working and living conditions of fisher girls.

### 2.7 *The Church of Scotland Home and Foreign Mission Record*, 1 December 1898 (344–5)

#### DEPUTY WORK AMONG OUR
#### FISHER LASSES

To some inland folk it may be interesting to know something of the life our fisher lasses live when the silvery herring visit our shores. Many can hardly realise the difference those denizens of the deep make to an ordinary quiet fishing town. But picture the arrival of six or seven hundred girls gathered from all parts of Scotland as an instalment of more expected, and follow them ashore – tired, and many still suffering from the effects of the voyage – into the barracks provided for their accommodation by the curer; see them lay their aching limbs in the bed, or rather berth, composed solely of straw, tucked in by a sheet, six to twelve in a room, having berth above berth, steamship style, with all the dust of last year's tenants still about them, then you will understand how the work of the season begins.

Next morning two are told off to clean up and make something like order appear, but soon it may be that the word comes round that a big catch has come in with the morning boats, and waterproof skirts must be donned whether the day be fair or foul, fingers are rolled up not quite so neatly as at a hospital, and the short, sharp "gutter" is seized, and off they run eager for a start. If the fishing is heavy the work becomes very hard on the girls, for no hours are kept, no Factory Act applies to the herring; the girls are kept at it often for twelve to eighteen hours on a stretch, with hardly a moment to snatch even the cup of tea. This overwork soon begins to tell on the weaker ones, and the Lady Deputy on her rounds finds some of them in bed . . . Much suffering to sick ones is caused owing to the numbers of women who live in one building, constructed as they are of wood, and so badly partitioned off that a voice sounds from end to end of the building, and also from lack of attention when a very busy time comes, and all are in the yards hard at work.

And few would believe the suffering caused, too, by salt sores, those who pack the herring being specially subject to these; and even cases of salt poisoning of the hands occur, and much careful treatment is needed to get them cured. To do this is especially the work of the Lady Deputy, and she earns much gratitude for her services . . .

A. M. WATT.
HILLVIEW HOUSE
WEST CULTS, ABERDEEN

In the extracts below, Ada Goodrich-Freer depicts the pattern of movement to summer pastures which had previously been a feature of life in South Uist. This is followed by an account of women's employment in the fishing trade in the north-east of Scotland which was current with the time of writing. Goodrich-Freer had a particular interest in psychic phenomena, and this appears to have been one the motivations for her visit to the Hebrides. Her book provides a very readable account of life in the Hebrides in the 1890s, is illustrated, and is well acquainted with previous literature on the Highlands and Islands and their social and economic problems.

## 2.8 A. Goodrich-Freer, *Outer Isles* (Westminster: Archibald Constable and Co. Ltd, 1903) (161, 163, 166)

A fine day in the month of June would be chosen for the start, and at an early hour in the morning the procession formed, the men, lads and young girls, driving the sheep, mares, and calves, their simple provision packed in creels strapped on the backs of a few mountain ponies, the older women, knitting as they walked, following with the young children, while half-grown boys and girls, full of wild anticipations of fun, ran backward and forward like excited dogs, probably of all the party most conscious of responsibility.

On arriving, there would be small repairs to make to the shealings of last year, all of the simplest and most elementary description, often of the bee-hive shape, but on occasion adapted to the material available – stones roughly piled against a large rock, or against a bank, supports of disused oars or parts of masts, a roof of the roughest thatch of heather or bent grass, a shelf in the thickness of the wall for keeping the milk cool on hot summer days, the floor as Nature may have provided, turf or sand or beaten earth.

. . . .

During the three months or more of their stay, the principal work of the women would be to make butter and cheese for the winter store. The flocks could ramble all day at will, feeding in the freshest and greenest spots; the calves and lambs would be growing fat and strong on the sweet hill pasture, and the cows would be yielding of their best. Spare hours would be occupied with the distaff, getting the wool ready for the winter's task of weaving their warm durable cloth which was their only wear. The young folks enjoyed the fun and freedom of an existence without even the responsibility of herding, and none of the folk-songs are so blithe and gay as those in praise of the shealings and the shealing life.

. . . .

The people have an absolute craving for work, and it is chiefly from these islands that the young women go every year to the east-coast fishing, mainly now in Aberdeen, though formerly largely to Fraserburgh and Peterhead. They are expert fish-curers. They receive £2 on engagement, in mid-winter, when money is scarcest, and this probably tempts away many a woman who repents of her bargain later. However there is no work for them to do at home, the change and better food, now that there is no shealing-life, is good for their health, and they bring home not only money but enlargement of notions. Many of the domestic details of life have improved greatly since the women have been away from the Islands. They bring home crockery and articles of clothing, and their lives have gained in order and in complexity. Their life at the fishing is necessarily of the roughest. Sometimes they work for two or three nights without sleep. Their conduct is said to be excellent.

I have travelled with them two or three times between Oban and their own islands. They were always neat and modest in their dress and orderly in their conduct, but, poor girls, strange to say, they were horribly sea-sick!

Concern about economic conditions in the Highlands and Islands led to several investigations. The report quoted below described local economies, and the respective contributions of men and women, often making comparisons with opportunities, wages and conditions in the towns. As well as the weaving and tweed-making in the Highlands and Islands, the report also discussed lace-making initiatives in New Pitsligo in Buchan and Tarbert in Argyll. The extract below describes women's role in tweed-making. The report is available at House of Commons Parliamentary papers online.

2.9 *Report to the Board of Agriculture for Scotland on Home Industries in the Highlands and Islands* (1914) [Cd. 7564] (77–8, 79–80)

Labour in the Making of Tweed.

The accounts in the foregoing pages of the methods of producing tweed and of the organisation of the industry will have afforded glimpses of the condition of the workers. This aspect of the industry is of such interest that it is worthy of more detailed treatment. From the point of view of employment, tweed-making is an occupation for women. It is only in weaving, save in exceptional cases, that male labour is used. Sometimes old men, or those who are unable to do any other work, help in the preliminary processes, such as teasing the wool. In St Kilda able-bodied men assist the women in this work. Spinning is women's work. Weaving, on the other hand, is divided between the sexes. In Harris, nine out of ten weavers are women; while in Lewis, in Shetland, and on the mainland most of the weavers are men.

. . .

According to the author of the report, while women's earnings were lower in the Highlands and Islands than in the towns, their working conditions were better:

Apart from the question of earnings, the tweed-worker has some advantages from her occupation. Her surroundings are healthful. In the older type of cottage she had an abundance of air, even though it was mixed with peat smoke. Her occupation was interesting in itself, and of such a nature that it could be interrupted to permit of attention being given to any household task that required it. In the long winter evenings work could be carried on while any neighbour talked or sang or told interminable Gaelic tales. For those who are able to appreciate the simple and satisfying things in life, an occupation of this kind has much to recommend it. In it there is not the pressure and speeding up of the factory, while there is a sufficient element of skill and artistic work in some of the processes to enable the tweed-maker to take a pride and a pleasure in what she produces. No doubt she suffers from what Professor Marshall calls "monotony of life," but here one has to distinguish between two different things. To a person brought up in a city, Highland life would be unbearably monotonous; but to the people themselves there is a wide range of interests, arising out of the varied life of the township, which they find pleasant and even exciting. Then, too, they preserve the almost lost art – at least in this country – of introducing what Schiller called "the play-instinct" into their work. Thus, in tweed-making, "the waulking party" is not only the finishing of the web – it is also a social gathering of great interest to those who participate in it. There are, however, signs that the younger women are feeling the insistent call of the great centres of population. Some go to domestic service, and many take part in fish-curing. During the years 1909 to 1911, 6736 women and girls were employed regularly in the latter occupation for periods varying beween five weeks and twenty-nine weeks. This work brings high money earnings to those who are skilled at it, and it provides variety and change of scene, since the herring-gutters follow the shoals of fish. This employment cannot be described as an agreeable one, and it requires good physique to stand the exposure to the weather which it involves. Tweed-making, on the other hand, is more suited to those who have home ties, and it can be continued by workers far past middle life . . .

### Section 3: Domestic service

Domestic service was a major source of employment for women in the nineteenth century. Some aspects of domestic service have been illustrated in Chapter 3, and the small selection of extracts here illustrates other varying perspectives on domestic service. The reactions of domestic servants to their employment conditions is also illustrated at 6.2 below.

Mairiread Ghriogarach [Margaret MacGregor] was born around the mid-eighteenth century, and became a recognised poet in her community.[5] As a young girl, as was common with indigent gentlewomen, she spent some time in service in the household of a relative, MacGregor of Strathspey, where her status was somewhere been that of servant and dependant. She also spent time at school in Perth, and it is to this period that the poem refers. To her the outdoor life was preferable to the training in domestic skills required for service and household management.

3.1 Margaret MacGregor, *Co-chruinneach dh'Òrain Thaghta Ghaeleach nach robh riamh ann an clò-buala*, ed. by Duncan MacKintosh (Edinburgh: John Elder, 1831)

'Òran 's i san sgoil am Peart' [A song composed while she was at school in Perth]

Air fonn 'Tha Ceapach na fòsach'

To the tune 'Tha Ceapach na fòsach'.

1

'S mi 'm shuidhe an seo fuaigheal
'n uinneag uasal taigh mhòir,
's mòr gum b' annsa bhith 'sa bhuail'
'g èisteachd nualaich nam bò,
leaga' ghabhar is chaorach
's crodh laoidh tighinn mun chrò,
na bhith an seo air mo dhaoidheachd
's an snàthad chaol ann am dhòrn.

1

I am sitting here sewing
at an elegant window in a great house,
but I would far rather be at the fold,
listening to the lowing of the cows,
milking the goats and the sheep,
and the cows and calves around the pen,
than be sitting here discontented
with a fine needle in my hand.

2

Thug mi tamall an toiseach
gun sprochd orm no sgìos,
rè an latha ri fuaigheal
gun smuaineach air nì,
gus an cual' mi na dearcan
bhith gan reic airson fiach,
ghrad bhuail e am bheachd-sa
Coir' a Bhacaidh nam fiadh.

2

I spent a while at first
not feeling low-spirited or weary,
sewing all day
without a thought,
until I heard that berries
were being sold,
and suddenly the thought struck me
of Coir' a' Bhacaidh of the wild deer.

3

'S truagh gun bhith an Leitir Dhubh
      Lachlainn
's ann a chaisginnn mo mhiann,
gheibhte iomadach meas ann
gun neach a' farraid am prìs.
Còir gaolach mo chridhe
's am biodh iasg is sitheann gun dìth,
meadhg is bainne gun airceas
's cha b' iad na drapagan tì.

3

It's a pity I'm not at Leitir Dubh
      Lachlainn,
that's where I would satisfy my longing.
There are plenty of berries there
with no one asking the price.
It's a corrie dear to my heart
where there's fish and game in plenty,
whey and milk without limit
and not just dregs of tea.

4

Nuair dh'èigheas iad am bainne
bheir mi sealladh a-mach,
's ann chì mi a' bhairle
air a ceangal an cairt,
ged a thèid mi ga cheannach
Rìgh, cha mhilis a bhlas!
's fheàrr am meadhg bhios sa
      Ghaidhealtachd
na bainne blàth bhios am Peart.

4

When they shout 'Milk' here,
I look out
and I see the barrel
tied to the cart.
Though I go to buy it,
Goodness – it does not taste sweet!
The whey of the Highlands

is better than the warm milk of Perth.

5

Cha robh neach air bhith 'g iarraidh orm
triall gu machair nan Gall,
ach thuig mi gum b' fheàrrd mi
ràidh an t-samhraidh thoirt ann.
'S mòr an stàth tha san ionnsach'
bheir e toinnsgal don dràic,
's neach sam bith ga bheil tùr
cha leig à chuimhne e gu bràth

5

No one asked me
to travel to the Lowlands,
but I knew that I would be better
for spending a summer season here.
There is great benefit in learning,
it gives common sense to careless girls,
and whoever has understanding
will never forget it.

6

Ged bu leamsa Siorrachd Pheart
na bheil mi faicinn ma cuairt,
no h-uile mìr dhen a' mhachair
th' eadar Glaschu is Cluaidh,
bheirinn trian deth Shir Raibeart
nan gabhte' e uam,
chan ann am malairt na h-Appan
ach na th' aige mu thuath.

6

Though Perthshire were mine
and all that I see around it,
or every scrap of the Lowlands
between Glasgow and Clyde,
I would give a third of it to Sir Robert
if he would accept it from me,
not in exchange for Appin,
but for what he has in the north.

Translation: Anne Macleod Hill

The broadside below on the strike of Edinburgh maidservants is contained in a scrapbook of Edinburgh broadsides, and probably dates from around 1825. A later version, dating from March 1840, appears in a further collection of broadsides. The later version is almost identical, with one or two changes, including a reference to contemporary circumstances affecting the price of tea, the 'quarrel with the Chinese'. Satirical in intent, it suggests a popular notion of uppity servants, doing rather well from the perks of their position. It is available online at http://digital.nls.uk/broadsides/

## 3.2 IMPORTANT Strike, of the Maidservants OF EDINBURGH

Just Published, upon good Authority, an account of the Meeting of the MaidServants of Edinburgh, which took place on Friday last, and who have formed themselves into an Union Society, for the purpose of making a general Strike for a rise of wages at the ensuing Term; with a Copy of 12 Resolutions formed by the Chairwoman, and Office-bearers.

Taken from the Evening Post, of Saturday last.
We understand that it is contemplated by 'The Maid Servant Union Society' of this City, to make a 'strike' on the 14th of next month, with a view to obtaining higher wages; and really after perusing the resolution of that respectable feminine institution, we hesitate not to confess that they have strong grounds for standing out. The following are the resolutions: –
1 – As labour is voluntary, wages should be liberal.

2 – As maids are generally delicate, both in regard to constitution and feeling, lenity, sympathy, and kindly feelings ought to be exercised towards them.

3 – That of late years the perquisites which custom and long usage had converted into 'Very ['Vestry' in later version] Rights,' have been decreasing, and in many case withdrawn.

4 – That Sundays being days of rest, these days are to be entirely at the disposal of the maid-servants – no questions asked.

5 – That mistress's old clothes have ever been, and must continue to be the property of maid-servants, and that when a gown or any other piece of dress has been worn a sufficient time, it must be considered as old clothes.

6 – That in case of any difference of opinion between the mistress and the maid about the condemnation of the dress – the servants of the house and those of the two adjoining houses to be appointed judges.

7 – The hare and rabbit skins, kitchenfee, fat, dripping, shall continue to be considered the property of the cook, and no skinned hare or rabbit to enter the house.

8 – That no young women under 16 shall be allowed to take service, and that no wages shall be under L2 10s, the half year, and L1 1s, for tea money; those taking less to be considered KNOB STICKS, and treated accordingly,

9 – That in consequence of the late strike among silk manufacturers at Lyons, the price of that indispensable article has risen to a great hight, and that this circumstance, coupled with the exorbitant prices of fur and tooth powder, has obliged the Union to resolve on demanding a higher rate of wages.

10 – That after the 14th of May, the wages should and must be advanced 25 per cent: – that is, those who engaged at L4. must now insist upon L5. the half year – tea money to remain as it is until the arrival of the free tea trade, when a change may be deemed necessary of which due notice will be given.

11 – That in the event of mistresses refusing to comply with this small advance, the maids are to strike work, and refuse to serve those who will not go into these resolutions. Joseph Hume's Act will protect the maids should they be brought before the Justice of the Peace (generally known as McFarlane's) Court.

12 – That each maid servant shall be supplied by the Union with a copy of the above resolutions, to be hung up in the kitchen along with the Police Regulations, that all concerned may see them.

FORBES, PRINTER, RATTRRY'S COURT, COWGATE

Discussion of the conditions of domestic servants was a recurrent feature of the nineteenth century. The article below was published in *Tait's Edinburgh Magazine*, whose readers would have been largely middle class. It indicates that prominent public figures took an interest in the question, recommending good practice in the treatment of servants. Published under only the initials A.J.H., it appears to have been written by a woman who herself had experience of domestic service.

A poor, weak woman, with none of the qualities of strong-minded women, who address meetings, and pass resolutions, and seek votes, can only state a case of helplessness. I cannot set loose a gang of commissioners over the country to examine our beds, and the rooms where the beds stand, and the hours through which we work, and all the other matters connected with the state of a third part of all the young women in the land, down to the potatoes that they eat . . . I can only tell people that there are grievances in our lot, if they would look to them. (22)

The article begins by giving an account of a speech by Free Church reformer Dr Thomas Guthrie at a soirée during a fair in Biggar in February 1861 where he argued that, for a servant, character was capital which could be devalued by inconsiderate treatment by mistresses.

> ### 3.3 A.J.H., 'Domestic Service', *Tait's Edinburgh Magazine*, 28: 324 (May 1861) (19, 20, 21, 22)

[Dr Guthrie] denounces the habit of seeking servants with "no followers." Perhaps he never liked it. At any rate he speaks the truth of it now. Nothing is more common than for married ladies to want a cook or housemaid with "no followers." What does it mean? Has the lady herself had no followers? How did she come to be married? Was she bargained for like a Levant damsel, or bought and paid for in coins like a jet black maid of Africa? The advertisements of female servants wanted with "no followers," are requests that only old or ugly women should reply to, unless they are issued by ladies who desire to turn their houses into refuges for the bereaved or the disappointed; or for females crossed in love, who have vowed never to love again; or into incipient nunneries; but very few female servants under forty years of age, have any decided preference for the life of a nun.

Hours of work could be very long:

Servants are often the only persons on all the earth for whom their mistresses have no pity. I have heard ladies express their anxiety for the salvation of the heathen whom they never saw; and yet, to my knowledge, they did not in ten days speak ten words calculated to advance the salvation of those other persons who made their dinners, or were in their house, maids-of-all-work, at all hours, from the Dan to the Beersheba of the live long year. I have known others extremely anxious to help short-time in factories, who had no notion of short-time at home. Gentlemen will sometimes sing "the Song of the Shirt," without considering for a single moment, that they keep persons out of bed for hours beyond midnight in their homes, who must be up and busy at six in the morning. A ten hours bill for domestic servants would revolutionize the country.

Living conditions could be cramped and insalubrious:

Dr Guthrie has a neighbour, Dr Begg, who has laboured hard to improve the accommodation of farm labourers; and, as one man cannot do everything, he will be justified in continuing to work on this field; but there are evils in the district of Newington, not worse than other evils out of it, connected with the accommodation of female servants, that cry for an agitation. The middle classes have palatial mansions, cut up in flats, and each flat has a kitchen, and each kitchen has a large box, called a bunker, for coals, and a hole in the wall, for two or more servants to sleep in, without light or air, except as much air as comes in or out through the leaves of this box bed . . . If no other place can be contrived in the architecture of these places for the dormitory of servants, except the kitchen, could not the coals and the servants change positions, so that the coals would be kept in darkness, to which they have been long accustomed, and the servants would get the light, which is needful for them?

Finding a means to improve conditions appeared insurmountable, and servants at home might envy the 'heathens' abroad:

> If we could strike work, or do something of that kind, good might come of it; but then we have no homes, and would have to sleep on a lea-rig or the roadside, and we might as well do that on some rainy night as not. I have often been half tempted to wish that the larger class of servants, female servants, were only heathens, or Hindoos, or had been born on "Greenland's ice mountains," if not on "India's coral strand," because then we would have been so interesting in our impertinences and wickedness; and an excuse might have been found for the first, and something might have been done for the second.

### Section 4: Business, enterprise and 'women's industries'

The position of women running businesses or as self-employed craftworkers or artists remains poorly defined, and represents a challenge to researchers. Women did not write about their businesses or enterprises or experiences of a commercial life, and, in fact, this is not a gender-specific issue, with male entrepreneurs similarly leaving few records reflecting on their business experience as such. The one exception to this is the histories of successful businesses or family firms, relatively few in number, and often conforming to a masculine model of business success, one dimension of which was the scale of the business concerned. Women's businesses were typically smaller scale. This section offers examples of types of sources which may be used to build up a picture of women's business activity: newspaper adverts, legal agreements, post office directory listings, and promotional material.

Newspapers were a common location for advertisements for women's businesses. The advert below suggests that Miss Allan's business included several employees and trainees:

4.1 *The Scotsman*, 7 November 1835

#### MILLINERY
**MISS ALLAN** takes the liberty to announce, that she has resumed business, and just received a splendid variety of **PARISIAN MILLINERY**, of the newest style.

> By devoting her attention to Millinery exclusively
> she trusts she will be enabled to give satisfaction to
> those who may favour her with their orders, and
> respectfully solicits an inspection of her patterns.
> **WANTED,** Two good **MILLINERS**; also, Two
> **YOUNG LADIES** as **BOARDERS**, to whose
> comfort and morals every attention will be paid.
> 23, Alva Street, 7th Nov.

A further source of information about women's business activity are legal records such as bankruptcy proceedings. These could also occasion public announcements in the press, as the following example shows.

### 4.2 *The Scotsman*, 7 March 1835

> **MRS JOHNSTONE'S SALE** by **AUCTION**,
> under a *fiat of bankruptcy, and without any reserva-*
> *tion whatever*, commences at her late Premises,
> **No. 4 CHARLOTTE SQUARE**, on **TUESDAY,**
> **10TH MARCH**, and to continue till all is sold off.
> To enumerate the whole of this *most costly Stock*
> *of Goods* is beyond the limits of an advertisement,
> but without saying too much, there *never* was
> such a Stock of rich Goods brought to public
> sale in Edinburgh. Many of the Silks cost from
> 8s to 9s a yard. The Sale is to be conducted by
> **MR WALKER** of the Agency Office, who begs
> to call the attention of Ladies, the Trade, and
> Dressmakers, to the sale.
> *No reserve – no Auction Duty –* and for *ready*
> *money only*. Catalogues in due time.
> The elegant Showroom **FIXTURES**, all of
> Mahogany, will be Sold after the goods are dis-
> posed of, and thereafter the **HOUSEHOLD**
> **FURNITURE**.

An unusual source identified by Stana Nenadic is a legal agreement of co-partnership between Margaret Cameron and her brother John.[6] Cameron ran a firm of milliners, dressmakers, stay- and corset-makers, was active in business in Edinburgh between 1826 and 1870, and was 'a significant entrepreneur'. She had a partnership with her brother John which lasted for twenty-two years and which was legally defined in the extract quoted below. This agreement placed the direction and control of the business largely in Margaret's hands but is also indicative of the role male family members might play in supporting businesses run by women.

### 4.3 Articles of Co-Partnery between Margaret Cameron and John Cameron [Cameron and Violard: 1835] [Scottish Record Office, Edinburgh. CS280/1/1]

* Capital stock consisting of stock in trade, furniture in shop and dwelling house, cash and debts are valued at £1300 [2/3 belonging to Margaret Cameron].

* Profits to be divided equally between the partners, and each shall pay on half of any merchandise or furniture purchased by the partners, or any losses on the business and dwelling house.

* Regular books showing the transactions of the company shall be brought to a general balance every six months, and a clear and distinct balance every twelve months.

* All cash received for sales should be entered into the books, which shall be kept in the shop, and when cash in hand amounts to £30 should be paid into a bank account in the name of the firm.

* The business shall be carried out on the principle of ready money business, and no credit given without the consent of both parties. Hours of business, 10.00 am to 8 pm, and one hour for dinner, except during the busy season when the partners shall give such attendance as shall be required.

* Respective duties–

    *John Cameron*: shall keep books, papers, accounts and other documents of the company, make out the inventories, balance the books and attend to the cash concerns of the company, rents, wages etc.

    *Margaret Cameron*: shall purchase goods and merchandise, and for that purpose shall visit London and Paris for the purpose of purchasing goods and learning the fashions as often as both parties shall consider necessary. Shall superintend the dressmaking and millinery departments, shall attend to the sales and orders, and have full power and authority to order, check and control the clerks, servants and others employed by the company.

* Company to be dissolved in the event of death of either party, and on the marriage of either, neither the husband of one, nor the wife of the other, shall be allowed to interfere in any way with the said business without the consent of both parties being previously obtained.

A major source of basic data about women's business activity (and other forms of women's employment) are the listings in post office directories [now available online at the NLS website http://digital.nls.uk/directories/]. By the second half of the nineteenth century, post office directories for the larger cities had become substantial volumes, boasting separate commercial and trade directory sections and advertisements. The Glasgow Directory for 1868–9, for example, indicates that the sectors in which women were most likely to be in business were: boarding and day schools, coffee houses, drapers, dressmakers, lodgings, milliners, stay- and corset-makers, and straw hat makers.

By the later nineteenth century the category of 'women's industries' seems to have become a common usage, and such industries were featured at trade and international exhibitions, such as the Edinburgh International Exhibition of Industry Science and Art in 1886, and the Glasgow Exhibitions of 1888, 1901 and 1911. The women's sections of exhibitions brought together a range of goods and artefacts manufactured by women, from different types of employment situations; businesses run by women and men, employing women and girls, and craftwork by individual women. At the Edinburgh exhibition of 1886, the Scottish-based 'industries' included embroidery in Ayrshire, wood engraving in Edinburgh, knitting from the Zetland [Shetland] Islands, [as illustrated at 2.6 above] and the Isle of Harris, needlework in Wemyss and Edinburgh, and wool manufacturing in Scotland. Some of these initiatives were sponsored by aristocratic ladies, a feature also in evidence in the 'home industries' of the Highlands and Islands. Some women were employed by shipbuilding firms in the design and upholstery work for passenger accommodation on ships, and also in departments concerned with mechanical calculations required for designing vessels. The types of employment gathered together under the heading of 'women's industries' were a real mix in terms of their conditions and pay, and the class background of the workers; what they had in common was a craft or skilled occupation. The following extract indicates that middle-class women earned some income from needlework, arts and crafts.

4.4 *Women's Industries, Edinburgh 1886 International Exhibition of Industry Science and Art* (22)

Needlework (Edinburgh).
Ladies' Repository for the Sale of Gentlewomen's Work,
Albert Buildings, 6 Shandwick Place, Edinburgh.
This Repository is under the charge of a small acting committee of ladies elected by a large general committee. The acting committee appoints a lady superintendent to look after the sales. She is responsible to the acting committee. The articles are priced by the working ladies themselves. Work of all kinds is sold at the Repository. Plain, fancy, and art needlework, embroidery on children's dresses, etc., wood carving, oil and water-colour paintings, Christmas, New Year, and Birthday Cards. The Repository also undertakes the copying of manuscripts, translation of letters, transposition of music, copying of paintings, colouring of photographs, mending and getting up of lace, cleaning and dressing feathers.

## Section 5: Professional employment

Throughout the period covered in this volume, there were always middle- and upper-class women who earned a living out of economic necessity, while the development of various forms of professional employment in the later decades of the nineteenth century opened up opportunities to women on a larger scale. The most typical areas of professional employment or creative work for women were teaching, nursing, midwifery and, later, medicine or literature and art. Despite growing numbers of women occupied in this manner, there seem to have been few women who commented on their working experiences, as such, though there are some autobiographical works by writers such as Margaret Oliphant‡ (1828–97). The extract below, from Catherine Helen Spence's‡ (1825–1910) autobiography (inspired by Oliphant's example) describes the education she received from a Miss Phin in the Borders in the 1830s. Spence was to become a well-known writer and public figure in Australia, herself being employed as a governess for some years before earning a living as a writer.

> 5.1 Catherine Helen Spence, *An Autobiography.* Reprinted from *The Register* (Adelaide, Libraries Board of South Australia, 1975) (9, 10, 12, 18)

Catherine Helen Spence's two elder sisters, Agnes and Jessie, went to a boarding school with their aunt, Mary Spence [who was their teacher], at Upper Wooden, half way between Jedburgh and Kelso. She was sent to another teacher, however:

> I was not sent to Wooden, but kept at home, and I went to a dayschool called by the very popish name of St. Mary's Convent, though it was quite sufficiently Protestant. My mother had the greatest confidence in the lady who was at the head of it. She had been a governess in good situations, and had taught herself Latin, so that she might fit the boys of the family to take a good place in the Edinburgh High School. She discovered that she had an incurable disease, a form of dropsy, which compelled her to lie down for some time every day, and this she considered she could not do as a governess. So she determined to risk her savings, and start a boarding and day school in Melrose, a beautiful and healthy neighbourhood, and with the aid of a governess, impart what was then considered the education of a gentlewoman to the girls in the neighbourhood. She took with her [her] old mother, and a sister who managed the housekeeping, and taught the pupils all kinds of plain and fancy needlework. She succeeded, and she lived till the year 1866, although most of her teaching was done from her sofa. When my mother was asked what it was that [made] Miss Phin so successful, so esteemed, she said it was her commonsense. The governesses were well enough, but the invalid old lady was the life and soul of the school. There were about 14 boarders, and nearly as many day scholars there, so long as there was no competition.
>
> . . . .
>
> The school in which as a day scholar I passed nine years of my life was more literary than many which were more pretentious. Needlework was of supreme importance, certainly, but during the hour and a half every day, Saturday's half-holiday not excepted, which was given to it by the whole school at once (odd half-hours were also put in) the best readers took turns about to read some book selected by Miss Phin. We were thus trained to pay attention. History, biography, adventures,

descriptions, and story books were read. Any questions or criticisms about our sewing, knitting, netting, &c., were carried on in a low voice, and we learned to work well and quickly, and good reading aloud was cultivated.

Earning a living by writing was one option open to women from aristocratic or middle-class backgrounds. Being driven to this by circumstances, such as widowhood and the necessity of supporting a family, made earning a living acceptable, and a number of women were to take this path: for example, Mrs Grant of Laggan‡ (1755–1838), Susan Ferrier‡ (1782–1854), Christian Johnstone‡ (1781–1857), Margaret Oliphant‡, Isabella Fyvie Mayo‡ (1843–1914). Given the prevalence of anonymously or pseudonymously published work in this period, it is reasonable to assume that there were many more women authors than appear at first sight, and many who would have been occasional authors, rather than earning a living by it. The nature of publishing was to undergo changes in the course of the century which rendered the relationship between authors and publishers more of a commercial contract. Earlier in the century, it was more important to seek sponsorship and patronage.

The extract below outlining Mrs Grant's career indicates how she sought support for the publication of her writings. Born Anne Macvicar in 1755, she spent part of her upbringing in the United States. In 1779 she married the Reverend James Grant, minister to the Highland parish of Laggan. After her husband's death in 1801 she embarked on a literary career to support her family. The extract is from an article by Christian Johnstone (originally published anonymously) in *Tait's Edinburgh Magazine*. Johnstone, herself a woman who earned a living editing and writing, takes a lively interest in the circumstances of Mrs Grant's career, as well as in her memories of the Edinburgh literary scene.

### 5.2 Christian Johnstone, *Tait's Edinburgh Magazine*, Vol. 15, 11, March 1844 (175–6)

Memoirs and Correspondence of Mrs Grant of Laggan.

. . . In 1801, she lost her excellent husband: and was left with a family of eight children, and not altogether free from debt. But she had firm faith and high courage, and the talent of attracting and attaching admirable friends, who again interested other friends in her behalf and in that of her family. Nor were her literary talents without their influence. From almost childhood she had scribbled verses; and now, her patrons and friends issued proposals for publishing a volume of her poetry. It proved the most successful attempt of the kind ever made, we believe, in Scotland; and was but an earnest of the very remarkable kindness which Mrs. Grant afterwards met with in quarters where she could have no claim, save that conferred by her virtues and talents, and the condition of her family. Through Mr. George Chalmers, the author of "Caledonia," she received, in one sum, three hundred pounds, the contribution of three princely London merchants, Messrs. Angerstein, Thomson, & Bonar. A number of ladies in Boston published her Letters by subscription; and transmitted her, at different times, considerable sums. Other generous individuals appear to have materially assisted her in her struggles; and her publishers, the house of Longman & Co., acted towards her with a liberality of which she was warmly sensible. They not only gave her a fair share of profits on her "Letters from the Mountains," to which she was entitled, but, as a free gift, a considerable part of their own profits. In her latter years she obtained considerable legacies from old pupils; and a pension of a hundred a-year; and one of her patrons, Sir William Grant, Master of the Rolls, left her an annuity to the same amount. This, with her other funds, and annuity as the widow of a Scottish clergyman, with her moderate tastes, rendered her old age easy and independent.

   –To return: soon after the death of her husband, Mrs. Grant removed, with her large family, to Stirling, in which she resided for some years. Her elder daughters, who had received many more advantages of education than their mother, were now of an age to assist her in any plan of active usefulness; and she received into her family some little boys, of a class that could afford to pay her handsomely, in order to prepare them for school. This scheme was afterwards relinquished for one more suitable to her family circumstances; and, settling in Edinburgh, she received a select number of young ladies of good fortune, who had finished their school, if not their mental education, but who needed the care and protection of a mother, on their introduction into life, and the affection and society of sisters. For many years, her house was the home of a succession of young ladies of this description; and she appears to have had much satisfaction in the character and affection of these pupils, or inmates, whose presence threw a brilliancy around her family circle.

A series of articles on 'Woman's Work', in *The Ladies' Edinburgh Magazine* in 1875, argued the case for middle-class women to be granted opportunities in a range of professions and occupations. Opening with an overview by Phoebe Blyth, quoted in Chapter 7, there followed articles on different professions. The extracts at 5.3 and 5.4 discuss teaching and nursing. Louisa Lumsden‡ (1840–1935) demanded greater access to teaching, though her article drew largely on the situation in England. Lumsden was born in Aberdeen in 1840; in her teens she lived some years in Cheltenham, returning to Scotland in 1857. She studied at Girton from 1869, subsequently tutoring there, before becoming classics teacher at Cheltenham Ladies' College. In 1877, with her friend Constance Maynard, she was recruited to head a new school for girls in St Andrews; this was to become St Leonards.

### 5.3 *The Ladies' Edinburgh Magazine*, Vol. I (1875) (208)

II – Girls' Schools.

Among the many fields of remunerative labour which are now beginning to be thrown more or less unreservedly open to women, the profession of Teaching offers almost without question the highest advantages. This was, as we know, far from being the case formerly; and it is to the reformation which the education of girls is even now undergoing that both the present change in the profession and the large possibilities of development in store for it in the future are due. Few people surely will deny, whatever may be said for or against a woman's entering other professions, that the teaching of her own sex at least is one which seems stamped by nature as most unmistakably hers. And yet women are only now beginning to claim their full share in, if not exclusive right to, one of its most important and certainly most honourable branches, school-teaching. That this has hitherto been to a surprising extent in the hands of men, cannot be gainsaid; indeed, the ordinary phrases with which we are all familiar in school prospectuses, "the advantage of the best masters," "First-rate masters," &c., sufficiently prove how universally women have been ousted from a province which it seems the merest truism to say is theirs. But public opinion is at last changing, and people are beginning to admit the, one would fancy, self-evident truth that woman is the proper instructor of women, and that she is capable of undertaking every branch, elementary or advanced, of education.

The article on nursing was signed 'A Probationer'. Whether the author wished her anonymity to be preserved because she was still a trainee, or for some other reason, is not known. The article argues the case for middle-class women to go into nursing – there is a 'constant cry from hospitals for the best sort of women to undertake nursing,' – and it describes the work routine of trainees.

### 5.4 *The Ladies' Edinburgh Magazine*, Vol. I (1875) (302–3)

. . . In the Edinburgh Infirmary there are already several ladies, and the Lady Superintendent expresses herself most warmly in their praise, and is only anxious to obtain more of the same stamp. In addition to the practical training in the wards, the probationers, as nurses of the first year are called, are taught in a class by Miss Williams, the Assistant Lady Superintendent. They have lectures from different physicians and surgeons, and once a-week they have the very great advantage of going round the surgical wards with Dr. Joseph Bell, who lectures to them over each patient. The probationers on day duty rise at 6 A.M., breakfast at 6.30; remain in the wards from 7 to 9.30, when they have lunch, return to the wards till 3, the dinner hour. Exercise is taken either from 10 to 11.30 A.M., or 3.30 to 5 P.M. Tea is at 5 P.M.; then wards till 8.30; supper at 8.45; bed at 10; and lights out at 10.30 P.M. Those on night duty rise at 7 P.M.; have tea at 7.30; go to the wards at 8.30 P.M., and remain there till 9 A.M.; dinner at 10 A.M., exercise 10.30 to 12, and bed at 12 noon. These are the hours; and now for the work. First of all, the patients' beds have to be made. The probationer leaves her own bed to air when she first leaves her room, but the room must be dusted and the bed made by 10 A.M. Then all wounds have to be dressed, bandages replaced, medicines given, and the rooms and patients made fresh and comfortable for the house surgeon's or physician's morning visit. The sweeping and scrubbing are done by ward assistants, and the patient's dinner is brought into the wards and removed by them; so what is considered hard manual labour is not required from a probationer, but there is constant occupation for her. One patient requires a fresh poultice, another fomentations, another more beef-tea, and so on; thus there is seldom time to weary. But when all the patients seem pretty easy and comfortable – and there are many cases where simply rest and a recumbent position are necessary for recovery – then the weariness and monotony of a ward can be relieved in many ways by an educated, cheerful person. Miss Pringle, the Lady Superintendent of the Royal Edinburgh Infirmary, has been highly trained herself, and is working on the experience gained in other hospitals to carry out all the best possible arrangements in her present sphere. She is ready to give all further information to any lady applying to her, in the kindest and fullest manner. The rooms for the nurses are tiny, and the food plain, but till the new building is ready these rooms cannot be altered; and it has been already proved that the most delicately nurtured women can stand the life without suffering.

A brief typewritten memoir of work at Elsie Inglis's‡ hospice in the High Street, Edinburgh, held at Lothian Health Services Archive, also provides an interesting insight into nursing work in the early twentieth century.[7] Written by Agnes Davies, at that time a probationer, it describes the staffing and work of the hospice, including the establishment of the infant welfare department, one of the first of its kind, by Dr Beatrice Russell. This supplied 'Humanised Milk', made up in feeds for babies of mothers living in the area. Davies commented that they had few resources and that Dr Inglis had to exercise great economy; it was, however, 'a wonderful bit of pioneering work by women doctors'.

### Section 6: Trade unionism, reform and regulation

The example of the Aberdeen Female Operative Union, quoted above at 1.1, indicates that there were attempts to organise women workers from at least the 1830s onwards, though they were often short-lived until later in the century. Women workers were not passive in the face of exploitation or difficult conditions, however, and there were many examples of spontaneous protests and strike actions outwith formal union organisation. Sources that provide information about protest actions and strikes are most likely to be local newspapers, business archives or even court records, but it is difficult to locate direct testimonies from women themselves. By the later nineteenth century, the growth of trade union organisation among women changed this situation though it was still quite common for working women's demands to be articulated by male supporters or by middle-class women. In this period, too, middle-class philanthropists and activists in organisations such as the Scottish Council for Women's Trades campaigned for improvement of women's working conditions. They carried out investigations into women's conditions and lobbied for legislative change. One result of union and labour agitation over the years was the introduction of legislation, and of regulatory frameworks such as factory inspection; by end of the nineteenth century, this included women factory inspectors. The photograph of Jewish women workers in Harry Furst's clothing business (Fig. 4.2) represents one form of workshop or small-scale factory employment in which many women were employed. Conditions in such workshops could vary greatly; the image, while posed for the camera, suggests that these women had a reasonably good working environment.

The extracts below illustrate women's trade unionism, factory inspectors' reports on working conditions, and the Scottish Council for Women's Trades' investigatory role.

> ## 6.1 Aberdeen Female Operative Union, *Proceedings of the Operatives*, &c. (Aberdeen, 1834) (2)

Proceedings of the Aberdeen
### FEMALE OPERATIVE UNION

In consequence of the determination of the Managers of Broadford Mill to reduce the Weekly Wages of the Reelers and Spinners in their employment, it was deemed necessary by the Operatives, in order to protect themselves from unjust oppression, to turn out in a body and resist the tyrannical interference of their masters. A Meeting of 156 Female Operatives was held in the afternoon of the same day, (Friday the 7th curt.) near Elmhill, for the purpose of considering what was to be done, and after due consideration, it was thought advisable, to form themselves into a Co-operative Union with the other Operatives employed at the different Manufactories in Aberdeen and neighbourhood. A Meeting was accordingly held for that purpose, in Robert's Hall, Queen Street, on Saturday 8th inst. at half-past six o'clock, P.M. to make the necessary preliminary arrangements for the proper formation of the Union.

While the conditions of domestic service were a perennial subject for debate, as indicated by A.J.H. above, it was particularly difficult to institute any kind of regulation of conditions, and organisation of domestic servants was rare. Indeed, the Dundee Maidservants' Strike of 1872, illustrated by the extract below, appears to have been unique in Britain though it stimulated widespread interest in the press outside Dundee.[8] The *People's Journal* gave considerable coverage to the dispute, and this included correspondence from women, and letters written in dialect that purported to be from women. The extract below is from an article about the second meeting of maidservants, written by a male reporter in a somewhat tongue-in-cheek style. Nonetheless, it gives a flavour of the atmosphere of the meeting and of the conditions of work which the women found most irksome.

> ## 6.2 *People's Journal*, Friday, 26 April 1872 [Dundee Public Libraries, Lamb Collection 278 (1–4)]

### THE DOMESTIC SERVANTS' AGITATION
### LARGE MEETING IN DUNDEE

Last night a meeting of domestic servants belonging to Dundee and neighbourhood was held in Mather's Hotel. There was a large attendance.

Strict silence was maintained for a considerable time, until at last they began to look for each other for some one to break the ice.

A SERVANT – I think it is time we were making a beginning; we needn't sit here like dummies. There was no use coming here if we weren't to say anything. (Hear, hear.)

ANOTHER – I vote for every second Sabbath to ourselves.

A THIRD – And a half-holiday weekly, or a whole one fortnightly. (Hear, hear.)

A SPEAKER – I think the Sunday cooking is most disgusting! (Great applause.)

A MEMBER – They should have it all cooked on Saturday night, and we would be willing to cook potatoes on Sunday.

ANOTHER – That is if they have cold meat.

A VOICE – Of course; there must be no cooking of meat on Sunday.

A SECOND – I vote for a rise of wages! (Hurrah! laughter, and hear, hear.)

ANOTHER – I second that.

A THIRD – I beg to be excused. I'm a stranger here, and wasn't at last meeting; but I saw by the newspapers that you had been speaking about the hours. The papers said from 6 to 10. Do you all agree to that? I decidedly object! (Hear, hear.)

A FOURTH – So do I. It's far too long.

A MEMBER – From 6 to 7 is long enough, or from 7 to 8.

A SECOND – I propose from 7 to 7.

A THIRD – But if we got extra pay I wouldn't object to work extra time.

A FOURTH – Nothing of the kind. There's no use of slaving the whole week from 6 to 10.

ANOTHER – Sixteen hours a day are far too many.

A SPEAKER – I object to extra time. There is no use for extra time to servants. Let them make their engagement and stick to it. I hope every one will give in with what they hear here, and not yield to mistresses in their fine flattering way! (Great laughter and applause.)

A SECOND – There could be no objection to serve at extra parties and the like of that.

A THIRD – We can't object to that. If mistresses would give their servants more liberty – (hear, hear) – it would be better for both mistresses and servants. There would be a far better house.

A FOURTH – We should be paid quarterly.

A FIFTH – Make your engagements for that.

A SIXTH – But there is no use for one doing it and not the rest. (Hear, hear.)

ANOTHER – I really wonder why mistresses can think their servants are able to do what they expect of them. I do not believe they actually think we are made of the same material! (Roars of laughter.) From 6 to 10! It's quite absurd. I don't know why any one could persist in such a thing. It's very hard labour that servants have to do. You haven't a moment you can call your own. If any one objects to what I have said I will be happy to hear her.

A general chorus – Not at all! not at all!

At the end of the meeting it was agreed that a union should be formed, and that it should be designated The Dundee and District Domestic Servants' Protection Association. As Merchant has commented, the Dundee servants' action may well have been encouraged by other strikes occurring locally and by growing support for the Nine Hours Movement. The extract below, also from the *People's Journal*, provides a commentary on a strike against wage reductions in the jute mills that occurred two years' later.

### 6.3 *People's Journal*, 1874 (no day or month given) [Dundee Public Libraries, Lamb Collection, 196D Wages and Conditions]

#### LETTER FROM A MILL LASSIE ON THE LATE STRIKE
#### TO THE EDITOR OF THE PEOPLE'S JOURNAL

Sir, – Altho' no bein' vera weel versed in grammar, I've ventured tae throw mysell on yer generosity tae insert this wee bit scribble in yer worthy paper. Bein' only a mill lassie ye ken ye canna expeck great things fae me. Weel, Maister Editor, I wis lookin' ower the *Advertiser* o' the 15th, an' saw there a letter purportin' tae be frae a "West-End Millowner," wha seems to find his defeat raither sair, and like mony a ane mair disna hae sense tae hide it, for he seems tae tak' a pride in terrafeein' the workin' class wi' the stopage o' machinery. But I will advise him tae nurse his wrath till the time comes, and then he'll hae the mair satisfaction. What a plisky he's in at the gentleman wha made the compromise wi' his workers in the reduction of ten per cent. I may say wi' confidence that it wis the greatest surprise that his workers could hae got whan it wis intimated to them that he had taen part in sic an act o' injustice as that wid hae been had it been successful – seein' that the rises are only by 2, 3, and 5 per cent. A "West-End Millowner" ca's on his brither tradesmen tae get up an Association tae keep us doon, and keep their ain heads aboon the water. Noo I've been thinkin' that as they need sic a thing tae keep them thegither, hoo wid it dae if we, the workin' women of Dundee, should be aforehand wi' them an' hae ane o' oor ain. Gin ilka worker wid gie the matter o' 2d or 3d a week for three months, and after that a penny – no tae touch the first three months' money, but tae let it lie dead for strikes alane – and aye mair tae be clappet to the back o' that, I think in a wee while we could keep oor ain ground. Always in justice let us be willin' tae rise when the maisters rise an' fa' as they fa'; but, as I said afore, there's nae use o' us fa'in' when they are standin' still. I dinna see what's the use o' us as women that we dinna hae a Union, since a' the men, even the vera scaffies, hae ane. Gin we could only get some chap tae tak' it in hand an' get it startit I'm sure there's no ane o' oor number but wid jump at the idea o't; an' if we canna get ony o' the men fouk tae tak' it in han', let twa or three sensible women come forward an' help on wi't. Unless there's something like this done oor wages will never be in a settled state. Sincerely trustin', Maister Editor, that every public worker will tak' this intae consideration,
I am                                                             A MILL LASSIE.

By the late nineteenth century legislation regulating conditions in factories and workshops had been introduced, and factory inspectors began to be appointed. The extract below quotes from Mary Paterson's report on conditions in laundries. Paterson and May Tennant were appointed in 1893 as the first

**Figure 4.2** Jewish women workers in Harry Furst's tailoring workshop, Glasgow, *c*.1890.
Courtesy of Harvey Kaplan, Scottish Jewish Archives Centre.

two women factory inspectors. Paterson, born in 1864, came from an affluent
Glasgow family. She subsequently became one of the first National Health
Insurance commissioners for Scotland in 1911.[9] Paterson's findings covered
facilities in the major cities and towns, and gives some indication of the scale
of services in different locations and of their clientele. The extract gives the sections on Glasgow and Edinburgh. The report is available at House of Commons
Parliamentary Papers Online.

### 6.4 *Laundries: Reports of H. M. Inspectors of Factories as to Hours of Work, Dangerous Machinery, and Sanitary Condition* (1894) (8–9)

(d) – Miss Mary. M. Paterson

| | |
|---|---|
| Glasgow, &c | Laundries generally clean, but washhouses often in dirty and insanitary |
| Excessive heat | condition, the heat being excessive and ventilation defective. |
| Gas irons injurious | The use of gas irons* observed to be injurious. [*Gas irons are in use in Leeds from which no fumes escape] |
| | Overcrowding rare. |
| | The *nominal* weekly hours as shown in tabular form, not excessive, being mostly under 60, except in a few instances where they reach 85, 74, 66, &c. hours. |

Hours irregular and excessive | But, as shown by numerous instances of excessive hours given below, these hours are not adhered to, and the meal times are both deficient and irregular.

The hours, &c. are most irregular in the smallest places.

Proprietors in Glasgow in general in favour of more regular hours, but not unanimous in advocating the application of the Factory Act. All are willing that the *weekly* hours should be limited, but not the *daily* hours.

> Proprietors favour a weekly limit.

Difficulties in securing greater regularity are: –
(1) Apparent impossibility of getting work early in the week.
(2) Necessity of sending clean clothes home on Saturday.

> Difficulties in securing regular work.

There is a class of laundries who devote themselves to late washing sent in on Thursday or Friday, as many laundries refuse to take it in.

> Lateness in sending clothes to the wash a matter of habit.

This lateness in sending to wash, like late shopping, is principally the result of mismanagement, and there is no remedy for it but in legislation.

Instance given of a laundry in which it is usual for washers not to have any work on Monday, but in Friday and Saturday they always have to work till 10 p.m., and frequently 12 p.m.

> Long hours at the end of the week.

Instances of ironers working four times a year from Friday morning until Saturday at midnight continuously.

It is thought by proprietors that more regular hours would prevent the drinking induced by exhaustion.

> Long hours worked by ironers. Drinking induced by exhaustion.

A general feeling exists among the workers that the late hours are a hardship: question raised by Miss Paterson whether enforcement of more regular hours would reduce wages. To some the hard and irregular work is compensated for, by their being able to get a day off sometimes early in the week, but the more sensible of them, wish much for the Factory Act to be applied to their case.

> Glasgow. Feeling that late hours are a hardship.

Most women who have been on laundry work three or four years, have at least on one occasion worked all night. Instance given of a woman working 42 hours at a stretch (less than three hours for meals) in washing and ironing.

> Working all night not uncommon.

Many instances given of working early and late on Friday and Saturday, sometimes as long as 7 a.m. to 12 p.m.

> Long hours on Friday and Saturday. Edinburgh.

Many laundries situated in area flats of private houses, mostly deficient in ventilation.

Here again want of employment for ironers in beginning of week the chief difficulty in regulating work.

Very late work at end of week exceptional here.

Few holidays given, and those have to be made up for.

General feeling is in favour of some limitation of hours, but opposed to Factory Act.

> Want of employment early in the week. Few holidays given.

Some overcrowding in hand laundries, ventilation neglected in
them and in large places too.

Smell of gas irons noticed as being offensive. Most hotels give               Gas irons
their washing out.                                                                                    offensive.

Many proprietors of small laundries had tried to regulate their
work better but failed, and thought it would be inconvenient to
enforce restrictions.

Suggestion was made that ships and hotels doing shipping trade      Night work in
would have to keep double supplies of linen unless work could be     shipping trade.
done at night.

. . .

The extract below, describing a tour of Scotland made by Marion Tuckwell, was
published in the *Women's Trades Union Review*. A London-based periodical, published from 1891 to 1906, it printed findings from factory inspectors' reports,
listed prosecutions under factories acts, and carried articles on disputes, and on
developments in trade union organisation among women. Marion Tuckwell was
the younger sister of Gertrude Tuckwell, of the Women's Trade Union League,
which merged with the Trades Union Congress in 1921. The *Women's Trades
Union Review* is available at 19th Century UK Periodicals Online.

### 6.5  *The Women's Trades Union Review*, 1 October 1895 (15)

Trades Unionism in Scotland

Having promised to attend and speak at the Annual Meeting of the Alva Textile
Workers' Union, I took the opportunity of inquiring into the condition of Trades
Unionism amongst women in Scotland and visiting all our affiliated Unions. In
Edinburgh, where I made my first halt, things are even worse than in London; it can
boast only of one little Union of about ninety women from various trades, though,
as I was informed by the Secretary of the Trades Council, there are some thousands
of women in the book-binding trades. The Secretary, Miss Jessie Bell, is an energetic
worker, and possibly the Trades Congress next year may do something to rouse
interest in Trades Unionism. This Union is not affiliated to the League. The Alva
meeting was crowded and enthusiastic. The Union, which in its present form is only
six months old, has already 400 members, and the standard of wages is being maintained, whereas in Menstrie and other small towns in the neighbourhood having
no Unions, wages, they told me, are "sore broke." A really delightful concert was
given by members and friends of the Union, many of whom had excellent voices
and sang their plaintive Scotch songs very sweetly to violin accompaniment. After
the meeting we had a tea party, at which I was presented by the Committee with a
beautiful shawl of native manufacture. From Alva I went to Dundee. A meeting was
held under the auspices of the Trades Council, but was not well attended. Dundee
is a house divided against itself, and though Mr. McConnell, the Secretary, is very
much in earnest, and Mr. Phillip, the President, has superabundant energy, out of
60,000 workers not one per cent. belongs to any Union, and wages are consequently
very low.

From Dundee I paid flying visits to Alyth, Forfar, and Brechin. At Alyth, a beautiful little town up amongst the hills, about two-thirds of the workers are organised; the Union was formed out of a strike against a reduction in wages of 5%, which the workers were able to recover when combined. Their steady progress was easily traceable to their officials, who are shrewd, determined men. The same applies to Forfar, where there is the strongest textile Union in Scotland, 20,000 out of 26,000 workers being organised. Forfar is peculiarly fortunate in possessing, beside its own Secretary, the excellent General Secretary of the Federation, Mr. Rose.

At Brechin again, where I spent a brief but very pleasant afternoon, there is a strong and growing Union, and I had a long and interesting talk on the prospects of Trades Unionism with Mr Hendry, the Collector.

In Arbroath on the contrary, in spite of its active Secretary, Mr. Addison, apathy prevails regarding Trades Unionism, and the organisation languishes. We had, notwithstanding, a successful though small meeting, and the members make up in enthusiasm for what they want in numbers.

Aberdeen was the Northern limit of my tour, and here, though the men in other trades are well organised, the Textile Workers' Union remains very small. I lost no opportunity of going over factories and mills in places I visited, and through the kindness of Mr. Johnstone I was taken through a large cotton mill employing hundreds of women, numbers of whom are earning in the spinning department from 6s. to 7s. a week. I think if the Federation could see its way to paying an organiser to devote him or herself to that work alone, the additional expense involved would be more than compensated for by the added membership . . .

MARION TUCKWELL.

A key figure in the Scottish Council for Women's Trades (SCWT) was Margaret Irwin‡ (1858–1940) who served as Secretary to the SCWT from 1895 and who was elected first Secretary of the Scottish Trades Union Congress in 1897. She was the most active commentator of her times on the conditions of working women in Scotland, was author of many SCWT publications, and also contributed to the *Glasgow Herald* and *Westminster Review*. The pamphlet, quoted below, provided research evidence to support the campaign for a Parliamentary bill, drafted by Scottish and London councils, and promoted by Colonel Denny, MP for Kilmarnock. The bill aimed to regulate the conditions in which home work was undertaken, through a system of licensing premises to protect public health.

### 6.6 Margaret H. Irwin, *The Problem of Home Work*, 3rd edition (Glasgow, 1906) (8,11)

. . . Recent investigations into the nether world of the home worker, that great industrial *terra incognita*, have revealed a state of things full of grave and subtle danger to the health of the community at large; and it seems strange that, while so many precautions to safeguard the health are taken when a dread epidemic is at our doors, the community in general should not be more alive to the terrible risks to which they are at all times exposed from the making of clothing and other things for common use in insanitary and disease-infected houses. The "Song of the Shirt" is probably the most effective labour report which has ever been written. It struck a chord in the heart of the nation that still vibrates readily enough when touched; but surely, if the purchasing public once clearly realised what are the actual conditions of home work as it is carried on in our midst to-day, and what it may involve to themselves as well as to the makers of the garments, they would "wear their rue with a difference," and feel that the matter demands not merely sentiment and philanthropic effort, but the speedy application of remedial measures in the form of Acts of Parliament.

. . .

A number of case studies were cited, such as the following:

Mrs. A., a shirt finisher, is an elderly woman, the widow of a labourer. She has in the house with her a married daughter and two grandchildren. The former is a deserted wife, whom her mother, with the beautiful helpfulness to one another we so frequently see among the very poor, has taken home. The daughter is employed in a calender work during the day, and helps the mother a little at night with the shirts. These are paid at 2½d., 4d., and 6d., a dozen for finishing, and take respectively two, four, and five hours a dozen. She cannot estimate the time given per day, but earnings average from 5s. to 6s. per week. Mrs. A. lives in a one-roomed house, the condition of which is very dirty, and the rent of which is 7s. 6d. per month. When I visited I saw the work piled on the bed where the two young children were lying ill of some unknown disorder.

## Select bibliography

T. M. Devine, 'Women Workers, 1850–1914', in T. M Devine (ed.), *Farm Servants and Labour in Lowland Scotland, 1770–1914* (Edinburgh: John Donald, 1984), pp. 98–123.

Eleanor Gordon, *Women and the Labour Movement in Scotland, 1850–1914* (Oxford: Clarendon Press, 1991).

Eleanor Gordon and Esther Breitenbach (eds), *The World is Ill-Divided: Women's Work in Scotland in the Nineteenth and Early Twentieth Centuries* (Edinburgh: Edinburgh University Press, 1990).

W. W. Knox, *Hanging by a Thread: the Scottish Cotton Industry, c.1850–1914* (Preston: Carnegie, 1994).

Jane McDermid, *The Schooling of Girls in Britain and Ireland, 1800–1900* (Abingdon: Routledge, 2012).

Jan Merchant, '"An Insurrection of Maids": domestic servants and the agitation of 1872', in Louise Miskell, Christopher A. Whatley and Bob Harris (eds), *Victorian Dundee: Image and Realities* (East Linton: Tuckwell Press, 2000), pp. 104–21.

Lindy Moore, 'Education and Learning', in Abrams et al., *Gender in Scottish History*, pp. 111–39.

Stana Nenadic, 'The Social Shaping of Business Behaviour in the Nineteenth-Century

Women's Garment Trades', in *Journal of Social History*, Vol. 31, No. 3 (spring, 1998), pp. 625–45.

Siân Reynolds, *Britannica's Typesetters: Women Compositors in Edwardian Edinburgh* (Edinburgh: Edinburgh University Press, 1989).

Deborah Simonton, 'Work, Trade and Commerce', in Abrams et al., *Gender in Scottish History*, pp. 199–234.

## Notes

1. The sections quoting Janet Cumming and Jane Peacock Wilson also appear in R. H. Campbell and J. B. A. Dow, *Source Book of Scottish Economic and Social History* (Oxford: Basil Blackwell, 1968) along with other sources about the mining industry and legislative reform.

2. We are very grateful to Anne Macleod Hill for information about Anna Gobh, and for the translation of her poem from Gaelic into English.

3. John Ord, *The Bothy Songs and Ballads of Aberdeen, Banff and Moray, Angus and the Mearns* (Edinburgh: John Donald, 1974), p. 16.

4. Ian MacDougall (ed.), *'Hard work, ye ken': Midlothian Women Farmworkers* (Edinburgh: Canongate, in association with Midlothian District Council, The European Ethnologocial Research Centre and the National Museums of Scotland, 1993). See also Ian MacDougall, *Bondagers: Eight Scots Women Farm Workers* (East Linton: Tuckwell Press, 2000), which gives testimonies of women farm workers after World War I.

5. We are very grateful to Anne Macleod Hill for information about Mairiread Ghriogarach, and for the translation of her poem from Gaelic into English.

6. Stana Nenadic, 'The Social Shaping of Business Behaviour in the Nineteenth-Century Women's Garment Trades', *Journal of Social History*, Vol. 31, No. 3 (1998), pp. 625–45. The agreement is quoted in this article, and Margaret Cameron's business career is discussed in detail.

7. Agnes Davies, typescript of memoir, Lothian Health Services Archive. [LHB8/14/34A, 34B]. The archive is located in the Centre for Research Collections, University of Edinburgh.

8. Jan Merchant, '"An Insurrection of Maids": domestic servants and the agitation of 1872', in Louise Miskell, Christopher A. Whatley and Bob Harris (eds), *Victorian Dundee: Image and Realities* (East Linton: Tuckwell Press, 2000), pp. 104–21.

9. Biographical information about Paterson is from the *Oxford Dictionary of National Biography* online: www.oxforddnb.com (accessed 12 October 2012).

# Chapter 5

# Crime and Punishment, Immorality and Reform

*S. Karly Kehoe*

## Introduction

What counts as 'crime' and 'immorality' has been subject to contestation and has shifted across time, as have discourses and practices designed to contain behaviours deemed to be socially threatening. This chapter focuses on behaviours that contravened laws or transgressed the dominant moral norms in the long nineteenth century; it does not discuss women as victims of crime, such as domestic violence, which was widely condoned in this period.[1] While women were less likely to be accused of breaking the law than men, they could be punished more harshly if their behaviour breeched gender norms, such as the use of violence. They could also be punished and scapegoated for sexual activity that threatened the sanctity of marriage. The rising middle classes, in particular, held a narrow view of sexuality as demonstrated by writings on prostitution, 'fallen women', and illegitimacy; but these 'self-appointed custodians of the nation's morality' did little to change 'the sexual mores of the masses'.[2] Thus, while middle-class discourses dominate within this chapter, the concerns expressed in their writings were not shared across the social spectrum.

It is a particular challenge within this field to identify the female voice itself, and this is true not only for working-class and rural women who came before the courts but also for middle-class reformers. On the one hand, the voices of women accused of crime are mediated by the standard practices of legal documentation and yet, on the other, while reports of institutions and voluntary bodies do give many indications of women's role within them, they provide little in the way of examples of women's authorship of texts. Conversely, court records provide a rich source of information about women's criminal behaviour, as Anne-Marie Kilday has shown in her study of Scottish Justiciary Court records between 1750 and 1815.[3] Indictments (written accusations charging individuals) and precognitions (distinctive in Scots law, these are factual statements taken from witnesses in preparation for a possible trial; they are not admissible as evidence) often include the female voice and, in this chapter, we have quoted extracts from both. Other sources include government enquiries and reports, newspaper articles, broadsides and ballads, annual reports of institutions, memoirs, and correspondence.

### Section 1: Crime and punishment

This section gives examples of crimes of which women were accused and often tried, and illustrates the penalties and punishments handed out. It includes extracts relating to child murder and concealment of pregnancy which were regarded as unnatural and often evoked public condemnation; extracts relating to these crimes have been grouped together as sources 1.1. to 1.5. The incidence of infanticide and concealment of pregnancy was low; the crime which women were most likely to commit was, like men, that of theft, as the crime statistics in *The Scotsman*, quoted in source 1.7, indicate.

By the nineteenth century, infanticide was viewed as the archetypal female crime and features in the nation's rich tradition of balladry. Ballads were almost always narrative and, at a time when the use of written records was limited, people relied on oral tradition both to acquire and to pass on information. 'The Cruel Mother' probably dates from the late seventeenth century but was still being sung in the nineteenth century when Francis Child recorded Scottish and English ballads. There are numerous versions of this ballad, thought to be of Scottish origin, which tells the story of a noblewoman who killed her babies, fathered by a servant, and buried them in the woods.

1.1  James Francis Child (ed.), 'The Cruel Mother', in *English and Scottish Ballads*, Vol. II (Boston: Little, Brown and Company, 1857) (269–71)

There lives a lady in London –
All along, and alonie
She's gane wi' bairn to the clerk's son –
Doun by the greenwood sae bonnie.

She has tane her mantle her about –
All along, and alonie
She's gane aff to the gude greenwood –
Doun by the greenwood sae bonnie.

She has set her back until a brier –
All along, and alonie
Bonnie were the two boys she did bear –
Doun by the greenwood sae bonnie.

But out she's tane a little penknife –
All along, and alonie
And she's parted them and their sweet life –
Doun by the greenwood sae bonnie.

She's add unto her father's ha' –
All along, and alonie
She seem'd the lealest maiden among them a' –
Doun by the greenwood sae bonnie.

As she lookit our the castle wa' –
All along, and alonie
She spied two bonnie boys playing at the ba' –
Doun by the greenwood sae bonnie.

O an thae twa babes were mine –
All along, and alonie
They should wear the silk and sabelline –
Doun by the greenwood sae bonnie.

O Mother dear, when we were thine, –
All along, and alonie
We neither wore silks nor the sabelline –
Doun by the greenwood sae bonnie.

But out ye took a little penknife –
All along, and alonie
And ye parted us with our sweet life –
Doun by the greenwood sae bonnie.

But now we're in the heaveans hie –
All along, and alonie

And ye have the pains o' hell to dree –
Doun by the greenwood sae bonnie.

Before 1809, cases of suspected child murder were treated as capital crimes. Such cases were prosecuted in the sheriff court and, as in the instance of Marion Henrysdaughter, members of the Church were often prominent witnesses. Control of female sexuality was regarded as a central aspect of the Church's disciplinary role until the early nineteenth century, and kirk session elders might request to examine a woman's breasts to ascertain whether she had recently given birth. This is probably one of the last examples of this practice being carried out by an elder; by the early nineteenth century, a midwife was more likely to undertake the task. The statement by the accused is contained in the extract below; it was accompanied by statements from the accused's father, the father of the child, and kirk elders. Henrysdaughter was found guilty but it is not known what penalty she suffered.

---

1.2  Child murder: Sheriff Court, Shetland, 1794. Marion Henrysdaughter, resident of Noss, Dunrossness, age 23 [Shetland Archives, SC 12/6/1794/17]

### Declaration by defendant

That upon a Sunday morning about nine months before her delivery after mentioned while she was gathering her father's cows in a barn a little distance from the house, Malcolm Malcolmson, tenant in Noss aforesaid came in to the barn and forcibly had carnal knowledge with the declarent. That from this connection she conceived and upon the ninth day of October last was delivered of a dead female child. Declares that she never told any person she was with child but that she remembers Henry Sinclair her uncle an Elder once asked her the question, to which she answered that she was not with child. Declares that there was no person present when she was delivered, nor did she call for any assistance. That she kept the corpse of the child in her own bed all day, and without the knowledge of any person whatever next day about noon carryed it to a skeo or small open house where fish are usually hung up to dry in which she dug a hole and buryed the corpse and covered it with a flat stone. declares that about eight days after Robert Allason an Elder came to her the declarents house and told her that he wanted to see whether there was some milk in her breasts. That she came out of the house showed the Elder her breasts and satisfied him there was then no milk in them, but says that he asked her no more questions. Declares that she was summoned to attend the kirk session of Dunrossness and that upon Sunday last the second current she declared in the session before the Minister and elders nearly to the effect above written. Declares that upon the day Allison the elder came to her, John Malcolmson, the brother of Malcolm Malcolmson the father of the child, James Leisk, Jacobina Hendrydaughter and Grizel Sinclair all in Noss went in to the skeo, took up the corpse of the child and buried it in the churchyard of Dunrossness. Declares that she never told Malcolm Malcolmson that she was with child nor does she think that either her father or her mother knew it. Nor did they know of her delivery until the day she was accused by Allison the elder. Declares that she never made any preparation whatever for her delivery nor had she provided any clothes for the child.

Declares that she cannot write.

The next case took place in Creich [Creech], Sutherland, after 1809 and the woman concerned was charged with concealment of pregnancy. Bessy MacKay, aged twenty, gave birth to a daughter, whose father was Bessy's cousin, John MacKay, aged eighteen or nineteen, who had come north from Strathspey to work for his relatives. Bessy had not made her pregnancy known to anyone, apart from John, but a number of women in the community would later admit to the kirk session that they had suspected it. John and Bessy were initially held in Dornoch's jail while evidence was gathered but it was decided that a case against them would not be pursued. In a brief note, Andrew Clephane, advocate and sheriff of Fife explained:

> This is not a case I am inclined to try. The question [of] whether the revealment of pregnancy to the father of the child takes the case out of the statute is a very nice one, but the present is not a case to try it; the poor girl seems to have had no desire whatever to conceal her pregnancy for the purpose of destroying the child. To try the father for murder is entirely out of the question.

### 1.3 Minutes of the Kirk Session of Creech, 22 March 1814 [NAS, AD14/14/13]

At Inveran the sixteenth day of March 1814. The Session of Creech having met and being constituted by Prayer . . . The said Betsy MacKay being summoned to the Session appeared and being interrogated by the Moderator has the same time in the cause of last winter or spring been with child answered that she had. She was asked who was the Father of her child answered John MacKay of Inveran. She was asked where and at what time she had criminal connection with him and answered on the Week of the Ledichan or Kincardine Market. She was asked what was the reason of her concealing her pregnancy. Answered that no person put the question to her whether she was with child therefore she did not tell. She was asked did she bring forth a living child. She answered that she did not, nor did she believe the child to be alive while she was pregnant with it. She was asked how long since she brought forth the child. Answered five weeks from Friday first. She was asked who visited her while she was unwell. Answered the neighbours – such as Bessy MacKay [aunt] spouse of John Bethune at Inveran [ferryman], Margaret MacKay her aunt at the Lairg of Tain, Christian MacDonald widow at Inveran, Janet MacDonald widow of the late Alexander Bethune at Inveran, Christian Ross widow of the late Simon Fraser at Inveran [midwife] who upon one of the visits tied a napkin about Bessy Mackay's middle and examined her breasts. Upon Bessy Mackay being thus interrogated the moderator desired Alexander Gray at Wester Linseidmore [tenant] Kirk Officer to call in John MacKay. John MacKay did not appear the Moderator asked the reason – he was answered that John Mackay was confined to bed. The Moderator then desired Alexander Gray, Andrew MacKay and Alexander Ross to go to Donald MacKay's house where John MacKay was lying indisposed . . . Upon this the Session adjourned to Donald MacKay's house where they found John MacKay lying indisposed in bed. The Moderator then interrogated John MacKay was he the Father of Bessy MacKay's child. He answered that he was. He was asked when he had the first criminal connection with Bessy MacKay. He answered about the time Inveran Tenants were beginning to sow the oats, i.e. about the 13th day of April 1813. NB Bessy MacKay forced her way to the room where we were interrogating John MacKay upon hearing him say that this was the first time he had criminal connection with her – said that he had no criminal connection with her till the week of the Kincardine Market. He was asked was he present when Bessy MacKay was delivered. He said he was. He was asked had he any further criminal connection with Bessy MacKay than what he had on or about the 13th day of April. He said he had not but some day of the week of the Kincardine Market. He was asked was there any person in the Room but themselves both when Bessy MacKay was delivered. He said there was not. He was asked was it a male or a female child Bessy MacKay brought forth. He said a female child. He was asked was it a heavy child – he said that it was not. He was asked what was become of the child – he said that he took a dead female child from Bessy Mackay. He was asked was it she that gave it to him, or did he take it himself. He said he took it himself . . . He was asked what was become of the child. He said that he took the child, and that he wrapped it up (to use his own expressions) in a lawn napkin and kept it in a trunk for three days.

. . .

Upon his being thus interrogated the members of Session repaired to the workshop and searched for the corpse. Upon searching the body was found at the north wall of the work shop wrapped in the lawn napkin. As soon as Bessy MacKay saw the napkin in which the child was wrapped she like a woman bordering upon a frantic state sprung from the south side of the workshop and said Oh! This is the first sight I got of my child – and when the body was taken up out of the place where it was deposited altho' covered over almost with the earth grasped at it like a ravenous bird when seizing upon its prey – kissed and embraced it and squeezed or pressed it so much to her breast that immediately those present laid hold her and forced her to give up the child for fear of its being bruised by her – all that were present in consequence of the manner she embraced her child, were much affected and declared that it was more than probably she had not seen her child till then. And the poor unfortunate mother has repeatedly declared she did not . . .

Though rare, prosecutions for child murder occurred throughout the nineteenth century. Quoted below is a High Court indictment, following the standard form, giving a statement of the alleged crime. Annie Wilkie, a woman from Ravenswood in Cumbernauld Parish, was accused of child murder in 1872. Although the body of the baby was never found and she pleaded not guilty, Wilkie was found guilty of culpable homicide and sentenced to ten years penal servitude. The verdict was probably a response to the level of violence she was said to have used against the child.

### 1.4  High Court Indictment against Annie Wilkie for Child-Murder: Glasgow, September 1872 [University of Glasgow Library, Special Collections, Mu Add f50]

Annie Wilkie, now or lately prisoner in the prison of Dumbarton, you are Indicted and Accused, . . .

. . . you the said Annie Wilkie are guilty of the said crime of child-murder, or of the statutory crime above libelled: IN SO FAR AS, you the said Annie Wilkie, having, on the 1st day of July 1872 or on one or other of the days of that month or of June immediately preceding, in or near the farm-house or premises of the farm in Ravenswood in the parish of Cumbernauld, and the shire of Dumbarton, then and now or lately occupied by George Paton, farmer, then and now or lately residing there, been delivered of a living female child, you the said Annie Wilkie did, time above, libelled, immediately, or soon after the birth of the said child, then in there, wickedly and feloniously, attack and assault the said child, and did with a hatchet or spade, or a hay-knife, or with some other weapon to the prosecutor unknown, inflict one or more cuts or wounds on or near the neck or throat of the said child, whereby its head was nearly severed from the body, its right shoulder or arm fractured, and its back and legs cut and wounded, and it was otherwise mangled and injured, in consequence of all which, or part thereof, the said child was mortally injured, and did immediately or soon thereafter die, and was thus murdered by you the said Annie Wilkie: OR OTHERWISE. Time and Place above libelled, you the said Annie Wilkie did bring forth a female child, and you did conceal your being with child during the while period of your pregnancy, and did not call for and make use of help or assistance in the birth, and the said child was afterwards found dead in or near a garden situated at or near said farm-house or premises, or the said child has since its birth been amissing: . . .

As noted, court and church records presented cases in a standard form such as the examples above. A small number contain statements from the accused that offer a glimpse of the female voice. The following example is the recorded statement of Alice Robertson, a domestic servant from Edinburgh, who was indicted for concealment of pregnancy in 1873. The father of her baby, when told of her pregnancy, disappeared. She pleaded not guilty and was found not guilty.

### 1.5  High Court Indictment against Alice Robertson for concealment of pregnancy, 1873 [University of Glasgow Library, Special Collections, Mu Add f50]

First Declaration – 5 July 1873 – 28 years of age . . . when delivered of a male child at Blackford [farm] when a servant on Sunday morning 29th June last – No one present or assisted at birth. I never told anyone that I was pregnant except the father of the child, James Graham a labourer in Berwickshire – I told him sometime in March last and he then ran away and I have not seen him since and I do not know where he is – I did not expect the birth to take place until 3 months after the time it did take place – I cannot say whether the child was born alive – It was dead when I first saw it.

Second Declaration – 18 July 1873 – Adheres to first Declaration in all aspects and further declares I first became acquainted with James Graham the father of my child about 2 years ago – he was then lodging in the town of Berwick from which he used to come to see me at Cothill where I was a servant – he continued to live at Berwick all the time I knew him but I did not know his particular address – I understand him to be a mason's labourer – he was a tall dark man – I have heard him speak of going to New Zealand – I can give no other clue as to where he may be heard of – when Graham visited me at Cothill it was after bedtime and no one saw him to my knowledge.

While the statute on witchcraft had been repealed in 1736, the crime of pretended witchcraft remained on the statute book. Though rare, its occurrence indicated the legacy of earlier times and the continuing vitality of popular belief in supernatural powers. The example below suggests that the accused made use of her supposed powers to manipulate her victim. Jean Maxwell had foretold that her victim, Jean Davidson, would bear a bastard child to a certain Hugh Rafferton, and got Davidson to hand over money, clothes, and food to her. Davidson denied there was a possibility of her being pregnant, though she was in courtship with Rafferton. Among other things, Maxwell induced Davidson, a domestic servant, to steal a shirt from her master. The extracts below quote from the indictment against Maxwell, from Jean Davidson's statement, and the verdict against Maxwell. [The 'pannel' is the accused]

1.6 *Remarkable Trial of Jean Maxwell, the Galloway Sorceress; which took place at Kirkcudbright on the Twenty-eighth day of June last, 1805; For Pretending to Exercise Witchcraft, Sorcery, Inchantment, Conjuration, &c* (Kirkcudbright: Printed by Alexander Gordon, 1805) [NLS, Shelfmark L.C. 2097] (7–8, 14, 24)

Jean Maxwell did . . . at Little Cocklick in the parish of Urr and Stewartry of Kirkcudbright, pretend to Tell Fortunes by Tea Cups and the grounds of Tea; and did tell to Jean Davidson, servant to Francis Scott, farmer in Little Cocklick aforesaid, that she would soon bear a Bastard to a certain young man, Hugh Rafferton; which you said you could prevent by certain means. And you the said Jean Maxwell, caused the said Jean Davidson to rub, or anoint her forehead and other parts of her head with a liquid contained in a bottle produced by you, which so much intoxicated and disordered the said Jean Davidson, that she would have done any thing that you the said Jean Maxwell had asked her to do; and you the said Jean Maxwell availing yourself of the situation that she the said Jean Davidson was in, declared to her that the Devil would speedily appear and tear her in pieces, unless she obeyed you, the said Jean Maxwell, in every particular.

Jean Davidson's deposition described the fortune telling:

. . . the witness depones that, the Pannel first came to the house of Little Cocklick on a wednesday before new-years-day last, new stile. – That the Pannel staid at Little

Cocklick all that night; and having heard that the Deponent and her Master had been detained late in the Town of Dumfries on that day, on account of a young man named Hugh Rafferton, the pannel on the thursday morning, at breakfast, pretended to tell the Deponent's Fortune, and offered to cast a Tea Cup for that purpose, and the Deponent having accepted the offer, the pannel proceeded to Cast a cup, and thereafter told the Deponent that her Fortune would be bad, and that Hugh Rafferton meant to deceive her.

. . .

Kirkcudbright, 28th June, 1805.

The Steward Depute having considered the Verdict of the Assize bearing date the 21st Day of June current, and returned into Court that Day against Jean Maxwell, the Pannel, whereby she is found Guilty of pretending to exercise WITCHCRAFT, SORCERY, INCHANTMENT, and CONJURATION, and of undertaking to tell Fortunes, contrary to the Enactments and Provisions of the Act of Parliament passed in the 9th year of the Reign of King George the Second, Chapter fifth, in the manner charged against her in the Indictment, at instance of the Procurator Fiscal of Court; the Steward Depute, in respect of the said Verdict, Decerns and Adjudges the said Jean Maxwell to be carried back from the Bar to the Tolbooth of Kirkcudbright, and to be imprisoned therein for the space of One Whole Year, without Bail or Mainprize; and Once in every Quarter of the said year, to stand openly upon a Market day in the Jugs or Pillory, at the Market Cross of the Burgh of Kirkcudbright, for the space of one Hour, &c.

(Signed) ALEXR. GORDON

There is much statistical data that sheds light on women's criminal behaviour, such as prison reports, court statistics, and so on. Such data was commonly reported in the press, as illustrated below. The statistics indicate the incidence of different types of crime, as well as gendered patterns of crime, and it provides a breakdown of the crimes tried in different courts: the High Court of Justiciary was the place in which serious crimes, such as murder and assault, were tried, whereas lesser offences were tried in the sheriff court, or local police and magistrates' courts.

### 1.7 *The Scotsman*, 13 August 1836

#### CRIME IN SCOTLAND

We have a newly published Return before us, which presents a view of the state of crime in Scotland for the year 1835. We select a few facts.

| | | Males | Females |
|---|---|---|---|
| Persons committed for trial | CHARGES | 2226 | 612 |
| Murder, | | 15 | 5 |
| Culpable homicide | | 25 | 2 |
| Child murder | | 1 | 6 |
| Concealment of pregnancy | | – | 8 |
| Robbery | | 23 | 13 |

| | Males | Females |
|---|---|---|
| Persons committed for trial | 2226 | 612 |

CHARGES

| | | |
|---|---|---|
| Robbery and assault | 6 | – |
| Rape | 17 | – |
| Wilful fire-raising | 12 | – |
| Forgery | 42 | 10 |
| Issuing base coin | 25 | 16 |
| Horse, cattle, and sheep-stealing | 11 | 2 |
| Theft | 793 | 376 |
| Theft by housebreaking | 193 | 33 |
| Reset of theft | 38 | 38 |
| Fraud and wilful imposition | 52 | 9 |
| Assault | 700 | 46 |
| Deforcement of public officers | 7 | 1 |
| Mobbing and rioting | 50 | 2 |
| Breach of peace | 55 | 9 |
| Malicious mischief | 28 | 5 |
| Exploiting infants | – | 16 |
| Killing game by night | 36 | – |
| The crimes are classed under 61 heads in the Return: the above are the most important – | | |
| Liberated without trial | 485 | 123 |
| Tried by the Court of Justiciary | 149 | 34 |
| --------------- Circuit Court | 344 | 76 |
| --------------- Sheriff, with a jury | 372 | 146 |
| --------------- Sheriff, without a jury | 586 | 133 |
| --------------- Burgh magistrates | 186 | 85 |
| --------------- Justices or other Court | 39 | 5 |
| Total number tried | 1677 | 479 |
| Convicted | 1475 | 427 |
| Outlawed | 15 | 1 |
| Acquitted | 185 | 49 |
| Found to be insane | 4 | 1 |
| Sentenced to death (all for murder) | 5 | 1 |
| Executed | 4 | 1 |
| Sentence commuted | 1 | – |
| Transportation for life | 21 | 3 |
| --------------- 14 years | 57 | 7 |
| --------------- 7 years | 162 | 42 |
| Imprisonment 3 months or less | 787 | 241 |
| --------------- 3 to 6 months | 216 | 85 |
| --------------- 6 to 12 months | 129 | 31 |
| --------------- above one year | 28 | 9 |
| Fined | 64 | 2 |
| Under caution to keep the peace | 6 | – |

Up until the mid-nineteenth century, one of the punishments for serious or persistent offenders was transportation to Van Diemen's Land [Tasmania] or New South Wales. The typical female transportee had been convicted of theft or robbery, and had previous convictions. Such convicts could be very young, for example, sixteen-year-old Christian Macdougall was sentenced to seven years' transportation for stealing a silver watch, because she was a thief by 'habite and repute'.[4] The extract below comes from the precognition for the trial of Mary Bentley, and gives her statement of events. Bentley was sentenced to transportation along with two others accused of robbery, Thomas Wilson and Mary McVicar. The case involved an assault and robbery committed in Dalkeith in 1836. The victim of the robbery, James Taylor, had been drinking but insisted that he was not drunk. The accused denied the crime and the two women also said that they had left James Taylor in the street because he had 'used liberties' with them. Taylor declared in his statement that Bentley had urged Wilson to murder him, and it appears that this accusation of violence was what led to Bentley's sentence of fourteen years' transportation; McVicar was sentenced to seven years' transportation and Wilson to transportation for life. It was this aspect of Bentley's behaviour that was focused on in *The Scotsman* (22 February 1837) which reported that, in the course of the assault on Taylor, 'Bentley exclaimed, "Kill him where he lies"; and proceeded with a pair of scissors to cut away Taylor's pockets'. The extract constitutes the Pannel statement for Bentley.

### 1.8  Precognition Thomas Wilson, Mary Bentley and Mary McVicar [NAS, AD14/37/393]

Edinburgh 5 December, 1836, in presence of George Tait esq. Sheriff Substitute of Edinburgh shire.

Mary Bentley at present in custody who being examined declared that she is twenty two years of age and she was born in Linlithgow and she resides in Dalkeith with her mother Mrs Helen Nimmo or Bentley a widow – Declared that on Saturday night the 3d current about ten O clock she fell in with the prisoner Thomas Wilson in Amos Close and he was then in conversation with a man whose name she does not know – That the man said he would give Wilson a dram and Wilson asked her to go with him and they all three went to the public house of one Simpson in the Back street in which they had a gill and a bottle of small beer for which the man paid – That they were not half an hour in that house and in coming out they met the prisoner Mary McVicar at the door – That the man asked them to go to Hares public house with him – That Wilson refused to go and said he had shown the man Hares door before and that the man would not go in – That the man said he would go with McVicar and the declarant and gave Wilson sixpence to go away and leave them by themselves – That Wilson went away and McVicar and the declarant went with the man to show him Hares door but he began to use liberties with them and they left him before going half way and loitered about the street for about half an hour and proceeded to the house of Wilson's father and they saw Wilson at the

head of the close in which his father lives, and he went to his fathers house with them – That they did not remain above a few minutes and McVicar and she came away by themselves and went to the house of the declarants mother and were there informed by a little girl named McComb that Angus McLeod Sheriff Officer was in search of them – That McVicar and she then went down the town and on seeing the officers coming McVicar and she concealed themselves in an entry as they were afraid of being ill used, and were there apprehended – Interrogated declared that she was not in Peter Allans house that night or on the Sunday morning – That when they went to the home of Wilsons father they saw there Peter Porteous a labourer who followed them out of the house and he gave them a half mulchkin of whisky – That it was not untill McVicar and she were in Gaol that she heard that Wilson had been apprehended – That the man had three bundles one of which he dropt several times when on their way to Hares house and the declarant always picked it up and gave it to him – That she did not knock or throw that man down, or take any money from him and does not know of McVicar or Wilson having done so – She now sees a knife to which a label is attached signed as relative hereto – Declares that she saw it in Wilson's possession after McVicar and she had left the man – That he said he had found it that evening opposite the Gaol – That she did not see him have the knife till after she had left the man – That when Wilson showed her the knife McVicar was present – That she does not know of McVicar having seen the knife before she saw it – That Wilson McVicar and she were sober but the man was much the worse of drink – That she had a shilling and three pence in her possession when she was apprehended – That she did not see Wilson have any money, and all this she declared to be truth and declared that she cannot write.
Signed: G Tait, Archd Scott, R I Mozey, A McLeod

When Bentley arrived in Van Diemen's Land, she stated her offence as highway robbery, and said 'she had been on the town for twelve months'.[5] After a period of servitude, however, Bentley was able to leave Van Diemen's Land and to enjoy a long life free from further contact with the law. As Lucy Frost's research has shown, Bentley married an English convict from Liverpool, William Peeler, while still serving her sentence. Following Peeler being granted freedom and Bentley being granted a conditional pardon, they left for New South Wales in 1848, by this time with four children. In 1851 they moved to the goldfield diggings in Launceston Gully, and William and two of his sons made a living as miners. Regarded at twenty-two as an incorrigible offender by the Procurator Fiscal, Mary's life story stands as a refutation of this view; she lived to be eighty-two.

The following extracts concern a case of kidnapping [plagium]. Prosecutions for this crime seem to have been rare though there were reports of parentless children being taken and shipped off to places such as North America and the West Indies as indentured servants. The case below refers to the kidnapping of Mary Morrison who, at two years and ten months, was lured away from her play area by the promise of sweets. Her parents were John Morrison, a pattern drawer,

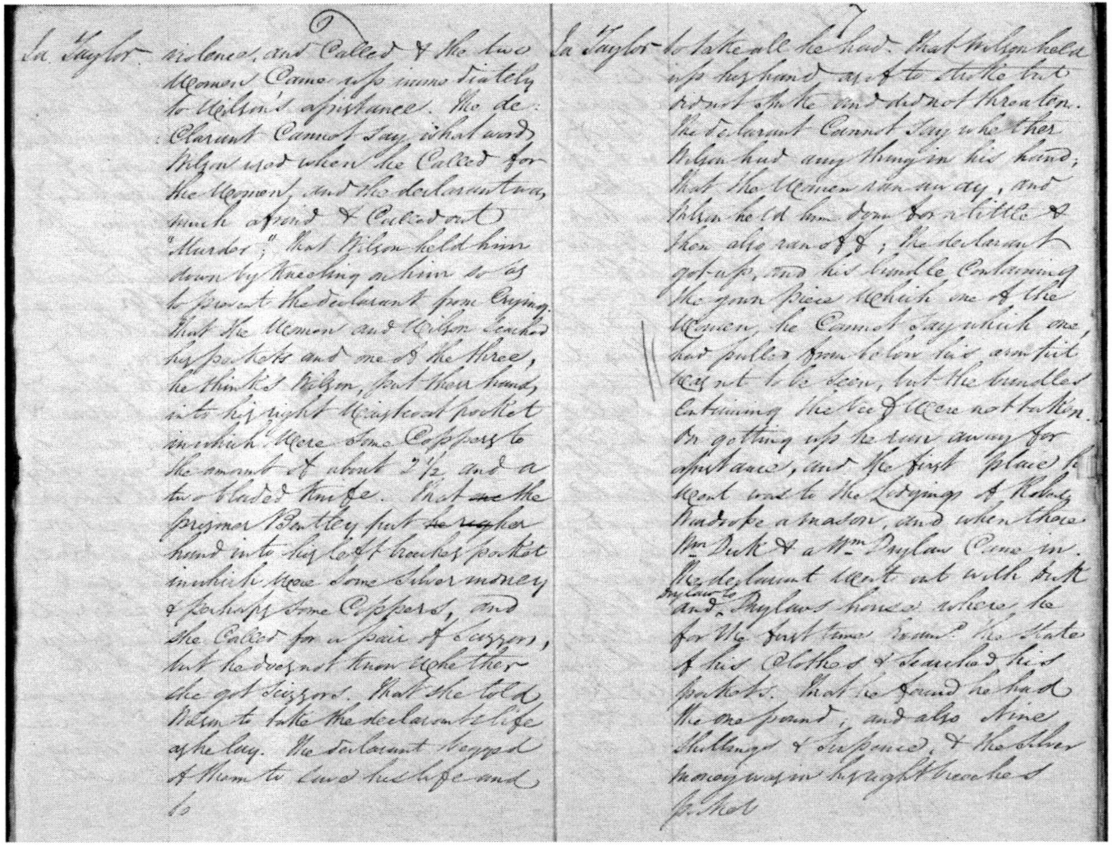

**Figure 5.1** Precognition against Thomas Wilson, Mary McVicar, Mary Bentley for the crime of robbery, 1837. Courtesy of the National Archives of Scotland.

and Elizabeth Morrison (née Craig), of Glasgow. The first extract is Elizabeth's statement. The second extract comes from the Declarant, Margaret Park. Park had previous theft convictions and admitted plagium.

> 1.9  Glasgow Autumn Circuit 1848. Precognition relative to a charge of
> plagium and theft against Margaret Park, previously convicted of theft.
> Glasgow, 20 July 1848 [NAS, AD14/48/116]

Elizabeth Craig or Morrison says I am 41 years of age, Wife of John Morrison, Pattern Weaver, and I reside with him in Love Loan in or near Glasgow. My daughter, Mary Morrison was [born] on 31 August 1845, so that on Friday the 7th July 1848 she was aged two years and ten months or thereby. My husband's house is situated up one stairs & about 1 o'clock p.m. of said Friday I let Mary out of my house to play about the doors as usual. I looked over my window about ten minutes afterwards to try if I could see Mary but then I continued to do so for sometime and afterwards went out and enquired among the children in the neighbourhood I could not find her or get any trace of her. I went to the central police office about ¼ to 3 p.m. and informed of Mary being missing and as there was still no trace of her information as to her disappearance was lodged at the various police offices in or near Glasgow, and I got no trace of her till the following Sunday evening being the 9th July when the witness William Fotheringham brought her to my house about 7 o'clock accompanied by my son George Morrison aged 15. When she was so brought home I found the articles after mentioned were missing which she had on her person when I let her out of my house on the aforesaid Friday viz.=
A checked frock
A printed pinafore
A pair of shoes and
A pair of stockings
Mary cannot speak very plain but when she was so brought home she spoke in a manner which was quite intelligible to me and said that a 'Wife' had taken her away and given her 'goodies' and taken of her Frock, Pinafore, Shoes and Stockings from her and put them into a basket, but she did not and could not tell me where the Wife has taken her to, or how the Woman had disposed of the articles. When Mary was brought home on the aforesaid Sunday evening I was told that the woman was in custody in the Calton Police office charged with having carried Mary off and stolen her shoes and apparel and I went to the Police Office the next day and saw the prisoner Margaret Park in custody but I did not hear her say anything as to the charge against her.

Declaration of Margaret Park at Glasgow, 11 July 1848. In presence of Henry Glassford Bell Esquire Advocate Sheriff Substitute of Lanarkshire [NAS. JC26/1848/340]

Appeared Margaret Park who being judiciously admonished and examined declares that she is a native of Londonderry, Ireland – thirty one years of age, unmarried. A

Weaver and she resides in Bell Street of Calton in or near Glasgow. Declares and Admits the charge stated against her of having on Friday last the seventh current stolen and carried off in or near George Square Glasgow a child, and with having the same day stolen and carried off from the person of said child in Ann Street of Port Dundas a pair of shoes and a pair of stockings; – as also from the said child in or near North Street of Anderston the same day a checked frock – that the stockings dropped from the Declarant so that she lost them, but she the same day sold the shoes in the shop of Smith a broker in Ann Street aforesaid for sixpence, and she sold the frock the same day in the shop of Kennedy a brokers in North Street of Anderston for four pence, and the Declarant —— and identifies said shoes and frock, and labels attached thereto, are do equelled and subscribed as relative thereto. – Declares that the Declarant took said child home to her own lodgings in the house of William Kerby a Weaver in Bell Street aforesaid, and kept it there till Sunday last the ninth current when a man and woman said to be friends of the child came and took it away. And all this she declares to be truth and that she cannot write.

Theft was the offence of which women were most commonly accused and convicted, though the crime statistics quoted in 1.7 above imply that it was rare for women to be involved in stealing livestock. Below is an example of a woman being prosecuted for sheep stealing in South Uist. As with many women's crimes, poverty was likely to have been the driving factor. The extract quotes the statement of Janet Steel, an illiterate Gaelic speaker, who, desperate for food, stole a lamb and wedder (wether, castrated ram) with her sister, Marion. Imprisoned while they awaited trial, Janet's statement was given orally in Gaelic and then translated and recorded by Alexander McLeod, Inspector of Police. Steel initially denied the theft but later admitted it.

### 1.10 Precognition relating to Janet Steel, Marion or Sarah MacLellan for the crime of sheep stealing, South Uist, 1849 [NAS, AD14/49/220]

Declaration of Janet McLeod or Steel, and Marion or Sarah McLeod or MacLellan of Lochmaddy the 23rd day of June 1849 years in presence of Charles Shaw Esq. sheriff substitute of the Long Island District of the County of Inverness.

. . . Sometime after sunset my said sister and I went to the hill that it is to the south of our house for the sole purpose of stealing sheep – I left in my house two inferior codfish and three cod heads, two small fish, and as much meal as would make two cakes of bread – my said sister and I went direct to the cot in which Alexander Campbell residing at Bunalicky in said Island parish and county keeps his lambs – when we came to the said cot I caught a lamb which I carried away, my sister did not assist me to catch it – on our way home, and when we were nearly a mile from my house I observed a wedder which as being on the farm of John MacLellan Tacksman of Drimore in said Island parish and county I presumed to be his property – the wedder was lying in a ditch, its leg broken, but it was alive – on observing this wedder I have the said lamb which I was carrying to my said sisters, and I caught the said wedder put it on my back and carried it to my own house – my said sister carried the said lamb upon her back, and also brought it to my house – we did not see any person while we were away – on our arrival at my house my husband was in bed and he got up and slaughtered the said wedder and lamb – my said husband gave my said sister a quarter of the wedder and two quarters of the lamb and some of the entrails – immediately after the said wedder and lamb had been slaughtered I took the meat off the heads of both carcasses and boiled them, and we ate them immediately – I took the wool off the shins next forenoon and folded it up in a blanket and tied it with —— – we nearly ate all of the flesh that day except what my sister got –

It was rare for women to be tried for murder, and when such cases arose they tended to excite much popular interest. As well as being reported in the newspapers, such cases were often the subject of broadsides. Probably the most publicised trial of a woman for murder in nineteenth-century Scotland was that of Madeleine Smith‡ (1835–1928), a young, middle-class woman accused of poisoning her lover, Emile L'Angelier. Smith was acquitted with a not proven verdict, a verdict received with much public sympathy. Among the most sensational aspects of her trial was the use of her love letters to L'Angelier as evidence of Smith's character, with their implications of an active sexual relationship. Numerous accounts of this case have been published, both popular and academic. Readers are referred in particular to Eleanor Gordon and Gwyneth Nair, *Murder and Morality in Victorian Britain* (2009). Gordon and Nair use Smith's letters, along with a range of other sources, to depict the lives of middle-class girls and women at the time, and to question how transgressive her behaviour was. They argue that many accounts of the case reveal more about prevailing discourses of sexual morality than they do of the actualities of Smith's life and times, and that an understanding of the case has been distorted, rather than clarified, by persistent stereotyping of the role of women in Victorian society.

At the time of Smith's trial in 1857, a murder conviction was likely to elicit the death penalty, and it seems likely that public sympathy for Smith was conditioned by knowledge of this. If a woman had children, sentencing her to death was a particularly difficult decision, and courts needed to be seen as being as lenient as possible within the rule of the law. The case cited below is that of Mary Reid or Timney, the last woman to be publicly executed in Scotland. Attempts to have her sentence commuted were unsuccessful and, though the public was outraged at the offence committed, sympathy for the young mother grew as her execution date approached.

1.11 *Dumfries and Galloway Standard*, 30 April 1862 [Dumfries Archive Centre, GGD422]

The Report of the execution of Mary Reid, or Timney, in public, at Dumfries on Tuesday the 29th April 1862.

The nature and circumstances of the crime for which Mary Reid or Timney suffered the last sentence of the law yesterday morning in Dumfries are so fresh in the memory of our readers that we do not need to do more than refer to them in the briefest terms. The deed for which she was condemned and executed was of a truly horrible description. Her neighbour, Ann Hannah, was found, on the 13th January, lying weltering in her blood on the floor of the little farmhouse at Carsphad, in the lone district of Glenkens, under circumstances which, though purely circumstantial, pointed out Mary Timney as the perpetrator of the deed.

No one was present save the two women when the destructive outrage was committed; and no one is able to describe all that passed ere the fatal blows were struck which deprived the unfortunate Ann Hannah of life.

She was dreadfully beaten on the head and otherwise wounded; and died unable to name her assailant; breathing twice only, 'Oh dear!' before she expired. Strange to say, the person who first discovered the deceased in this condition had been sent for by the convict Timney, to come and bake for her that day; and but for this circumstance, the crime would probably not have been discovered till the evening, when the brothers of the deceased, who lived with her, came from their work, and by that time all the silent evidences of the convict's guilt might have been destroyed. This in itself favours the idea that the murder was not premeditated or deliberately intended, but committed in a paroxysm of fury. Mary Timney on being apprehended denied all knowledge of the crime; but her blood stained garments, and a mallet also stained with blood, found hidden in her house, supplied powerful testimony of her guilt. She was tried at the late circuit court in Dumfries on a charge or having murdered Ann Hannah, was found guilty, and sentenced to death, without the hope of mercy, by presiding judge, Lord Deas.

Strenuous exertions were made with a view to getting the capital sentence commuted; it is superfluous to repeat that these were unavailing.

. . .

However it may be accounted for, we simply state a fact which all the prison officials would readily substantiate, that the woman who was depicted on the day of the trial as a savage and implacable monster, without a single redeeming feature in her characters or her crime, exhibited during the latter days of her imprisonment, when not visited by the thoughts of her approaching doom, a subduedness of disposition allied to that of those who in country districts are called 'innocents', because they are harmlessly idiotical. On Wednesday the prisoner, as we have previously stated, was visited by her husband and her youngest child save one, and by her mother and sister. Her husband had a parting interview with her on Monday; and her farewell words to him were to 'Remember the weans', and see that they were brought up well . . .

. . . At twenty minutes past eight o'clock, the culprit was brought out under the superintendence of Mr Stewart, governor of the prison, and accompanied by Mr Cowans, the chaplain, whose kind administrations followed her even to the drop. On being brought out, the prisoner seemed in a most frantic and distracted state. The crushing agony of the last three weeks seemed to have had a great effect on both mind and body.

Her countenance had lost all the firmness, stolidity, or stupidity which it wore during the trial; and was pale, vacant and distorted with terror: fear of some great and incomprehensible danger was impressed in every lineament, and she seemed to have grown twenty years older since the day of her trial. When she reached the open air, she gazed round her, and looked up to the blue sky and the objects around with a kind of idiotic, maniacal, or hysterical stare. It was remarked in our hearing that she had become insane, and had it not been for the words she uttered in her great distress, it would have been difficult to convince us that the 'lamp of reason had not wavered and gone out'. She screamed aloud, in tones that brought a shudder to the hearts of those who heard her. 'Oh, no, no! Oh no!' 'Oh! My four weans. Oh! My four weans.'

She was just beyond the prison wall on to the platform when a packet, in apparently great haste was delivered to the governor of the prison. The eyes of those who witnessed its delivery were riveted upon Mr Stewart, and recollections of reprieves to prisoners when on the scaffold flashed like electricity through the minds of everyone. With a disdainful toss the papers were cast aside, and it appears it was merely a request from some imprudently enterprising newsagent in London for news of the execution in time for the evening papers.

While the convict was being brought forward to the steps leading on to the drop, she caught sight of the gentlemen in the courtyard of the prison, and looked toward them with an imploring look, crying out, 'Oh! My four weans!' Uttering this cry in accents which were piteous and heart rending in the extreme, she was assisted on to the drop. On her appearing there, the state of excited suspense in which the crowd had been held was broken by wailing ejaculations of pity and commiserations, which rose like a great sigh in the quiet morning air. She continued in plaintive, beseeching accents to cry 'Oh! No!' 'Oh! My four weans!' and asked to get standing a little, while the hangman was busy about his preparations. She was supported while Calcraft with considerable dexterity, and great coolness and deliberation, took off her mutch or cap, drew the white cap over her face, adjusted the noose upon her neck, fastened the rope to the cross-beam, and at twenty minutes past eight o'clock drew the bolt. The unfortunate woman dropped about fifteen inches. Death to all appearances was painless and easy, and the executioner, who must be allowed to be a good judge in such matters, said she died instantly. She only gave one desperate convulsive struggle after the drop fell, and the twitchings of the fingers apparent for some time after life was extinct were supposed to arise solely from nervous or muscular action.

## Section 2: Women in prison

In the early nineteenth century the prison population in Scotland was small, the sexes were mixed together in jails, and the physical conditions were poor.[6] Because serious crimes were penalised by execution, banishment or transportation, many prison inmates had actually only been convicted of petty offences or had been imprisoned as debtors. In the course of the nineteenth century, attitudes towards penalties for crimes changed and, overall, penalties tended to become more lenient but a transformation of prison regimes resulted in harsher treatment. Confinement was to become more common as a form of punishment and reform through both imprisonment and the growth of other non-penal, but penitentiary, institutions, as discussed in Section 4 below. As in England, there was a prison reform movement and, when reorganisation of the prison system came, it adopted the Benthamite approach favoured by reformers. The new regime placed prisoners in separate cells, and often in solitary confinement, and during their long hours of labour, prisoners were under constant surveillance. By the century's end, there had been a great increase in new statutory offences, and thus the net of incarceration was widened.

Many more men than women were imprisoned, and often those who were incarcerated were persistent petty offenders without the wherewithal to pay fines, rather than the perpetrators of serious crimes. Poverty was thus an important factor in women's imprisonment. It is very difficult to find testimony of women as prison inmates, the only evident exception being women imprisoned on account of their political activity, such as militant suffragettes Ethel Moorhead‡ (1869–1955) and Arabella Scott, whose accounts of forcible feeding are described by Leah Leneman in *Martyrs in Our Midst*.[7] Included in Chapter 7 on Protest and Politics is Lila Clunas's‡ (1876–1968) account of her time in Holloway after being charged with criminal damage. There are, however, many sources that provide insight into prison regimes for women, such as prison reports, governors' journals, police records, and newspaper coverage of prison reports and debates about policy. The writings of the prison reform movement are another source of information, though these appear to reveal little that was written by women. Middle-class women, including religious communities of women, were participants in this movement, often acting as prison visitors; an account by Mary White in *Scottish Women's Temperance News* outlined such work carried out over twenty years.[8]

Quoted below is an article, from the *Inverness Journal*, which reports both the imprisonment of Katherine Mackenzie for concealment of pregnancy and her lawyer's description of conditions in the local gaol.

### 2.1 *Inverness Journal*, 1 October 1824

Katherine Mackenzie, accused of concealment of pregnancy, pleaded guilty. Her Counsel, the Hon. Leslie Melville, in mitigation of punishment, stated that the prisoner had suffered six months imprisonment in the gaol of Tain previous to trial. That three days after her delivery, she was put into an apartment there with bare stone walls, in which she was exposed to the inclemency of the weather, there being a hole for a window, and no glass; there had been a shutter, but it was broken previous to her confinement. The floor is of clay. There being neither bedstead nor bedding, bench nor chair. He spoke from his own knowledge, having inspected the gaol . . . In addressing the prisoner, he stated, that the sense of shame had no influence in leading her to the commission of her crime, as he observed from her declaration that she had been leading a very improper life; he exhorted her to amendment, and sentenced her to six months imprisonment in the gaol of Inverness, as he said that he would not send her back to Tain, and he found that the gaol of Dingwall was in no better condition – her maintenance to be of course defrayed by the County of Ross.

The English prison reformer, Elizabeth Fry, paid close attention to the condition of Scottish prisons. She believed in separating the sexes within prisons and felt that female prisoners should receive visits from men only in the company of a female officer, and she advocated the establishment of ladies' committees for prisons. The memoir of her life published by her daughters contains an account of a meeting in Aberdeen in 1838.

2.2  Katherine Fry and Rachel Elizabeth Cresswell (eds), *Memoir of the Life of Elizabeth Fry* (London, 1848) (247–8)

After a morning engagement, we were occupied with the principal officers of the gaol who visited us, desiring to have some private conversation with Elizabeth Fry. Then came on the large meeting of ladies; nearly two hundred assembled. She had only meant to receive them in our drawing room, but they flocked in to such a degree, that a large assembly-room in our Hotel was got ready on the spur of the moment. There was much reading from reports, & c., as well as valuable communication from Elizabeth Fry, to this interesting assembly. Her excellent tact and remarkable facility on these occasions, are admirable. A society was formed for the prisons of Aberdeen and its vicinity. The Countess of Errol is Patroness; the Lady of the Provost, President; very respectable persons take the other functions. The Provost, Sheriff, and many other gentlemen were in attendance, but, to their evident disappointment, were most politely dismissed by our dear friend, who feels it important, as a woman, not to overstep the line which restricts her public addresses to those of her own sex, excepting only in the exercise of the spiritual gift of the Ministry. Between the formation of the association, and proceeding to select the various officers, Elizabeth Fry read a psalm, spoke very nicely upon it to the ladies, and was then engaged in prayer. This meeting satisfactorily over, we went, accompanied by a large party of gentlemen, magistrates, and others, and many ladies also, to visit the Bridewell. A thorough inspection was made, indeed this visit employed an hour and a-half; all met afterwards in the Committee-room, to hear what Elizabeth Fry had to remark upon the state of this large and important establishment; she made an excellent address.

As the statistics for 1835, quoted above in extract 1.7, suggest, most women who were imprisoned had not committed serious offences, and the majority received short sentences. While prostitution itself was not a crime, some of the associated activities, such as soliciting and causing a nuisance, were. By the 1840s, there were growing concerns about the number of prisoners who were prostitutes, as this extract from *The Scotsman* shows.

The article was an abridged version of the report of the governor of the Edinburgh jail and bridewell, Mr Hill.

### EDINBURGH PRISON

. . . The number of prostitutes sent to this prison is very great. Of 240 female prisoners lately in confinement at one time the governor believes that 200 were prostitutes. The governor attributes the great number of this class of prisoners in part to the difficulty which females have in getting employment in Edinburgh, owing to the want of manufactures. He states that if a servant once loses her situation with an injured character she has scarcely any other resource than prostitution. The House of Refuge and Shelter meet the difficulty to some extent, but a much larger provision appears to be necessary.

In 1860, the report of the Prison Board of Aberdeenshire on the Repression of Prostitution, written by the Convenor, Alex Thomson of Banchory, voiced similar concerns. The report attacked 'female licentiousness', and contained an appendix on the numbers of female prisoners engaged in prostitution.

2.4 *Report by a Committee of the Prison Board of Aberdeenshire on the Repression of Prostitution* (Aberdeen, 1860), [Edinburgh University Library, Centre for Research Collections, P. 206/14] (23)

*Memorandum respecting Females committed to the Prison of Aberdeen, during the years* 1856, 1857 and 1858.

| | |
|---|---|
| 1856, – Total commitments | 276 |
| Of these were recommitments within the year, | 55 |
| Individuals committed, | 221 |
| Of whom known prostitutes, | 92 |
| Other classes, | 129 |
| 1857, – Total commitments | 342 |
| Of these were recommitments within the year, | 84 |
| Individuals committed, | 258 |
| Of whom known prostitutes, | 91 |
| Other classes, | 167 |
| 1858, – Total commitments | 354 |
| Of these were recommitments within the year, | 97 |
| Individuals committed, | 257 |
| Of whom known prostitutes, | 94 |
| Other classes, | 163 |

There can be no doubt that a good many of the "other classes" were prostitutes, but as they were following some occupation, they were not entered in the prison books as prostitutes, but as "factory workers," "sempstresses," &c. as the case might be.

(Signed) AL. W. CHALMERS

From the late 1830s or early 1840s women appear to have been active in prison reform and welfare; some further examples are cited in Chapter 5 on religion. Ladies' committees were typically motivated by religious convictions and, similarly, prison visiting formed part of the social and welfare work of some religious communities of women (Roman Catholic sisters and nuns). The Ursulines of Jesus in Perth and the Franciscan Sisters of the Immaculate Conception in Glasgow were active in the 'prison mission', and the extracts below refer to the work of the Ursulines at the General Prison of Perth which housed male and female prisoners. In an age when hostility towards Roman Catholicism was common, securing official support for Catholic religious personnel to visit Catholic prisoners, hear confessions and offer spiritual instruction, was often difficult, as the second extract suggests.

### 2.5 Letter from Sr M. Angela to Reverend John Strain, 5 June 1865 [Scottish Catholic Archives, Edinburgh. ED/3/177/2]

My first visit Sunday at the prison, which I was dreading so much is passed, and very satisfactorily, and next Sunday I shall be quite up to the mark. Sister Mary and Sister —— went for the first time to visit the sick and then joined me in the classroom. Today in leaving the penitentiary we all agreed in thinking that our time was far too short, and wished we had half as long again to give to our poor prisoners.

### 2.6 Statement of Reverend John Strain, c.1867 [Scottish Catholic Archives, Edinburgh, DD/1/34/1]

The General Prison of Perth has been established to receive convicts who have been sentenced to long periods of imprisonment, during which they may have time and opportunity to be instructed and reformed before they may again mix with society. Convicts are sent to it from all parts of Scotland, male convicts to pass the first year of their sentences before being transferred to Millbank, and female convicts to pass the whole of their time. In 1862, the Secretary of State, under whom the Prison is governed, ordered a Catholic chaplain to be appointed for the benefit of the Catholic prisoners. The Rev. G. Rigg, the Catholic clergyman at Perth, was appointed and is succeeded now by Rev. Dr MacPherson, at present the senior clergymen at Perth. The Chaplains soon perceived that the assistance of Religious Sisters, who might daily visit the Prison, would be of the greatest benefit for the instruction of the female convicts, of whom there is an average of 120, constantly in Prison. He therefore proposed to the Secretary of State, to admit the member of a religious community to discharge this duty. The proposal was assented to by the Government, and on 1st June 1865, six nuns from St Margaret's Convent, Edinburgh, under a Lady Superioress (Miss Langdale), proceeded to Perth to undertake it. A suitable residence, formerly a Scottish Episcopal seminary was, at considerable expense, provided by the Bishop for them, and is now their home, under the name St. Joseph's Convent. The convent was furnished by themselves, and £250 a-year, the lowest at which the establishment could be carried on, was guaranteed to them for two years, that a fair trial might be made of so interesting and deserving a project. The trial has been made, and it has proved eminently successful, so far as the good done to prisoners is concerned. This is acknowledged by all who have the means to judging it. But there is now the prospect of the withdrawal of the Nuns, and a stop being put to the good work at the end of the two years, unless further support be obtained for it.

### Section 3: Discourses of female immorality

There were certain types of behaviours among women that tended to excite public censure, though such behaviours did not necessarily constitute criminal acts in themselves. Sometimes, however, they were associated with behaviours that crossed the boundaries into illegality. Women who had incurred moral censure and those who had committed certain types of crime might find themselves institutionalised together. Perhaps what was most important here was the dominant idea of what was appropriately feminine, with the key markers being sexual propriety, sobriety, and the absence of physical aggression. The section below illustrates various representations of female behaviours that transgressed conventional mores and, again, this is a sphere wherein it is difficult to locate the female voice either commenting on other women's behaviour or as direct testimony of their experiences. While male voices dominated public discourses about female behaviour and morality, the fact that many middle- and upper-class women were involved in the running of institutions and reformatories, and gave energetic support to the temperance movement for example, suggests that they shared the views of their menfolk.

Not all commentary on female behaviour was pious and moralistic. Popular broadsides, whether sensationalist or satirical, often provided commentary on gendered identities, including accounts of women criminals, cross-dressers, uppity servants, and so on. Women fighting was a topic of ribaldry as illustrated in the satirical broadside below. Physical fights and brawling among women would not have been uncommon, resulting sometimes in court appearances for breaches of the peace. The broadside depicts the altercation in Aberdeen as an amusing public spectacle; it is available online in the NLS 'Word on the Street' collection, at http://digital.nls.uk/broadsides/

### 3.1 Milling among the Fair Sex, 1825 [NLS. Shelfmark LC.1268]

A Full and Particular Account of that Gallant and most Extraordinary BATTLE, that was Fought on Thursday last, 30th day of June, 1825, in the Market Place of Aberdeen, between a Soldier's Wife, and a Dandy young Fish Wife, at that place.

On Thursday last a scene, very rarely witnessed here, although among the Billingate Ladies in the south, it is nothing uncommon, accured in the Fish market in this Town. It was not premeditated, and therefore there was no betting on either side though there might be several of the fancy present.

A Soldier's wife having, as is often the case, accasion to go to the market to lay out her scanty pittance in the most beneficial and economical manner, by some means or other, fell into a dispute with a young aspiring dandy Fish wife, to whom she applied an epithet, which it may be as well not here to repeat; suffice it to say, that it had the effect of rousing all the Amazonian courage in the blood of her antagonist. The insulted dame considered it her imperative duty to vindicate her character and respectability, and instantly rushed on her traducer, and gave her such a blow on the breast, that sent her a reeling among the creels of the fish women. The Soldier's wife, loth to be behind, and also considering the whole British army to be grossly insulted in her person, gave the retort uncourteous, when instantly a ring was formed by the females in the market, and a regular set to commenced.

The dreadful conflict now commenced in grand stile, and if they could not boast of using so much science as was lately displayed in the neighbourhood, by Robinson and Crosbie, they certainly shewed they were real game, and produced, at least, as much claret. The Battle continued a considerable time, neither of the combatants seeming inclined to give up; but the Soldier's wife, who seemed to have most wind, as well as better science, snatching up a Native from her opponent's creel, by a dexterious manoeuvre, thrust it, tail foremost, down her rivals throat. This, for the fish woman, was a complete finisher; she fell in a moment, and instantly grew black in the face; and, if she had not been relieved by some of the bystanders on the instant, she must have been choked.

Concern about 'fallen women' and the likelihood of their resorting to prostitution led to the establishment of Magdalene Asylums in Edinburgh and Glasgow in the late eighteenth and early nineteenth centuries, as illustrated in Section 4 below. Rapid urbanisation in the early decades of the nineteenth century generated significant public debate about the increase in prostitution. The visibility of prostitutes soliciting for customers in particular areas of the main cities added to the sense of panic. Discourses on prostitution consisted of a mixture of the economic, moral, legal, and salacious. In the earlier part of the century commentators seemed more sympathetic to the economic circumstances driving women into prostitution but this faded as the century progressed and attitudes about femininity and respectability hardened. As with many areas of working-class women's experience, it is perhaps impossible to find sources which give direct expression to women's perspectives, and the extracts below are from male commentators.

3.2 William Tait, Surgeon, *Magdalenism. An Inquiry into the Extent, Causes, and Consequences of Prostitution in Edinburgh* (Edinburgh: P. Rickard, South Bridge, 1840) (107—8, 110, 114)

William Tait was House Surgeon to the Edinburgh Lock Hospital, and had previously been Surgeon to the Midwifery Dispensary at High School Yards,

Edinburgh. Tait recognised the economic circumstances that led to prostitution, and here discusses the problem of low wages.

One causal factor was 'Inadequate remuneration for needle and other kinds of work in which females are employed':

> In no city in Europe, perhaps, is there less employment for the female part of the population than in Edinburgh. In most of the large towns in Scotland there are manufactories of various descriptions where females are employed; but in the capital scarcely anything of that kind exists. It is true, that within the last few years a silk manufactory has been established to the west of the city; but as yet the benefit which has accrued from it to the females of this place, is too small to be observed. The whole of the young women, with the exception of those who are bred for house-servants, are consequently trained up as sewers, dress-makers, milliners, bonnet-makers, stay-makers, colourers, book-stitchers, shoe-binders, hat-binders, &c. &c. The market for the employment of these different classes is thus completely overstocked, and the price of labour reduced to the lowest rate.
>
> The weekly sum which girls can realize in the ordinary kinds of needlework, has already been alluded to when speaking of the love of dress as a cause of prostitution. The trifling sum of 6s. a-week is there mentioned as being about the income of the great majority of sewing girls . . .
>
> . . . If inadequate remuneration be a cause of prostitution – and there can be no doubt of the fact – then prostitution is an evil of such a nature that its effects must be experienced by all classes; and every penny or shilling which is imagined to be saved from the pocket of the poor seamstress or dress-maker, may be paving the way for the ruin of some member of the family of the person whose rigid economy permitted such an action. Probably the merchants are also in some instances the cause of this undue reduction in the price of needlework. It is well known amongst sewers themselves, that higher prices are allowed for the same kind of seam in some shops than in another; yet both sell the articles at the same price, obviously showing that the difference must be pocketed by the merchant. How can a woman maintain herself when she is only allowed 5d. or 6d. for sewing a man's shirt? Every person, whether merchant or purchaser, who is accessary to the bringing down of labour to such a contemptible degree, is at the same time giving his countenance to the encouragement of vice.

Over twenty years later, James Bertram publicised his views on prostitution. Bertram, a journalist and editor of the *North Briton*, the first penny paper in Edinburgh, wrote under many pseudonyms, and was author, among other things, of erotic books. While not dismissing economic circumstances as contributing to prostitution, his attitude to women practising the trade appears both harsher and more ambiguous than that of Tait. Bertram's pamphlet opened with a description of court proceedings where women were being charged with soliciting, and went on to argue that prostitution in Edinburgh had increased, and become more brazen. He also condemned the Forbes Mackenzie Act (1853) (an act applying to Scotland for regulation of public houses) which he saw as having contributed to the problem, as brothels were all able to operate as shebeens. Bertram contended that there were women bred and apprenticed to the trade, and he condemned the desire for clothes and finery. His preferred solutions were more Magdalene Asylums, and better regulation on the Parisian model.

> ### 3.3 Editor of the *North Briton, The Whole Truth and Nothing But the Truth about the Social Evil, being deeper glimpses of the business of prostitution in Edinburgh* (Edinburgh: Henry Robinson, 1866) (17, 23)

An idea – it is a very sentimental one to be sure – has been gaining ground during late years, that a very large proportion of our street women are victims of seduction; have been lured from the parental home, perhaps, under the pretence of marriage, and then, after being "ruined," had no alternative but to seek the streets and become common prostitutes.

There are, no doubt, women "on the town" who have fallen victims to the crime of seduction, but they are so few as not to make it worth my while to consider their cases at all; they are mere exceptions to a general rule that prostitution in Edinburgh has become a trade to which girls serve an apprenticeship – the same as they would have to do if they learned millinery or shoe-binding. In fact, prostitution in Edinburgh is an established institution that is daily becoming more and more dreadful in its character. It is a trade young women of their own free-will take up, and week after week, month after month, and year after year, is becoming more and more formidable to deal with.

. . .

Prostitution is, I regret to say, one of the avenues of social employment; and, according to that inexorable rule of supply and demand, of which so much has been said and written lately, society has made it such. Property is secured by prisons, bayonets, and halters. Charity is bestowed in driblets, and accompanied with dishonour. Poverty is a crime. But the selfishness of our present social condition produces a new avenue of employment, and truth blushes to say that avenue is prostitution. The demand exists, but where is the supply? It is the old sentimental story of seduction, but seduction has very little to do with it. There is a force at work more powerful and more general by far than seduction; that is, cheap goods, stinted wages, and starvation . . .

He discussed the economy of the brothel, and the exploitation of women by madams and brothel-keepers:

The greater number of the young women engaged in prostitution in this city are little better than slaves. Many of them are drunkards, and so entirely in the hands of the house-mistresses or brothel-keepers that they never have one penny-piece to rub upon another. The girls are nearly always in debt to the owners of the houses in which they live, and their lives are so irregular – they take part in so many drunken orgies – that it is almost impossible for them to know what money they receive or what becomes of it.

Bertram attempted to quantify the numbers of prostitutes in Edinburgh, and offered the figures quoted below, though cautioning that it was 'greatly an underestimate':

| | | |
|---|---|---|
| Public women in houses known to the police | | 500 |
| Other women in houses not yet known | | 200 |
| Stray public women | (say) | 250 |
| Sly prostitutes | (say) | 400 |
| Servant women who occasionally err | (say) | 200 |
| Other women (kept mistresses, &c.), | (say) | 150 |
| Total | | 1700 |

Premarital sex and illegitimacy had long been the focus of attempts at regulation, both through the surveillance of kirk sessions and their public rebukes and through the criminalisation of concealing a pregnancy. Despite moral strictures against illegitimacy, it was by no means uniformly treated as a cause for social ostracism and local cultures and social structures varied both in their tolerance of illegitimacy and in their levels of support for unmarried mothers. Nonetheless, from time to time, levels of illegitimacy were the subject of public debate, and the Aberdeenshire Prison Board report on prostitution, also quoted in 2.4 above, provides a striking example of middle-class moral outrage about levels of illegitimacy. The civil registration of births was introduced in Scotland in 1855 and, in 1859, the Registrar General's report enumerated illegitimacy rates for counties for the first time. Thomson's views, reported here, were shared by many other writers at the time. The idea that Scotland was less moral than England was one factor provoking reaction, though it transpired that this was erroneous and was due to an omission of some 20,000 illegitimate births per annum from English statistics.[9]

---

3.4 *Report by a Committee of the Prison Board of Aberdeenshire on the Repression of Prostitution* (Aberdeen, 1860) [University of Edinburgh Library, Centre for Research Collections, P.206/14] (7–8, 9–10)

The publication of annual returns of illegitimate births, in our own and other countries, has of late drawn much attention to one branch of this subject.

We had long been accustomed to consider Scotland as a kind of model country in respect of morality: and we are not very willing to admit the contrary, but the hard facts of statistics on this subject are not to be denied.

. . . .

When we turn to the Scottish returns, the state of female morality is found to be far worse than in England.

The number of illegitimate births for all Scotland last year was 9,256, out of a total of 104,195, or about 9.2 per cent. or nearly one half more than in England. For the quarter ending 30th June, 1859, the number was somewhat less, 2,455 illegitimate to 26,101 legitimate, or 8.5 per cent.; and for the last quarter, a little more, or 8.8 per cent. Of course the number varies, but the general fact stands out undeniably that from 8 to 10 per cent. of the children born in Scotland are illegitimate – and that without taking any account of the many cases in which marriage between guilty parties legitimises their children in the eye of the law.

Now this state of things proves something very far wrong in the state of society, and it is more closely connected with our duties as members of a Prison Board than may at first sight appear – these unfortunate illegitimate children being one of the great supplies of criminals in after life. Their treatment as a class is altogether different from, and inferior to that of legitimate children. They are very rarely well brought up. The fathers regard them only as a burden, and the mothers can never look upon them but as memorials of their disgrace. Their education is neglected – they enter life with a bad mark upon them – and experience tells us how rarely they prosper in the world. Illegitimate children furnish more than their numerical proportion of the inmates of our prisons and poor-houses. Daughters are also very apt to follow the evil example of their mothers. In country parishes, it is well known how often licentiousness is hereditary, passing on from one generation to another.

In Scotland, as in England, the number of dissolute women is distributed very differently in different districts; and from this diversity, we may, perhaps, ultimately learn something of the producing causes.

The most northerly are the most virtuous districts of Scotland, viz. the Orkney and Shetland Islands, where the illegitimate births vary from 2 to 3.5 and 3.6 per cent. in different quarters; and in Ross and Cromarty from 3.1 to 4.7.

. . . .

On the whole, female immorality, taking illegitimacy as the criterion, is somewhat greater in the rural than in the town districts of Scotland; the rural per centage being 8.7, and the town 8.4; but it must be remembered that the number of these births in towns is considerably increased by unmarried females endeavouring to hide their shame, by leaving their homes in the country, and seeking shelter in the towns, at the time of their confinements.

Concern about rising levels of drunkenness and alcoholism fuelled the growth of the temperance movement, a mass movement in nineteenth-century Scotland, and one in which many women were active, as illustrated in Chapter 7. While many focused on the problems caused by men's drinking, which was often associated with domestic and other forms of violence as well as financial insecurity and general fecklessness, the overconsumption of alcohol was a problem for women, too. It was a problem that crossed class boundaries, and the emergence of institutions, public and private, whose purpose was to treat alcoholism, helped to raise awareness about the broader cost of addiction but sometimes they simply served as a way to offer families a break.

Public authorities introduced new forms of regulation and institution-alisation to deal with the problem, with attitudes to public drunkenness hardening towards the end of the century. There were several parliamentary inquiries on the subject: the following extract is taken from evidence given to the Select Committee on Habitual Drunkards of 1879. Dr Alexander Peddie, an Edinburgh physician, spoke about addiction which was, in his opinion, the inability to help oneself, and about healing. To illustrate his points, he discussed the condition of an unnamed Edinburgh woman whose father, two brothers and son were all alcoholics:

3.5 *Report from the Select Committee on Habitual Drunkards, together with the proceedings of the committee, minutes of evidence, and appendix. Minutes of Evidence Taken Before the Select Committee on Habitual Drunkards. Tuesday, 19th March 1872. Parliamentary Papers.*

I may here mention the case of a lady, regarding whom I was consulted, who is at present detained in a licensed private house, a small institution, against her will. That is a bad case. She was well-educated, and early in life, I believe used to drink. She has been a confirmed drunkard since 1862. Her conduct was always most violent when under the influence of drink, she going into great paroxysms of passion when it was withheld from her. She has several times threatened to take her husband's life, and once she set her son on fire. When she was able to rise from the sofa to dinner, she would often throw plates, hot water jugs, decanter, &c., at her husband, servant, or anyone who happened to be in the room. The consequence was that no servant would stay in the house, and her young family were utterly neglected, suffering all the miseries that a drunken mother can inflict. She was also very cruel to them, at times endangering their lives by blows, &c. Her habits latterly became most shockingly filthy. When in her drinking fits, no matter what room she would be in, she would not use a chamber or go to the water-closet; the consequence was that the house became almost unfit to live in. Everything was tried to reform her: change of air, also keeping no spirituous liquors in the house, but all was of no avail, as she either sent for or ordered herself the drink from shops in the neighbourhood, or would even bribe a beggar at the door to bring it to her. She had several times nurses from asylums in the house attending her, when she had reduced her system by excessive drinking for weeks altogether, but this was found to be perfectly useless, for when she got well again in a short time she was as bad as ever. She was placed under control in a licensed house in August 1869, against her own will and that of some of her relations, where she remains comparatively happy. It is quite evident that if she were at liberty to-morrow she would soon commence drinking again and be as miserable and as annoying as ever.

As noted, there was widespread public debate about drink and morality, including a voluminous newspaper output by the temperance movement itself. Concerns about the problem were expressed across the denominational spectrum. In 1889 the *Glasgow Observer* printed a series of letters that debated the relationship between women and alcohol. While the true identity of the authors is not known (both used pseudonyms), the issues they identify highlight the inherent tensions between perception and reality. The second letter, in particular, reveals the frustration that some women felt when their integrity and respectability were called into question.

## 3.6 Letters on 'Intemperance Amongst Women. To The Editor', *Glasgow Observer*

10 August 1889.

Sir, – "Solitaire" deserves the thanks of all. The dangers and temptations by which our Catholic working-girls are surrounded in the factories and the workshops cannot be minimised. Intemperance, however, on the part of the girls themselves, I think, works more evil to body and soul than all the non-Catholic surroundings to which your correspondent refers. The evil wrought by drink among our Catholic girls is not confined to any one stratum of society. Among the better-to-do of our people I should say the evil is more prevalent. What can be gained by blinking facts? Absolutely nothing. A foul soul-destroyer is in our midst, and parents cannot be too watchful over the conduct of their daughters. So long as it is possible "the thing is kept dark" by the unfortunate girl herself. The unhappy being conceals her vice as long as she can, and even when it has become obvious to her people it is hidden from the outer world. For, once it gets to the world, the girl is marked. She is an object of contempt and pity. Worse than all the harshness and unkindness which she experiences from those of her own sex maddens her and too often drives her on in her insane career to a life of shame. To what depths of degradation girls, good and kind-hearted, can fall by drink most of us have seen. Many a young man hesitates to enter the marriage life at the thought of his wife should prove a drunkard. And is there any need for wonder? Intemperance is a curse in many, but it is thrice doubly a curse in a woman. What is to be done and how can it be done? Individual example and individual effort are the only means by which we can hope to eradicate this evil. The surest and safest preventive from excess in intoxicating liquors is in total abstinence. Prayers and the holy sacraments will fortify and render impregnable the resolution to avoid drink and the man or woman who does not utilise both has little chance of remaining true to the principles of Total Abstinence. Those who can "take it or leave it alone" do more mischief than they are aware of. It is their boastings that make weaker mortals delude themselves in the belief that they too can do the same . . .

    . . . Yours, etc.,
      Felix.

17 August 1889.

Sir, – In your last issue there appeared a letter, signed "Felix," in which among many telling truths, he makes the following assertions: – "The evil wrought by drink among our Catholic girls is not contained to one stratum of society. Among the better-to-do of our people, I should say, the evil is more prevalent." He then asks – "What is to be gained by blinking facts?" and his reply is "Absolutely nothing."

Few men, even after much experience and exhaustive consideration, would care to venture so strong an assertion as the second, and through a medium that carries so wide an area and introduces it to the notice of so many people. The columns of the newspaper, in the age of nervous intellectual activity and desire for startling events, are eagerly scanned; and, unhappily, society is at present so constituted that it pays most attention to those incidents of frailty and viciousness which the Press, in general, is too ready to place before us in all their revolting details.

Strictures such as those of "Felix" are sure to receive general notice and to do some injury, and it is a pity that he did not, before making such sweeping charges, give the subjects fuller thought. The charges certainly came as a disagreeable shock to those among us who, from a wide experience throughout the Kingdom, can, and without "blinking facts," speak justly and firmly, and who express a decided dissent from his statements. But there is yet time for atonement, and it is to be hoped that one who – if we are to judge by the general tenor of his letter – is animated by a desire to benefit rather than to injure the name of the middle-class Catholic girls – who are, indeed in every sense, the best class of Christian womanhood in the world – will acknowledge his hasty judgment and express regret for it, – I am sir, faithfully,

Solitaire

## Section 4: Institutionalisation and reform

This section illustrates the development of a variety of institutions designed to reform women's behaviour. It should be noted that admissions to institutions such as Magdalene Asylums were voluntary; some inmates entered after they had served gaol sentences but others sought help without having fallen foul of the law. This may be because the homes did, indeed, provide a refuge and offered some means of security on a short-term basis. Once a woman entered such an institution, however, it could be hard to leave because the discharge criteria were stringent. Directors sought to place the women in domestic service but it was difficult to find enough households willing to take them on. Others absconded after a while and could be fined for taking asylum clothes with them or refused readmission. Discipline, surveillance, labour and religious instruction were the hallmarks of such institutions.

The Edinburgh Magdalene Asylum, established in 1797, was the first of its kind in Scotland. The extract below, from the Asylum's 1804 report, outlines the reasons for its establishment.

4.1 *An Address to the Public in Favour of the Magdalene Asylum in Edinburgh instituted in the year 1797* (Edinburgh: printed by James Ballantyne, 1804) [University of Edinburgh, New College Library, Special Collections] (5–7)

ADDRESS.

The institution of the *Magdalene Asylum*, which has now existed in this city for several years, was at first suggested by the compassion of a few benevolent individuals for those wretched females, who gain a dishonourable and precarious subsistence by prostitution; and it is intended, not only as a place of refuge to such of them as are desirous of abandoning their vices, but as a school for training them to industry, to virtue, and to religion.

. . .

To open an asylum for the reception of such of these poor unfortunates as feel compunction for their crimes, and wish to escape from utter ruin, is not merely an act of compassion to the individuals, – it is of incalculable advantage to society. While they follow their dissolute courses, they are dangerous to others, as well as lost to themselves. They prowl about our streets, corrupting the morals, infecting the bodies, and ruining the souls of our inconsiderate youth; and suffer themselves the miseries which they inflict on others, in the consciousness of guilt, the feeling or the fear of want, the pains of loathsome disease, and the pangs of remorse. To reclaim them, therefore, from their vices, is to prevent those crimes to which their manner of life leads, – is to restore to society members, who not only had ceased to benefit it by useful labour, but were a burden upon it by their idleness, and a nuisance by their debaucheries, – is to diminish the number of temptations to the young and thoughtless, – to pour consolation into the hearts of parents, mourning the ruin of beloved and once hopeful children, – and "to save souls from death, and hide a multitude of sins."

Included in this report was a drawing of the design of the new building to be erected in Edinburgh's Canongate (Fig. 5.2 below). As the report noted, the asylum's current accommodation was not adequate to take in the number of women applying to the institution:

These considerations induced the managers some time ago to purchase a piece of ground adjacent to their present house, with the view to erect on it a plain economical building, capable of lodging seventy persons, and fitted up in such a manner as should at once be adapted for carrying on the various labours of industry in which the women are employed, and affording them sufficient opportunity for retirement. A plan of the intended building has been submitted to the managers and approved; . . .

While women were not directors nor members of the board and, indeed, the Glasgow Magdalene Institution did not permit women to become board members until 1913, they were actively involved in running these institutions and in contributing funds. Reports were most probably written by male office holders but offer evidence of women's involvement, whether naming prominent supporters, such as the Duchess of Buccleuch and Lady Eleanor Dundas, or through references to the ladies' committee. The Edinburgh asylum report for 1814 laid out in great detail the regulations governing the running of the asylum, including the criteria for admitting women, their employment and the organisation of their working day, and conditions of discharge. These regulations furnish a description of an arduous labour regime, of close surveillance, and of the use of religious indoctrination as the means of reform. It also outlined the duties of the Committee of Ladies:

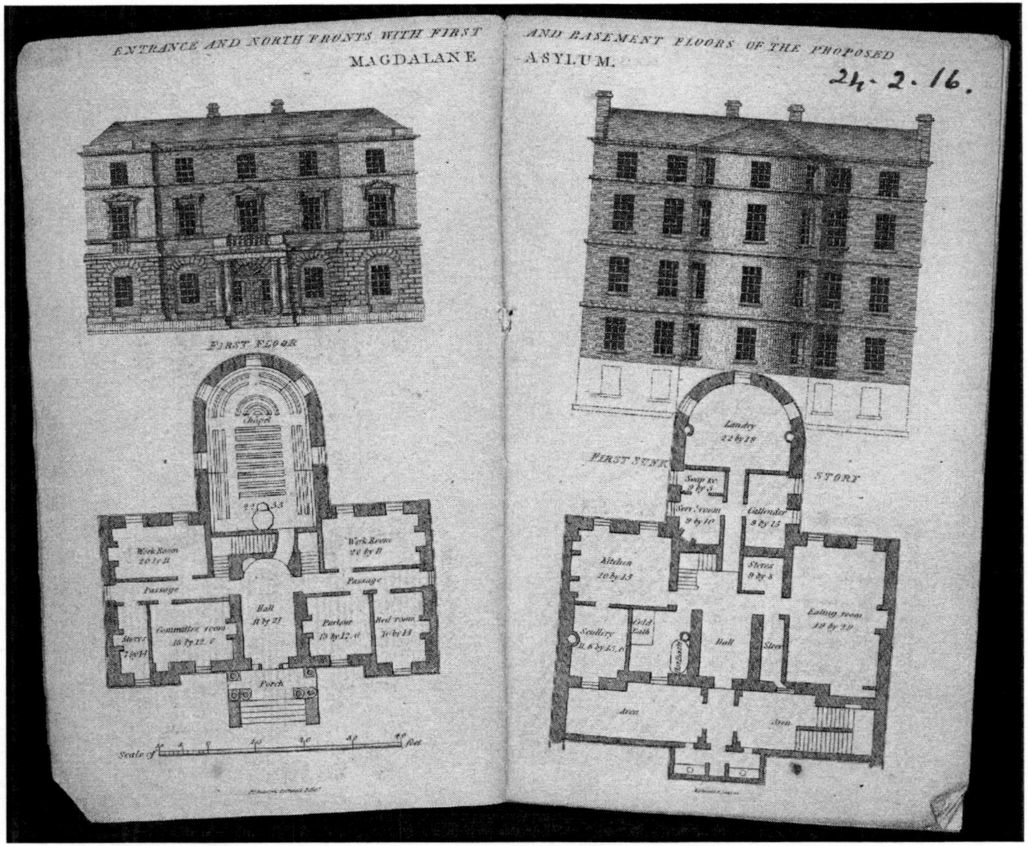

**Figure 5.2** Entrance and north fronts with first and basement floors of the proposed Magdalane Asylum, Edinburgh, 1804. Courtesy of University of Edinburgh, New College Library.

### 4.2 *Regulations of the Society for the Support of the Magdalene Asylum* (Edinburgh, 1814) [University of Edinburgh Library, Centre for Research Collections, P.92/14] (6–7)

III. *Duties of the Committee of Ladies.*

1. *Sub-Committee of Ladies.*

1st, They shall visit the Asylum weekly, or oftener, on any days, and at any hours which they shall think proper.

2d, They shall superintend the employment and diet of the women, ascertain that all the regulations with regard to the cleanliness of the rooms and beds, and the inventories of the women's clothes, are strictly attended to; examine the different branches of work done in the House; and take every proper opportunity of giving the women serious and useful advice, by conversing with them, reading to them, or putting proper religious books and tracts into their hands.

3d, They shall enter a minute, at each meeting, in a book to be kept for the purpose, and suggest such improvements as may occur to them; which minutes shall be laid before the monthly meetings of the Ladies Committee, and the Sub-Committee, and Committee of Directors.

2. *Committee of Ladies.*

1st, They shall meet in the Asylum, on the Tuesday before the first Wednesday of every month, at twelve o'clock forenoon, or any other hour that may best suit their convenience.

2d, At these meetings, they shall receive the Reports of their Sub-committee, and make out a minute of their proceedings, in which shall be inserted any suggestions which occur to them as likely to prove beneficial to the Institution, which minutes shall be laid before the Committee of Directors at their next meeting.

3d, They shall, along with the Mistress, have the sole charge of determining what particular articles of clothing shall be purchased for the women out of their earnings, of fixing both the quantity and quality of such clothing, and of giving the necessary directions for the purchasing of the same.

4th, They shall weekly examine the quantity of work done by each of the women, and if on examination they are of opinion that any of them have not executed as much work, as, in the circumstances of the case, they ought to have done, they shall report this opinion to the Sub-committee of Directors.

To assure supporters of the efficacy of their work, asylum reports often included narratives of the progress of individuals or quoted letters from previous inmates. The following example comes from the Edinburgh Magdalene Asylum report of 1823, written to the institution's matron.

### 4.3 *Report from the Directors of the Edinburgh Magdalene Asylum for 1823* [University of Edinburgh Library, Centre for Research Collections. P.59/15] (7)

Dear Madam, – I avail myself of the liberty you gave me of writing to you, though I sensibly feel my unworthiness and incapacity. How much I have to thank you, for the kind admonitions which I received from time to time while under your care! I hope they will make a lasting impression on my mind.

I am very happy here; it is a good place. I have great cause of gratitude to God, that I am placed amongst those that fear him, and diligently command their household after them to keep the way of the Lord, and I hope to obey them in all things in simplicity of heart, fearing God; knowing that my condition has been assigned me by the over-ruling Providence of Him who has fixed the bounds of my habitation. He has placed me at the post which I occupy; and though it may be, in comparison with that of others, laborious, I will think on my great mercies, and remember what a poor miserable creature I was when received into those blessed walls. My heart rises in gratitude to God, and to those kind Gentlemen and Ladies that interest themselves so much in our welfare, and have provided an Asylum for such poor wandering outcasts as we were, and I hope they will be rewarded for their labours of love; for what would I have been had I not found refuge under that hospitable roof – I would have perished, with all the horrors of an ill-spent life, long before this time . . .

In Glasgow, a ladies' committee was similarly central to the operations of the Magdalene Institution, renamed the House of Refuge for Females in 1840. Indeed, the ladies had been responsible for suggesting that the institution should be extended, a proposal that was adopted, resulting in a new building. The extract below indicates the importance attributed to the role of the ladies' committee, and named the committee members who were to work with the directors.

### 4.4 *House of Refuge for Females, Parliamentary Road, Glasgow* (1840) [NLS, 5.1024(47)] (5–6)

The Committee, in a previous part of this Report, have alluded to the valuable services of the Ladies who have taken cognizance of young females who have departed from the paths of rectitude, and they beg to note the following Resolution that was made at a General Meeting of Subscribers to the House of Refuge for Females, held in the Exchange Rooms, on the 16th February, 1839: – "The meeting desire to record their opinion that the co-operation of the Ladies of the city and neighbourhood, in promoting the objects of the Institution, particularly in reference to the treatment, education and training of the inmates, and the procuring employment and situations for them when they quit the house, will be of the highest importance to its success, and that it be recommended to the Directors to endeavour to secure such co-operation."

The Committee having signified to the Ladies that it would be desirable that they would nominate the Committee which will act along with the Directors, the following names have been handed to your Secretaries:

Mrs. OSWALD, Abbotsford Place,
Mrs. Colonel FLEMING, 7, Woodside Crescent,
Mrs. HUNTER, 35, Abbotsford Place,
Miss HAGGART, 79, South Portland Street,

Miss JEFFRAY, College,

Miss ALSTON, Garnethill.

The work conducted at the Asylum is intended to be similar to what previously took place, viz.: – Washing and dressing, white seam, making of baby linen, &c. and your Committee beg to recommend in this respect this Asylum to the attention and support of the Citizens of Glasgow, and to give them assurance that every attention shall, on the part of the Matrons and Assistants, be paid to give complete satisfaction.

Among other types of provision aimed at girls and women coming into existence from the mid-nineteenth century were government-approved reformatories, houses of refuge, rescue shelters, industrial homes, homes for 'fallen' women, homes for deserted mothers, lodging houses and reformatories for inebriate women, and so on. The main cities all supported such provision, and also towns such as Greenock, Paisley and Perth.[10] The extract below, authored by Alexander Thomson, prison reformer and member of Aberdeenshire Prison Board, praises the work of Aberdeen women in developing reformatories for girls. By 1861 there were four industrial schools in Aberdeen, a boys' school, a mixed school, and two 'separate female schools'.

---

### 4.5 Alexander Thomson of Banchory, *Preventive and Reformatory Work in Aberdeen* (1861) (7)

As soon as the managers were tolerably satisfied of the soundness and practicability of their views as regarded male juvenile offenders and outcasts, it was obviously their duty to apply the same remedies to neglected girls, and to this work the ladies of Aberdeen have, from its first proposal down to the present day, given their hearty and unwearied exertions. The first girls' school was opened on 5th June, 1843, with only three girls, and the number was gradually increased to twenty, forty, fifty, and at last to sixty, the full number for which accommodation was provided. The results were, if possible, more satisfactory than with the boys. A poor half-starved outcast girl is felt by all to be a more painful sight than a boy in the same condition. She seems to have been forced farther below her right place in society than the boy, and to be less capable of struggling for herself. Experience, however, soon proved that ameliorating influences acted more rapidly, and perhaps more permanently, on the girls than on the boys. The change produced by a few weeks of careful feeding and training upon the most abject was so great, that the ladies who devoted themselves to the arduous enterprise had every encouragement in their labour of love.

In December, 1844, the first complete year's report of the girls' school stated the number on the roll at forty-nine; and in 1845 it was above sixty. During the third year, thirty-five girls left – sixteen, because their parents had become able to provide for them; five got employment in manufactories; and seven as domestic servants; seven deserted, and one died. During the fourth year the attendance varied from fifty-six to sixty-nine; twenty-three left for domestic service, and thirty-one were removed by parents, as in the previous year. This must always be regarded as one of the most satisfactory results of the schools, arising either from improved pecuniary circumstances, or from improved moral feeling on the part of the parents.

Around the same time, a new reformatory was established in Dalry in Edinburgh, benefiting from government support, as a consequence of recent legislation on industrial schools.

> ### 4.6 *Report of the Girls' House of Refuge, or, Western Reformatory School, Dalry, for Juvenile Female Delinquents. With a list of subscriptions and donations, 1862* (3, 5)

. . . When the last Report was published, the new and commodious premises at Dalry had just been taken possession of by that branch of the Committee's charge which had occupied the Reformatory at Boroughmuirhead. The Magistrates of the city and the public had generously come forward and assisted the Trustees and Committee to erect the House, which, having been certified as a Government Reformatory, it was expected would soon be filled with sentenced cases from various parts of the country, as well as from our own city. Accommodation has been provided for fifty girls, but as yet twenty-seven is the largest number of the sentenced class that has at one time been under the Committee's care, during that five years which have elapsed since the Institution was certified. There had been in the Reformatory at Boroughmuirhead, besides the sentenced girls, voluntary cases, that is, delinquents not convicted, and, consequently, not paid for by Government; and when the Committee found themselves in possession of larger accommodation at Dalry, it became a matter for consideration whether their doors should not be opened wider for the reception of girls equally guilty with the sentenced cases. Many such there are, who commit crimes of an aggravated nature, but who, not being brought under the notice of the police and the sentence of the Magistrates, are not convicted, and so not eligible for Government support.

. . .

On the 1st of January, 1862, there were twenty-two sentenced cases at Dalry: to these thirteen have since been added; making in all thirty-five. During the year, eight were permitted to leave the Reformatory before the term of their sentence had fully expired, their good conduct having warranted such a step. Of these, one was assisted to emigrate to Canada, and was sent out under the auspices of the London Reformatory and Refuge Union. A letter, written shortly after her arrival, announced that she was settled in a good place. The other seven were all placed in respectable situations in this country, where some, if not all, are doing well. Another has just finished her time, but remains in the meantime as a voluntary inmate. This leaves twenty-six Government cases in the Reformatory.

By mid-century, communities of women religious were becoming noticeable in urban Scotland. The first communities of sisters were focused on education and came from France and Ireland. The second wave – those who arrived from the late 1850s – had a different mission and, though education was part of it, there was more attention paid to women's moral improvement. When the Good

Shepherds arrived in Glasgow and established a convent at Dalbeth in 1858, they also opened Scotland's first Roman Catholic Magdalene Asylum. Their decision in 1892 to close their reformatory school and open an industrial school, illustrated in the extract below, probably reflected low numbers of convictions and declining support.

### 4.7 'Convent of Our Lady of Charity of the Good Shepherd, Dalbeth', *Glasgow Observer*, 20 February 1892

We are authorised to publish that the Sisters of the Good Shepherd, Dalbeth, have decided to close their Reformatory School for girls, and with the approval of his Grace the Archbishop, have applied for a certificate as an Industrial School for Girls instead. The Sisters have been compelled to close the Reformatory owing to the decrease in the number of girls sent, which may be accounted for by the general feeling of dislike of the imprisonment of girls sentenced to reformatories. It may not be generally known that the Sisters of the Good Shepherd, have at Dalbeth, three separate institutions within their grounds, distinct from one another. 1st, A Reformatory School for girls, with its own kitchen, reformatory, laundry, playground, church gallery, &c. 2nd, the Refuge or Home for penitent women and destitute girls, again comprising refectory, playground and church accommodation, &c. 3rd, the Convent proper belonging exclusively to the nuns, and into which visitors are not admitted. There are usually over 160 inmates in the Refuge who are supported principally by their own work in the laundry and sewing rooms, but it is greatly to be deplored that the supply of both laundry and needlework is totally insufficient, and the Sisters most earnestly solicit the charity and favour of the public. Those who send means of employing materially forward this great and noble undertaking . . .

The Girgenti Inebriate Reformatory was established in 1900 by the Glasgow Corporation, following the 1898 Inebriates Act. The Corporation purchased Girgenti House and Estate in Ayrshire for £7,000 and converted it into a facility for 'habitual drunkards' of the 'criminal class'. Though initially intended for men and for women, in 1901 its sole focus became women. Most of the women housed there were 'paupers, and about half of them had been convicted of importuning'. The following extract highlights the daily routine that governed the lives of the inmates. As with many other institutions, religious instruction and labour, which included sewing, knitting, housework, laundry, farm, garden and orchard work, were important elements of the reform process.

### 4.8 *First Report of Committee on Inebriates Acts on Girgenti Inebriate Reformatory, for the period ending 31st December, 1901* [University of Glasgow Library, Open Shelves. Statistics BB 1444.G5] (5, 12–13)

The following is the time-table of work, &c., which has been in operation since the opening of the Home, viz.: –

6 a.m. – Inmates to be called.
7 a.m. – Breakfast and prayers.
7.45 a.m. – Work.
12 noon – Dinner.
1 p.m. – Work.
5.30 p.m. – Tea.
6.30 p.m. Recreation and time for private work.
8.45 p.m. – Prayers.
9 p.m. – Bed.
9.30 p.m. – Lights out.
During the winter months, inmates may be called at 6.30 a.m., with a dinner at 12.30, and tea at 5.
These hours may be varied in the case of inmates who, for the time, are engaged on household work, or in attending to cattle, &c.

Admittance to the institution was not voluntary and, as a result, some of the women found it difficult to adjust to the strict routine. In his report to the committee, William King, the reformatory's superintendent, noted the frequency of escapes over the course of 1901:

> Escapes from the Home have been rather numerous, but, owing to the fact of there being no walls or unclimbable fences round the estate, it is practically an easy matter for an inmate, who is determined to bide her time and take the first opportunity that presents itself for escape, to effect her purpose. The managers, however, notwithstanding the determination of a few, whose conduct seems to indicate that they will not be controlled, are resolved not to recede from their purpose to conduct the Home as a real home for inmates who will appreciate or can be taught to appreciate home comforts. The number of escapes is as follows: – five have escaped once, one has escaped twice, and one thrice. Eight of these have been remitted to the Sheriff; one has been admonished, and sentences have been passed on others varying from 10 to 30 days' imprisonment. I might say here that short sentences are in most cases treated with contempt . . .

The press regularly covered the activities of the Magdalene Asylums and the plethora of other refuges, homes, and reformatories that were to mushroom after the mid-century. Magdalene Asylums, such as those mentioned above, continued in existence throughout the nineteenth century and well into the twentieth. Annual meetings, for example, of the Edinburgh Asylum Board continued to be reported; by 1913 numbers of inmates were declining. Board member Bailie Rose saw this decline as resulting from better employment conditions, and attributable 'to the fact that the Insurance Act contributions and benefits gave them more stability in their employment, and gave them an additional reason for remaining at it'.[11] This comment serves to underline how much the precariousness of economic circumstances shaped poor women's entanglements with the law and with agencies of moral reform.

## Select bibliography

Yvonne Brown and Rona Ferguson (eds), *Twisted Sisters: Women, Crime and Deviance in Scotland since 1400* (East Linton: Tuckwell Press, 2002).

Carolyn Conley, *Certain Other Countries: homicide, gender, and national identity in late nineteenth-century England, Ireland, Scotland, and Wales* (Columbus, Ohio: Ohio State University Press, 2007).

Russell P. Dobash and Pat McLaughlin, 'The Punishment of Women in Nineteenth-Century Scotland: Prisons and Inebriate Institutions', in Esther Breitenbach and Eleanor Gordon (eds), *Out of Bounds: Women in Scottish Society, 1800–1945* (Edinburgh: Edinburgh University Press, 1992), pp. 65–94.

Lucy Frost, *Abandoned Women: Scottish Convicts Exiled Beyond the Seas* (Sydney: Allen and Unwin, 2012).

Eleanor Gordon and Gwyneth Nair, *Murder and Morality in Victorian Britain: the story of Madeline Smith* (Manchester: Manchester University Press, 2009).

Anne-Marie Kilday, *Women and Crime in Enlightenment Scotland* (Woodbridge and Rochester: The Boydell Press, 2007).

Linda Mahood, *The Magdalenes: Prostitution in the Nineteenth Century* (London: Routledge, 1990).

Linda Mahood, *Policing Gender, Class and Family in Britain, 1850–1940* (London: Routledge, 1995).

Rosalind Mitchison and Leah Leneman, *Sexuality and Social Control: Scotland, 1660–1780* (Oxford: Basil Blackwell, 1989).

Deborah A. Symonds, *Weep Not for Me: Women, Ballads, and Infanticide in Early Modern Scotland* (Pennsylvania: Pennsylvania State University Press, 1997).

Deborah A. Symonds, *Notorious Murders, Black Lanterns, and Moveable Goods: Transformation of Edinburgh's Underworld in the Early Nineteenth Century* (Akron, OH: University of Akron Press, 2006).

## Notes

1. Annmarie Hughes, 'The "Non-Criminal" Class: Wife-beating in Scotland (*c.*1800–1949), *Crime, Histoire & Sociétiés/Crime, History & Societies,* Vol. 14, No. 2 (2010) pp. 31–54.

2. Andrew Blaikie, *Illegitimacy, Sex and Society: Northeast Scotland, 1730–1900* (Oxford: Clarendon Press, 1993), p. 212.

3. Anne-Marie Kilday, *Women and Violent Crime in Enlightenment Scotland* (Woodbridge: The Boydell Press, 2007).

4. Indictment against Christian Macdougall, AD14/36/212, NAS.

5. Lucy Frost, *Abandoned Women: Scottish Convicts Exiled Beyond the Seas* (Sydney: Allen and Unwin, 2012), p. 178.

6. Joy Cameron, *Prisons and Punishment in Scotland from the Middle Ages to the Present* (Edinburgh: Canongate, 1983).

7. Leah Leneman, *Martyrs in Our Midst: Dundee, Perth and the Forcible Feeding of Suffragettes* (Dundee: Abertay Historical Society, 1993).

8. Mary White, 'Prison Work in Glasgow', *Scottish Women's Temperance News*, 15 April 1897.
9. Blaikie, *Illegitimacy, Sex and Society*, p. 11.
10. Linda Mahood, *The Magdalenes: Prostitution in the Nineteenth Century* (London: Routledge, 1990).
11. *The Scotsman*, 24 December 1913.

# Chapter 6

# Religion

*Lesley Orr*

## Introduction

Religious institutions, belief systems, social power and personal convictions were immensely significant shapers of women's experiences and identities. In many domains of life, religious structures and discourses made an impact on their roles and activities, and the meanings ascribed to those. Women actively reinterpreted faith and created religious cultures in a religious landscape which was significantly reconfigured throughout the nineteenth century, as noted in Chapter 1. Following the fragmentation of the Church of the Scotland at the Disruption of 1843, there were three main Presbyterian denominations: the Church of Scotland, the Free Church and the United Presbyterian Church. The Church of Scotland's claim to be the national Church and custodian of a 'godly commonwealth' was further undermined as responsibility for poor relief (1844) and education (1872) passed to the state. Evangelical congregations became hubs of organisation and activity, particularly of the rapidly expanding urban middle and aspiring working classes, and, by the 1880s, non-denominational city missions and the Salvation Army were part of the mix. A growing Roman Catholic Church, strengthened by Irish immigration, sought to nurture devotion, welfare, education and a respectable Catholic community. Revivalism was a recurring feature in many areas, rural and urban, though the impact of smaller Protestant sects was often limited and localised. By the late nineteenth century, Churches were criticised for failing to respond adequately to economic and social problems, while a progressive minority developed a Christian social vision for reformation of Church and society. Also by the end of the century, Jewish communities were becoming more established in Scotland. International connections were also giving rise to interest in other faiths, though this remained the preserve of a small minority.

Though there were women writing about religion throughout the period, the nature, scale, provenance, purpose and readership developed and changed considerably. Before *c.*1830 published authors of fiction, poetry, and didactic literature [Joanna Baillie‡ (1762–1851), Elizabeth Hamilton‡ (1758–1816) and others] sometimes included overtly religious themes in their work. Other sources, including letters, journals and memoirs, were typically personal or for private circulation. From the 1830s, as notions of feminine piety and benevolence mobilised women for mission, the development of mass-circulation religious literature opened up acceptable avenues for women to publish in various genres, including instruction, tracts, pamphlets, reports, hymns, devotional writing, biblical and morally improving stories. Women's church and mission periodicals (for example, *The Eastern Female's Friend, The Helpmeet, Life and Work Woman's Guild Supplement*), letters for circulation and organisational records were central to the development of female associational culture, especially from the 1880s. The reformist women's movement gave scope for more reflective, critical and literary writing, such as in the journal, *The Attempt*, and its successor, the *Ladies' Edinburgh Magazine*, about belief and practice and more broadly interpreting claims and campaigns in Christian terms. Religion was an important, if ambivalent, contextual factor for feminism. Most literature reflects the privileges of dominant Christianity, class, education and position which gave unequal access to writing and publication. It has, for example, proved virtually impossible to find written sources emanating from women of the Jewish community in this period. Other women's voices and beliefs may to some extent be accessed through oral history, images and material culture. This chapter draws on a range of sources to give an impression of diverse women's religious convictions, doubts, concerns, cultures and activities.

### Section 1: Religious faith and practice in the lives of women

Women's personal lives of faith and practice, though influenced by prevailing norms of female piety, were inflected by class, location, theology, affiliation, tradition and life history. The extracts in this section give a flavour of religious beliefs, preoccupations and aspirations, and their impact on women's lifestyles across the century. They include accounts of religious struggle, conversion and spiritual yearning, strong opinions, everyday life and organised activity.

A small number of faithful women, brought up in an assertively Protestant environment, encountered Roman Catholicism as both compelling and challenging. Drawn to its doctrine and rituals, they worried about the consequences of conversion, including possible alienation from their family, friends and community. This narrative is from the autobiography of Ann Trail [Agnes Xavier Trail]‡ (1798–1872) a minister's daughter and artist who was received into the Catholic Church in 1828 while in Italy. She entered the Ursuline order, taking the name Agnes Xavier, and, in 1834, she founded St Margaret's, Edinburgh, the first post-Reformation convent in Scotland.

> 1.1  *The Revival of Conventual Life in Scotland. History of St. Margaret's Convent, Edinburgh, the first religious house founded in Scotland since the so-called Reformation; and the autobiography of the first religious, Sr. Agnes Xavier Trail* (Edinburgh: John Chisholm, 1886) (324–6)

Extract from Letter IV

Then the situation in which I should be placed, should I change my religion, arose to my mind in all its horror; slighted and condemned by those who had hitherto honoured and courted me; regarded as an outcast from grace, and pointed out as a beacon to warn others, by those religious persons who had heretofore marked me as an example to be followed, and for whose esteem and regard I had most value; perhaps abandoned by my friends and relatives, many of whom I knew to be most hostile to the Catholic faith. But what wounded me most deeply was the thought of the affliction into which I knew I must inevitably plunge my beloved parents and family – perhaps I may bring my father's grey hairs with sorrow to the grave, perhaps I may break the tender heart of my affectionate mother, of whom I have hitherto been the pride; my own will break soon, too, thought I, but no matter, I must follow the dictates of my conscience; but, if my conscience be mistaken, what then? To lose *all* for *this* world and the *next*! Yet, would my Saviour suffer this, when I am willing to sacrifice everything I value most, even life itself, for His sake? Nay, when, were I even sure of being saved in the Protestant faith, yet should the Catholic faith be more pleasing to Him, I would embrace it as the hazard of all I possess in the world. Surely No!

Ah, my dear Father, would you but conceive half of what I then suffered, you would weep with me now. Without a friend to whom I could reveal my distress; – in fear whether God was not at that moment forsaking me, I could only cling closer to Him and entreat Him not to abandon me. If stones could speak, those of St. Giovanni would bear witness to my sighs and tears; for there, usually as I returned from my painting, I retired to pray and meditate; and I sometimes withdrew into the most obscure chapel, where, throwing myself down on the pavement, with my forehead on the cold marble steps of the altar, I would truly pour out my heart before God, to beseech Him to preserve or deliver me from error, and to enlighten me with the light of truth – the whole truth. Then, my God! Let me suffer what Thou wilt – nay, I would rather suffer, should it be more for Thy glory and the honour of religion. From two things alone, I think, I prayed God to spare me; that, should the Catholic religion be the true one, and God enabled me to perceive and embrace it, I might not be doomed to break the hearts of my parents, nor be reduced to the necessity of accepting a partner. I know I prayed likewise that I might have no worldly inducement, that I might feel more sure about my own sincerity, and that the world might not be able to impute an interested motive. How graciously my Heavenly Father heard and answered all these prayers. Ah, pray for me, that I may correspond to so much mercy by an entire devotion of myself, body, soul and spirit, to God.

Christian Watt's‡ conversion took place around 1858 during a period of lay evangelical fervour in north-east fishing communities. Her memoirs, begun in 1880, tell the story of a difficult, varied and fascinating life; her account of women's work in fishing is quoted in Chapter 3. Hardship and tragedy informed her fierce anger at injustice and religious hypocrisy. But she was also a woman of profound Christian faith, and her writings resonate with plain speaking, wit and courage.

### 1.2 *The Christian Watt Papers*, edited and with an introduction by David Fraser (1983) (97, 110)

During the weeks of waiting, [for fish-curing work in 1858] I read nothing but my Bible, and to my own joy and astonishment I found the Lord Jesus as my own personal saviour. Only in my own personal experience did I discover how man was alienated from God, and how we were reconciled by his death on Calvary's cross. In my own room that night I knew I had passed from death unto life. 'Oh joyous hour when God to me a vision gave of Calvary, my bonds were loosed my soul unbound, I sang upon redemption ground.'

My duty lay in carrying out my betrothal contract, for whatever happened nothing could separate me from the love of Christ, whose very purity can see through the false, swicks, liars and cheats. His very majesty can make the greedy, envious and covetous hang their heads in shame.

. . .

. . . One thing I have learned in this world, 60 per cent of folk who call themselves Christians are fakes, especially round north-east Scotland and the Moray Firth seaboard. Their Christianity is a form of Godliness and respectability, but it is absolutely necessary it be applied to prosperity! Poor Christians are not the thing, for who wants to be seen with folk with barefoot bairns. I have beheld the saints on a Sunday night forming little groups in parting at their kirk doors, with that 'holier-than-thou' kind of tone of voice. They are either discussing herring or harvests or houses, but not the Lord Jesus who had not a place to lay his head. My mother-in-law was a typical example. She thought that heaven might be as far as Finechtie. Man cannot envisage the height or breadth of God's domain. We do not know, but there may be seven suns, ten million light years away from the Earth, and one day man may go there, God willing, for the power of the Almighty goes beyond the highest heaven and transcends the lowest hell. The same power that lifted Christ from the grave can send the planets hurtling through space. How many go into the highways and byways to help the poor? . . .

Mary Anne Paterson (née Rogerson) was a farmer's wife from Upper Annandale. Her youthful 'Meditations' are typical of the introspection encouraged by orthodox Calvinism. Pious Christians were expected to examine their behaviour, thoughts and inner disposition for evidence of election. Rogerson initially kept her Sabbath evening diary almost every week, but entries tailed off rather dramatically after marriage and the arrival of her first children. Mother's Diary was printed for private circulation. Like many such publications, it was intended primarily for family use, not only to preserve her memory but as a source of religious example and guidance.

### 1.3 *Mother's Diary, from 1853 to 1858: Sabbath Evening Meditations by Mary Ann Paterson (née Rogerson)* (Edinburgh: Andrew Elliot, n.d.)

SABBATH EVE, *December 3rd, 1854.* – Sabbath Eve indeed. Yes, 'tis another week run its ample round, and I am spared to see its successor begun. Oh may I be better fitted for my duty now and henceforth. How short yet how momentous are its results to some of my friends who began it. It has seen them laid out for their last long sleep in the tomb. Oh how solemn is the lesson to us all. May we all profit. Youth and health are no safeguards against the fell destroyer. No! he has snatched from my young friend the partner of her married life, and that too in a few short days. Oh how true there is but a step between us and death. Oh may my slumbering energies be aroused, and may I be made more watchful in future. I am soon, if we are spared, to stand side by side with one and own him as my partner for life. O how solemn is the thought – we are spared and thus allowed to be. May the blessing of God rest on each of us. May we seek it earnestly, and we have the assurance, we shall not be disappointed. Oh may the hand that has wounded heal the heart of my friend, and support her under her sore trial. May it be for her eternal good.

. . .

HEATHERYHALL, SABBATH EVE, *March 18th, 1855.* - yes, Sabbath has again come round, and I am found resuming my for-a-time neglected Journal, if worthy of such a name. Oh how many changes have I experienced since I last traced a few lines. Yes, since then I have experienced mingled seasons of joy and sorrow, some sweet hours of earthly bliss. Yes, but how unsatisfying is even this, with the most affectionate of husbands, united by the strongest and tenderest tie, for even our very blessings become our curse when they come between us and our God. And how ought my feelings of unhappiness during the past week teach me the lesson that no earthly good can satisfy the wants of my immortal soul. And I know I have been careless and indifferent in duty, those hours which were my happiest, have been neglected or almost so. And how can I be happy forgetting that God in His Providence is ordering every event in my life, and now when in His Providence His will is running counter to my will?

The daughter of a professor, Helen Menzies was brought up in Edinburgh. In 1871 she married James McFarlan, minister of Ruthwell parish church in Dumfriesshire, and lived there until he died in 1889. Her journals and letters, also quoted in Chapter 3, describe family, church and community life within the 'narrow limits . . . of parish and glebe and walls of the manse'. It is a pattern shaped within mainstream Scottish Presbyterianism, critical of the extremes and enthusiasms of less moderate Christians. These personal writings are imbued with the commonplace: relationships, everyday encounters, joys and sorrows.

> 1.4 Helen McFarlan, *Selections from Letters and Journals of Ruthwell Manse Life 1871–1889* (Edinburgh: privately printed, 1914)

November 6th
Three elders came to dinner yesterday; one of them is eighty-eight years old. J's service was very beautiful. But one cannot rightly enjoy the communion in a manse. All the bustle and preparation takes away somewhat from the peace and solemnity one has been used to.

Saturday night, though, was very solemn and beautiful. Towards midnight my husband called me to be with him while he cut and prepared the loaf for Holy Communion. I followed him with a feeling of awe, and was surprised to see a loaf like any other. He gave me his sermon, and I read it to him while he cut and shaped the loaf. Then we sang a psalm together, and he read his prayers over. His face was radiant and peaceful as he said good-night. Turning at the door, he made me put the bread away. Left alone with that holy Bread of Life, I felt it too sacred to touch. Putting a white linen cloth over it, I wrapped it up and carried it upstairs to my room, and laid it on a small table by itself. There seemed to be a radiance from it in the darkness.

On Sunday morning, before service, the elders came to the manse for 'the elements'. No feelings of solemnity or awe oppressed *them*! They chatted gaily about parish matters while they uncorked the wine and filled the flagons, and then one of them, taking the bread from the silver platter on which it lay, drew the napkin more tightly round it, took a pin from his vest to fasten it, and then tucked the whole under his arm and carried it over to the kirk! The communion table is also the stove! Or rather the grating in front of it, a most curious and horrid arrangement.
. . .
September 9th 1874 Ruthwell Manse To J.M'F. :–
We had a beautiful day yesterday, and a very full church to hear young Mr. ———. A wagonette full of men with beards and knowing eyes from Annan. The sermon was dreadful – all the vices of the rich dwelt upon with the assurance that they would indulge in them no more in Hell! There were to be no card-tables there, and that, I hoped, would go home to my mother's gambling spirit, but – she was sound asleep! His voice nearly ca'd the roof off, and he seemed to enjoy it all immensely himself. Maclean said, 'He was pitten his best foot foremost.' Good old Mr Coulthard, you will be glad to hear, remarked that he thought it rather impudent of a young man

like that, 'a stranger too, to be coming and hanging us all over the brink of Hell!' The day for that kind of preaching is past, he says. The collection was 12s.6d.

May 29th 1886 Edinburgh. To J.M'F.:–
The meeting of the W.A.F.M. [Church of Scotland Women's Association for Foreign Missions] was yesterday. We had an Indian missionary lady who spoke in a very ladylike voice, and she brought with her a native teacher, a dark descendant of Shem wrapped in picturesque drapery, who spoke to us in her own language – rather fascinating to listen to.

Mrs. Clement Scott comes up to one's ideal of a missionary – a little, spare young thing, too shy to speak, and not able to answer Miss Phoebe Blyth's cross-questioning as to creeds, but full of hard-working enthusiasm.

Miss Jamieson on the Jews was vigorous, and Mrs T. G. Murray is always delightful to listen to.

I got through my effort quite well; it was short, and the audience attentive. Mrs Phin patted me kindly afterwards and said, 'You read your paper very nicely.' So I pleased Mrs. Phin at all events.

After that I heard Mr. Clement Scott of Blantyre at a drawing room meeting – a handsome young man, refined, full of devotion and most interesting.

The first communities of Catholic sisters to arrive in Glasgow were principally concerned with the provision of female education and ran Sunday and evening schools, private convent boarding schools and parish schools. The efforts of these women did much to validate Scotland's democratic tradition of schooling, endeavouring to give Catholic girls and young women a stronger educational foundation.

1.5  Convent life: Charlotte Street Convent, Glasgow, and Franciscan novices [Franciscan Sisters of the Immaculate Conception, Glasgow. Box: 012.2, Beginnings and Early History, Box: 015.1, Photographs of Historic Value]

As indicated above in the introduction to extract 1.1, the first convent was reestablished in Scotland in 1832, and others followed from the late 1840s. The image below, which dates from the early 1850s, illustrates the first purpose-built convent in Glasgow for the Franciscan Sisters of the Immaculate Conception, and shows the small cell-like rooms for the nuns. The photograph shows a group of Franciscan novices from the Charlotte Street Convent, Glasgow, and dates from the 1870s (see Figs 6.1 and 6.2 overleaf).

Orangeism was a sectarian movement associated with communities of the Irish Protestant diaspora. Organised into lodges with distinctive rituals, the most public manifestation of the order was the summer marching season. Though its ethos was patriarchal, it functioned as an important cultural and associational nexus for women and children as well as for men.[1] The first female Orange lodges in Scotland were granted warrants in 1909, and there were thirty-four by 1914. The following exchange shows the resistance women encountered when they

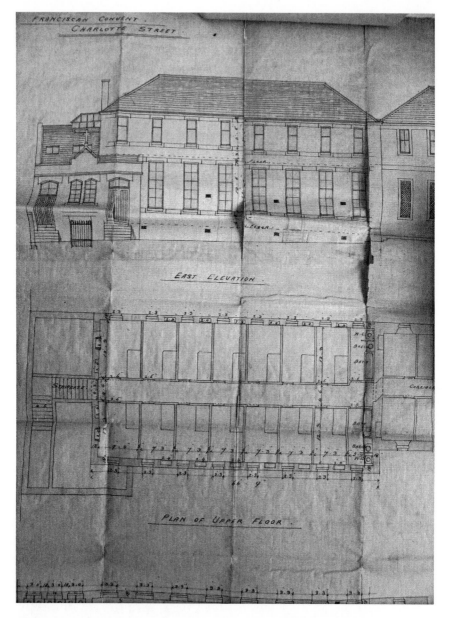

**Figure 6.1** Franciscan Convent, Charlotte Street, Glasgow: east elevation and plan of upper
floor, 1850s. Reproduced by permission of the Franciscan Sisters of the Immaculate
Conception, Glasgow.

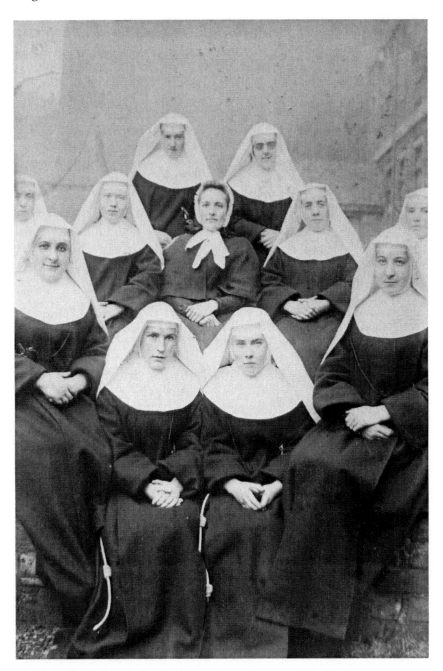

**Figure 6.2** Photograph of Franciscan novices, *c.*1870s. Charlotte Street Convent, Glasgow.
Reproduced by permission of the Franciscan Sisters of the Immaculate Conception,
Glasgow.

claimed the right to participate in parades, and not just to raise funds or make the tea.

## 1.6 'Female Orange Lodges', *Belfast Weekly News*, 1910

30 June 1910
from William M'Lean jun, 27 Marquis Street, Bridgton, Glasgow
'Female Orange Lodges',

It is not my intention at present to criticise the value of Female Orange Lodge, but I do not approve of women taking part in an Orange church parade. It is out of place, and spoils the look of a procession to see a body of women, say 30 or so, followed by a large number of brethren. I would also like to draw the attention of those responsible that there is a considerable number of Orangemen who will not demonstrate on 9th July in consequence of the feeling that the Orange regalia should not be publicly worn by women. Moreover, I hold that the Orange Institution was never intended for young women. What our Order wants is young men, not young women. By attending to their domestic duties women have enough to do without identifying themselves with the Orange Order.

7 July 1910
from Annie J. Wilson, secretary 'Scotland's First' Female Loyal Orange Lodge. Does Br M'Lean think for a minute that he and the few he makes mention of – I say few, for I am in a position to know – will hinder the women from walking in procession? I consider that women wearing regalia and walking at the head of a procession honour that procession. I would also like to draw Br M'Lean's attention to the fact that there will be more than a hundred women marching in procession. This will assuredly cover the loss sustained by the absence of the few mentioned. Br M'Lean states that our regalia should not be worn publicly. What does he mean? Does he think that we Orangewomen intend to hide our light under a bushel? Never! Do the women of other societies hide their colours? Even Roman Catholic societies have taken the women into their ranks, and why not the Orange Order? I would like to ask Br M'Lean if he has read any history? Where would the men have been if the women had not helped in times of national distress, and threatened calamity? Had the Orange Order taken the women into their ranks years ago there would not have been so much talk of the changing of the Declaration Oath, for there would not have been so many weak-kneed Protestants today . . . No matter how many household duties a woman has to perform she can always find time to attend an Orange meeting. By publicly adopting Orange principles, a woman will be better fitted to discharge the duties of life in whatever sphere it may please God to place her.

A more ecumenical spirit emerged in the late nineteenth and early twentieth centuries. Awareness of other religions and traditions, experience of travelling abroad, the Celtic renaissance with its romantic interest in pagan and Christian myths and symbols, a search for spiritual teaching and community more in keeping with aspirations for equality, were all factors influencing this. For some women, involvement in the suffrage movement had a quasi-religious significance. A few were drawn to the esoteric spiritualism and philosophy of theosophy. One example of this desire to go beyond traditional Christianity is Jane Whyte (1857–1944) whose interest was in the Baha'i faith. The daughter of Margaret Stewart Sandeman (see source 2.4 below), she was married to a leading United Free Church minister, Reverend Professor Alexander Whyte. Jane belonged to a circle of progressive intellectuals and artists, including Patrick Geddes and Phoebe Traquair‡ (1852–1936). While on holiday in Egypt in 1905, she was invited to visit Abdu'l-Baha, leader of the Baha'i movement, who was a prisoner of the Ottoman Empire. It was a key moment in her spiritual journey, and her account of the visit, written in March 1906, has been published in A. Khursheed, *Seven Candles of Unity: the Story of Abdul-Baha in Edinburgh* (London: Baha'i Publishing Trust, 1991). By 1912 Whyte had become a member of the 'Council' established to promote Baha'i in Britain, and invited Abdu'l-Baha to visit Edinburgh. Along with the Scottish Theosophical Society, the Whytes were responsible for organising his programme which generated large attendances and considerable interest. Abdu'l-Baha's translator, Ahmad Sohrab, also stayed in the manse, and wrote letters to an American follower. These extracts are from this correspondence, and are available at www.paintdrawer.co.uk/david/spirituality

## 1.7 'Abdu'l-Baha in Edinburgh: The Diary of Ahmad Sohrab'

January 7 1913

. . .

We have just returned (11.30 pm) from the beautiful meeting in the Theosophical Society. There was a most lovely spirit of love and sympathy manifest there. Everything was warm and hospitable. The audience running into several hundred of people most sympathetic. Members of the Society have come from all parts of Scotland and even from Ireland to hear the Master talk. It is one of the most wide-awake Theosophical Centers of Europe . . . On arriving the Master was taken into a private room. Here He met a Mrs Brown who has been born in Ramleh from a Scottish father. She is a Theosophist and devotes much of her time and her means to the maintenance of this establishment. The Master talked with her and prayed for her that she may soar to the heaven of Reality, a heaven whose sun never sets, whose moon never disappears, whose stars never fall. Afterward a mother with seven daughters, the first of whom has in turn nine daughters, came in to receive the Blessing of the Master. "I hope your daughters may form a blessed family. Abraham was one single soul. God blessed him and today he is represented in millions of souls."

Jan 9 1913
Women and Equality Meeting
At 4 o'clock Mrs Whyte had the meeting of Edinburgh women (150) in her own spacious Library. The Master came down. At first in an adjoining room, some noble Ladies were introduced . . . Then Our Beloved was conducted by Mrs Whyte

in the other room. All arose from their seats. His talk was first devoted upon the Unity and Spirituality, then He branched off to the equality of women, the stories of several Baha'i heroines etc. It was a dramatic address in many of its passages. In the audience there were suffragists, suffragettes and anti-suffragists. It was a most difficult thing to talk in a way that all of them may be pleased, all of them may co-operate with each other. But after the meeting Mrs Whyte said that all of them were highly satisfied.

## Section 2: Religious poetry, hymns and blessings

The language of prayers, poetry and hymns offered an important way for women to express and disseminate their faith. This section begins with material from the *Gàidhealtachd*, where spirituality had for centuries been shaped around the natural environment, the rhythms and hardships of everyday life. Charms and rituals were gendered, combining influences from Roman Catholic Christianity and folk belief, and persisted even where evangelicalism became dominant.[2] The papers of pioneering folklorist Alexander Carmichael (Centre for Research Collections, University of Edinburgh) show the significance of the oral tradition for Hebridean women. Gaelic Protestant women also composed religious poetry and songs (see 2.3 below). Austere Presbyterian services used only biblical psalms and paraphrases but, by the 1860s, desire for more aesthetic worship and the influence of the 'salvation industry' led to the introduction of hymns, organs and choirs to enliven praise, and they became vital for popular devotion and diffusion of Christian culture, particularly after American evangelists Moody and Sankey visited Scotland in 1874. A number of women were productive hymn composers and translators. Later, Women's Missionary College students (see 3.5 below) widely performed hymns arranged by the principal, Annie Small‡ (1857–1945), and compiled in *Missionary College Hymns: Being Hymns Oriental, Missionary and Devotional* (Edinburgh c.1914).

Sources 2.1 and 2.2 are charms collected by Alexander Carmichael whose anthology, *Carmina Gadelica* (the first two volumes of which were published in 1900), was a key text in the Celtic Twilight Movement of that time. Carmichael collected the charm to protect unbaptised infants in 1867. A later transcript, dating from around 1884, begins with a passage recording that Mrs MacIsaac presented him with a tropical Molucca bean, washed ashore and cherished for its powers. The Gaelic text below is a transcription of Carmichael's handwritten notes.

2.1  Anna MacIsaac née MacLellan, Ceann Langabhat, An t-Ìochdar
18.10.1867 [University of Edinburgh Library, Centre for Research
Collections, CW MS 87 fos 16v–17]

Cha bhaolaichte leana gun bhaiste aig taigh am bitheadh an Arna so, cha bhaolaichte bean mu m bitheadh e agus cha mhu reachadh taigh am bitheadh i ri theine

(Baol = accident, mishap.) Cha tugain de m' aon nighinn an Earna agus ion cha tugain eir ceud gini oir i ged tha mi cho gorach agus gu bheil mi ga toirt duibhse leis a ghaol tha agam fhein agus aig Eachann oirbh. Chaidh an Arna bheannaichte so a bheannachadh air an altair leis an t-sagairt agus ann an suilean Dhia agus dhaoine tha i naomh. Ged bhitheadh eathar an cunnart dol a dhi cha rea'adh i dhi ach an arna so bhi innte. Cha tig baol air bean gu brath air am bith i . . . Gu ma buan an te gheibh sibh agus gu n robh piseach air a ceann agus gu math curamach a gheibheas i an Arna phriseil ghaolach.

*An unbaptised child cannot be harmed in a house where this bean is, no woman can be harmed while wearing it, nor will a house where it is go on fire. I wouldn't give the bean to my only daughter, nor would I sell it for a hundred golden guineas, although I am so foolish as to give it to you because of the love myself and Hector feel towards you. This blessed bean was blessed on the altar by the priest and in the eyes of God and the people it is sacred. A boat in danger of being wrecked wouldn't be wrecked were she carrying this bean. No misfortune shall ever strike a woman who wears it. . . . May the woman you get have a long life, may she enjoy good fortune, and may she keep the precious beloved bean very carefully.*

The next charm was collected in Malacleit township, North Uist, *c.*1871. It was published in the *Glasgow Herald* in 1872, and subsequently in *Carmina Gadelica.*

### 2.2 Mary Stewart née MacPherson (Mairi Bhreac), 1824–98

Charm for Blessing Cattle

Cuiridh mise 'n spréidh so romham
Mar a dh-òrduich Rìgh an Domhain,
Muire ga'n gleidheadh o fheith' nan coimheach;
Air thùs a Bhrìde mhìn bi mariu,
Le d' bhata 's le d' lorg bi rompa
'S gun glacadh tu ciabh as d' fhalt,
O rinn thu dhuibh eolas 'as earail,
Gan gleidheadh o chall 's o lochd,
O bhathadh, an oilt 's o gharadh cam,
Na o mhilleadh sluic;
A Bhride mhin fagam h-agad,
Muire tilleadh thugam,
Le luas Dhia 's Challum-Chille
Casan cuiribh fothaibh
'S drochaid Mhuire romhaibh

*I will (now) drive this (flock of) cattle before me,*
*Even as the Lord of the Universe has commanded;*
*The (Virgin) free them from dangerous pitfalls –*
*First of all and before them with thy rod and thy staff,*
*Be thou Saint Bride of gentlest nature;*
*Since by a tress of thy golden hair*

*Thou did'st make for them a spell of watch and ward,*
*To keep them from every evil and harm;*
*From being drowned in mountain torrent, or lost in tortuous cavern,*
*And from the misfortune of every pitfall;*
*Gentle Saint Bride to thy care I commend them,*
*Saint Mary do thou restore them to me in safety;*
*With the confidence of cattle under the care of God and St Columba,*
*Put your feet (fearlessly) under you,*
*A safe pathway (bridge) being provided for you by the Blessed Virgin.*

Translations: Domhnall Uilleam Stiùbhart

Mary McDougall Macdonald‡ (1789–1872) was a crofter's wife from Ardtun, near Bunessan, Ross of Mull. She composed poems and hymns which she sang as she sat at her spinning wheel, and is known for 'Leanabh an àigh', roughly translated into English as 'Child in the Manger' for the 1888 collection by Lachlan Macbean, *Songs and Hymns of the Scottish Highlands,* which is quoted below. The English translation was by Macbean.

## 2.3 Mary Macdonald, *Leanabh an àigh* (Child in the manger)

Leanabh an àigh!
Leanabh bh'aig Màiri
Rugadh an stàbull,
   Righ nan dùl!
Thainig don fhàsach,
Dh'fhuiling nar na 'àite
Son' iad an aireamh
   Bhitheas dha dluth!

Child in the manger!
Infant of Mary;
Outcast and stranger,
Lord of all!
Child who inherits
All our transgressions,
All our demerits
On Him fall.

Ged a bhitheas leanaban
Aig righrean na talmhainn
'N greadhnachas garbh
   'Us anabarr muirn,
'S gearr gus am falbh iad
'S fasaidh iad anmhuinn,
An ailleachd 's an dealbh
   A searg' 'san uir.

Monarchs have tender,
Delicate children,
Nourished in splendour,
Proud and gay;
Death soon shall banish
Honour and beauty,
Pleasure shall vanish.
Forms decay.

Cha b'ionnan 's an t-Uan
A thainig g'ar fuasgladh,
Iriosal stuama,
   Ghluais e'n tus;
E naomh gun truailleachd,
Cruithfhear an t-sluaigh,
Dh' eirich e suas
   Le buaidh o'n uir.

But the the most holy
Child of Salvation,
Gently and Lowly
Lived below;
Now as our glorious
Mighty Redeemer,
See Him victorious
O'er each foe.

So leanabh an aigh
Mar dh' aithris na faidhean,
'S na h-ainglean ard,
    B' e miann an sul;
'S e's airidh ar gradh
'S ar n' urram thoirt dha;
Is sona an aireamh
    Bhitheas dha dluth.

Prophets foretold Him –
Infant of wonder;
Angels behold Him
On His throne;
Worthy our Saviour
Of all our praises,
Happy forever
Are His own.

Margaret Stewart Sandeman (1803–83) of Perthshire was a niece of the song-writer Lady Nairne. 'Quitting the Manse', written in her journal on 26 May 1843, meditates upon the consequences of the 1843 Disruption. Those who chose to join the Free Church lost their church buildings, and ministers' families had to leave their manses.

> 2.4 Margaret Stewart Sandeman, 'Quitting the Manse', from Robert Ford (ed.), *The Harp of Perthshire: A Collection of Songs, Ballads and other Poetical Pieces*, chiefly by local authors (London, 1893) (186)

We are leaving the scenes of our happiest hours
So gay and so lovely with spring's opening flowers
Our children's last look to their homes has been given
And faith's eye is fixed on her mansion in heaven.
Now, Scotland, our task is accomplished for thee,
And the Church of our country is faithful and free!

Last week in His house we united in prayer
And we felt that the God of our fathers was there.
Yet 'twas solemn and sad thus in parting to pray
And the *last* song of praise on our lips died away.
Now, Scotland, our task is accomplished for thee,
And the Church of our country is faithful and free!

Yes, secured to thee now is the Gospel's sweet sound
And our conscience is peaceful, our fetters, unbound;
The shield of His truth He will over us fling
And that shout that ye hear is the shout of a King!
The crown on his brow shall forever endure,
His throne as eternity stedfast and sure.
Now, Scotland, our task is accomplished for thee,
And the Church of our fathers is faithful and free!

The poem quoted below, a tribute to Sister M. Veronica Cordier and the Franciscan Sisters, Glasgow, was written in 1854 by Bishop Alexander Smith, vicar apostolic of the Roman Catholic Church in Scotland, Western District. The house was founded in 1847 by nuns from France, and he feared that the city was 'not yet prepared for the good sisters'. But, by the mid-1850s, he was persuaded of religious communities' importance in providing education and socialisation for the rapidly expanding Catholic population.

---

**2.5** Bishop Alexander Smith, *A Notre Mère*, 'A Poem for the Franciscan Sisters of the Immaculate Conception' (1854) [Franciscan Sisters of the Immaculate Conception, Glasgow. Box 012.2, Beginnings and Early History]

> From the home of her sires she has wandered alone
> To the land of the Celt and the Saxon she's gone
> The olive branch waves in her white gentle hand
> And her accents of peace greet the cold frozen land
>
> Midst the foe, and the stranger she seeks not renown
> She courts not their smiles, and she heeds not their frowns
> Could she only impart unto childhood and youth
> The science of God, of religion, and truth . . .
>
> See her stand in the midst of the listening young
> While they hear the blessed words in a sweet foreign tongue
> How they gaze with delight on the form that imparts
> Their duties to God, to their innocent hearts
>
> The black cloud of ignorance now disappears
> Where darkly it brooded for numberless years
> Blind heresy weakened will also decay
> As the light of instruction illumines the way.

Religious poems written by women regularly featured in religious periodicals. Several of Elizabeth Clephane's‡ (1830–69) verses for children were published posthumously in *The Family Treasury* between 1872 and 1874. While in Scotland in 1874, evangelist-musician Ira Sankey read 'The Ninety and Nine' in a newspaper, set it to music and sang it that afternoon at a service in the Free Church Assembly Hall. This poem, and 'Beneath the Cross of Jesus' by the same author, became widely popular hymns on both sides of the Atlantic.

---

**2.6 'The Ninety and Nine'**

> There were ninety and nine that safely lay
> In the shelter of the fold;
> But one was out on the hills away,
> Far off from the gates of gold,
> Away on the mountains wild and bare,
> Away from the tender Shepherd's care.
>
> "Lord, Thou hast here Thy ninety and nine –
> Are they not enough for Thee?"

But the Shepherd made answer, "This of Mine
Has wandered away from Me;
And although the road be rough and steep
I go to the desert to find My sheep."

But none of the ransomed ever knew
How deep were the waters crossed;
Nor how dark was the night that the Lord passed through
Ere He found His sheep that was lost.
Out in the desert He heard its cry,
Sick and helpless and ready to die.

"Lord, whence are those blood drops all the way
That mark out the mountain's track?"
"They were shed for one who had gone astray,
Ere the Shepherd could bring him back."
"Lord, whence are Thy hands so rent and torn?"
"They were pierced tonight by many a thorn."

And all through the mountains, thunder-riven,
And up from the rocky steep,
There arose a cry to the gate of heaven,
"Rejoice, I have found My sheep!"
And the angels echoed around the throne,
"Rejoice, for the Lord brings back His own."

Marion Bernstein's‡ satirical rant may be atypical of Victorian women's religious writing but stands in a long European tradition of provocative sectarian verse. The author's own religious affiliation was complex. She was a Glasgow music teacher, feminist and prolific published writer, and is also quoted in Chapter 3. The context for 'What the Pope Said' was controversy in the wake of a decree declaring papal infallibility a dogma of the Church.

2.7 Marion Bernstein, *Glasgow Weekly Mail*, 12 December 1874 (7)

WHAT THE POPE SAID
Said the Pope (so he did), if all Papists agree,
To be guided by me,
What fine times shall we see
If they'll do all I tell them, set up I shall be.

We will soon have another Bartholomew's day;
Such slashing away;
As good as a play.
Best answer to Protestant logic, I say.

But if Catholics once for themselves dare to think,
I shall certainly sink;

For I'm close to the brink
Of that which might surely make any Pope shrink.

Then Catholics all, rally round at my call;
Let our enemies fall:
Send the Book to the wall.
Then we shall look big, and the truth will look small,
And long live myself, to grow fat by it all.

## Section 3: Women's religious work

Through the long nineteenth century, the idea that women had a special calling as moral and religious exemplars to exercise good works gathered momentum and was widely disseminated in tracts, published sermons and addresses, journals, novels and biographies. 'Woman's Mission' was presented as prescription, rhetoric, scriptural teaching, aspiration and divine blessing. It was the justification for women's personal and organised interventions into other's lives. Sources 3.1 to 3.4 illustrate the work carried out at home, while sources 3.5 to 3.10 illustrate the work of foreign missions. Both home and foreign mission work was reflected in the pages of church periodicals from the early nineteenth century though women themselves rarely authored articles at this time. The first Scottish missionary periodical exclusively about women's work was the *Eastern Female's Friend* launched at the time of the Indian Mutiny in 1857. The main Presbyterian denominations all subsequently published similar periodicals to which women increasingly contributed. Biographies of women missionaries were rare, however.

Agnes Duncan Renton (1782–1863) was married to an Edinburgh merchant and belonged to the dissenting tradition which, in 1847, became the United Presbyterian Church. Agnes is portrayed in her son's *Memorial* as a strong, intelligent and devout woman, involved in a remarkable range of activities, including the anti-slavery movement.

3.1 Henry Renton, *Memorial of Mrs Agnes Renton. For the Private Use of her Family*, Kelso 1866 [NLS. Shelfmark OO.8/2] (66, 69)

In what has been advanced several indications must have been apparent of her Benevolence, than which no attribute of character was more prominent, and which therefore claims special and particular notice. It was, indeed, so much a part of herself, that it is difficult to think of her in any relation of life without recalling it. It might have been originally a strong natural disposition, but it was nourished, purified, and strengthened by love to Christ, and through constant exercise it acquired all the power of the strongest habit . . .

. . . Mr. Smith, the excellent Governor of the Prison, writes – "Mrs. Renton visited the prison, for the purpose of imparting religious instruction to the female prisoners, for upwards of thirty years, and the great patience and self-denial implied in these few words can only be fully known and appreciated by those who have been earnestly and perseveringly engaged in the same kind of arduous duty . . . Severe domestic affliction, and even bereavement in her own family, was not allowed to stand in the way of active duty in her labours of love among the poor unfortunates of the prison; and she has been known to leave her own house to attend to them under circumstances which an ordinary Christian would have considered as a more than sufficient excuse for giving up all labours beyond the circle of her own family. But she was *not* an ordinary Christian. Deeply impressed with the importance of religious truth herself, she made an earnest, sustained and continuous effort to impress the minds of others. She appeared as if continually saying to herself, and acting accordingly, 'My Saviour *died* for me, I must *live* for Him – I must work while it is day – the night cometh.'"

One of the most striking instances of the fruits of her prison labours is given in the following extract from a letter of one of her granddaughters: – 'While A——— and I were staying with grandmamma in 1848 she took us repeatedly to the prison, when visiting Sarah Brannon, who was then awaiting her trial. She was a very ignorant woman, of Irish extraction, could neither read nor write, and beyond knowing there was a God and hell, was without religion. In a drunken quarrel with her husband, she had flung a stool at him and killed him. On coming to her senses, and finding what she had done, she was in great grief for her husband, but felt none for her sin. When brought to prison she was so ignorant and brutish as to seem incapable of understanding right from wrong; and because her case seemed so desperate grandmamma took her in hand, visiting her almost daily for many weeks, talking and praying with her, and by the time her trial came on she had learned to view her crime in a proper light. Passing over grandmamma's conferences with her counsel, all that could be done in her behalf was done, and she was sentenced to imprisonment for life. As she shewed herself increasingly grateful for all that was done for her, and attentive to all that was spoken to her, grandmamma got her detained as long as possible in Edinburgh, and ere she was transferred to Perth had the joy of seeing her a converted woman . . .

Helen Lockhart Gibson was from Kirkcaldy and belonged to a wealthy manufac-turing Baptist family, actively engaged in religious and public issues. In 1859 she committed herself to engage in Christian work 'to advance the Kingdom of God by faithful dealing with individual souls'. She married a Free Church minister in the town, and his memoir, drawing upon her extensive diaries, letters, addresses and Bible lessons, exemplifies a common genre of religious literature. Believing in the saving grace of Christ, Mrs Gibson understood the redeemed life to include self-discipline, sharing her faith, good works and benevolence, to which she committed her personal income.

### 3.2 Reverend W. Gibson, *Not Weary in Well-Doing: The Life and Work of Mrs H. L. Gibson* (Paisley, 1889)

*From a paper read to fellow Sabbath school teachers*

I think it is of the utmost importance that we should keep before them that Jesus is a <u>real living</u> person, who has done a real work, as sinners' substitute, and who is ready to save them <u>now</u>, not at some future time.

. . . We can also pray for our scholars, individually. [In my first class] I knew that fourteen out of sixteen were converted. One died unsaved. She was often in deep anxiety about her soul, but anxiety is not conversion. Love of dress, of dance and bad companions were the snares that kept her out of the Kingdom of God. The last time I saw her, I told her she could not have both Christ and the dance. She said "I can't give up the dancing". "Then" I said "you must lose your soul". Very soon after she was suddenly cut down by smallpox.

*Article about her young women's Bible Class, March 1878*

I live in a town where there are a great many mills and factories, and consequently many young women. I often wished to do something for the spiritual good of this interesting class of the community, but did not know very well how to begin . . .

From the beginning the class has been quite unsectarian. I would never waste any time in merely seeking to gather members to any particular church, much as I love my own. My aim has ever been higher, even to win souls to Christ . . . At the close of the first session, there were 56 girls on the roll, and the next year 77. The kitchen of my house became too strait for us . . . we in a short time removed to the hall of the Church . . . The Hall soon became as crowded as the kitchen . . . more than 200 young women each year.

. . . The class is based strictly on the Word of God . . . I prepare very carefully – about seven or eight hours each week . . . But while I give instruction, my chief aim is conversion . . . I also give an opportunity at the close of each meeting to any who may wish to converse with me, besides setting apart an evening each week, on which young women may come to my house to get counsel and direction on the all-important matter of their salvation . . . I look upon this personal dealing as a most important part of the teacher's work . . . I try to know all by name and to take an interest in all that concerns them . . . There is a prayer meeting for 20 minutes before each class, when two or three plead for the presence of the Holy Spirit on the lesson to be taught . . .

Many look upon our mill and factory workers as a sort of LOWER SPECIES. It is a great mistake; for while there are many who are rough and uncouth, there are also many of the finest specimens of womanhood amongst them, ay! And many noble Christians too. The way to raise them is to teach them God's truth . . . It is not amusement they need, but something that will satisfy them, not only in time but throughout eternity. They require earnest and faithful dealing and warning; for their temptations are many and great.

From the 1870s, the Church of Scotland developed a national programme to organise mission work with particular communities, including itinerant farm workers and the fishing industry, and Jewish immigrants who had settled in Glasgow. The deployment of lay personnel, including women, was central to this approach which was regularly featured in church periodicals and reported annually to the General Assembly, as in the next two extracts.

### 3.3 *Church of Scotland Home and Foreign Mission Record*, Vol. XVII, January 1889–December 1890 (9)

'Among the Fisher-folk' by Miss M. Park, Glasgow
During the months of August and September, Fraserburgh is a chief centre of those interested in the fishing trade and for the time being it becomes the rallying point of about 12,000 fishermen and fisher-girls.

Although life among the fisherfolk is uneventful, they're an interesting people to work amongst. They are a distinctive class, wearing a special dress and many of them speaking a language of their own. The girls come from all parts of the Highlands and Islands of Scotland, and even from England, from which country come the 'kipper-ers' whose trade has been successfully established in Fraserburgh. Different from the custom at other fishing places, many entire families come here, living together in single rooms, which are scarcely habitable, sometimes not even rainproof . . . but somehow they all get shelter and from their pleasant happy looks, no one would think but that it was all sunshine with them. We have in former articles protested against the poor accommodation provided, the small ill-ventilated houses, or the great unkindly barracks . . .

In dealing with these fisher-girls, we the Lady deputies of the Church of Scotland, endeavoured to show as much interest in them, collectively and individually, as we could. We took a record of their names as much as possible, and do them as much good as lay in our power, and we were often cheered by hearing them say after a visit, "Haste ye back again."

We visited one family from St Monan's, who were superior to the ordinary run of fisher-people. They were working for a bazaar for their church and were much interested to find that we, along with some other ladies in Glasgow, were working for it also . . . At another time we came upon a "crew" of Highland girls who were delighted by our saluting them in a few Gaelic phrases which we had picked up. We gave them some Gaelic tracts, but after glancing at them their manner completely changed, and they became indignantly clamourous. We discovered that they were Roman Catholic, and were glad to make our escape.

We only refer to one other visit – a most pleasurable one – to a crew of Cromarty girls. At their request we held a meeting in their room on Sabbath afternoon, the hour fixed not interfering with church services. Although the day was most unpropitious, on our arrival we found the room well filled with young men and women, all seated around on the girls' trunks, a herring barrel being placed for a table. All seemed to appreciate the service . . .

May this work not be labour in vain, as water spilt upon the ground, which cannot be gathered again! God grant that in the great harvest day, it may not be nothing but leaves, but many gathered sheaves from among those toilers of the deep whom it has been our privilege to serve for Jesus' sake in the name of the Christian Life and Work Committee of the Church of Scotland. M.M.P.

The extract below quotes from the report of Mission Sister Miss Margaret Salkerson who worked with the Glasgow Mission to Jews.

3.4 *Reports on the Schemes of the Church of Scotland for the Year 1900. Home Mission Committee, VI – Mission to Jews in Glasgow and Neighbourhood*

During the past winter a beginning was made with work amongst the many hundreds of Jewish women in Glasgow. It had been curious to observe some of them when they came to the mission hall for the first time. They seemed so frightened and so suspicious. One, after a first visit, declared she could not come again, as we would "change her faith" if she did so. Others say that it is needless for them to come, as their husbands attend. All consider it quite superfluous, however interesting, to hear the message of salvation, "for," they say, "being Jews, Jews they must remain." Still, out of seventy families visited, in only three cases was a second call forbidden, and the welcome is generally cordial. Especially when the visit is due to sickness in home, the presence of the "nurse" is valued. Twenty-six patients have been attended in their own homes, and with their words of gratitude frequently surprise has been expressed that Christians should care enough for poor Jews to employ a nurse to look after them. The suffering caused by poverty is very great, and is not alleviated by Jewish friends if a member of the family is known to attend a mission hall. The women know, as a rule, very little English, and some have been in this country for years without having learned to speak it. They are glad to meet with someone who understands Yiddish and can converse with them. Lessons given in English are appreciated by a very few, but domestic claims or the fear of hearing too much about Jesus prevents any great progress. Many women can read Yiddish, but not a few are frightened when they see a book, and to them "the old, old story" has to be told "as to a little child". One who had listened very attentively for some time made the rather disappointing comment, "It is very beautiful, but of course it cannot be true, or everybody would believe it." In this branch of the work the winter has been altogether one of "beginnings." When or where the fruit may appear cannot yet be told.

The foreign mission enterprise included women from the outset; in the early years, a few women travelled as wives or sisters of male missionaries. In response to pleas for single women to dedicate their lives to work in India and Africa, and to raise funds for the cause, female missionary associations were established from the 1830s. These were linked to the main denominations, and were active in developing a network of support at the 'home base'. Missionary correspondence, reports and publications were instrumental in fostering the growth of this movement, disseminating but also reshaping perceptions of women's sphere at home and abroad. By the turn of the twentieth century, women (if married women working unpaid are included) constituted the majority of Scottish missionaries.

The extracts that follow include writing intended for different readerships and purposes. Personal letters give insights into challenges for women living in trying or hostile circumstances, for example, sources 3.5 and 3.9. Material for public consumption told colourful stories portraying missionary women as heroines struggling against heathen customs and practices to bring education, healing and salvation to their benighted sisters. Such material sought both to vindicate and to inspire. The National Library of Scotland holds extensive foreign mission archives, and many missionary materials and publications are also held by New College Library, University of Edinburgh, and by the University of Aberdeen.

Margaret Wilson‡ (née Bayne) (*c*.1795–1835) was the gifted wife of a pioneer Church of Scotland missionary to western India. She established several girls' schools, translated and wrote educational and theological works, and regularly supervised the Bombay mission while her husband was away. Her advocacy helped to establish the first Scottish Association to support the work of female agents. This extract from a letter to her husband conveys her Christian fervour for female education and her interest in engaging intellectually with the challenges of Hinduism, while struggling with constant ill-health.

3.5  John Wilson, *A Memoir of Mrs. Margaret Wilson of the Scottish Mission, Bombay, including Extracts from her Letters and Journals* (Edinburgh, 1840) (308)

*May 3d.*—I was prevented from writing to you yesterday by a slight bilious attack, accompanied by spasms. It confined me to bed a great part of the day, but is now entirely removed; and I feel as if I should be much better afterwards. I rejoice you have decided on remaining a little longer at Khandala . . . I trust the result will prove favourable, and that you will return with new strength to the performance of your duties, and to declare to the natives that blessed Gospel, which is for the ennobling and renovating of our race in every region of the earth. The fitness of Christianity for universal diffusion, is certainly a most convincing argument for its divine origin. It clams no particular locality, but finds a habitation in every region and clime under heaven.

I have read the Darpan [journal], and now send it to you. You will be indignant at the proposal made to Hindudharmadhwansak, and still more so, at the letter of D.K.* What a profound production!!! It savours of ——'s school, or rather of every school whose object it is to oppose the pure light of the Gospel. It has not the merit of being an *ex parte* statement, for it is altogether false. It embodies, however, the unphilosophical and antichristian sentiments of an immense number of people; and I trust it will be met with an able and argumentative reply . . . I could almost reply to him myself, if it would not be unseemly for one of my weak sex, and still weaker capacities, to enter the lists with such a *rude* antagonist . . .

How little does D.K. know of the sublime and holy religion of Jesus; and what a phantom, or airy nothing, in comparison, is that knowledge, the door of which he would open to the Hindus.†

[John Wilson adds the following footnotes]:

*A letter attacking Missionaries, and extolling the virtues of the Hindus
† Mr Nesbit and I sent in replies to this letter, which were never answered. Mrs Wilson also wrote the following note, which was duly published in the Darpan:–

'SIR,– Female education is of great importance as it respects the moral and intellectual improvement of India; and I would earnestly solicit you to call the attention of your readers to it. I have had much pleasure in hearing that the Raja of Satara has set a noble example to his countrymen in this respect, and has instructed his daughter in the elements of reading and writing. When his example is generally followed, many will hail the commencement of a brighter and happier era to the subjects of this vast empire. It is a fact, that, throughout the whole of India, no institution has been formed by the natives for the improvement and culture of the female mind; and that she, who was formed for endless happiness or misery, and "who was originally destined to be the depository of man's thoughts, his solace in affliction, his counselor in adversity and prosperity, is reduced to the level of a slave, or of the brutes he has domesticated for his service." It is a received maxim in all countries, that nothing is unimportant which affects, immediately or remotely, the character and condition of man; and it cannot be denied that to woman belongs, in an eminent degree, the power of imparting to the minds of her children, those impressions and associations which abide with them through all the changes of their history, and contribute, in a powerful degree, to the formation of their habits. Where the character of woman is degraded, we invariably find deceit, demoralization, and the absence of every domestic and social virtue. Where, on the contrary, woman has been elevated to a participation in the religious and moral privileges of man, as in every country into which the light of Christianity has penetrated, we find all that is pure in morals, exalted in feeling, and beautiful in the arrangements of social and domestic life. All the female schools at present in India have been formed by, or are placed under the superintendence of, missionaries, who have been ignorantly or designedly represented as shutting the doors of knowledge to the rising generation. They may be said, in an emphatic sense, to have opened wide the gates of her temple, and to be beckoning to all to come in, and receive of her boundless treasures. – *Mata.*'

The *Eastern Female's Friend* was the first Scottish women's missionary periodical to be published (1857–62), being succeeded by other publications such as *Women's Work in Heathen Lands, News of Female Missions,* and the *Zenana Quarterly.* These are in the St Colm's College archive (NLS Acc. 113001/225–8).

3.6 *The Eastern Female's Friend*, 1 July 1859, New Series, No. XI (37–8)
[NLS, Acc.113001/225]

LETTER FROM MISS M'CARTER
MADRAS, 26th *April,* 1859.
I visited the day-school, a scene of busy, animated interest, and quite a pattern for order and arrangement. I was much struck with the intelligent manner in which the

children gave answers to questions of Scripture, – the truths which we are accustomed to hear from our infancy seemed to be presented in such a suitable point of view to the heathen mind. It was *particularly* gratifying to observe the distinct knowledge which the children seemed to have of man as a lost, fallen sinner, and Jesus Christ as a perfect Saviour. Altogether, there is a freshness about Christianity here, and a simple looking up to God, which strikes the mind in coming from a land of prevailing light, abounding privilege, and much outward profession. The first Sabbath which I spent in India, the Lord's Supper was dispensed to the native congregation for the first time in the Tamil tongue. Though I could not follow the precious truths that were spoken, the scene was one of very deep interest. Mr Rajahgopaul officiated at the whole service, Mr Braidwood and Mr Campbell as elders. The text was Zech. xii. 10. The Lord grant that his own appointed ordinance may continue in the native tongue, accompanied by a living power, till His own second coming!

 . . . The scholars presented the most varied appearance of anything I had ever seen in one assembly. There were the sons of Ishmael, the followers of Mohammed, and Hindus with lines painted on their foreheads as the badge of their respective castes. Varied were they in shade, and endlessly varied in garb. To see these young persons seated, quietly and attentively listening to the native teacher declaring to them the great name of Christ, and themselves repeating that blessed name given under heaven whereby man can be saved, was a picture fitted to encourage the hopes, strengthen the faith, and increase the earnestness of prayer amongst Christians at home. I could not help lifting up a prayer that these labourers may have very many gathered from amongst this people, to share with them the eternal reward. I have seen most of the native Christians here, and visited some of them in their houses; and all that I have seen has had only the effect to deepen one's interest, and draw out the heart to them. The whole work tells unquestionably of much bygone labour followed by the blessing of God.

Euphemia Miller (Mrs Sutherland) (*c.*1820–81) was orphaned as a child and worked as a domestic servant in Glasgow. After hearing an address about a planned mission to West Africa, she resolved to become a missionary herself, and worked for the United Presbyterian Mission in Calabar from 1849 until her death. Waddel's book is typical of the biographies designed to evoke the heroism, self-sacrifice and adventure of missionary lives, and to inspire young Scots to follow in their footsteps, but unusual in the Scottish context both in being a biography of a woman missionary and being written by a woman.

### 3.7 Agnes Waddel, *Memorials of Mrs Sutherland, Missionary, Old Calabar* (Paisley: J. & R. Parlane, 1883) (79–83)

Duke Town has from six to eight thousand inhabitants, and amongst this dense heathen population Mrs Sutherland found ample scope for her labours in behalf of the women. The Gospel light seemed yet but as a glimmer in the surrounding darkness of heathenism. Part of her regular work was to visit the women in their own

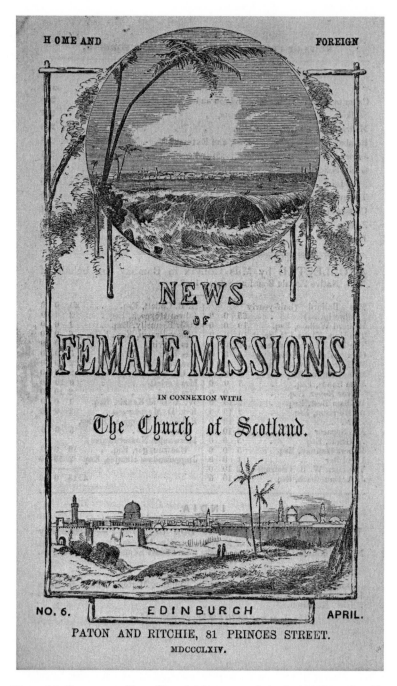

**Figure 6.3** Front cover, *News of Female Missions*, no. 6, April 1864. Reproduced by permission of the Trustees of the National Library of Scotland.

houses . . . Inside, a certain amount of cleanliness is seen; but outside, all the garbage and filth are thrown with an entire disregard of pestilence or disease; smells of all kinds pollute the air; and to a European lady visiting daily in the Town, the trials must have been very sore . . . The soil of human minds she had to cultivate . . . was encrusted with the superstitions of generations of barbarism. Coldness, indifference, ingratitude, joined to low cunning, were often all the return to be had for the most painstaking labour bestowed on the people. But Mrs Sutherland did not dwell much on this side of the work, certainly not in her letters, nor even, we believe, in her own mind. She had a wonderful spring of hopefulness in her nature. Believing devoutly in God, she fully expected that He would yet visit Calabar with the outpouring of the Spirit, and cause the dry bones to live. Her love for the people made it easier to believe that God loved them, and *that* is the secret of successful missionary effort.

Mrs Sutherland was readily welcomed into the harems of the chiefs. She read and prayed with the women, gave them elementary instruction in knowledge, both secular and sacred; taught them to pray, and to read the Word of God for themselves; encouraging them, at the same time, to come out to public worship where they were allowed to do so. One class that greatly moved her compassion were the women "sitting in Mbukpuisa". These were widows who, being shut up in one apartment for months, sometimes for years, were not allowed to wash or dress themselves until a ceremony called 'devil-making' had been performed for their late husband. If slaves, they were frequently reduced to starvation when the time was long protracted.

Religious instruction, offered in such circumstances, would seem but a mockery. However, Mrs Sutherland had a wonderful "bag" out of which she would produce a little parcel of rice, or something of the kind, with which to allay the all-dominating claims of hunger, and then try to instil into the darkened minds of these poor creatures a little hope, some notion, faint it might be, but yet true, of Him who came to be the light of the world.

Jane Waterston‡ (1843–1932) was the first of many missionaries belonging to the pioneer generation of women to qualify as medical practitioners. Their skills were considered important in opening up new avenues and access for missions.

3.8 *The Free Church of Scotland Monthly Record*, 1 August 1879 (187) 'Work for Women in Connection with The Ladies' Society for Female Education in India and Africa' by Mrs Murray Mitchell [Maria Hay Flyter Mitchell]

Many of our readers are already well acquainted with the name of Miss Waterston. Her successful career at Lovedale, where for seven years she acted as superintendent of the female seminary, will be fresh in the remembrance of all who follow with intelligent interest the work of our society. We have now bidden her "God-speed" as she enters on a new and still more difficult and self-denying enterprise; and many will follow her with their earnest good wishes and prayers when we announce that she has already started for Lake Nyasa to join the Livingstonia Mission, as a fully qualified medical missionary. Miss Waterston is thus among the first European females who have ventured to take up residence in the wilds of Central Africa. The only other lady who has gone to Livingstonia is to be the wife of the well-known missionary Dr. Laws, who so ably conducts the Free Church Mission there; and at Blantyre, the station of the Established Church of Scotland, there already resides wife of one of the missionaries – Mrs Duff McDonald.

. . .

Her success at Lovedale, and the deep spiritual need of poor Africa, fired her with a holy ambition to do yet something more for its regeneration – to penetrate to its further recesses, and get at new peoples and tribes. So she came home, gave herself to thorough medical study, worked hard; and now, with diplomas and testimonials in abundance, she has gone forth fully equipped to help to carry Christian civilization, with healing for both body and soul, to the dark and untrodden "regions beyond." Who will not follow her with heartfelt sympathy and interest, and earnest prayer for the success of her noble enterprise?

Waterston left Livingstonia after only six months, believing that the mission head, Dr Laws, and his colleagues did not understand her, and were professionally jealous. She was frustrated that her qualifications and experience were not utilised. Waterston's apparent crisis of faith and fears for the future did not, in the longer term, hinder her medical career or her continued involvement in church and missionary affairs. When she died in 1932, she had become one of Cape Town's most prominent citizens, renowned for her medical, philanthropic and political activities, and her commitment to women's rights.

### 3.9 Lucy Bean and Elizabeth van Heyningen (eds), *The Letters of Jane Elizabeth Waterston, 1866–1905* (Cape Town: Van Riebeck Society, 1983)

A long letter written on 14 February 1880 describes the strain and her sense of isolation:

Now for my last piece of news. *I have resigned.* My honour as a Doctor will prevent me from leaving until the unhealthy season is over but my year is out on the 5th June and I go then. I will never repent having come here but once, and that is to the last day of my life, for it has shattered my faith in God and man and I fear I will never recover it. If I fall, don't let any humbug of self denial be written about me for, if I lose my life here, I grudge it sadly, and it is from no missionary spirit of any kind I stay up here for the next few months, but simply the same feeling that would prevent me deserting my post during an epidemic at home.

My resignation runs after this manner, that I find I must either give up my profession or give up teaching. I cannot do the amount of teaching and looking after needed here and also practice medicine without simply killing myself, (what is worse, killing someone else by bad doctoring that is not in the nation), that unless the doctors were to knock about more, there is only work for one here and therefore one is enough, and that I refuse utterly to give up what I have learnt thoroughly and know how to do work (teaching the alphabet and looking after girls demoralized by idleness and bad ways before I came) which a girl at a much lower salary could do. Of course my resignation is more smoothly worded, for the formal one is handed to Dr Laws.

I was judged fit to teach Anatomy in London. I am thought fit for the Alphabet here. There are about eighty in the school. The highest twenty go to Mr Gunn, and the next to Mrs Laws and the forty beginners to me. Most of the medical work is done by me and I do all that needs tramping.

Waterston wished to return to Lovedale to work as a doctor but was worried that she would not be accepted back:

> . . . If I don't go to Lovedale I have to pay a heavy fine to the Committee and will land in London with shattered faith, very probably impaired health, and empty pocket, such being the price of nearly a year's Missionary work in Central Africa. If I were a man I would add anything but a soft expression here. It is the shattered faith in God and Missionary work that I feel most of all. Life is no longer what it was to me and never will be again. If I come to Lovedale you will want me to conduct worship and turn up at Church and services and I can't do that at present. What I want is to be let alone and left to fight out doubts, if that be possible, and get back, not some fragments of the old belief, that is not possible, but some standing ground on which to work in the present and have some slight hope for the future. I will not sham what I don't believe for any consideration. I have got a horror of religious humbug that will last me the rest of my days. I just hate being up here . . .

In June 1894, a new 'Institute' was established by the Free Church Women's Foreign Missionary Society to prepare female candidates for missionary service. The experiment was unprecedented in the British Isles. The first principal, Annie H. Small‡ had served as a missionary in India. As head of the Institute (from 1908, the Women's Missionary College), she was instrumental in developing an innovative and integrated approach to missionary preparation, emphasising the responsibility and creativity of women embarking upon a vocation. Small's leadership and the college were regarded as models of good practice, not least through their involvement in the World Missionary Conference, held in Edinburgh in 1910. By 1914 there had been 245 students from many countries and denominations. The extract comes from the large St Colm's College Archive (including material pertaining to women's foreign missionary work from 1839) at the National Library of Scotland [Acc. 133001]. It gives an account of Small's years as principal (1894–1914), written by her as a gift to the college.

3.10 'Our First Twenty Years', written by Miss Annie H. Small and presented to House Guild, Women's Missionary College, Inverleith Terrace, Edinburgh, 1 November, 1916 [NLS, Acc.133001/180]

Chapter IV
OUR VISION OF MISSIONARY PREPARATION
The calling of a missionary of Jesus Christ, whether Home or Foreign, is to a life, not to a mere life-work or profession; not only so, but it is to a life highly specialised.

She preaches, teaches, heals, and those duties must be truly and finely done, done too with a delicate understanding of their ultimate significance; for this reason, that they are the exterior expression of something interior and immeasurably great.

For, the missionary of Jesus Christ is, if I may so express it, the embodiment of all for which we believe Him to stand to our world, her voice is His, her eyes, looking into the eyes of hearer, pupil, patient, are His, her hands and feet are His; and the only way of it for her is that she should herself find herself in Him, and then in all simplicity go out and make her offering to His world, the offering of a real imaging forth of the Lord who thus possesses her being. She, every bit of her, and all the time, not her words and acts for so many hours a day, must make her Blessed Lord desirable to His people.

A college which should help women to become such missionaries was not easy to evolve. It would have been fatally easy to make it that which we most dreaded, a sort of hothouse for "forcing" a certain type of missionary character, which would be self-conscious and unnatural, and which would have defeated the end for which the college had been founded.

Here the College itself came to our aid. I wonder whether I can explain.

It was not long before we began to realise that the college was itself an organic thing, a living, growing thing. It therefore soon began to express itself in terms of its purpose . . .

There were meantime certain obvious lines of action: the students must know their Gospel, and they must know also something of the very wonderful world of thought and experience and need to which their Gospel must appeal, they must find themselves within the great succession of those "sent forth", they must test their powers in various directions, all of this was comparatively easy. College, evolving its own purpose, did the rest. We learned, for example, that we could not train missionaries, but we learned that life, corporate life, under simple and natural conditions, with the missionary idea as its centre, could and did train missionaries . . .

. . .

We took the – then subversive – method of entire belief in our students' good will and power to make the very best they could of the help we offered them. They were responsible women, offering themselves for the greatest calling in the world; we therefore trusted them entirely . . .

There is another view of the evolution of the College which I must not omit. From the beginning we have felt that as far as it was in our power our students should be brought into relation with the great world and its happenings. If we wished them to have that greatest of all missionary qualities, an understanding heart, they must have the chance of learning and understanding. Visitors of note have spoken to us, we have gladly broken in upon routine to go out and meet passing events. Some of these events have been Scottish, as when we stood in pouring rain to watch the historic streams of Free Church and United Presbyterian Church and became one united stream . . . And again, when the World Missionary Conference of 1910 was in prospect, we had not only the interest of the fact that I was a member of the Commission on the Preparation of Missionaries, but we gathered to the College itself as our guests ten men and women who might well be said to have brought us into the closest intimacy with the Conference . . .

This linking of our College life with the happenings and doings of the greater world has a vital connection with the future life of missionary candidates. A missionary with a little mind or a little heart is an unthinkable person. She goes out to the great old world to help build a great new world, and she must see life not only as a whole but as a great whole, if she is to do any justice at all to her own apparently infinitesimal share in it.

### Section 4: Women and religious authority

As the previous sections show, women through the long nineteenth century were increasingly active in church life and mission. This marked feminisation of religion was of service rather than authority: in all mainstream denominations, ordination to ministry or priesthood was restricted to men. But this subordinate position was contested by women claiming their right in disparate contexts: to vote in a call (source 4.1), to preach and minister (sources 4.2 and 4.6) to participate in church governance (source 4.5). Most disturbing for patriarchal Presbyterianism, which emphasised good order, was the spectre of women rejecting its authority and asserting divine vocation. Elspeth Buchan‡ (1738–91) convinced a seceding minister from Irvine and a small group of followers that she was 'the woman clothed in sun' (Revelation 12: 1) gifted with the power of prophecy and able to confer the Holy Spirit by breathing on them. The notorious Buchanite sect was regarded as warning of the dangers when women disobeyed the Pauline injunction to keep silent in church,[3] and there was a similar reaction from the religious establishment to Owenite utopian socialist women (1830s– 40s) whose lectures attracted thousands and included outspoken attacks on religious doctrines and institutions.[4] Itinerant female preachers were also a feature of mid-century millenarian revivalism (source 4.2) and, by the 1870s, Salvation Army 'Hallelujah lassies' started to appear on city streets. These challenges to convention, and the growth of Roman Catholic convents, provoked debate on the vexed question of 'woman's ministry', and the Protestant churches responded by establishing officially sanctioned organisations, notably the Woman's Guild (source 4.3) to foster distinctive but subordinate forms of vocational ministry, including deaconesses and church sisters (source 4.4). By the 1900s large numbers of church women were active in the suffrage movement, and some contended that their exclusion from church governance and ordination was at odds not only with secular aspirations for equality but also with the gospel message itself.[5] In 1914, as the mainstream denominations embarked on protracted debates on these questions, a Glasgow University theology graduate and Pentecostalist became the first woman in Scotland to be ordained to the ministry of word and sacrament (source 4.7).

Primary sources are extensive. Reports of, and responses to, 'disorderly female preaching' (especially *c.*1866–70) are found in Presbytery minutes and church journals (such as the Free Church's *Watchword*). Discussion about the role and ministry of women recurs in denominational magazines and General Assembly Reports, particularly the Kirk's Life and Work Committee and publications such as, from around 1890, the *Life and Work* Guild supplement and branch/ presbyterial council minutes and reports (NAS), and the United Free Church's *Monthly Record*. There are also biographies of individual churchwomen (for example: Mrs H. Macrae, *Alice Maxwell, D.C.S.* (1917); Lady Frances Balfour, *Ne Obliviscaris* (1912).

A foundational principle of the Free Church of Scotland was the right of congregations to call their own minister (an Act of 1833 gave power of veto) but the extent of democracy became a contested issue. At the first General Assembly of the new denomination in 1843, there was a heated debate about whether women in full communion with the Church could be counted as individual members, with full rights and responsibilities, or whether male relatives should vote on their behalf. Women contributed anonymously to the wider debate, arguing that their contribution to the new project entitled them to representation, and the eventual outcome was a recognition of the principle (if not always the practice) of their claim.

4.1  *Present Crisis of the Free Church; or, A Scriptural Examination of the Question, Ought Females to have a voice in the calling of pastors in the Church of Christ?* (Edinburgh: John Johnstone, 1843)

Appendix B – letter which appeared in the *Witness* newspaper, June 1843, from 'A Female Friend and Member of the Free Church'

TO THE VERY REVEREND THE MODERATOR OF THE GENERAL ASSEMBLY OF THE FREE CHURCH OF SCOTLAND

VERY REVEREND AND HONOURED SIR, –

. . . I am sure it is not your wish, nor that of your distinguished colleagues in the work of restoring and renovating your church, to overlook any of those who are members of Christ, and whose interests come under your care, in studying for the general welfare. I speak of the *Christian women* of your community; and I am persuaded, that though withdrawn from the governing sphere of the church's affairs, and though silent hearers of the Word in the mixed congregation, you will admit that they stand equally near the Redeemer, and have an equal interest with the other sex, in the character and adaptation of those who preside over them in holy things.

Many felt the *Veto Law* to be defective in this respect. There was something harsh and exclusive, when neither Scripture rule nor expediency seemed to enjoin it, in the term *male heads of families* as solely entitled to give expression to their wishes in the settlement of their ministers. The faithful daughters of the Church of Scotland rejoiced in the Veto Law, as a good attainment for the time in which it was achieved; they would not have raised a finger to add to the embarrassment of those who had the task of defending that measure in high places, or by any pretension of theirs given colour to the charge of its being too popular and favourable to democratic influence. We were silent through the period of those anxious discussions in the General Assembly, while the Act was passing, and since, while it was subject to Parliamentary animadversion. No murmur of ours would have been heard, could the measure, imperfect as it seemed to many of us, have cleared its way, and established itself in undisputed authority. It is only now, when, through the pangs of a second birth, our church starts to a new race, free of all extraneous weight, and bound by no tie in framing her regulations, save that of fidelity to her own glorious Head and faithful people, that we, the attached, jointly-protesting fellow-sufferers with you in the cause, would humbly submit our claim to your and our brethren's consideration.

What we ask is not a voice in the church's legislation, – not a hand in the church's government, – but simply room for the expression of our choice, as members of the body of Christ, in the calling of our ministers. We are fully aware that there may be a *virtual*, where there is not an *actual*, representation of opinion; that religious society does not divide itself into the male and female sects; and that the interests and opinions of various classes may be protected and take cognisance of, where the elective franchise is confined to a specified few . . . It is not a superfluous power for which I plead, – a right of which the fruits may be as well enjoyed without the ostensible possession, – but a substantial interest, to be exercised for the good of the parties concerned, and with advantage to the community.

There is no occasion to interfere with the order and subordination of families to this end. Where families are united, connected with the same church, the *male head* of the family, the husband and father, he being a communicant, may sign the call as representative of his house. In the case of a Christian wife, united to a careless husband, she a communicant and he not, let her exercise the right of a member of the church. She has her family to watch over, and is not the less anxiously interested in their religious instruction, that her care for them in this respect is undivided. Christian widows, with or without families, rank often among the church's most inseparable friends and fairest ornaments, having faithful children nurtured with prayer, and hands practised in good works. Why should not these, loving ordinances, and waiting continually on the means of grace, have a voice in the selection of their pastor? Single women, also householders, often stationary in the places where their parents dwelt, which their male relatives revisit only at long intervals, have a status in a parish. They are acquainted with the resident poor by constant intercourse, know their histories, and are relied on by them. These form the friends of the minister's family, are profitable to him in many of his undertakings; and no class of persons is more concerned to find in their pastor a man whom they can regard as a friend, and look up to as a leader and coadjutor in every labour of love and plan of usefulness. They may chance to obtain the minister they would choose, through the suffrages of others; still the reason remains to be shown, why they should not act for themselves in the matter, and have the measure of credit with their neighbours and future pastor, which their aid in his election might give.

The women of your church, noble Sir, have responded promptly to your call.
. . .

We love the principle of your free Church; we rejoice greatly in the pastoral tie, formed by the choice and concurrence of the Christian people; but still the thought will occur, are not *we* also the Christian people?

Millenarian female preachers were a distinctive feature of the revivals of 1859–73. A few, including Jessie Macfarlane‡ (1843–71) from Edinburgh and Isabella Armstrong‡ (b.1840), who was based at the Newmains Assembly near Wishaw (a congregation of seceders from the Evangelical Union Church), challenged convention and propriety by addressing 'promiscuous gatherings' of men and women. Armstrong preached to hundreds every week and, in 1866, wrote a tract in defence of her ministry. While not directly challenging or claiming institutional leadership and authority, she contended that the public ministry of women was a sign of the 'last days' prophesied in Joel 2: 28–29. She was an eloquent advocate for the equality of women, and later engaged in temperance and suffrage campaigns.

> ### 4.2  Isabella Armstrong, *Plea for Modern Prophetesses, Glasgow*, 1866
> [University of Edinburgh, New College Library, P.g. 14/1]

That prophetesses were called of God cannot be doubted; that their mission was to men as well as to women we know for certain; that their office was public as well as private is clear; and that they taught with an authority no female now, so far as I know, desires or contends for, is evident. How Christian women can now be charged with "unsexing themselves" and a host of other appellations sometimes freely used, I am at a loss to know . . .

. . . Instead of Christian forbearance, I have met with worse treatment than I might expect if I were an evil-doer . . . when I have met those who, in clerical finery unknown to the Apostle, clamoured loudly in the pulpit, and extended my hand as one Christian to another, it was not accepted . . . Where God's servants stand while they deliver their message of love and salvation, is of no importance; but for ease and comfort . . . it is of great advantage to have an elevation, call it what you please. But to believe females must not occupy a pulpit, because it is more holy than many other places, or that a female member is less holy than a male member, is surely blind and absurd to no common degree . . .

I am not contending that women ought to form churches and preside over them, ruling however diligently and exercising official ecclesiastical authority, however wisely and moderately. But leaving this field clear, we have ample margin to prophecy . . .

The disciples marvelled that Jesus talked with the woman at the well (John 4: 27) . . . and it is evident that the disciples still marvel, that the Great Shepherd speaks so graciously to the female members of His body, though it is to be regretted that they do not evince the same circumspection in allowing him to manifest in His own time His own God-like purposes.

From 1887, when the Church of Scotland's Woman's Guild was founded, all three Presbyterian denominations implemented schemes to organise women's work. The arrangements for these gave women a measure of local and national autonomy under the authority of exclusively male church courts. Despite these limitations, organisations such as the Woman's Guild were of central importance in providing space and encouragement for women to develop an impressive range of initiatives, services, institutions and publications. The rules and regulations outline a threefold structure, including an order of deaconesses, which was presented as the appropriate biblical model for a distinctive full-time ministry of women. The second level of women workers was soon abandoned.

### 4.3 *Rules and Regulations of the Church of Scotland Woman's Guild* (adopted by the Church of Scotland General Assembly, 1887)

#### WOMAN'S GUILD

1. The Association shall be called "THE CHURCH OF SCOTLAND WOMAN'S GUILD".
2. The general object of the Guild shall be to unite together all women who are engaged in the service of Christ in connection with the Church, or desire to give help to any practical Christian work in the parish, as well as all who are receiving Christian teaching and looking forward to Christian service.
3. Parochial branches, therefore, may take whatever form may seem most desirable to the minister and kirk-session for making a Parochial Union with the above-named object in view. It is intended that the members of Bible-classes, of young women's congregational associations, of mission working parties or Dorcas societies, as well as tract-distributors, Sabbath-school teachers, members of the church choir, or others similarly occupied, shall be incorporated in a branch, or in separate branches, and the members of such branches regarded as individual members of the Guild. Other workers might also, in special circumstances, be enrolled as individual members, though there were no branch of the Guild in the parish or congregation. (*Note* – All members are requested to make the welfare of their fellow-members of the branch, and of the whole Guild, a subject of special prayer.)

#### WOMAN-WORKERS' GUILD

1. This Association shall be called "THE CHURCH OF SCOTLAND WOMAN-WORKERS' GUILD" and shall consist of experienced workers not less than twenty-one years of age.
2. Enrolment shall be made by authority of the kirk-session, after that court is satisfied of the member's Christian character and devotion to service for a period of not less than three years.

. . .

**DEACONESSES**

1. Deaconesses, after their qualifications have been approved by the presbytery, shall be solemnly set apart by that court, at a religious service in Church.

2. There shall be an Institution or Home which shall be in connection with the Church of Scotland, and under the direction of the Christian Life and Work committee, unless the General Assembly shall otherwise direct.

3. There will be two classes of deaconesses, equal in position, but having different spheres. *A) Those whose qualifications have been attested by their work while residing in their own home* – (1) They shall have been known for not less than seven years as active workers, giving their life during that period very largely to Christian work. (2) They shall be free to work where they find themselves most useful in connection with the Church of Scotland, and subject to the minister and kirk-session of the parish. (3) It will be possible for those whose work has mainly been at home to reside for a time in the Institution, on conditions to be arranged, with a view to special training. *B) Those who have been trained in the Institution* – (1) They shall have been not less than two years connected with it on probation and in service. (2) If accepted as candidates, they shall during the first three months contribute £— for their own support; if thereafter taken as probationers, they shall, during their time of probation, be maintained in the Institution. (3) While being trained in it they shall be subject to the rules, and shall be prepared to go where sent for temporary service.

*Life and Work* magazine was established in 1879. This extract from an article by a minister's wife indicates the perceived nature and purpose of 'women's ministry' and, in particular, the revived Order of Deaconesses (DCS, who received training under the guidance of Alice Maxwell‡ (1856–1915) at the newly established Deaconess Institute). Their availability and presumed ability to transcend class barriers were elements of the Church's strategy, such as it was, to respond to the 'Social Question' which preoccupied Scotland in the late nineteenth and early twentieth centuries.

---

4.4  Flora Blair, 'How to bring the east and west ends of our large cities together', *Life and Work*, 1892 (94)

---

I have considered very carefully the methods now in process of endeavouring to elevate the condition of the poor . . . Let me say I have failed to find any method which in its plan of ministering Christianity to rich and poor is fulfilled so broadly and completely as by that ideal and highest mission for women – the Order of Deaconesses . . . To such as these, quoting the beautiful words of Miss Maxwell, the ministry of the Deaconess of the Church of Scotland (DCS) will be "to speak God's gospel in mission hall and poor man's home; to tend the sick, soothe the suffering, comfort the sorrowful, reclaim the erring, to feed and clothe the needy in a spirit of sisterly charity that will not pauperise." . . . What we need here, and what the deaconess has to give, is her religion of love, for it is only by living the true human life alongside the poor, ignorant and sorrowing in this world, that they will believe her about the next . . . The obligation between rich and poor involves sacrifice on both sides: the rich to descend without condescension, the poor to aspire without pretension. That ladies of culture and position and intellectual power, under the seal of the Diaconate, should be willing to throw themselves into the work of bridging the deep social gulf, is one of the best signs of promise for the expansion of Christianity, for linking east and west ends, and for the continuing stability of the Church of Scotland. Training and discipline must do much more than untrained effort. The essence of the work in relation to men and women (not in the mass) will forever preclude the Diaconate from becoming mere professionalism. The presentment of the DCS is that of a character not so much powerful as delicately strenuous in bestowing the highest service upon an individual, not upon a mass of individuals. Take away the tambourine, the street preaching, the storms of excitement in prayer, of the Salvation lassie, and how much is there left? Scanty spiritual nourishment, I fear, for the reclaimed drunkard and penitent sister. I say this without prejudice . . . While those of our sisters . . . are going out into the world upon their divine mission of mercy to the dying and others both rich and poor, we under the shelter of our happy homes, would do well to consider the arduous toil with which they follow their vocation. Let us help them with prayer, sympathy, interest . . . Theirs is essentially a life of devotion and sacrifice. As Mary, most honoured of women, lived a life of obscurity and sacrifice, we remember the strange fact that she is not present at the moment when Christ breaks bread . . . But she is with him at the last when, abandoned by his own . . . He bows his head. To minister in affliction was the service left for women – the last, highest and best. In this lies the glory of the Deaconess of the Church of Scotland.

The United Free Church (UFC) was formed as a union of the Free Church of Scotland and the United Presbyterian Church, in 1900. A significant minority of members was supportive of progressive political and social movements, including Woman Suffrage. The UFC united with the Church of Scotland in 1929. The *Monthly Record* provided an important forum for discussion of women's changing roles in church and society, especially 1913–14, through its 'Matter to the Women' section. By 1914 momentum for change to Church polity to include women in official governance structures resulted in petitions from UFC presbyteries to the General Assembly.

4.5 'Matter to the Women' – *a monthly section written by and for women, United Free Church Monthly Record*

*October 1913*
We women are comrades of our ministers and office bearers, and probably we hardly realise to how great an extent we influence their work . . . a large proportion of home and foreign missionaries are women. According to the distribution of labour, funds distributed by men in the committees and church Courts are largely supplied and collected by women . . . Our preachers supply religious thoughts and teaching . . . we women, according to our gift and opportunity, largely supply public opinion . . . Might not our contribution be more conscious, ordered, purposeful than it is?

*November 1913*

God created man male and female – not two, but one human race . . . We have evolved an elaborate civilisation based upon the conception of a man race and a woman race; nor, even in this late year of grace, 1913, has our consciousness of the purpose of God for the social order been clear enough to prevent the reproach that only through a contest within the twofold unity of the race can ancient and grave wrongs be righted . . . The stately bow has given place to the warm mutual handclasp . . . Just so far as are asked to cooperate, we learn to cooperate . . . The demand for fellowship must become entirely mutual.

The extract below is from an article published a month before the General Assembly received a petition calling for consideration of 'the place of women in the church's life and work'.

## 4.6 'The Church and the Women's Movement', *United Free Church Record*, April 1914 (151)

. . . There are many movements agitating and disturbing human life today, creating controversy and dissension and embittering the relations of men and women, class and class, nation and nation. Should the Church keep aloof from these, or should it study them, apart from the political aspect, discover what contribution they are making to the cause of righteousness, or otherwise, and take a definite stand in regard to their spiritual content and possibilities? Is it the duty of the Church to give members a lead in such matters?

For the moment let us take the claim of women to greater recognition in public life. Everywhere we see them bursting the bonds and conventions that have dominated them since the beginning, rising above old narrow ideas of sex, and desiring a position as co-workers with men in the task of governing the world. Is this an abnormal phase, or is it in line with the natural order and an inevitable corollary of the passing of brute force, and the freer action of the mind in the region of public service?

Is it an abrogation of their position and function in the social organism, or merely a continuation of the finer and quieter work they have hitherto accomplished into a wider and larger sphere, a broadening of the base of spiritual influence? There are some who take one position and some the other, but it is the duty of the Church to note the movement, and if it find it to be on the side of righteousness to give it the benefit of sympathy and support.

. . . There is the more reason for directing attention to this question, because the claim of women is now beginning to make itself felt within the Church. Many are restless and dissatisfied with their position, particularly among the younger class, which is constantly being recruited by girls passing out of school imbued with new ideas. They might have hitherto been content to do what might be called the drudgery of Church work, and it is universally admitted that they have done it with a self-abnegation, patience and thoroughness beyond praise. They are the chief machinery for collecting funds; their services are requisitioned for any special effort. But apparently the time is coming when they will no longer be satisfied to do this work, fine as it is, without some ampler responsibility than they have at present. We do not know whether any precise policy has been formulated in their minds, but from what is stated in some quarters the assumption is that they will wish some sort of say in Church government – a principle which, by the way, one at least of our City congregations has already conceded by admitting a woman as manager.

The whole question merits serious consideration. It is perhaps hardly one for piecemeal treatment in Presbyteries, but rather for a quiet and dignified pronounce-ment one way or the other by the General Assembly. The easiest course is to let it 'lie on the table' and await developments; but one is inclined to doubt whether it is the wisest. The problem is reacting on the spiritual life of thousands in the Church, and the Assembly would probably earn greater respect by taking up a definite stand, according to the light given it, than by ignoring it altogether.

By the 1890s, new critical approaches to theology and the Scriptures offered potent arguments against the notion that women should be barred from ordina-tion to ministry, and universities finally opened up divinity faculties to women. In 1910, at St Andrews University, Frances Melville‡ (1873–1962) (Church of Scotland member, educationalist and leading suffragist) was the first in Scotland to graduate with a degree in theology. The possibility that she and others might be able to test their vocation was no longer something that could be ignored. Eunice Murray‡ (1878–1960), Frances Simson and Lady Frances Balfour‡ (1858–1931) were among the women's rights campaigners who were activists for women's ordination, especially after 1918. For most in the Presbyterian churches such a consideration was beyond contemplation, but the unthinkable was begin-ning to happen in smaller denominations, and was acclaimed in some quarters as a feminist advance, as an article from the Women's Freedom League paper, *The Vote*, indicates, in this report of a woman minister officiating at a marriage in Glasgow.

### 4.7 *The Vote*, Friday, 24 April 1914 (9)

'Scotland's First Woman Pastor: Rev Olive May Winchester, B.D.'

From the *Glasgow Weekly News* of April 18 we take the following interesting particulars: –

'She is truly a remarkable personality, and her attainments are as remarkable. She obtained her B.D. degree after passing through the Divinity Hall at Glasgow, an honour which she shares with Miss Melville of St Andrews.

Miss Winchester not only took the degree and passed brilliantly, but she has been ordained to the ministry of the Pentecostal Church. She is, there is little doubt, the first woman to become a fully qualified and acting pastor in Scotland.

The story of her career is most interesting. She was born in the United States of America, her father being a lawyer in Maine. On the death of her father she and her mother moved Eastward, and after studying in Harvard University, she became a teacher in a theological school, the Pentecostal Collegiate Institute at North Situate, Rhode Island. Here she had the unique experience of training men for the ministry.

Miss Winchester arrived in Glasgow five years ago to assist in the work of the Pentecostal Church, and during that time she entered the Divinity Hall of the University. Her entrance to the classes was treated as a huge joke by the male students, but Miss Winchester fairly turned the tables by proving herself at least a match for them. She gained the gold medal and several other honours, and one can well imagine the chagrin of the discomfited mere men students at being beaten by a woman! The Pentecostal Church admits women to the pastorate, and in America there are a number of women ministers: but the ordaining of Miss Winchester as a fully-qualified minister is an event unique for Scotland. In Glasgow Miss Winchester has acted in all the capacities of a pastor, though the wedding at which she officiated recently was the first in which she has taken part. The bridal couple were attached to the Pentecostal Church. She has often conducted the entire services at the Parkhead Church. Her duties, too, have included baptism. Her work in Scotland being now completed, Rev Miss Winchester is now on her way back to America, having sailed almost immediately after the wedding at which she officiated. She is returning to the Theological School to which she was formerly attached. Though a born American, Miss Winchester has Scottish blood in her veins, her ancestors having been natives of the Land O' Cakes. She is but little over thirty years of age, yet has attained these great distinctions.'

The only fact to be regretted in that she has left the land where women ministers are unusual and returned to work where they are already recognised and doing good service.

Rev Olive Winchester's attainments and ordination, and the establishment of the Woman's Church at Wallasey, at which the Rev Hatty Baker officiated, will prove to men that what has so long been regarded as their monopoly is no longer safe!

## Select bibliography

Esther Breitenbach, *Empire and Scottish Society: The Impact of Foreign Missions at Home c.1790–c.1914* (Edinburgh: Edinburgh University Press, 2009).

Callum G. Brown, *The Death of Christian Britain: Understanding Secularisation 1800–2000* (London: Routledge, 2001).

Callum G. Brown, 'Religion', in Abrams, Gordon, Simonton and Yeo (eds), *Gender in Scottish History Since 1700* (Edinburgh: Edinburgh University Press, 2006), pp. 84–110.

S. Karly Kehoe, *Creating a Scottish Church: Catholicism, Gender and Ethnicity in Nineteenth-century Scotland* (Manchester: Manchester University Press, 2010).

Lesley Orr Macdonald, *A Unique and Glorious Mission: Women and Presbyterianism in Scotland c.1830– c.1930* (Edinburgh: John Donald, 2000).

Rhonda Semple, *Missionary Women: Gender, Professionalism and the Victorian Idea of Christian Missions* (London: Boydell and Brewer, 2003).

## Notes

1. See D. A. J. MacPherson, 'The emergence of women's Orange lodges in Scotland: gender, ethnicity and women's activism, 1909–1940', *Women's History Review*, Vol. 22: 1 (2013), pp. 51–74.
2. See Elizabeth Ritchie, '"A Palmful of Water for your Years": Babies, Religion and Gender among Crofting Families in Scotland, 1800–1850', in Jodi Campbell, Elizabeth Ewan and Heather Parker (eds), *The Shaping of Scottish Identities: Family, Nation and the World Beyond* (Guelph: Centre for Scottish Studies, 2011), pp. 59–75.
3. See Joseph Train, *The Buchanites from First to Last* (Edinburgh and London, 1846) which includes extracts from Buchan's letters.
4. See Barbara Taylor, *Eve and the New Jerusalem: Socialism and Feminism in the Nineteenth Century* (London: Virago, 1983).
5. See Lesley Orr, '"Impudent and Mannish Grown": "Women's Ministry" in the Church of Scotland', *Practical Theology*, Vol. 2: 1 (2009), pp. 7–25.

# Chapter 7

# Protest and Politics

*Lesley Orr*

## Introduction

Throughout the long nineteenth century, Scottish women indicated their engagement with political debates in a variety of ways, ranging from participation in spontaneous and short-lived protests, to decades-long campaigns, such as the anti-slavery and women's suffrage movements. Women also progressively enlarged their role in public life through membership of philanthropic bodies and charitable organisations, often concerned with welfare provision or regulation of crime and morals, as Chapter 5 indicates. By the late nineteenth century, they were seeking public office as members of school boards and parish councils, ever more vociferously demanding the right to vote and to stand for Parliament, and making their presence felt within political parties. This chapter represents various aspects of women's political activity, with claims to equality and the demand for the suffrage being dominant themes. As with other chapters in this book, it remains a challenge to find sources giving direct voice to working-class women's views, and the extracts quoted here are largely from middle-class activists.

## Section 1: Popular protest and social movements

Popular protests were a feature of Scottish life in the late eighteenth and nine-teenth centuries, occasioned by a variety of causes including rising food prices or food scarcity, the imposition of road tolls, opposition to the Militia Act, politi-cal and industrial disturbances, resistance to clearances in the Highlands, and involvement in the Crofters' War. Women were frequent participants in such events, sometimes among the ringleaders. A major source of information about women's participation in protests are court records and official reports; as Logue has shown, women were less likely than men to be prosecuted but their pres-ence was still notable.[1] Another major source of information is contemporary newspaper reports. Poetry and song were also an important means of codifying working-class and rural communities' experience, and of transmitting knowledge of local traditions and history, and some examples are illustrated here.

The major working-class political movement of the first half of the nineteenth century was the Chartist movement which demanded universal male suffrage and political reform, and which also attracted women. There were over twenty female Chartist associations in Scotland, and at least some of these were active in the 1830s and well into the 1840s. Some of these demanded female emancipa-tion, such as the Gorbals Female Universal Suffrage Society, formed in 1839.[2] The movement was in decline by the 1850s, and there is little research on the forms that working-class women's political action took between this period and the later nineteenth century, though there is some evidence of trade union activ-ity, as illustrated in Chapter 4. The Chartist movement had its own newspapers but there was also much coverage in the mainstream press.

The anti-slavery movement, represented in sources 1.5 to 1.8, emerged in Scotland in the late eighteenth century though there is little evidence of women's participation before the early nineteenth century. While women were likely to have been active in auxiliary organisations before the late 1820s, it was not until then that female emancipation societies, as such, began to be formed. The Edinburgh Female Anti-slavery Association, established in 1830, was possibly the first female society in Scotland. Some female societies attracted working-class support but the movement was largely middle class. Evangelicalism was important as a driving force of the movement but the Scottish movement suffered divisions between its evangelical and radical abolitionist [Garrisonian] factions, influenced by the politics of the American movement; this also caused splits among women supporters, as illustrated by the formation of the Edinburgh Ladies' New Anti-Slavery Society, quoted below. The anti-slavery movement acted as a precursor to the women's suffrage movement, articulating a discourse of rights adopted by women, and providing a training ground for organisation and campaigning. It should be noted that, given Scottish interests in the Caribbean, pro-slavery posi-tions were supported among sections of Scottish society, represented in particular by the Glasgow West Indian Association.[3] There were undoubtedly women who shared these views but this has not yet been the subject of research.

With regard to popular protests, it is hard to find women's voices, apart from their presence in witness statements, though knowledge of their role has sometimes survived through local history and traditions. One of the best known of these episodes is the anti-Militia Act riot in Tranent in August 1797 (the act had been passed in July of that year, and legislated for a compulsory levy of men for the army). A number of women, beating drums, led the crowd, against which soldiers opened fire, killing twelve people; two were women Joan ('Jackie') Crookston[e]‡ (1768–97) and Isabel Roger. Crookston[e]'s role in the riot has been memorialised in a statue in the Civic Square, Tranent. The extract below is from the official report of the deputy lieutenants, who were responsible for the suppression of the protest.

1.1 *Narrative of the proceedings at Tranent, on Tuesday the 29th of August, at the Meeting of the Deputy Lieutenants of that District of East Lothian, for carrying the MILITIA ACT into execution* [NAS, RH2/4/81/82] (105, 106–7)

The affair at Tranent, it appears, had been for several days in agitation. On the evening of the 28th of August, the day preceding the district meeting, a number of disorderly people of Pencaitland and the neighbouring parishes made a violent assault, on the house and property of James Saunderton, Schoolmaster at Pencaitland . . .

Every effort had been for some time employed to inflame the minds of the People, and even children, by the roadside, were heard asking their mothers – "When the Gentlemen would be put to death?" The Colliers in particular were remarkably assiduous; on Monday parties of them went round the country, and engaged all their brethren to attend. Monday night was spent in making preparations for the attack. Great magazines of stones were collected at Tranent; the town drum was forcibly seized, and a large party paraded with it round the neighbouring villages, requiring the inhabitants to assemble next day at different appointed places, and then to march in bodies to Tranent . . . Intimidated by these threats, the people, men and women, turned out next day in great numbers, and joined the tumultuous mob; and many who had no mischief in view until collected in this unlawful manner, assisted in the outrages which were committed.

*Letter signed by Anderson, Gray, Cadell and Wright: Deputy Lieutenants*
. . . About 11 o'clock we proceeded from St G[ermain's] to Tranent, escorted by the Cinque Ports cavalry and Yeomanry as before mentioned. After entering the town, and as we approached the junction with the Post Road, we found ourselves surrounded by Crowds of people chiefly women, who were extremely clamorous and threatened the Deputy Lieutenants in general, mentioning some of us by name, and amongst other expressions of a like nature it was said that we should not leave the Town alive, and that they would have our Hearts blood before an hour was over.

About the same time a Drum was beat by some of the populace – on alighting at the Door of the House appointed for our meeting, Mr Grey and Mr Cadell, two of our number, who happened to be last, were insulted, and their persons pushed and laid hold of . . .

The following extracts, from the radical Scottish Chartist press, are unusual in that they report women speaking or singing on public platforms, in support of the Chartist cause, but also defending their right as women to participate in the struggle. A Female Chartist Association was established in Dunfermline, as a direct response to the opinion of a writer in the *True Scotsman* (24 November 1838) that women would be better off hearing lectures on domestic economy than attending Chartist meetings. This extract comes from a letter, signed only 'L', written to repudiate these views.

### 1.2  *True Scotsman*, 22 December 1838

The Women of Dunfermline in their own defence

Has the very talented writer yet to learn that political economy stands in about the same relation to domestic economy as fourpence does to a groat – that national affairs is but an aggregate of household affairs – that until woman becomes an independent creature, not the subservient slave of man, but a fit companion and assistant in all his undertakings – that until they become acquainted with the results of imprudence, and the want of a sound system of education – until she herself be fit to give the greater part of that education there can never be a sound constitution and enlightened nation. But what the writer's reason be for endeavouring to prevent us taking part in this great struggle, I know not . . . I challenge him or any man in Scotland to show we have no right to interfere with the laws of our country, when our homes are comfortless, our purses and our presses empty, our children naked, ill-fed and uneducated . . . If he will show there is evil in it, I pledge my word that we will instantly give it up, but if they do not, each stone they cast to press us down, will serve us as for a prop, and make our roof the firmer.

The Aberdeen Female Radical Association held a meeting at the Temperance Hotel on 29 April 1839. A Miss Johnston was reported as condemning all who did not support the Charter

### 1.3  *True Scotsman*, 11 May 1839

We have no confidence in the government of Queen Victoria because they spurn the just demands of the people. We have no confidence in our magistrates and rulers because they are deaf to suffering humanity. We have no confidence in the aristocracy or middle classes who will not join the people. We have no confidence in the teachers of religion who deny us our civil rights. We have no confidence in working men who will not join their brothers and sisters in bondage to achieve their just demands and win their political emancipation. In short we have no confidence in none who deny the People's Charter.

At a meeting held the following year in Dunfermline, in honour of three national Chartist leaders, a Mrs Collie was reported as declaring:

### 1.4 *Scots Times*, 11 November 1840

I know it is neither common nor customary for a female to come before a public audience, but hearing that Collins, McDouall and White were once more to visit this place, I resolved to lay aside some of those feelings which generally belong to my sex . . . Do they think that by persecuting the friends of the people they could crush the demand for the Charter? No, they cannot. The victims of oppression are awake; the barriers of corruption are assailed, and liberty yet shall reign triumphant.

Mrs Collie then sang:

The time draws nigh, and is at hand,
When females will with courage stand!
Each heart united will decree,
We'll have our rights, we will be free!
We'll sever ne'er, but steadfast be!
We'll die to have our liberty!

The extracts below represent various phases of women's activity in the anti-slavery movement: the formation of the first female emancipation societies illus-trated by the rules of the Edinburgh Association formed in 1830; the Glasgow women's petition to Queen Victoria in 1837 which praised the emancipation of 1833 but deplored the apprenticeship system (which was abolished in 1838); the formation in the 1850s of the Edinburgh New Anti-Slavery Association after the split with the radical Garrisonians; and the celebration of the abolition of slavery in the United States by the Edinburgh Ladies' Emancipation Society, and anticipation of the end of the association's lifespan in the late 1860s. Surviving primary sources exist mainly in the form of annual reports, and copies are scat-tered across a number of Scottish archives: several are available electronically via Glasgow University Library. The Wilson Anti-Slavery Collection, held at The John Rylands University Library, the University of Manchester, holds a number of reports from the Edinburgh and Glasgow Ladies' Associations, and these can be downloaded via JSTOR [a digital archive for scholars, researchers and students accessed via universities and other educational institutions].

### 1.5 *Resolutions and Rules of the Edinburgh Female Anti-Slavery Association* (Edinburgh: printed by Ballantyne and Company, 1830) (10–11)

RULES

1st. That this Association be termed the EDINBURGH FEMALE ANTI-SLAVERY ASSOCIATION.

2d. That the object of this Association be to circulate such books or tracts as give a correct view of the system of slavery and its results; also to contribute, as opportunities occur, towards the relief and improvement of the Africans and their descendants.

3d. That the business of this Association be conducted by a treasurer, secretaries, and committee; five of whom shall be competent to act.

4th. That every subscriber of five shillings and upwards annually, be a member of this Association, entitled to attend the committees, and to receive a copy of the Anti-Slavery Monthly Reporter.

5th. That two or three members of the committee be appointed to propose tracts and papers for circulation, and to select portions of works for reading in the committee.

6th. That the committee meet once a month, or oftener, as occasion may require, arrange for the diffusion of information, and attend to any other business that may claim their notice.

7th. That the members of this Association be requested to use every means in their power to awaken in the minds of those with whom they have any influence, a lively sense of the injustice, inhumanity, and impiety of the present system of colonial slavery.

8th. That the members of this Association be also requested to encourage the use of sugar produced by free labour, in preference to that obtained by slave labour.

9th. That the funds raised be employed in the purchase of books, tracts, &c., in defraying incidental expenses, and in promoting the Christian education of Negroes, either by this committee separately, or in conjunction with other Associations.

---

1.6  *Petition to Her Majesty, Queen Victoria, from the Ladies of Glasgow and its vicinity, adopted at the public meeting held in the Rev. David King's Chapel, 1st August* (1837)

TO VICTORIA, QUEEN OF THE UNITED KINGDOM OF GREAT BRITAIN AND IRELAND

*May it please Your Majesty*
We, the undersigned, a portion of your Majesty's dutiful and loyal Female subjects resident in the City of Glasgow and vicinity, under a deep sense of our duty to God and our fellow-creatures, beg leave, most respectfully to address your Majesty, in the language of deep sympathy and earnest solicitude in behalf of upwards of seven hundred thousand of your Majesty's subjects, held as Negro Apprentices in the British Colonies.

Your Majesty is aware, that, after years of anxious toil, and by the payment of Twenty Millions of Pounds sterling, an Act was obtained which declared, that from and after the 1st August, 1834, the Negroes of the British Colonies should "be to all intents and purposes free, and discharged of and from all manner of *Slavery.*"

The day when this Act came into operation was hailed by the British people as the commencement of an era of personal freedom, of intellectual improvement, and social prosperity for those who had previously suffered in a state of unjust, degrading, and cruel bondage.

. . .

. . . we at the same time feel it to be our solemn duty to represent to your Majesty, that, with reference to the Negro population of the Colonies generally the Act has signally failed of its declared object.

Facts the most abundant – collected from the dispatches and circulars of Colonial Governors; the returns of punishments furnished by Special Juries; the public statements of numerous Missionaries long resident among the Negroes; the testimony of highly respectable and disinterested individuals, who have investigated on the spot the workings of the system; and the minutes of evidence taken before a select Committee of the House of Commons, have clearly demonstrated that the condition of the Apprentices, especially the Women and Children, is, in many respects, worse than during the legalized continuance of Colonial Slavery.

As *mothers* and *daughters*, our hearts have been deeply affected by the knowledge we have obtained of the treatment of the *female* Apprentices, and their helpless offspring.

We can now no longer doubt that many of our sex are indecently and inhumanly flogged: – worked upon treadmills, so constructed as to be instruments of indescribable torture, and condemned to toil on the highway chained together by the neck with iron collars.

These punishments are inflicted without regard to age, condition or constitution, and are annexed to alleged offences of the most trifling character.

On the plantations, Females are subjected to hardships before unknown. Mothers of large families, who, under the former system, were exempted from labour, are driven back into the field. Others, with infant children, are deprived of the nurses usually allowed them, and compelled to labour with their little ones upon their backs, or are reduced to the necessity of neglecting them altogether.

. . .

As *females* we deeply feel the dishonour done to our sex by the continuance of such a state of things.

As free born *British* females, happy and protected under the glorious constitution which has placed your Majesty on the throne of this Empire, we earnestly desire to see the blessings which we enjoy bestowed upon all our fellow-subjects without distinction of Colour or condition, and we fervently pray that the commencement of your Majesty's reign may be distinguished by an act of justice and benevolence, which would be a bright example to other nations, and shed a hallowed lustre around our beloved sovereign's name – even the breaking of every yoke, and the setting of the oppressed free.

The report, quoted below, indicated that an Edinburgh Ladies' New Anti-Slavery Association was formed in 1856, though the split that occasioned the formation of the new organisation took place five years previously; at that point, the women concerned had formed an association auxiliary to the Glasgow Association for the Abolition of Slavery. The extract below indicates their rationale for continuing to campaign against slavery.

### 1.7 *Report of the Edinburgh Ladies' New Anti-Slavery Society for the years 1856 and 1857* (Edinburgh: 1857) (7–8)

It is not from any overweening or enthusiastic notion of their influence that the Edinburgh Ladies' Association is organized to oppose the slave power; but if this and similar Institutions give utterance to their strong and earnest protest against slavery, and do what they can to cheer on the noble and philanthropic men who, in the face of obloquy and scorn, and all the formidable array of the pro-slavery section of the community, stand forth as the friends of the slave, and assert his right to freedom, the influence of even our little association may not be unfelt. The Abolitionists of America can operate with far greater effect against the system than the people of this country; but they do not despise, nay, they highly value the aid and countenance of Christian friends on this side of the Atlantic . . .

Viewing the abolition of slavery as a cause which must finally be successful, in spite of the opposition of enemies, and in spite of the scarcely less dreaded errors of friends this association would go forward, unmoved by the ever-changing political aspects and sectional successes or reverses of the conflict.

In 1866 the Edinburgh Ladies' Emancipation Society celebrated the abolition of slavery in America, and mourned Lincoln's death. The report gave a lengthy account of developments in the United States of America and, regarding this as the major goal of the movement, speculated as to whether the society would continue to exist.

### 1.8 *Annual Report of the Edinburgh Ladies' Emancipation Society* (Edinburgh, 1866) (26–7)

Even from our very imperfect sketch of the progressive events of the memorable year that has just gone, it must be evident that Slavery is fast passing away from the civilized world; and surely we have cause for thankful rejoicing.

Whether this shall be our last Report we cannot tell. The constitution of our Society announces that "its object is to promote the abolition of Slavery *throughout the world*," and this not being altogether accomplished, we feel it our place to continue at least one year more, at the close of which, may it be granted us to witness the *complete* overthrow of Negro Slavery. Whether this be the case or not, we would now gratefully thank those friends who have sustained us in times past; who have been united with us in sympathy for the slaves for more than thirty years; who have watched the struggle for his emancipation, at times hoping against hope, and who to so large an extent have been permitted to see their hope ripened into assurance. We would enlist the co-operation of these kind friends a little longer, to extend a helping hand to the suffering freed people of America; to stand by them with the means of advancement in learning and citizenship, till they shall be fully able to stand alone . . .

The extract below is taken from Mary MacPherson's‡ (1821–98) poem, *Eilean a' Cheò*. The core of this extended song (228 lines, 22 stanzas) was probably composed in the mid-1870s, though possibly amended and updated into the mid-1880s. It expresses her deep attachment to Skye, her pride in its people, her

ANNUAL REPORT

OF THE

EDINBURGH
LADIES' EMANCIPATION SOCIETY,

AND SKETCH OF

ANTI-SLAVERY EVENTS

DURING THE YEAR ENDING 4TH MARCH

1862.

AM I NOT A MAN AND A BROTHER

AM I NOT A WOMAN AND A SISTER

" Can we behold, unheeding,
Life's holiest feelings crush'd ;—
While *woman's* heart is bleeding,
Shall *woman's* voice be hush'd ?"

EDINBURGH:
PRINTED BY H. ARMOUR, 54 SOUTH BRIDGE.

1862.

**Figure 7.1** Front cover, *Annual Report of the Edinburgh Ladies' Emancipation Society*, 1862. Reproduced by permission of the Trustees of the National Library of Scotland.

anguish at the clearances, and her powerful call to arms to struggle for crofters' rights. Popularly known as Màiri Mhòr nan Òran (Big Mary of the Songs), MacPherson was a native of Skye but moved to Inverness *c*.1845. She left in 1872 after the death of her husband and her 'humiliation', when she was imprisoned for stealing clothes from her mistress's chest (almost certainly an unjust conviction). She then worked as a nurse in Glasgow, retiring home to Skye in 1882. She was a significant and galvanising voice in the 1870s to 1880s crofters' struggle for land rights and justice.

### 1.9  *Eilean a' Cheo* ['The Island of the Mist']

No. 59 in Donald Meek (ed.), *Caran an T-Saoghail: The Wiles of the World Anthology of 19th century Scottish Gaelic Verse* (Edinburgh: Birlinn, 2003) (370–2)

| | |
|---|---|
| Ach cò aig a bheil cluasan | But who has ears to listen |
| No cridh' tha gluasad beò | Or a heart that throbs with life |
| Nach seinneadh leam an duan seo, | Who would not sing this song with me |
| Mun truaigh' a thòinig oirnn? | About our most piteous plight? |
| Na miltean a chaidh fhuadach, | The thousands who have been banished |
| A' toirt uath' an cuid 's an còir, | Having lost their lot and right |
| A smaointinn thar nan cuantan, | Whose thoughts now cross the oceans |
| Gu Eilean uain' a' Cheò. | To the green Island of the Mist |
| | |
| Ach cuimhnichibh gur sluagh sibh | Remember that you are a people |
| Is cumaibh suas ur còir; | And stand up for your rights; |
| Tha beairteas fo na cruachan | Wealth lies beneath those mountains |
| Fon d'fhuair sibh àrach òg | Where you spent your early life |
| Tha iarann agus gual ann, | Iron and coal are stored there, |
| Is luaidhe ghlas is òr | And grey lead, and gold, |
| 'S tha meinnean gu ur buannachd | And mines to bring you profit |
| An Eilean uain' a' Cheò. | In the green Island of the Mist |
| | |
| Cuimhnichibh ur cruadal, | Remember now your toughness |
| Is cumaibh suas ur sròl; | And hold your banner high; |
| Gun teid an roth mun cuairt duibh | The wheel will surely turn for you |
| Le neart is cruas nan dòrn; | By the strength and power of fists; |
| Gum bi ur crodh air bhuailtean, | Your cattle will yet have pasture, |
| 'S gach tuathanach air dòigh, | And each farmer live in style, |
| 'S na Sasannaich air fuadach | And the English will be banished |
| A Eilean uain' a' Cheò. | From the green-clad Misty Isle |
| . . . | . . . |

### Section 2: Feminist claims and campaigns

The anti-slavery movement, as noted, facilitated the emergence of nineteenth century feminism in Scotland, as elsewhere. Claims to equality for women began to be articulated some decades before the establishment of women's suffrage societies as such. The early example of Marion Reid's‡ (1815–1902) *A Plea for Women* is illustrated here, together with extracts from Christian Johnstone's‡ review of Reid's work. Reid made the case for women's access to civil and political rights, while Johnstone also stressed the importance of economic independence, a theme taken up later by Phoebe Blyth in the *Ladies' Edinburgh Magazine*. The other extracts in this section focus on education; the women's suffrage movement is treated separately in Section 3. Alongside the demand for the vote, the issue of education was central to the women's movement, encompassing the demand for access to higher education for women, feminist views about the school curriculum for girls, and the role of women on school boards. The extracts quoted here come from the writings of women already well known in the history of the nineteenth-century women's movement: Sophia Jex-Blake‡ (1840–1912) who campaigned for the right of women to study medicine; Phoebe Blyth, campaigner for the employment of women, and school board member; Flora Stevenson‡ (1839–1905), teacher, educationalist, and school board member; Mary Crudelius‡ (1839–1877), founding member of the Edinburgh Ladies' Education Association; and Agnes Husband‡ (1852–1929), who served as a parish councillor and school board member in Dundee.

Marion Reid's *A Plea for Women* was published in 1843, and argued for women's fitness for civil and political rights. Reid had been present at the World Anti-Slavery Convention in London in 1840, and this is thought to have influenced her views on women's rights. Several editions were published in the United States following its publication in Britain and Ireland. It was reprinted as Marion Reid, *A Plea for Women* (Polygon 1988).

2.1 Mrs Hugo [Marion] Reid, *A Plea for Woman: being a vindication of the importance and extent of her natural sphere of action; with remarks on recent works on the subject* (Edinburgh: William Tait; London: Simpkin, Marshall & Co.; Dublin: John Cumming, 1843) [NLS, Shelfmark ABS.1.89.96] (48–50, 53, 53–4, 55)

Chapter V. Woman's Claim to Equal Rights

"To see one half of the human race excluded by the other from all participation of government, is a political phenomenon which, according to abstract principles, it is impossible to explain" – *Talleyrand*

We shall now proceed to enumerate more precisely the disadvantages which, in this country, we conceive woman in general labours under. The principal of these seem to be: –

I. Want of equal civil rights

II. Enforcement of unjust laws

III. Want of means for obtaining a good substantial education

The second and third of these grievances are, in themselves, and essentially, evil and unjust. The first is, perhaps, principally of importance, because without it there are no sure means of obtaining and securing the others; but although the results of legislative powers are what renders those powers chiefly desirable, still they are also desirable on their own account; free institutions being one of the most important and elevating influences which can be brought to bear on the human mind. We, therefore, place the deprivation of civil rights first; being the fertile source of many other evils, as well as being most injurious in itself.

The ground on which equality is claimed for all men is of equal force for all women; for women share the common nature of humanity, and are possessed of all those noble faculties which constitute man a responsible being, and give him a claim to be his own ruler, so far as is consistent with order, and the possession of the like degree of sovereignty over himself by every other human being. It is the possession of the noble faculties of reason and conscience which elevates man above the brutes, and invests him with this right of exercising supreme authority over himself. It is more especially the possession of an inward rule of rectitude, a law written on the heart in indelible characters, which raises him to this high dignity, and renders him an accountable being, by impressing him with the conviction that there are certain duties which he owes to his fellow-creatures. Whoever possesses this consciousness, has also the belief that the same convictions of duty are implanted in the breast of each member of the human family. He feels that he has a *right* to have all those duties exercised by others towards him, which his conscience tells him he ought to exercise towards others; hence the natural and equal rights of men.

We do not mean to enter into the question of the claim of all men to equal rights, but simply to state the foundation on which that claim rests, and to show that the first principles on which it does rest apply to all mankind, without distinction of sex . . .

Our readers will, doubtless, soon observe, that throughout all the arguments we have used in these pages runs the idea of the equal right of all men to be represented – actually and really represented – in Parliament . . . Of course, we do not mean that all women should possess a privilege which has, at yet, only been conferred on particular classes of men; we only mean to insist that the right is the same in both sexes. If there be any particular reason for the exclusion from this privilege of a certain class among men, we would allow it to have weight for excluding the corresponding class of women, but for these alone . . .

The exercise of those rights would be useful in two ways: it would tend to ennoble and elevate the mind; and it would secure the temporal interest of those who exercise it.

No doubt can be entertained of the debasing nature of slavery. Its tendency to crush and extinguish the moral and spiritual, and to elevate the animal in human nature, is now generally acknowledged; but it does not seem to be so clearly perceived, that every degree of constraint partakes of the same tendency. Perfect liberty, we should say, is that which allows as much freedom to each individual human being, as is consistent with the same degree of freedom in every other human being. Everything short of this liberty, however far it may be from absolute slavery, yet partakes of its nature, and of its power of crushing, cramping and debasing the human mind; of implanting a slavish spirit, and of substituting cunning for true wisdom.

It prevents the human being from developing its powers; forbids independence of thought and action, without which there can be no virtue; and exercises, in a thousand baneful ways, the most pernicious influence on the formation of individual character. What a cramping and keeping-down effect on the mind of women must this remark have, "What have women to do with that?" – the matter in question being one of interest to the whole human family, – "let them mind their knitting, or their house affairs!" Now, this remark is, perhaps, only occasionally expressed in words, yet the spirit of it runs through all society: if not *spoken* in conversation, it is constantly acted on by our institutions.

. . .

The possession of the franchise would tend to raise woman above the bonds of this intolerable restraint; would give free play to her faculties, energy and individuality to all her powers. It would remove that inert and subdued state of mind which must be the result of a belief, that one is not fit for this or that thing of common sense and every-day life.

Christian Johnstone‡ was a journalist and author who published, and was effectively editor of, *Tait's Edinburgh Magazine*. Following the convention of the time, articles in the magazine were published anonymously – Johnstone made many contributions to the journal. Further extracts from Johnstone's article are reprinted in Dorothy McMillan (ed.), *The Scotswoman at Home and Abroad: Non-fiction Writing 1700–1900* (Glasgow: Association for Scottish Literary Studies, 1999). This extract considers the arguments advanced by Reid and broadens the discussion of women's rights.

## 2.2 Christian Johnstone, 'Mrs Hugo Reid's Plea for Women', Review Article, *Tait's Edinburgh Magazine*, Vol. 11, Issue 127, July 1844, pp. 423–8 (424–5, 427)

. . . But although women were to attain the solid and good preparatory education which we take for granted everyone now allows they should have, another and far more difficult change in their condition is required to raise them to social and civil equality. Nor are we sure that this grand change must not be preliminary to judicious female education. It is one of which Mrs Reid has not spoken, and which must appal many, – a complete revolution, which shall place women of every rank above the necessity of contracting marriages of convenience, or mere mercenary marriages; above the humiliating necessity of being, in the colloquial phrase, "provided for", or "well provided for"; of obtaining "a good establishment"; or the climax, "a great match". This necessity is the main root of their debasement. By the present laws or customs of society, no woman is wholly independent of unsuitable or unhappy marriage, save the few heiresses, and perhaps well-conducted clever maid-servants. Now, while this rule holds, women must, we fear, to a great extent be trained to meet and suit their destiny. While half, or a great proportion of the human race, in civilised society, depend for the very means of subsistence upon the contingency of marriage, there can be neither civil nor social equality. Women, therefore, require

not only a better education, but to be placed in circumstances where they may turn that education to account for their individual benefit – like men. They must be made to understand that upon themselves, *like men,* devolves the great duty of their own maintenance by their own exertions. A revolution of opinion which should make female labour as profitable and honourable as that of men; the exercise of female talents, ingenuity, and mechanical skill, commercial enterprise, or professional ability, a source of emolument and credit, and a recognised part of the social system, contains the only true principle of female emancipation . . . We can see very little objection to women participating, as Mrs Reid contends they should, in the same political franchises that men enjoy: as it is not easy to perceive danger accruing to society from the increase of the educated minds that watch over, or have an active voice in the conduct of its affairs; while we see a positive and great injury in the system which renders it necessary that women, from having their minds stunted, and their hands tied up, should remain for ever under the thraldom of the marriage-necessity. Why should not women, like men, be permitted and encouraged to assume a social position which should enable them, – still like men, to decline marriage, until free choice, preference, exclusive affection, nay *love* – though Mary Wollstonecraft disclaims the weakness – determined their fate in wedlock.
. . .

. . . But we have wandered too far from Mrs Reid's able and useful little book. We trust that many women will read it, for all must benefit by the ideas it develops. They will find no trimming to please men: no trite, commonplace preachments showing women how to gain and retain empire over man: but many eloquent exhortations to become cultivated and estimable human beings, regardless of mere sex. She has also settled the great boundary question of "woman's sphere". The sphere, even in its most circumscribed sense, is a noble one; but Mrs Reid enlarges its verge, or rather, throws down the partition walls . . .

Having campaigned unsuccessfully for the right to be awarded degrees in medicine from the University of Edinburgh, Sophia Jex-Blake‡ and her fellow campaigners approached St Andrews University requesting admission for a medical degree. While this request was not granted, it was instrumental in influencing St Andrews to consider its position with regard to women's entry to higher education and, in 1877, it began to award the degree of Lady Literate in Arts.

> ### 2.3  Sophia Jex-Blake, et al.: Letter to St Andrews University (St Andrews University Special Collections, UYUY459/Box D/Bundle 1871–73)

To the Senatus Academicus of the
University of St Andrews.

July 17th 1873

Gentlemen,

   We venture to request your sanction to the admission of women as students of medicine in the University of St. Andrews, and beg to submit to you the following grounds, among others, on which we rest the present application:

1. A large and increasing demand exists among women for the medical services of their own sex, and a corresponding desire is manifested by a considerable number of women to fit themselves for medical practice.

2. It is most desirable that if women enter the profession of medicine they should be thoroughly qualified to perform its duties, and should receive such education and pass such examinations as will deservedly command public confidence.

3. No practitioner is recognised by law as legally qualified unless his or her name is entered on the National Medical Register. Similarly, the Medical Council of the United Kingdom require that every student shall be registered, after passing the required preliminary examination, and before commencing medical study.

4. The Medical Act of 1858 makes no distinction between male and female practitioners of medicine, and at the present moment two women are entered on the national Register as legally qualified practitioners; and at least fourteen other women are registered as medical students.

5. In order to obtain registration as medical practitioners, a licence or degree must be obtained from the Examining Boards recognised by the Medical Act of 1858.

6. As the University of Edinburgh must now be considered as closed by the recent legal decision, there is at present no Examining Board in the United Kingdom prepared to examine women, and thus enable them to place their names on the Register.

7. The decision of a majority of the Court of Session, that women cannot be considered lawful students of the University of Edinburgh, rests on the fact that the sanction of the Crown was not obtained previous to their admission, it not being disputed that with such sanction they could be admitted to any University.

8. The most general objection to the admission of women to Universities lies in the supposed difficulty of educating them jointly with male students of medicine, the latter being taught already in every University of the United Kingdom except that of St. Andrews.

9. As the University of St. Andrews possesses the power to grant degrees, and has a complete staff of examiners, and a partial staff of medical professors, but no medical students, it seems to possess facilities for admitting women to the study and practice of medicine which no other University enjoys.

10. It appears clear that, with the sanction of the Queen in Council, the University of St. Andrews would have full power to admit women to matriculation and graduation; or, if even a supplementary charter should be needed, this could be obtained with little delay, and we beg hereby to intimate that we are quite willing to make ourselves responsible for all contingent expenses.

11. The present regulations of the University only require that two out of the four years of medical study should be passed at a University, and the courses of the present medical professors of St. Andrews would be sufficient to form two complete <u>Anni Medici</u>.

12. We are in a position to state that at least fifteen ladies would at once avail ourselves of the permission, if given, to matriculate at the University of St. Andrews

13. We may further state that we, with the assistance of the Committee formed in our favour, are prepared at once to hire or build suitable premises for a Medical

School; and are also in a position to arrange for a complete course of lectures on all the required subjects of medical education which are not taught in St. Andrews, if the University authorities will sanction such arrangements, and will subsequently admit us to examination and graduation.

Without trespassing further on your time, we beg most earnestly to commend the present application to your most favourable consideration, and remain

Yours obediently

Sophia Jex-Blake, Isabel Thorne, Edith Pechey, A. R. Barker, Alice J. S. Ker, Elizabeth J. Walker, Agnes McLaren, Isa Foggo, Jane R. Robison, Elizabeth Vinson, Jane Massingberd-Mundy

15 Buccleuch Place
Edinburgh

*The Ladies' Edinburgh Magazine* was published by a group of women who had formed the Ladies' Edinburgh Debating Society in 1865. Previously named *The Attempt*, the magazine was renamed in 1875. The extract below is from the first in a series of eight articles on the 'industries and employments open to educated women'.

## 2.4  Phoebe Blyth, *The Ladies' Edinburgh Magazine*, 1875, Vol. 1 (184–7)

### Woman's Work – I: Introduction

In former generations, when the proper sphere of woman was discussed, the question was generally decided by the consideration of any course of action being 'womanly' or 'unwomanly'. There was and is no fixed standard by which this term can be applied, but this did not render it the less decisive; and under shelter of it, strange inconsistencies were tolerated. It was "womanly" to dance or sing before assembled thousands, but it was "unwomanly" to speak to a small number, even if in behalf of the oppressed or wronged; it was "womanly" to write weak or sentimental novels, but "unwomanly" to approach grave and important subjects; it was "womanly" to appear in the hunting-field and to be present at the death of the fox, but "unwomanly" to come to the help of the sick and wounded; it was "womanly" to use the needle, but not the graver's style; it was "womanly" to starve for want of food, but "unwomanly" or at least unlady-like, to work for self-support.

Between the past and present of what is expected from woman, many points of contact exist. Now as then, she is considered as by nature the guardian of infancy, childhood, and youth; now, as then, it must be she who so regulates and overlooks domestic matters as to make the wheels of life roll smoothly under her care; now, as then, she must represent and defend the highest form of Christian morality, of self-denying religion, of all-pervading godliness; and should she ever withdraw from one or other of these high functions, it will be well neither for herself nor for society. But while this is so, and some would greatly limit women's field of action, many have now wider views regarding them. Statesmen refer to the number of women necessarily thrown on their own resources as a "grave social fact", and remark that among the questions which we have to answer are, "How to manage, when from year to year more and more of our women are becoming self-dependent members of the community? How to secure labour its due honour? How are we to make ourselves believe, and bring the country to believe, that in the sight of God and of man labour is honourable and idleness is contemptible?"

This change has been brought about by various causes: some ascribe it to the greatly increased and rapidly increasing wants of high civilisation, which make it difficult for the exertion of one to supply the needs of all that are connected with him even by family ties; others take a more gratifying view of the change, and consider that it has arisen from the higher estimate now made of woman, in her intellectual nature as well as social position, which would afford her varied powers full scope for development. Some importance is also attached to the progress of machinery, which has greatly interfered with the domestic character of female industry. We must admit too, that we sometimes look in vain for the chivalrous feelings of the middle ages, when men shielded and cared for all who were less strong than themselves. Experience has also shown that "capability" in various directions is not a question between *men* and *women*, but between *individuals* of either half of the human race; so that the question now arising in many quarters should not be, What *can* women do? But, What is it wise or expedient that women should do?

The conviction is now widely spread that it is neither wise nor expedient that a woman should leave unemployed any powers which she can exercise with comfort to herself and with advantage to others; nor is it now considered wise that she should exhaust her strength and injure her health by a continuance and excess of frivolous occupations aiming at nothing higher than amusement. With this conviction comes the enquiry how she can be more worthily employed? . . . We propose to consider woman's work on what may be termed its prosaic side – *i.e.,* as a means of providing a livelihood – "gaining money", some would call it; "being independent" is its definition by others.

Flora Stevenson‡, a member, like Blyth, of the Ladies' Edinburgh Debating Society, was elected along with Blyth to the Edinburgh School Board in 1873. They were the first women in Scotland to hold these positions. Stevenson took the view that girls should compete on the same terms as boys within schools, and argued that boys would benefit from taking domestic subjects.

### 2.5 'Cookery in Public Schools', *The Scotsman*, 28 September 1876

Sir – I have read with great interest the article in yesterday's Scotsman on this subject. That it is one of great importance most people will admit, and now that the school Boards have so far accomplished the work which they had to undertake in finding out and providing for the educational wants of the country, it seems reasonable to expect that attention can now be given to such questions as what special branches of training can best be added to the ordinary work of the school.

I believe that it was from no want of interest on the part of the members of the Edinburgh School Board that no decision has been come to on the question of teaching cookery in their elementary school, beyond the very general one, that if satisfactory arrangement could be made for giving this teaching it would be desirable to have it . . .

It should be borne in mind that besides the lessons which they share with the boys, the girls have already an additional class, attendance on which is compulsory. In every school under the Board five hours per week are given to sewing instruction, and unless some modification can be made in this arrangement it seems unfair to the girls to burden them with another extra subject . . . They must be presented for examination in the different standards at the same age as the boys, and with the disadvantage of having five hours per week less of teaching in the branches for which grants are given, for under the Scotch Code excellence in sewing is not recognised by payment of any grants . . .

I have no desire to undervalue the importance of this kind of training for girls, and I think we are greatly indebted to Miss Guthrie Wright and the other managers of the Edinburgh School of Cookery for all they are doing in providing instruction in cookery for all classes of the community. I do, however, deprecate the tone which so many people assume in speaking of the importance of teaching women the art of cookery, as if by this means, and by this means alone, society is to be regenerated, and an end is to be put to all intemperance and improvidence. I believe it is one means of promoting the well-being of mankind, but there is another side to the question which is too often lost sight of. By all means let the girls of this generation be trained to be good 'housemothers' but let it not be forgotten that the well-being of the family depends equally on the "house-father". It seems to me quite as important that the boys attending our public schools should be trained for their future duties as husbands and fathers, as that the girls should be trained to be good wives and mothers; and if boys are not trained early to habits of industry, self-denial, self-reliance, and thrift, it will be of little avail to train our girls to be perfect cooks and housekeepers. When the mother of the family is driven to be the breadwinner for the family, because of the idleness or intemperance of the father, it is not likely that she can be a model housewife.

. . . if the Edinburgh School Board arrange to have cookery lessons for girls, I hope that they will use every means they can command to train boys in such a way that when they come to undertake responsibilities as heads of families they may be able to provide a proper house, and money to carry on the expenses of a model home, to be presided over by a model housewife. – I am, &c.

FLORA C. STEVENSON

Mary Crudelius‡ was a founding member of the Edinburgh Ladies' Education Association, later Edinburgh Association for the Higher Education of Women, established in 1868 to organise university-level lecture courses for women, and to campaign for women's right to higher education. The editor of her memoir, Katherine Burton‡ (1829–98) (referred to in the entry for Mary Rose Hill Burton), was an active suffrage and education campaigner. The following extract is from a letter from her extended correspondence with David Masson, Professor of English Literature at the University of Edinburgh and the main supporter of the association.

## 2.6 Katherine Burton (ed.), *Memoir of Mrs Crudelius* (Edinburgh: Printed by Miller & Sons, for private circulation, 1879) (103–5)

November 21, 1868, Mrs Crudelius to Prof Masson:

. . . Is it the case that most of the Professors here are in favour of opening the University to us? I have a strong feeling that now we ought to put our strength to set the industrial wheel rolling. First get the bill for protection passed (ie Bill for protection of Married Women's Property and Earnings), and then set to work at getting professions thrown open. Mrs Burton has a good deal of right on her side, when she says "what is the *use* of this high education?" We must grant that the practical issues are not yet arrived at. These issues will commend themselves to the commercial or utilitarian, call it which you will, they seem to me to hinge on one another, – spirit of the age and nation. The education (by that I mean the true and right result of the most advanced teaching and training) *is* a real good in itself, but it is difficult to maintain it to be such to the mass without tangible proofs. At the same time, I always hold to my answer to Mrs Burton. I have felt all along that progress in education should be the leader in the trio (ie political, industrial and educational). When we are better educated, we shall feel the want of an end and aim, and be less and less satisfied with the emptiness of our present lives. Something to do will become a real demand, not as at present, a mere theory of what the demand should be. All that has been done yet (in the industrial question) is so petty and weak. All these 'Societies for the Employment of Women' fail so utterly in the elements of large organisation, at least so it seems to me from the miserable results, and they don't aim high enough, and they don't aim straight; however, it is easier to find fault than to mend matters; but of one thing I feel convinced, that any movement now must be clear of the existing societies; let them fulfil their duties as register offices for the lower classes, which is about all that they are, and that on a small scale, but don't let them interfere with and be a drag upon efforts of a different kind. I have been interrupted, and have just time to close. Don't think that I am *deserting* education, but I want its *uses* to begin to develop themselves. Tell me if you have thought much about that; I look upon you as our great friend and helper . . .

As noted above, Agnes Husband‡ was a parish councillor and school board member in Dundee. An Independent Labour Party activist and suffrage supporter, she contributed a column on school boards to the short-lived local ILP paper, *The Tocsin*.

## 2.7 Agnes Husband, *The Tocsin*, No. 7, October 1909

### School Board Notes

The Grim King laid a heavy hand on the School Board during the past month, and two members, with apparently a strong hold upon life, had to answer his claim and follow the great majority, a man and a woman, each with special gifts and characteristics, filling their niche as best they could.

The Man's Eulogium was not over-done, though a fitting tribute to his worth; the woman's short, very short, considering her long service; and it is well, perhaps, that a man's or a woman's value to life is not to be measured by the contents of these or in the memory of colleagues.

The man's place has been filled by an arrangement, which the Board accepted and confirmed on a plea of deference to the wishes of a section of the electorate. This, at least, was the guiding principle, and should hold in filling the woman's place, if any principle exists at all. That a man can represent women as well as a woman may sound well, but it is a specious argument which women themselves are not prepared to accept; besides, Miss Shaw was supported by the body of women electors, not a section, which should constitute a stronger claim on principle. The result will, of course, be still another lesson as to the measure of men's chivalry towards women.

The conference with headmasters relative to altering the morning hours of commencing school, to suit working mothers, was a curious illustration of the effect association may have on judgement. An unfortunate slip betrayed the fact – that the Board was intended to receive the combined testimony through arranged speakers, which was, of course, voted out, though it possibly accounted for the wonderful unanimity and caution of the several speakers. One speaker rather over-reached himself, however, by asserting that 'already there was too much done for the children under the present system,' while he was himself asking greater favours from that system, and providing another instance of how easy it is to have two perspectives while accepting common benefits, and two things only were made clear to the Board, 'that it takes half-an-hour for an effective lesson in religious instruction, and that many hundreds of children miss that benefit through the present arrangement and – poverty.'

## Section 3: The women's suffrage movement

The extent and activities of the women's suffrage movement in Scotland have been well documented by Elspeth King and Leah Leneman. The first Scottish women's suffrage society was established in Edinburgh in 1867 and, by the early twentieth century, there were many suffrage societies across Scotland. This included the constitutional Women's Suffrage Societies, militant organisations such as the Women's Social and Political Union (WSPU) and Women's Freedom League, and organised male support in the Northern Men's Federation for Women's Suffrage. Also represented here is the temperance movement which brought many women into campaigning activity from around 1870, with the British Women's Temperance Association Scottish Christian Union [BWTA (SCU)] being established in 1876. While the temperance movement emphasised women's moral contribution to society, it also articulated views on women's rights to citizenship, and, in particular on women's right to vote, a right that they could use in support of legislation to regulate alcohol.

The extracts in this section illustrate arguments put forward for votes for women from the early 1870s onwards, and they indicate the forms of action taken from public meetings to court protests, and damage to property leading to imprisonment. They represent the views of prominent figures in the movement, such as Priscilla Bright McLaren‡ (1815–1906), a long-standing women's rights campaigner, married to Liberal politician, Duncan McLaren; Jane Taylour‡ (1827–1905) who undertook public lecture tours campaigning for women's rights; Flora Masson‡ (1856–1937) (see entry for Rosaline Masson), member of the Ladies' Edinburgh Debating Society; Catherine Forrester-Paton‡ (1855–1914), temperance campaigner and philanthropist; Lila Clunas‡ (1876–1968), militant suffragette, teacher and town councillor; Chrystal Macmillan‡ (1872–1937), suffragist and pacifist; Christina Jamieson‡ (1864–1942), writer and school board member, and leading light of the women's suffrage movement in Shetland; Ethel Moorhead‡ (1869–1955), artist and militant suffragette; and Dorothea Smith‡ (1872–1944), doctor and militant suffragette. Their positions ranged across the spectrum from constitutional to militant, and their political affiliations from Liberal to Independent Labour Party (ILP). There is also one example of an anti-suffrage position, that pronounced by Lady Griselda Cheape‡ (1865–1934) at the BWTA(SCU) annual conference in 1909. Cheape was a leading member of the Scottish National Women's Anti-Suffrage League. The sources represent a mixture of feminist, temperance and political publications, as well as newspaper coverage, which was extensive.

### 3.1 *The Scotsman*, 18 November 1873

#### WOMEN'S SUFFRAGE

A LECTURE on Women's Suffrage was delivered by Miss Jane E. Taylour in the Freemason's Hall yesterday afternoon, under the auspices of the Edinburgh National Society for Women's Suffrage – Mrs M'Laren presided. The audience was composed principally of ladies. Mrs M'Laren said their Edinburgh committee was the only one in the kingdom which never had a gentleman upon it; and she believed there was no committee that had done so much work with so little money. Much generous work had however been done by some of the best men in Edinburgh outside the committee; their city members had also been faithful to them from the beginning, and had helped them both here and in the House of Commons. They had good cause to congratulate themselves, for their agitation had made wonderful progress, and now ranked among the more important agitations of the day. As it was now acknowledged to be no fanatical idea that women should possess the franchise, they expected that this winter many influential ladies would join their ranks. Many women voted in the School Board election, and they were not the less feminine than they were before. (Applause)

Miss TAYLOUR then proceeded with her address. No reform agitation, she observed, had ever made so much progress in so short a period as the movement for obtaining the suffrage for women. It had been often asserted that women themselves did not desire the suffrage; but although this were true, it did not carry with it any weight whatever; for to argue the question, which was one of simple justice, on any ground but its own merits was unfair and illogical. (Hear, hear.) But last year at the English municipal elections women voted in a greater proportion than men; women also had exercised the franchise at the School Board elections; and what better proof than that could be given that they wished to exercise their electoral rights, and that they could do so without any inconvenience or injury to themselves. Considering the question from a constitutional point of view, it was, she said, incomprehensible how any person could oppose their movement; for was it not ordained by masculine decree that the franchise should be attached to property; and while women were taxed, it could not be alleged that they were outside the pale of the Constitution. Alluding to the Married Women's Property Act, she contended that it was too limited in its application. The laws that oppressed women would have been repealed long ago if the bulk of men had not refrained from taking advantage of these laws. If the suffrage was only to be given to one of the sexes, it ought to be given to the women and not to the men. The latter were strong and able to protect themselves; women, on the other hand, needed all the protection they could get, owing to their comparative weakness. But they only wanted equal rights; and public opinion was awakened to see that legislation could not be just which was the work of only one section of the community. (Applause.) A number of deplorable social, moral evils would also continue to exist if woman was not trained up to a higher sense of her dignity as a human being; and this she never could be until she had been restored to her proper place by man's side as his co-worker and help-meet in all things. It was also said that women were not sufficiently educated to use the franchise; but when the right was based on a property qualification that argument went for nothing. Many men who exercised the franchise were not educated at all; and that the Ballot Act recognised in having a special clause explanatory of the way in which illiterate voters were to vote. Replying to the statement that woman's sphere was at home, and that she ought to take no part in public life, she said such an argument sounded strangely in a country governed by a Queen, whose retirement from public life for many years past had been a source of great regret to her subjects. Those who met their arguments and their movement by raising a religious difficulty, and by quoting St Paul, could only do so by drawing the Apostle within the narrow bounds of a legality inconsistent with the grand principles enunciated by his Master. (Applause.)

Miss WIGHAM then moved : –

Resolved that, as in this country, taxation is the basis of representation, it is unjust in principle to exclude ratepayers simply on the ground of sex from voting for members of Town Council or of Parliament: this meeting pledges itself to promote, by petition and otherwise, Mr Jacob Bright's bill to remove the electoral disabilities of women; and that a petition to this effect be sent from this meeting, signed by the president on our behalf, and forwarded, for presentation, to the care of our city members whose systematic help we gratefully acknowledge.

3.2  Flora Masson, *The Ladies' Edinburgh Magazine*, 1876, Vol. II, pp. 97–102
(99–100, 101)

Woman's Work, VII – The Parliamentary Franchise for Women
. . . At this time there are many questions under discussion relating to the employ-ment, education, property and treatment of women, which of course are of more

immediate interest to women themselves than to men. Some people assert that the interests of men and women ought to be identified. They *ought* to be perhaps, but they are not; it is constantly found that laws have to be made for the protection of women, their lives and property, and it cannot be right that those laws should be made entirely by men, who are chosen by men.

. . .

It is sometimes said that, if the franchise were extended to women, they would become unwomanly, and would neglect their household cares, and we should indeed be sorry if this were the case. But of such evils we must not prophesy, but judge from our experience; and we have had a good deal of experience to help us. Women in England do vote at present at municipal elections (they are debarred from doing so in Scotland, because the municipal vote here carries with it the right of Parliamentary voting). They are allowed to vote in both England and Scotland at School Board elections; and in none of these cases have evil results been seen. No ugly transformation has occurred among the women of Edinburgh since three years ago, when they went up in large numbers to the polling-booths and voted for members of the School Board . . .

Masson described petitioning and the women's suffrage movement since 1866, and the increased numbers of signatures in favour: by 1875, there were 415,622 signatories. In the same year a bill brought before the House of Commons got 160 votes in favour but 205 against:

In Scotland the movement has gone on vigorously. Of the Scottish Members half are pledged in favour of WS, and some are neutral. Last year a memorial from 10,127 women of Scotland was presented to the Right Hon. B. Disraeli, and of the Scotch Town Councils no fewer than sixteen petitioned in favour of the Bill . . .

### 3.3 *Scottish Women's Temperance News*, No. 7, Vol. X, July 1906 (102)

Deputation to the Prime Minister on Women's Suffrage

This deputation has been so largely discussed in the daily press, and so universally reported, that it is unnecessary to go into details. All our readers must already know that no definite promise was obtained from Sir Henry C-B [Campbell-Bannerman], although his sympathies are evidently with us. Among the members of the deputation were Mrs Steele, Dundee, and Mrs Watson, Helensburgh. Mrs Watson said – "I have the honour to represent the SCU [Scottish Christian Union], of the BWTA [British Women's Temperance Association], an Association which has a branch in almost every corner of Scotland. Our membership now stands at 52,000. Scotland has contributed already in large measure to the progressive Parliament we now have. It has almost unanimously sent members to the present HC [House of Commons] pledged to social and temperance reform. We feel that legislation is being brought more and more face to face with social and economic problems – problems in which women would be most valuable. We have already proved our worth on School Boards, Parish Councils, and many other public bodies. There are many questions before the country in which we, as Scottish women, feel we ought to have a voice. From the temperance point of view, we feel that the termination of all vested interests in licenses, after a short time-limit, is a question we ought to speak about. We feel, also, the concession of direct power to inhabitants, to control the issue and renewal of licenses, is surely a question in which women ought to be able to judge . . .

Chrystal Macmillan‡ was one of the first women admitted to Edinburgh University where she was awarded a degree in law. She was secretary to the Women Graduates of the Scottish Universities Committee which argued that women graduates had the right to the parliamentary franchise within the university electorates. To establish this right they took a case to the Court of Session, and on its rejection, appealed to the House of Lords which also rejected their case. The lecture, from which the extract below is taken, was delivered shortly after the House of Lords decision and published as a WSPU pamphlet.

> 3.4 Chrystal Macmillan, *The Struggle for Political Liberty* (The Woman's Press, 4, Clement's Inn, Strand WC, 1909) [NLS, Shelfmark EL.3.93.6 (Miscellaneous Pamphlets)]

Men resist the claims of women professedly on the ground that they are acting, not only for the good of the country, but for the good of women themselves, and because they are anxious to save women from responsibility. Men base their claim on the natural order of things – sometimes even on divine order – forgetting that right is merely hereditary and founded on custom, and that what seems to their limited outlook to be the natural order of things is no more than the political custom of our own time and country. Women have to face the further difficulty that they are not yet recognised as 'the people' . . . Be the franchise wide or limited, it must not exclude women on the ground of sex. Women demand that they should be recognised as 'the people'.

The storm centre of the international movement for woman suffrage is this country . . . Today, the omission of our measure from the King's speech brings home to us most clearly that we are shut out from the common council of the kingdom – that we have no constitutional means of suggesting the amendment to that Speech we most need and desire . . . The House of Commons presumes to legislate for the people without having asked the consent of half of the people.

Women's interest is not considered to rank as of equal importance with men's. They are only considered of value in so far as they promote the interests of men . . . but the good of the country is best promoted when she, too, is considered of value, and when her interests are not made subservient to his, but when the capacities of both are allowed to be developed. This fallacy of assuming that woman is of no value in herself is the assumed major premise of writing, legislation and judicial decisions . . . It appears at every turn – women are only recognised as citizens in certain connections.

The Scottish Graduates Case
. . . 'Women' are not 'persons'. Here again we have the purely arbitrary setting aside of the obvious interpretation of the law. The interpretation by the House of Lords,

when applied to the statutes in question, produces contradictions and absurdities in these statutes. It was denied that the meaning of the statutes is to be inferred from them, as they stand. And why? Because the privilege is so exceptional, because it is a fundamental constitutional law and principle of the Constitution that women do not vote – a principle!

The highest court in the land has decided that courts of law may, at their discretion, draw an arbitrary line saying so much we may infer from the statutes and no more . . .

We need today, as men did seven hundred years ago, a great Charter setting forth the rights of women:

– That women as well as men are the people
– That privileges shall not be denied to women simply because they are great
– That women shall not be taxed without consent
– That Government be established deriving just powers from the consent of the governed, both men and women
– That such a Government can only be established by giving Votes to Women.

The report of the BWTA meeting, described in the source below, indicates that anti-suffrage positions were part of the public debate, and that opinion was divided on the question within the temperance movement, even if a majority was pro-suffrage.

### 3.5 *The Scotsman*, 1 April 1909

#### BRITISH WOMEN'S TEMPERANCE ASSOCIATION
#### ANNUAL MEETINGS IN EDINBURGH

The annual meetings of the British Women's Temperance Association (Scottish Christian Union) were opened yesterday in Lothian Road United Free Church, Edinburgh. The proceedings began in the forenoon with a devotional meeting, and in the afternoon the first of the business meetings was held – Miss Forrester-Paton presiding over a crowded attendance.

The President in her opening address reminded the delegates that the motto of the Association was "For God, for Home and Every Land." It was a sad fact, she said, that among their sisters the drinking habit was increasing. As members of such an Association, they had their work to do in connection with municipal matters, and even the suffrage, for they had a suffrage department, too, and as women she thought they ought to take their share in going to the poll and giving their votes. (Applause) In doing so, she asked, would they not be working for God? With reference to the use of non-alcoholic wine, they were glad that so many of their churches were now using that which would not any longer be a stumbling block to many who sat at the Lord's table. There was a great work open for them in connection with the home, and, referring to the question of infant mortality, said they looked forward to the time when they should be in the fortunate position of America, where twenty million children were under regular instruction in physiology, with special reference to the effects of alcohol upon the human body. (Applause.) Speaking of their interest in other lands, she wished that they as a country would be brave enough to banish the drink from their land as China was prepared to banish opium. (Applause.)

. . .

## ALCOHOLIC QUESTIONS

. . . Mrs Milne, Aberdeen, gave in the report on Parliamentary elections, and moved that the meeting welcomes the Temperance (Scotland) Bill, which embodied the principle of local veto, and which would enable the electors to veto all or a fourth of the licences in their respective districts; heartily supports the provision for the later opening of licensed premises in the morning, and urges all to sign the petition in favour of the Bill. The resolution was agreed to, and arrangements made for sending out lists for signatures.

## THE SUFFRAGE DEPARTMENT – AN OBJECTOR

Mrs Napier submitted the suffrage department report, which stated that the interest in this work was steadily growing.

Lady Griselda Cheape said she was expressing the opinion of many women when she said there were many who did not want the vote. She was president of the local branch of the British Women's Association at St Andrews, and also of the Anti-Suffrage League there, and they had sent up a petition to Parliament with 1103 names. Many of those who signed were working women – a charwoman had obtained 75 signatures – and they said they did not want the vote, for they did not understand the question, and it would do them more harm than good. Let the women, she urged, stay in their homes; let them do the Christian work as women that God had appointed them to do. (Applause)

Mrs Black, Aberdeen, said for the first time in her life she had seen an anti-suffragist. (Laughter.) She had no doubt that the women who signed an anti-suffrage petition did so consciencously, and that in all probability they would not use the vote if they had it, but she submitted that that was no reason why those who wanted it and believed it would be for the good of the country should be refused it. (Loud applause.) If one or two members of the family were not hungry and did not want bread that was no reason why the others should not get it. (Laughter and applause.)

Lila Clunas‡ was a member of the Women's Freedom League in Dundee, along with Annot Wilkie‡ (1874–1925), later to become an organiser for the Women's Labour League. In 1909 she was arrested while taking part in a deputation to Downing Street, and was sentenced to three weeks imprisonment.

### 3.6  Lila Clunas, *The Tocsin*, No. 5, August 1909

#### Life in Holloway

The Dundee Branch of the Women's Freedom League has always been very active; the credit of this is due to our first secretary, Miss Annot Wilkie, who, in the days when a suffragette was regarded as a hooligan, gave herself whole-heartedly to the cause in Dundee. But as we are all working women we have not hitherto been able to send a danger duty volunteer to London. When the appeal came for the first week in July it seemed to me, as I thought of women, who had been three and even four times in prison, that it would be a very small sacrifice for me to give up part of my holiday, so I offered for active service.

On Friday, 9th July, whilst picketing at 10 Downing Street, I was arrested, charged with obstructing the police in the discharge of their duty, and refusing to be bound over, was sentenced by Sir Albert de Rutzen – an old man who looked helpless and worried – to three weeks in the Second Division. We were a lively company as we drove off in Black Maria in charge of a friendly policeman, who seemed concerned at my quietness, and who attempted consolation by frequently offering me a basket of strawberries which had been given us. From Bow Street to Holloway in Black Maria is a most uncomfortable half-hour's drive, but as we did not know what lay before us it was all too short. Soon the gates of Holloway clanged behind us; we waved goodbye to the policeman, and realised that we were prisoners.

Second Division prisoners wear green skirts and blouses, blue and white checked aprons, white caps and very coarse black shoes and stockings. The under garments are many and varied, and what they were all meant for puzzled us considerably. Wing DX, the newest part of the prison, has been given up entirely to the suffragettes. It is well lit, and consists of three floors, thirty-four cells on each; I was lodged on the second floor in cell 30, so for three weeks I lost my identity and became No. 30. Life in Holloway is deadly in its monotony; we rose at 6 a.m., breakfasted at 7, had dinner at 12, and supper at 5. As vegetarians we had special food, but specially nasty food is more correct. We attended chapel every day, were marched in before any of the ordinary prisoners, were seated quite by ourselves, and were only allowed to leave our seats when the others were safe in their cells. To me chapel was the most tragic part of prison life. The idea that the life of every woman there was wrecked – and there must have been four hundred, most of them young, and only a few with bad faces – haunted me day and night. Their familiarity with the service was uncanny, and meant either that they spent most of their time in prison, or that for practical purposes their religion was an utter failure. I never asked to see the chaplain, but I understand he went into the cells with his hat on, and was requested by a suffragette to take it off or walk out.

For one hour every forenoon we walked round and round the yard at a certain distance from one another, and we women, whom Mr Asquith feared were going to assault him, kept our bread from breakfast and fed the pigeons with it.

The only good thing about Holloway is the Library, and even here all the books I read were dated since women began to go to prison for political freedom. I read a great many very good novels, and for books of instruction we chose history. We petitioned Mr Gladstone twice. His first answer was that he had considered the case very fully and saw no reason to interfere. By the following week he had decided to remit the remainder of our sentence. What new facts had come to his knowledge in the interval we have not found out. The evening I was released I was taken to the Reception House, ordered to dress as quickly as possible, then although the prison authorities knew I was a stranger in London I was put into the street all alone, dazed and giddy, not knowing which way to turn. A wardress told me I need not wait

**Figure 7.2** Gorrie Album Collection: 1909 suffrage demonstration, Princes Street, Edinburgh. Reproduced by permission of the National Library of Scotland.

for the others as I would not see them, so I took a bus to the office. Next morning a letter arrived from Mr Gladstone stating we were to be released on Wednesday evening. To me it seems as if after four years the Liberal Government is at last beginning to realise that coercion has failed.

Christina Jamieson‡ contributed regularly to Shetland newspapers on suffrage campaigning, reporting on a variety of political, fund-raising and social activities. In the extract below she emphasises the importance of women's economic contribution in Shetland.

### 3.7 Christina Jamieson, *Shetland Times*, 11 November 1911

SHETLAND WOMEN'S SUFFRAGE SOCIETY

. . . A report of the year's work of the Society was also given by the Secretary, showing that the Society had secured petitions in favour of the Conciliation Bill from the County Council and one Parish Council; had distributed and sold literature; had contributed to the funds of the Scottish Federation of Women's Suffrage Societies; had sent a representative with the Society's banner to the great Women's Suffrage procession in London in 17th June; had prevailed on electors to question Mr Watson publicly on his attitude to Women's Suffrage; had kept "The Common Cause", the organ of their Union, in the public Reading-Room; and had brought the question of the movement before the public from time to time in the Shetland papers . . .

It was resolved that the Society continue working on the same lines, and that a conversazione, arrangements for which were left to the Committee, be held to raise funds.

This Society imposes no special or trying duties on its members, and it is hoped that those in favour of Women's Suffrage, who are not already members, will send in their names for enrolments (the fee is one shilling) among those who "stand for Suffrage" in the islands . . .

### SEAMEN'S WIVES

There is one reason for the enfranchisement of women that should tell strongly in Shetland. It is often urged that seamen have no votes – not necessarily that they are voteless, but they are seldom at home to exercise them. There are 4000 votes in Shetland – how many of these are here to vote at elections? The enfranchisement of women would enable seamen's wives to qualify for the vote. Shetland women have bitter cause to know how much of the accidents, disease, and death among seamen is due to preventable causes. If they realised that the vote would enable seamen's wives to bring pressure on legislation affecting the wages, safety and lives of seamen, surely they would do all they could to show they wished for the political enfranchisement of women. And in so doing they would be following in the footsteps of their foremothers of old, who managed the homesteads, gave counsel, and strengthened the hands of their men-folks. For we should remember that "we have in us the blood of a womanhood that was never bought and never sold; that wore no veil and had no foot bound; whose greatest heroine was the unconquered maid who gave counsel, the deepest that ever yet was given to living man – a race of women who knew no fear and feared no death, and lived great lives and hoped great hopes." Let us be worthy of them. C.J.

A report on the trial of Ethel Moorhead (alias Miss Morrison)‡ and Dorothea Smith‡ for breaking into, and attempting to set fire to, a mansion in Glasgow's West End appeared in the *Glasgow Herald* under the headlines 'Suffragist Outbreak', 'Missiles Thrown at Judge' and 'Three Women Arrested'. The extracts below illustrate how the women defended themselves and their interchanges with the judge, Lord Salvesen. After the sentence of eight months imprisonment for each was passed, there was a 'storm of protests' including the singing of a suffragette song to the tune of the Marseillaise.

### 3.8 'Riotous Scene in Glasgow Court', *Glasgow Herald*, 16 October 1913

#### ACCUSED DEFEND THEMSELVES

. . . On their names being called, they entered the dock. In view of the fact that both had declined to plead at the first diet of Court, Lord Salvesen informed them that if they adhered to that attitude the Court would regard their plea as being 'not Guilty'. Miss Morrison announced, in reply to His Lordship, that they would defend themselves. "We generally find" she added amid laughter, "that counsel make a muddle of it." She afterwards protested against a jury of men being empanelled, remarking that the only jury able to try them was one composed of voteless women. Lord Salvesen dismissed the objection with the comment that on such grounds every trial of a woman in the past would be illegal. Before calling the first witness, the Advocate-Deputy intimated that there were no witnesses for the defence. Evidence was then led regarding the charge of breaking into a house at 6 Park Gardens on July 23 with intent to set fire to it. Mrs Smith was arrested in the house in the night in question, and Miss Morrison was apprehended around eight o'clock on the following morning while she was in the act of climbing the area railings in order to leave the house. Her clothes were smeared with dust and soot, and the conjecture was that she had been hiding in a chimney place.

### REFLECTIONS UPON THE JUDGE

An objection to the indictment on the ground that no evidence has been led to justify the charge of housebreaking was submitted by Miss Morrison, who held that there was no need to put the issue to the jury. Lord Salvesen said that Crown counsel would have to be heard, since he would not sustain the point on the argument of one side alone. The Advocate-Depute, followed by the accused, then addressed the jury. Miss Morrison concluded her address by attempting to justify "this rebellion" in which she was taking part. "I am not an idler", she said. "Painting is my work, but I have come to the conclusion that reform is more necessary than oil painting."

Lord Salvesen described these remarks as totally irrelevant and asked the accused to confine herself to the facts of the case. In summing up he commented upon the cool and indifferent demeanour of the two accused. At one point he was interrupted by Miss Morrison, who exclaimed, "My Lord, you are making suggestions that are not in the proof. I do not think you are dealing quite fairly." Lord Salvesen took no notice of the interruption.

The jury, after an absence of about twenty minutes, unanimously found the prisoners guilty as libelled. On the Advocate-Depute moving for sentence, Miss Morrison vehemently protested. "You have" she said "misdirected the jury, my Lord, and they have brought in a verdict of guilty as you desired. They could not have done otherwise from your summing up. You know that in sentencing us suffragists you are sentencing us under this infamous 'Cat and Mouse' Act, not only to imprisonment but to torture. You can still retrieve yourself; you have done unjustly, but you can do justice now. You can refuse to sentence us. Do your duty." This injunction was greeted with a demonstration of applause on the part of sympathisers in court.

### Section 4: Women in political parties

By the late nineteenth century, political parties had begun to create affiliated organisations or women's sections to attract women members. This section illustrates some of these organisational developments, and the ways in which the debate on women's suffrage was having an impact across the political spectrum. It also illustrates the types of policy questions that women party members debated, such as the interest of women candidates and councillors in child welfare.

Women's Liberal Associations were being organised in Scotland from around 1890, with the Scottish Women's Liberal Federation being constituted at the same time. The federation was committed to women's suffrage. While suffrage was a central concern, the associations debated a range of issues, from disestablishment to the opium question. During World War I, women Liberals put their energies into the war effort, and raised funds for the Scottish Women's Hospitals. With legislation awarding the franchise to (some) women being anticipated, at the end of 1917, women Liberals approved the amalgamation of women's and men's associations. The extract below lists the objects and membership criteria of the Scottish Women's Liberal Federation.

### 4.1 *Constitution and Rules of the Scottish Women's Liberal Federation* [NLS, Acc. 11765/20] (2)

OBJECTS

1. To promote and extend the knowledge of sound Liberal principles.
2. To promote the formation of Women's Liberal Associations in Scotland, and to afford to them a centre from which information and assistance on political matters can at any time be obtained.
3. To promote intercourse and united action between the Women's Liberal Associations of Scotland, without compromising their independence, or in any way interfering with their Constitution, Rules, or Local Authority.
4. To secure just and equal legislation and representation for women, especially with reference to the Parliamentary Franchise, and the removal of all legal disabilities on account of sex, and to protect the interests of children.
5. To communicate information and arouse interest among women on political, social, and moral questions, both of general and local interests, and to advance these objects by meetings, lectures, and individual effort.

MEMBERSHIP

The Federation shall consist:

1. Of all organizations of Liberal Women numbering not less than 25 Members.
2. Of any Liberal Association which has admitted Women to its Membership.
3. Of Liberal Women in any district where there is no Local Women's Liberal Association, who shall pay not less than 1s. per annum to the funds of the Federation.
4. Of all Liberals who shall subscribe not less than One Guinea per annum to the funds of the Federation.

Each Association shall pay an Affiliation Fee of One Guinea per annum, the Executive having power to accept a fee of 10s. 6d. in special cases.

The activities of Women's Liberal Associations are illustrated by the following extract, the secretary's report to the Annual Social and Business meeting of the Edinburgh Women's Liberal Association Southern Branch, held on 16 November 1891.

## 4.2  Edinburgh Women's Liberal Association Southern Branch. Secretary's Report, 1891 [NLS, Acc. 9080/4]

The interest excited in the Southern district of the city in the objects of the Women's Liberal Association, has not abated during the past twelve months. The Executive meetings were well attended, and progress was made in the important work of organisation.

. . .

Federation.

After discussion at two separate meetings the Executive resolved to affiliate with the Scottish Woman's Liberal Federation . . . The Branch delegates supported a resolution of the Federation, asking for the appointment of Women Sub-commissioners by the Royal Commission on labour, as the only means of obtaining a true insight into the conditions under which women are compelled to labour for a living.

Mrs Ormiston Chant's Visit and other work.

The visit of Mrs Ormiston Chant to Edinburgh in January last, excited much interest, and the result was to give a great impetus throughout the branch to the cause of progressive liberalism in general, and to enlarge the sphere of Woman's work in the advance of political social, and educational reform.

Mrs Ormiston Chant addressed, under the auspices of the Branch, large and deeply interested meetings, at Canaan Lodge (Mrs Hodgson's), The Morningside Liberal Club, and in the hall of Viewforth U.P. Church, on strikes, Woman's Suffrage, prison discipline, and other questions at present attracting public attention.

Drawing-room and other meetings were also held, at which, papers by Miss Wigham on "Arbitration" Mrs Watson on the "Railway Strike" and "Temperance in the Home and the State", Mrs Carlaw Martin on "Disestablishment" and Miss Burton on "Education" were read, and discussed. Other meetings are to be held during the coming winter, and the committee are anxious to awaken an interest especially amongst the working women.

Elections

The School Board Elections called for energetic action, and the Executive having approved of the programme and principles of Miss Burton, and Messrs Burn and Pringle, did all in their power to secure the election of those candidates, and their efforts were crowned with success.

No more important municipal contests have taken place in Edinburgh than during the recent elections of Town Councillors. Liberal Candidates were strenuously opposed on the sole ground of their Liberalism, by candidates who loudly proclaimed "no politics" but, who were strangely enough, Tory or Unionist by profession, and pledged to exclude Liberals from the Lord Provostship, and their offices of honour or usefulness. In St Cuthbert's and St George's wards, members of the Branch gave material assistance in canvassing, and the Liberal candidates, Mr Russel, now Lord Provost, and Mr Scot, were elected by handsome majorities

. . .

Isabella Bream Pearce‡ (1859–1929) was invited by Keir Hardie to contribute to the *Labour Leader*, the paper of the ILP. Under the pen name 'Lily Bell', she contributed a regular column, 'Matrons and Maidens', between 1894 and 1898. The extracts below give a flavour of her conversational style, slightly arch witticisms, and her presentation of feminist ideas as a vital component of the work of the ILP.

> ### 4.3 Isabella Bream Pearce ('Lily Bell') 'Matrons and Maidens' column, *Labour Leader*, 1894

March 1894

. . . At first I objected. "Why," I asked, "should there be a special column for women in the Labour Leader? You don't set up a special column headed 'For men only,' and why should there be one headed 'Women only,' like a ladies' compartment in a railway carriage? You say you believe in the equality of the sexes, and yet here you are proposing to treat us like so many children."

The Chief smiled. He knew my arguments were unanswerable, and he did not therefore condescend to argue the point. He merely repeated, "I want at least one column a week devoted to women's affairs, and I want it well done, and I want you to do it." Of course, that settled the matter. Had he condescended to argue the point, I could have convinced him in five minutes that he was altogether wrong. But he didn't. He merely said in his slow fashion what I have recorded above, and I felt there was no appeal. I don't believe he really believes in the rights of women. If it isn't not only a right but a prerogative of the sex to argue with a man, then what is I would like to know? For the honour of my sex I determined to at least insist on the last word, a privilege which no sane man would dispute, and so I answered as meekly as could be expected under the circumstances, "Very well, but I shall use that column to abuse the men." "Oh! that's all right," answered he, "only see that it's well done," and with a laugh he walked away. These men are simply horrid betimes.

So here I am, enthroned in the editorial chair of the women's column of the Labour Leader. And now, what am I to say? Thousands of women will read these lines. What message has this paper for and to them? Will it prove a Leader in very truth? A Leader which will lead women away from the dreary, grinding poverty and sordid, squalid surroundings which to-day make life miserable? Will it lead us into a fuller realisation of those indefinable longings which we have all felt, but which we cannot express in words: longings after loving, free comradeship and companionship: longings for freedom from the narrowing prejudices of conventional folly.

Next week I will get to work in earnest. Meanwhile I invite confidences. I mean this column to be a real help to the women in the movement. Tell me all about your branches of the I.L.P. and your trade unions. Tell me about your domestic troubles and worries. It does one good sometimes to confess the troubles of life to a sympathetic ear.

June 30 1894

I suppose ignorance has been the main point men have relied on to keep women in subjection to them. With knowledge she would have looked on them with different eyes, and soon the semblance of authority would have had to be thrown aside, just as we find is becoming the case at the present day. No longer either could there be allowed to be one law of morality for one sex and one for the other. The subjection of woman and the idea of her inferiority to man are just the outcome of his physical appropriation of her to his use, or rather, to his pleasure, and no emancipation can do her much good which does not include, which indeed is not built upon, her absolute right to herself. So long as a man thinks he has a right, legal, moral, or religious – for religions have been woman's worst enemy in this respect – so long as he thinks he has a right to claim *anything* from her, which it is not her will to give, so long must her real freedom be delayed. Why are women so blind to this fact? Why can't they see the truth of it. None lies deeper; but we are little more than children yet, incapable of understanding anything but what lies uppermost, and so, even when we do feel that we want something we have not, we hardly know what it is that we do want, and we cry for this and for that, for more education, for the suffrage, for the right to work, and right to amuse ourselves as we please, not realising that what we want, and what we must have, is the right to ourselves, to the entire possession of our own bodies, and in this right all others are included, out of it all will surely come. We owe it to ourselves, we owe it to our children, we owe it to men as well, who are yet ignorant of what it involves to them no less than to us, to hold for this right, to fight until we have it. Who knows but out of it may come the salvation of the world.

Eliza Wigham‡ (1820–99), who had been a stalwart of the anti-slavery movement and of the women's suffrage movement, was a member of the Edinburgh Women's Liberal Association. On moving to Dublin, not long before her death, she wrote a farewell letter to the WLA in June 1898, stating the principles on which her politics were founded.

### 4.4 Letter from Eliza Wigham to Edinburgh Women's Liberal Association [NLS, Acc. 9080/8]

1 Palmerston Park, Dublin

25.6.98

To the Southern Branch of the Edinburgh Women's Liberal Association

Dear friends,

I have received your kind letter of farewell, which I very much appreciate, and for which I thank you very much. I hope I shall still continue connected with your association although not able to take any part with you in its working. As you say, I have been a Liberal in politics ever since I have known anything of political life; and I hope to remain a Liberal while I have the faculty of choice – but I am anxious that we should remember that being a Liberal does not merely consist in belonging to any party of that name (although it is useful for those who have the same views to unite in order to influence the people in the right direction) – but in each one, as far as possible, looking abroad on the things that affect the well-being of the nation, and the nations, and striving to be enlightened by best Wisdom to understand these things, and to do our little best to carry out our convictions. I think if this were more the method of politicians we should not have such terrible wars, destructions of brothers, and making widows and orphans of so many thousands. It surely is an irrational plan of settling disputes, to adopt the Canine plan of fighting; and then, in our case, the fighting is not done by the individuals aggrieved, but by thousands of human beings to whom the cause is almost unknown – who are paid on each side for the dreadful work; and those who destroy the largest numbers of God's creatures are considered the victors; and then questions are discussed, and immense sums of money are paid; questions which ought to have been discussed, and money paid before the additional costs of life and treasure had been spent. The true Liberal, as it seems to me, should adopt the Christian principle, so clearly enunciated in that wonderful book of political ethics – the New Testament – "Thou shalt love thy neighbour as thyself." Then the disposition to oppress the working classes should be met. Equal rights and representation would be accorded to all classes and both sexes. Temptations to evil would as much as possible be kept from the weak – wise care would be extended even to the erring – and the suffering ones would be the special care of those who adopted these great principles of Political life.

May we all seek more and more to be guided by these principles, and then, if we are not called publicly to express them except by our votes; our influence will be felt and extended, and the blessing of God will surely help us and rest on us, and enable us to take our place in the dispensation announced by the angelic messengers on that night at Bethlehem.

With love for you all, and thanks for your kindness,      I remain
Your affectionate friend
Eliza Wigham

The Primrose League, named after the favourite flower of Benjamin Disraeli, was set up in 1883 to promote Conservative principles though it was an independent organisation from the Conservative Party. It was a mixed-sex organisation, and succeeded in attracting male working-class and female middle-class members. A Scottish Branch of the League was established in 1885. The League in Scotland attracted a substantial number of members: by 1901, over 85,000 people had joined, and there were eighty-six Habitations (branches) in Scotland (Annual Report, 1901). In organisational terms it was a male-dominated group but one which had a clearly defined place for women in it. The league acted as a vehicle for women to acquire political knowledge and skills and, while the issue of women's suffrage is highlighted here, they also took up issues such as Tariff Reform, and opposition to Home Rule in Ireland. Indeed, in 1913, members in Scotland were active in supporting the 'Women's Covenant', opposing Home Rule and pledging support to women in Ulster in the event of hostilities breaking out.

The extract below indicates the position of women in organisational structures. There was a Ladies' Grand Council which oversaw the activities of women members. Subscription rates were differentiated between 'Knights' and 'Dames' and 'Associates'. Knights and Dames were required to pay an annual 'tribute' as well as membership fees, while Associates had to pay only the latter. The role of the Dames is illustrated in the section on 'The Ladies' Grand Council' in the Scottish Branch Manual.

4.5 The Primrose League, Scottish Branch, Manual, *Statutes and Ordinances, Model Bye-Laws for Habitations, &c. &c.*, Central Offices: 122 George Street, Edinburgh. [no date] [NLS, Acc. 10424/1] (37–8)

The Ladies' Grand Council.

The Ladies' Grand Council exists for the purpose of forming a bond of union between Dames of the Primrose League for the furtherance and support of its principles and objects.

It already numbers many hundreds, and the promoters rely on the ladies of Great Britain to maintain the enthusiasm and activity of this most important branch of the League.

Every lady wishing to be elected a member of the Ladies' Grand Council must first be a Dame, and then sign a Declaration expressing her willingness to join, and must be proposed and seconded by two existing members.

Every member joining in Scotland is entered in a separate roll called the Ladies' Grand Council, Scottish Branch. All members' names are published annually in a general list. A grant is made to the Scottish Branch of the League as representing the subscriptions of all Scottish Ladies.

The Annual Subscription is One Guinea, and the Badge (a blue enamel Brooch) costs Half-a-crown.

The funds are employed for speakers, literature, &c.

The administrative work of the Council is carried on by an Executive Committee elected by the members who, in their turn, can assist by attending and promoting meetings, starting and presiding over Habitations, lending carriages, encouraging their friends to join, and taking a general interest in the cause, *whenever possible*. Those, however, who are *unable* to give *active* help will be welcomed for the support of their names and subscriptions.

If Dames could be brought more generally to realise the usefulness of enrolling themselves in the Ladies' Grand Council, the rate of increase would be great. Many ladies are able to devote both time and attention to the work, but there are many others whose occupations render such work impossible. To these in particular the Ladies' Grand Council offers a means through which they may effectually carry out the engagements which they undertook when they subscribed themselves members of the League. They cannot give their time, we ask them, therefore, to give their money.

It must be obvious to every one that, considering the character and extent of the work undertaken by the League, the material support afforded by the Ladies' Grand Council is very valuable.

The names of all newly elected members are announced in the *Morning Post*, and a full list is also printed.

The Annual Meeting is held during May, when the report is presented, and there are speeches and music. A reception is also given during the London season.

Unity is strength, and in these important times the Ladies of Great Britain and Ireland can do much by thus uniting in their country's cause.

For Ordinance and Declaration Forms of Ladies' Grand Council apply to the Political Secretary, The Primrose League Office, 122 George Street, Edinburgh.

From 1890, a number of resolutions was put forward by Habitations to the Annual Meeting of the Scottish Branch, on the subject of the 'extension of suffrage to women'. In 1901, the Scottish Grand Council was asked to urge the government to prepare legislation entitling women ratepayers to vote in parliamentary elections. The typical response to earlier attempts to get the Scottish Branch to support women's suffrage was to say the time was not right, or that it was inexpedient at present. In 1901, however, the Grand Council, effectively ruled it out of order:

### 4.6 Minute of meeting of Grand Council, 11 February 1901 [NLS, Acc. 10424/1]

A letter from Mr Lane Fox was read acknowledging receipt of a copy of the Annual Report and congratulating the Scottish Branch on the progress of the League in Scotland during the past year. The letter proceeded as follows, "I am further desired to explain to you that the proposed resolution No. 2 which is to be considered at the meeting of the Scottish Branch Grand Habitation is really outside the scope of the Primrose League, just as a resolution advocating Protection, or antivaccination would be. Such questions are not discussed upon Primrose League platforms because members of the League are free to support or oppose them as they please." The Political Secy was instructed to acknowledge receipt of the letter and to say that Grand Council had made a note of the view entertained by Grand Council as regards the resolution in question.

By 1908 Women's Unionist Associations were springing up in various parts of Scotland, and Conservative women were shifting their allegiance to them, offering support to Conservative Associations in electioneering.

The Edinburgh Fabian Society was formed in December 1891, and the Glasgow society in 1892, with Sidney Webb speaking at the first regular meeting. Edinburgh socialist, John Gilray, referring to the period in the early 1890s, noted that, in the Edinburgh Fabian Society branch, 'two ladies, were most energetic and untiring in work for the cause'.[4] The minute book of the Edinburgh society refers to occasional discussion of 'women's' issues, as the following extract for 1910 indicates.

## 4.7  Edinburgh Fabian Society minutes, 1910 [NLS, Acc. 4977/7]

Fabian Rooms

4 Bristo Port
27th October.

On this evening the second meeting of the session was held, Mr J. Drummond Shiels, vice-president in the chair.

The minutes of the last meeting were read and approved.

Miss K. McKeracher then read a paper on "The Economic Position of Women's Wages"

After a brief summary of woman's economic position in past ages, the lecturer said that women's work might be divided into four classes – manual, routine mental, artistic, and intellectual, and stated that, except in the third class, which includes singers actresses and dancers, women receive much lower wages than men.

Public opinion seemed to be that they ought to receive less, and the possible reasons for this opinion were discussed.

Miss McKeracher thought that reform lay along the lines of Franchise, better training for women, and Trade Union organisation.

A lively discussion followed, in which almost all present took part. The question as to whether the present day idea of "the home" should be preserved occupied a considerable portion of the time.

Clarice McNab‡ [later Clarice McNab Shaw] (1883–1946), was the first Labour Party woman to be become a town councillor in Scotland, elected to Leith Town Council in 1913, having previously served on the school board.

## 4.8  *The Scotsman*, 22 October 1913

### LADY CANDIDATE'S VIEWS

A meeting of Leith Six Ward electors was held last night in Balfour Place School – Mr W. L. Sharp, a member of Leith School Board, presiding. The meeting was addressed by Councillor Edgar and Miss C. M. McNab, candidate for the ward. Miss McNab said that during the last few days she had received several letters, some wishing her success in her candidature, and others giving her advice. Part of that advice was that she should withdraw from that campaign, because the Town Council was not a place for a woman. (Laughter). That of course made her all the more anxious to get there. (Laughter.) She wished to try to dispel that sex prejudice. Among the things which she advocated were the introduction of a baby clinic, cheaper gas, and a municipal cooking depot.

Lavinia Malcolm‡ (1847–1920), a Liberal Party member, was the first woman to be elected to a town council in Scotland in 1907, and she subsequently became the first woman provost in 1913, in Dollar.

## 4.9 *The Scotsman*, 8 April 1914

### INFANT MORTALITY

Provost Mrs Lavinia Malcolm, Dollar, submitted the report on the work of the National Association for the Prevention of Infant Mortality and the Welfare of Infancy, on which body the Convention is represented. Mrs Malcolm said there was no doubt as to the wisdom of the Convention in being represented on that Association. Many agencies were at work for the saving of infant life, and their reward was clearly shown by the decrease in infant mortality. There was still much to be done. Until our poor had healthy, sanitary homes, and a living wage, it stood to reason that that blot upon our nation's legislation must still exist. (Applause.)

## Select bibliography

Anna Clark, *The Struggle for the Breeches: Gender and the Making of the British Working Class* (London: Rivers Oram Press, 1995).

Eleanor Gordon, *Women and the Labour Movement in Scotland, 1850–1914* (Oxford: Clarendon Press, 1991).

Sue Innes and Jane Rendall, 'Women, Gender and Politics', in Lynn Abrams, Eleanor Gordon, Deborah Simonton and Eileen Janes Yeo (eds), *Gender in Scottish History since 1700* (Edinburgh: Edinburgh University Press, 2006), pp. 43–83.

Elspeth King, *Scottish Women's Suffrage Movement* (Glasgow: People's Palace Museum, 1978).

Elspeth King, 'The Scottish Women's Suffrage Movement', in Esther Breitenbach and Eleanor Gordon, *Out of Bounds: Women in Scottish Society 1800–1945* (Edinburgh: Edinburgh University Press, 1992), pp. 121–50.

Leah Leneman, *A Guid Cause: The Women's Suffrage Movement in Scotland* (Edinburgh: Mercat Press, 1995).

Kenneth J. Logue, *Popular Disturbances in Scotland, 1780–1815* (Edinburgh: John Donald, 1979).

Jane McDermid, 'School Board Women and active citizenship in Scotland, 1873–1919', in *History of Education*, 38 (3) (2009), pp. 333–47.

Clare Midgley, *Women against Slavery: the British campaigns, 1780–1870* (London: Routledge, 1992).

Megan Smitley, *The Feminine Public Sphere: Middle-class Women in Civic Life in Scotland, c.1870–1914* (Manchester: Manchester University Press, 2009).

J. J. Smyth, *Labour in Glasgow, 1896–1936: Socialism, Suffrage, Sectarianism* (East Linton: Tuckwell Press, 2000).

## Notes

1. Kenneth J. Logue, *Popular Disturbances in Scotland 1780–1815* (Edinburgh: John Donald, 1979).

2.  Anna Clark, *The Struggle for the Breeches: Gender and the Making of the British Working Class* (London: Rivers Oram Press, 1995).
3.  See Iain Whyte, *Scotland and the Abolition of Black Slavery, 1756–1838* (Edinburgh: Edinburgh University Press, 2006).
4.  Edinburgh Fabian Society minutes: NLS, Acc. 4965.

# Chapter 8

# Empire Experiences and Perspectives

*Esther Breitenbach*

## Introduction

There is little literature as yet that focuses on Scottish women's experiences of Empire. This chapter aims to illustrate the lives of Scots women within a range of Imperial territories: colonies of settlement, India, and dependent colonies in the Caribbean and in Africa; and within different capacities and roles, such as emigrants, travellers, spouses or family members of colonial administrators or soldiers, and as missionaries.

## Section 1: Emigration – leaving, travelling, arriving

In the nineteenth century there was a voluminous literature on emigration: published accounts, handbooks, magazines and so on. Of this printed literature, very little was authored by women. Women's accounts of their experiences tend to be found largely in correspondence to family members at home, though some journals, letters and diaries were subsequently published. Other sources of accounts of the earlier decades of emigration can also be found in memoirs. In addition, a considerable range of sources can be used to study women's emigration, such as passenger lists, emigration society records, newspaper coverage and adverts and so on. The selection of extracts below covers: circumstances surrounding emigration; accounts of journeys; experiences on arrival; and support for women's emigration. Extracts refer to experiences in different territories, at different times, and of women from different class backgrounds. They represent emigrants who were coerced into emigration, whether by landlords or harsh economic circumstances, others who sought to better their circumstances, and some motivated to emigrate through family connections.

The extract below gives an account of emigration to Canada in the 1820s. Jessie Buchanan Campbell's father was a minister who moved with his family from Edinburgh to Beckwith, Lanark County in Canada in 1822. He was responding to the petition from Beckwith township to the Presbytery of Edinburgh for a Presbyterian minister. Jessie was probably about ten years old at the time. Campbell's memoir of her father's life was first published in 1900; Campbell died a few weeks after completing it. A copy is available as an online version via the UTL Canadian Pamphlets and Broadsides digital collection: http://link.library.utoronto.ca/broadsides/

> 1.1 Jessie Buchanan Campbell and John J. McLaurin, *The Pioneer Pastor: 'I will add a stane to his cairn'* (Franklin, PA, 1905) (16, 17)

The family sailed from Greenock in May 1822:

Nothing especially eventful marked the tedious voyage. Each Sunday father preached to a crowd of attentive hearers. Thirty-eight days brought us to Quebec, where our real tribulations began. Part of the route was by water and many a weary mile by land, over roads and through swamps almost impassable. Barges drawn by horses conveyed us and our goods through the canal. At Prescott the Rev Mr Boyd, who lived to a patriarchal age, invited us to his house, but we had to hasten forward. Rev William Smart welcomed us at Brockville, showing great kindness. Next morning, the fatiguing journey, in wagons heavily loaded with furniture and supplies, was begun. It lasted nearly a week, ending on August 10th at Franktown, three miles from our ultimate destination.

The first glimpse of Franktown dampened the ardor of the most sanguine of our party. McKim's log-tavern and three shanties, in a patch of half-cleared ground, constituted the so-called village. Some of my sisters wept bitterly over the gloomy prospect, begging piteously to be taken back to Scotland. Although not impressed favorably by the surroundings, father besought us to be patient, assured that "all things would work together for our good." Yet we formed a sorrowful group and ardently wished ourselves once more in Edinburgh. Certainly our faith was sorely tried . . .

On arrival, they were temporarily accommodated in a 'log-house' built by James Wall, 'a big-souled Irishman', though 'not a Presbyterian':

We were not burdened with household effects, having sold the bulk of the furniture in Scotland. "Necessity is the mother of invention." Quilts and blankets, hung over the openings and across the apartment, served as doors and windows and a partition. We cooked on the flat stone, at one end of the building, which did duty as a hearth in the chimneyless fire-place. More smoke stayed inside than found the way out. Millions of mosquitoes and black flies added to our discomfort, obliging us frequently to exclude nearly every breath of air to shut out the pests. The plague of flies in Egypt could hardly have been more tormenting. No one dared venture far at night, for wolves prowled around the house in the darkness, uttering dismal howls. Like the wicked, these ugly creatures "loved darkness rather than light, because their deeds were evil." But God watched over us, preserving our health and strength, and we hoped for the speedy coming of better days.

Settlement of New Zealand began to expand from the 1840s. Quoted below is the account of early settlement in Otago and Dunedin given by Isabella Anderson and Janet McKay. It forms part of the *Taieri Allans*, by James Allan Thomson, great nephew of both Anderson and McKay. Thomson's source was Hocken's *Contributions to the Early History of New Zealand*; Hocken had talked directly with Mrs Anderson and Mrs McKay.[1] Published in a volume on pioneer settler women collected by the Women's Institutes of New Zealand (founded in 1921), it is indicative of women's interest in preserving their own history.

1.2 A. E. Woodhouse (ed.), *Tales of Pioneer Women*, 2nd revised edn (Christchurch, Auckland, Wellington, Dunedin, Invercargill, London, Melbourne, Sydney: Whitcombe and Tombs Limited, 1940) (266–8)

Isabella Anderson and Janet McKay

James Anderson, his son John, and another young Scot, Alexander McKay, arrived in Wellington by the ship *Oriental*, in 1840. Between them they tested the possibilities of Wellington, Auckland, and Nelson, and when the New Edinburgh (afterwards, Dunedin) Settlement was mooted, resolved to try their fortunes there. In this decision they were doubtless as much influenced by the thought of living once more in a Scotch and Presbyterian community as by the lack of outlook in Nelson. When they heard of the abandonment of the scheme, they did not change their plans, for they had no doubt that it would ultimately come to fruition.

John Anderson married Isabella Allan in April, 1844, and in December of the same year Alexander McKay married her sister Janet. The Allan family had arrived in Nelson in 1842.

James Anderson, with his son and daughter-in-law, and Mr and Mrs McKay left for the south shortly after the second wedding, chartering the *Deborah* to Wellington, and the *Sarah Ann* to Otago, and taking with them a large quantity of flour, sugar, and such other stores as they thought they might require.

The voyage lasted three weeks and was a very stormy one. Frequently they thought the end had come, and once the women, sitting quietly in the cabin, heard McKay, in strong commanding voice, calling to the sailors to cut the ropes. At last they reached the Otago harbour, and anchored safely off Koputai, now known as Port Chalmers. Here, on December 30th, 1844, before they disembarked, Isabella Anderson gave birth to her first son, James, the first white child born in the Otago harbour.

Finding, on their arrival, that the tide of immigration was not yet in flood, and that there was little prospect of employment, yet having youth, and strength, and faith in the future, they decided to remain and encounter the certain hardships of their new condition.

McKay and his wife decided to stay at Koputai in readiness to do business when the settlement should at last be formed, and also with any chance whalers. He built the first public house, the 'Surveyors' Arms', which stood on the same site as the present Port Chalmers Hotel.

The Andersons circumnavigated the harbour, or the 'river' as the whalers called it, and finally decided to pitch their tent in that pretty little inlet named after them, Anderson's Bay. Here was a strip of clear land running from bay to ocean, with plenty of good bush in the vicinity, and they hoped to run a few sheep, and perhaps cattle; both the Andersons, father and son, were experienced sheep men.

They built a house of rushes and rough timber on that rising piece of foreshore now in the junction of two roads and forming part of the Cintra property. For food they eked out half a ton of flour brought from Nelson with potatoes and other vegetables of their own raising, as well as wild pork, fish, rock oysters, and birds. There was an abundance of native quail, which young Mrs Anderson, who soon learnt to shoulder a gun, brought down in sportsmanlike manner. She was sometimes accompanied on her shooting expeditions by a young Maori woman called Akina. Her sister Janet, at Koputai, not quite so accomplished with a gun, was content to carry the bag when her husband went pigeon shooting. Intercourse between the two families had to be by boat, for the bush came down close to the water's edge, and the only tracks were very rough ones. The scenery, however, was a constant delight, and it was a great grief to the pioneers in after years that it had been spoiled by the felling of the trees.

Time hung heavily on the hands of the young wives, their sole amusements being gardening, fishing and boating.

The original letter from Margaret McRitchie, quoted below, is held in the Australian Manuscripts Collection: State Library of Victoria, MS.10233 (the NLS holds a photocopy of the original). The Library was able, through newspapers and ships' passenger lists, to establish that the emigrant ship that the McRitchies travelled on was the *William Stewart* from London via Plymouth. There were two cabin passengers, and 234 steerage passengers, described as 'bounty emigrants', on the ship. Two emigrants were young unmarried women named McRitchie, from North Queensferry, Scotland: Christine, aged twenty-three and Mary, aged twenty-one. Both were described as Presbyterian, domestic servants and able to read and write. It seems likely that the letter was written by one of these women who were probably sisters.

### 1.3 Letter, 1848, of Miss [Margaret] McRitchie, Melbourne, to her father in North Queensferry, Fife [NLS, Acc. 7117]

Melbourn June 5th 1848

Dear Father

We are happy to inform you of our safe arrival in Melbourn on May 16th we had a good passage a good Captain a doctor & officers with Temperate sailors we intended keeping a Journal but our part of the ship being so dark many days we could not see. their was nothing of speaking about but we caute a few Fish and Shirks & they passed away the time cheerfully their was some Children died but none of the old people died it would have been a great deal worse if their had been but the Children were never much minded there was Eight Births no Marradges on board but their was two of the Children Baptised named Elizia & William Stewart.

Dear Father be shure & let us know the name of our last Sister that was born before we left home I hope you received our letters from Pleamouth & we dropt one by the way. we had Church on Board every Sunday weathersn permiting. we never wanted a meal of vitals all our passage, so you may consider what a passage we had, we may thank the Lord for our safe arrival. Their was 51 Singal Woman all in our room & we were very happy. their was but 16 English & 35 Scotsh were all ingaged on board but our-selves it was like a Fair. we went to whom we had our letter to & they found Situations for us & we got more wadges then was given on board, we have good Situations & we are getting £25 they year, the house maids have no grate to clean they all burn wood their is not such a thing as a grate to be seen, the work is not so haird as it is at home nor the mistresses are not so sassay, they are glad to get any person to work to them.

Melbourn is as large a place as Dunfermline the most of the houses are brick it is wonderful to se such a place only to be 13 years old it is all Buch round thousands of miles what we would call a plantations at hom the nataivs live their & large Sheep Stations and Barracks stations their, & the natives live like the soldiers. they ocopy so much ground & they have Kings and Chiefs & any of the rest of them goes on one anothers ground they fight with them. The Beef is 2d. per Pound Rice 6d per lb. Bread cheep Barly 6d per lb. Clothing & Drink very high. their is no Beggers hear. Rich & poor lives all alike if people is willing to work, they can get plenty to do, the people is greate Tea Drinkers, the tea is 1/6 per lb thay have it after every meal the weather has been very bad since we came & the streets is not for Femails to walk they are in such a state thay will not let us out thay bring everything to us that we want the people are so kind that we are quite ashamed of their kindness to us & as for Mr & Mrs Brown thay are afull kind to us & always to make their house our home at any time. be sure and tell Mr William Brown & the family that their both well they have three nice Children & let him know how much Obledged we are to him for his letters. With kind love to grandmother & all friends and acquaintances, that none need be afraid to come here but for the passage for it is so long, it is upwards of twenty thousand miles, we have never seen person that we knew of as yet.

Dear Father be sure and write and let us know how you are all at home. The money that we received from you that we never needed any of it, so we put it in the Bank and if you want any money be sure and let us know, and we will remitt it by a Bank order

The memoir of Ann Anderson, quoted below, provides a graphic account of her voyage to Australia, and goes on to recount her career there as a nurse. Anderson, born in 1833 at Garrisford Farm in the parish of Forgue near Aberdeen, was daughter of a working farmer. Her mother was Isobel Hay, a shoemaker's daughter from the neighbouring parish of Auchterless. Anderson was a domestic servant, before becoming a nurse, eventually becoming matron at the Paramatta District Hospital. She emigrated to Sydney with her sister after a letter arrived from Australia, telling them 'that our long-lost Brother was alive and well', had 'bought a small freehold Farm, about twelve miles north of Sydney

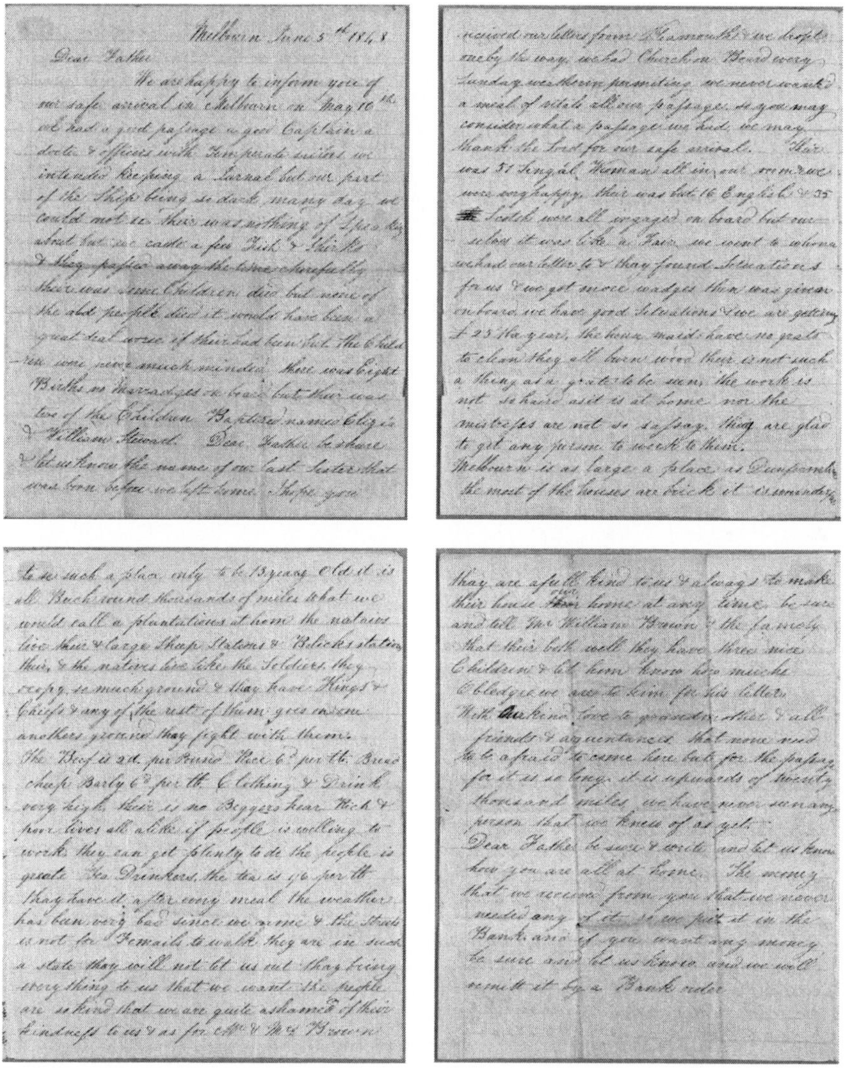

**Figure 8.1** Letter from Miss Margaret McRitchie, Melbourne, 5 June 1848, to her father in North Queensferry, Scotland. Courtesy of the State Library of Victoria, Melbourne.

City, and was in need of a Housekeeper'. They sailed from Plymouth in March 1877. The manuscript of Anderson's memoir is held by the NLS. An edited version of the manuscript has been published: Mary L. Elder, *Ann Anderson 1833–1906: The Enduring Spirit – Memoirs of a Country Lass from Aberdeenshire to Australia* (Edinburgh, Cambridge, Durham: The Pentland Press, 1992).

## 1.4 Ann Anderson, memoir [NLS, Acc 11468]

On a Sailing Ship to Australia in the 1870s

Upwards of ninety single women, most of them young, were now ushered into what might easily have been mistaken for a squalid and foul-smelling cellar. The disappointment – indeed incredulity – they felt as they contemplated their ship-board lodging was plain to see on every face. It took several days, and in some cases weeks, for the more discontented souls to accommodate themselves to such cramped surroundings.

. . .

The morning of our embarkation dawned bright and beautiful, a fact which I hailed as a good omen for the voyage to come. By twelve noon, however, it was raining heavily and it continued to do so with increasing intensity until after dark. We left the Depot about three p.m. carrying, each the best way she could, an incredible quantity of eatables and wearing apparel in our canvas bags. By the time we had been ferried to the ship in the open boat these were, of course, soaking wet. Many of us were feeling like convicts huddled together to await our doom. As the boat came alongside, orders were shouted at us to make haste. An official showed us single women the way to our quarters. Soon afterwards we found the two bunks – they were no more than coffin-like boxes – where we were to sleep, and to which our names had already been affixed. Isa's was raised about six inches from the floor or deck, while my own was about two feet above. In earlier days we had been accustomed to assure one another that anywhere we could get our heads down we would sleep. The difficulty in my case was how to get my feet down without raising them higher than my head, for in addition to my own person I had two bags, a box and a biscuit tin to accommodate. The latter contained the essential medical comforts which I would need if I suffered an attack of the tic douloureux. The food we were given constituted a further unpleasant surprise, though as time went on it did improve.

The diary and notes of Margaret Hinshelwood (née Charters) [Mrs Thomas Hinshelwood], quoted below, gives an account of their voyage on the *Nebo* from Glasgow to Rockhampton in 1883. The diary appears to have been written for publication in the *Jedburgh Gazette* in which extracts were published in December 1883 and January 1884. A number of extracts are quoted in Don Charlwood, *The Long Farewell: settlers under sail* (Allen Lane, 1981). There is much about the domestic economy on board ship, as well as treatments for illnesses. The passage clearly entailed risks for young children, several of whom died on the voyage as a result of an outbreak of measles; there was also one adult death. The extracts describe: some of the deaths; the catering arrangements on board ship; and the welcome they received on arrival in Queensland.

## 1.5 Margaret Hinshelwood, account of voyage to Queensland, 1883 [NLS, Acc. 12149]

The Hinshelwoods left Jedburgh in May 1883, proceeding first to Glasgow. Between Greenock and Helensburgh they boarded the 400 berth *Nebo*, which had a full complement of passengers. The journey was supposed to take ten weeks, but took three months, with the ship arriving in Rockhampton on 25th August. By early June measles had broken out among the children on board.

> Friday 15 – What a strange world we live in, one weeping and another rejoicing. Last night the sound of mirth and music ranged from forecastle to stern, and before dawn the wail of sorrow echoed over the peaceful sea. A fine little fellow of eighteen months was seized with croup and severe bronchitis in the night, and, though the doctor tried every remedy, it was of no avail. The poor mother was nearly frantic, it came so suddenly, so unexpected. I could not go on deck to see the little body consigned to the waves. I felt it would be more than I could stand. The captain desired as much quietness as possible, as there is so much illness on board.

> Saturday 16 – Still oppressively hot, as we are about the hottest just now. We entered the tropics on the 11th and passed under the sun yesterday, the 15th. We are about 900 miles from the equator today. The sun is on our north today instead of south. I was awakened this morning by a poor woman laying her trembling hand on my shoulder saying "Will you come Ma'am, my baby is dead". I went with her and prepared the little one for its watery grave. She bore up bravely but broke down terribly after the funeral; that makes two within twenty-four hours.

Passengers did not have regular access to the supplies they had brought with them; this was allowed only at certain points in the voyage. Given that the ship was full to capacity, cooking and eating arrangements needed to be well organised. Hinshelwood provides a detailed account of 'culinary arrangements':

> Wednesday 11 [July]
> NOTE: As I have been unable to write daily during the coarse weather, I think it may be useful to give some account of our culinary arrangements. We are divided into messes, with a captain over each mess, which includes 10 adults. This sometimes means four parents and twelve children. Tom is captain of our mess, comprised of ourselves and an English family with five children. The two men take week about to seek in provisions, and it is a constant run, especially on Saturday, when we get two days' provisions. We get flour, suet and raisins, and make our own duffs. They have to be in the pot by eight on Sunday morning, and boil till one o'clock. We also get preserved beef for Sunday, and can either eat it cold or make a pie, which, with the plum duff, makes a good Sunday dinner. We are allowed tea, with bread and biscuit and butter, for tea and breakfast. The purser calls the number of each mess, beginning with the young women, of whom there are eight messes, that is eighty girls. There are constables who receive their allowance and take it to the cook. As they are not allowed forward it is carried to them when cooked, and they are allowed to bake what they please, and they use vinegar off their pickles for want of baking soda. We are pinched for nothing but flour – I would strongly advise intending travellers to bring two or three stones of it, plenty of baking soda, a cheese, plenty of jam instead of the large quantity of clothing we brought. We have never used a sheet of our own yet. Just wash the ship's sheets to save our own.

The Scots emigrants received a warm welcome at Rockhampton:

> Tuesday 29 [August] – We had a splendid reception from the Caledonian Society
> last night. All the passengers were invited to tea in the School of Arts, which was
> finely decorated with flowers and banners, the Scotch tartan predominating. I never
> saw such a richly spread table in my life. The confectionary and fruit must have cost
> a large sum, while eggs and milk are so scarce and expensive. The refreshments were
> all provided by the ladies of the Society, who also presided at the tables each having
> some article of Scotch tartan about her dress. The Rev. Alex. Hay, who has been
> indefatigable in his efforts for the benefit of the Scotch passengers, and to whom
> we are all very much indebted, took a leading part in the entertainment, and with
> several other Scotch gentlemen, occupied the platform. The music was delightful
> – the songs all Scotch – while the addresses by Scotch residenters of twenty and
> thirty years, were full of hearty welcome, encouragement, and good, useful advice.
> They advised us to take the first of work whatever it was, and look out for a better
> opening as we got better known.

Assisted emigration specifically for women was a development of the later
nineteenth century. One organisation supporting emigration was the Aberdeen
Ladies' Union, formed in November 1883, 'with the object of uniting together,
in one body, all workers for the welfare of women and girls in Aberdeen'. First
named the Ladies' Union for the Care and Protection of Women and Girls, it
was subsequently renamed the Aberdeen Union of Women Workers in 1897,
when the Aberdeen Ladies' Union became a recognised branch of the National
Union of Women Workers. The ALU had an Emigration Committee (later
Emigration Branch) which sent girls from the north-east of Scotland to Canada
and Australia, mostly to go into domestic service.

---

### 1.6 Aberdeen Union of Women Workers, *Annual Report*, 1897 [Aberdeen City Libraries, Local Studies Section] (11–12)

There is as great a need as ever of thinning out our swarming population of young
women and of helping them in every prudent way, but the great and initial difficulty is *how* to do it. Too much help without corresponding effort on their part
is hurtful, and not true help.

All our girls are taken from the better class of mill girls and from public works
of various kinds, *not* domestic servants, as some people persistently continue to
think they are.

There is, however, a considerable stir on the other side as to how to get out more
good girls and women from Scotland. In Winnipeg there is now a "Girls' Home of
Welcome," and at the head of it is Miss Octavia Fowler, the daughter of a late Lord
Mayor of London. She writes that her Committee are very anxious to get out more
good Scotch girls, and that up to a certain point they are prepared to partly prepay
passage for suitable girls . . .

Then, again, in Montreal a new Committee has been formed in connection with
the "Canadian National Council of Women," and they hope that the Government

means to help them in their efforts to bring good women into the country. They have an idea that there are many young women in Orkney and Shetland who would like to emigrate if they could have their passage paid; of that we are not quite so sure. There are many girls in the Hebrides who would do well to leave those Islands, but the difficulty is to persuade of them of the advantages awaiting them, and their relations almost invariably object, though the poverty is deep and the future for them very dark.

### Section 2: Colonial life – colonies of settlement

Scots women living in colonial territories were keen to convey to those at home the character of their new surroundings, working and social lives. Such accounts included matters of finance and domestic economy, such as the costs of staple foods and goods such as textiles, clothing and tools, and also their availability. Women's accounts also included observations on the nature of agricultural work, including new technologies being employed and types of livestock being husbanded. In the earlier part of the nineteenth century, many emigrants came from agricultural communities, and part of the attraction of emigration was the capacity for acquisition of land in their own right, something many could never have aspired to in Scotland. Many accounts provide descriptions of living conditions, and the kind of housing available to them – from the building of log cabins in Canada in the early nineteenth century to the urban life of the early twentieth century. They also make reference to religious, cultural and political life. Other accounts of colonial life by Scotswomen include that of Elizabeth Macquarie‡ (1778–1835) (her travel journal and other writings are available online at http:// www.lib.mq.edu.au/digital/lema/)

The extracts below are from photocopies of letters from Marjorie [May] McNicol [Mackintosh] and John Mackintosh, on emigrant farms in Ontario, to James McNicol, by Nairn, describing their life and agricultural operations. McNicol's letter indicates that there were others from her home area in the place where she had settled in Canada, probably with some assistance from an emigration society: she asks if a recently widowed neighbour has a right to 'the Society's allowance'. It is also stated in the letter that it was being written by a John Tolmie: 'this is Tolmie's own handwriting'. Tolmie had been staying with McNicol's family but was due to take charge shortly of a 'fine large school'.

#### 2.1 Letter from Marjorie [May] McNicol in Ontario, Canada, to her brother James, a farmer in the Nairn area, August 1831 [NLS, Acc. 7020]

Southold, Riverroad, 2nd August, 1831.
Dear brother
I have the pleasure of reading your two last letters both in the same day, viz on the 12th April, dated 20th January, stating that you were all in good health.

... – I live since last January on my own one hundred acres of fine land and expect to buy some more very soon, wheat crop I raised this season looks remarkably well – The wheat is mostly all cut down in this quarter, and in most places is a very heavy crop. You may tell my Sister & Donald McPhail her son, that I do not advise them to come to this country but one thing I know that when people once get themselves properly settled that they are much better off here than at home. I tell you that it goes very hard with people at first, particularly with thoze who have no pieces of money with them after settling. When we settled here, there was not a single tree cut down, but now I have eight acres clear, and that the very best of land. I got built a fine large house to live in. I have about four acres under Indian corn, pumpkins, potatoes, kail and a variety of other things to tedious to be mentioned. Soon I intend to sow my wheat, from eight to nine acres. It cost me from forty five to forty six pounds before I got ourselves settled. If Donald McPhail has a mind to try it he better come by New York as it will be much cheaper than by Quebec. The land costs about eleven shillings and threepence an acre and a few other little expenses, but should he not take land, he would get 4/6 sterling per day & his victuals, which is no bad wages . . . Young girls do much better here than at home. If Donald and his mother come out, I will let them have twenty acres of my land, but mind you they will have to take up their hatchets and cut down the large trees, and then can have as many cattle and hogs as they like. You need not take any axes out with you, nothing but clothes and such thingz as you require on the voyage – you may take some pots as they will be very useful. John Cluny lives close to Mrs McIntosh has got two hundred acres and about fifty cleared and is doing extraordinarily well. Thomas his brother lives near him, and has got 100 acres of good land. There are all denominations of preachers here, you may go and hear whomsoever you please – such as Presbyterians, Methodists, Baptists, Episcopalians & Roman Catholics if you choose . . .

Christian Oliver's letter, quoted below, is in a collection of letters to James Scott, schoolmaster in Newstead, Roxburghshire, from his brother Henry and nephews and niece, James, John and Christian Oliver, in London and Burlington, Ontario, on life in Canada. Oliver's letter indicates the presence of other settlers from her home area in Scotland.

### 2.2 Letter from Christian Oliver, Burlington, Ontario to her uncle, James Scott, schoolmaster in Newstead, Roxburghshire [NLS, Acc. 11100]

Burlington                                                                  Octob. 25th 1834
Dear
Uncal we received your letter about the latter part of which gave us great pleasure to here from you one more as we had lost all hopes of geating one. I was about to write you that week we got your leatter. This leaves us all in our usual health hoping it will find you all in the same – which we have great reason to thank God for it the colera has been raging very severely in Canada – this season and some parts of the States.
    . . . You spok abou your son Adam coming to America. We should like very well to see him if you are willing and if he comes he must come here New York is the

safest harbour to sail to so he knows of a home to come to give my love to your son James when you write him and tell him to write us and give us an account of his travils. Their is a great many emigrants comed in here this season and settled from Roxburghshaire. I expect you have heard tell about them all that comes here liks the country very well and thinks they have made a good exchange. times was very dull last spring and the beginning of summer but they are rather better now . . .

. . . we had a very good hay and harvest time this season the summer was wet in the beginning of the season but July and August I believe we never had a wet day but very warm – I will give an account of our stock we have 160 sheep 40 head of cattal 4 working horse 2 young 10 feeding swine 10 keeping swine we will seend 6 or 7 to the Albany market we feed them to about 300 lb a peace . . .

. . . It is 400 miles from here to uncal henery If we have all our health next fall & that some of us will go and him he says he will come and see us If his family could take care of things in his absence. We have a very fine young man for a minister among us this season sent by the pesbetry as we are not able to keep one all the time but I hope we will soon be able to keep one he mets with the young people every sabbath night and a bible class every teausday evening their is all kinds of denominations her and a great many infidals our minister preatches in the Village a mile from our hous . . .

The extracts below from Jessie Campbell's letters are from a collection of edited and annotated extracts from letters and journals of eight women pioneers in New Zealand. Campbell was, with her husband Captain Campbell and their four children, an early settler in Wanganui. The letters discuss domestic and family life, work, cost of living, and relations with Maoris. The Campbells arrived at Port Nicholson in 1841, removing soon after to Wanganui. By 1848 Wanganui consisted of a church and around forty houses. Jessie Campbell's account of her journey out to New Zealand is available online at http://camclan.orconhosting. net.nz/trip.html

2.3  Alison Drummond (ed.), *Married and Gone to New Zealand* (Hamilton and Auckland: Paul's Book Arcade; London: Oxford University Press, 1960) (63–4, 64–5)

Wanganui, 27th June, 1843

My dearest Mother

. . . I am delighted at having so early an opportunity of announcing to you the birth of another grandson on the 27th May. I was safely delivered of a fine stout little fellow, and have only to repeat the tale of most women in this country, that I suffered nothing to what I would have suffered at home . . .

We got comfortably settled in our new house three weeks before my confinement. I was saying the other day, if you could have a peep at us, how pleased you would be to see us so very comfortable; the house is an excellent one for the country, commodious and well planned. Many a hot argument the Capt. and John Cameron had while planning it; the walls are of clay with a roof of shingle, all the partitions inside are of wood, the walls outside are whitewashed which gives it the look of a clean English cottage . . . The rooms are very warm; with a capital brick fireplace in the sitting room, and what is rare in this country, it does not smoke in the least . . .

Some purchases made last summer have increased our cattle to 40 head. I still get 3/- per lb for fresh butter and 2/6 for salt, 3d per pint of milk. I make a good deal by my dairy during the Summer and Autumn. We get nothing from our own land except the comfort of growing our own wheat and potatoes. As for raising crops for sale, it is not half so profitable as cattle.

Labourers' wages have lessened very much. The men we had working at this house got 15/- per week. A year ago they would not have worked under £1 and rations . . .

Wanganui, 17th March, 1845
My dearest Isabella,

I must now give you an account of some stirring events that have occured here lately. About the beginning of January, some 200 natives came down the river from the Taupo country (about 150 miles from here) with the intention of fighting a tribe who live 20 miles down the coast and who had killed and eaten some of their relatives 8 or 9 years ago. The Taupo natives on arriving here heard accounts of their enemies mustering so strongly that they dared not attack them, and here they remained to our great annoyance. Their chiefs were very friendly to the Whites, particularly the principal leader, a grey haired fine looking old man, but they could not control their men who took every opportunity of robbing the Europeans. They broke a pane of glass in our boys' room and hooked out all their blankets and the sheets. One of the chiefs recovered most of the things but poor John lost a new pair of boots.

They at last became so audacious as to break into some houses at night, and ten of the inhabitants were forced to take it in turn to watch.

Our Magistrate became alarmed that some collision might take place and wrote to the Superintendent in Wgton how we were situated. He immediately came down in the *Hazard*, sloop of war, at present commanded by Mr. Robertson, youngest son of Col. Robertson. He and the Lieutenant Governor or Superintendent, Major Richmond, had there been occasion for it would have landed 50 men from the vessel. Major Richmond was determined to take forcible means to make the natives leave the place.

Fortunately the sight of the vessel outside the bar was quite sufficient to frighten them into promising to go away – they did so 2 or 3 days later.

In case of an attack Major Richmond desired the Magistrate to swear in 40 or 50 of the inhabitants as special constables to arm them as best he could. Each Magistrate was to have 10 men under him and Capt. C. was to command the whole.

Such a rummaging there was for fire-arms of all kinds, John Cameron casting bullets with as much glee as if he were going deer stalking. The Commander in chief you may believe was very busy. He says he could compare his regt. to nothing else than Falstaff's ragged (horde). Some of them did not know how to load a gun. I must confess I placed my whole dependence for our defence on the Blue Jackets.

> It was arranged that on the firing of an alarm gun all the women and children
> were to take refuge in a large wooden house and an hotel. They were to be guarded
> by 100 of our own natives headed by our Bishop, Dr. Selwyn, and some of his black
> coats who were here . . .

Jane Blackwood Mack was the daughter of Scottish emigrant, Joseph Gardiner
Mack and his wife, Anna. She was born at Geelong on 17 October 1841
(sometimes given as 1842). She returned to Britain and married her cousin,
John Caverhill. She began her journal when she was living as a farmer's wife at
Greenburn, Reston, Berwickshire: it gives an account of her family life during
the years 1840–89. She knew she was ill and wrote the journal for her children.
She died in 1894. The Mack family is described in some detail in Joseph J.
Mack's book, *Chain of Ponds: a narrative of a Victorian pioneer* (Newtown,
Victoria: Neptune Press, 1983).

## 2.4  Jane Blackwood Mack, Journal: Early Days in Australia [NLS, Acc. 9754/1] (12–13, 5–6, 26–7)

Mack described her father as 'too openhearted and credulous for his own
welfare', having difficulty in prospering as a farmer and subsequently as the
keeper of The Wool Pack Inn. A further move to a dairy farm near Colac was
followed by the acquisition of a sheep station where the family settled. The sheep
farm had 'a funny long native name', Gherangemarajah. Her father, tired of
writing this name, renamed the farm 'Berry Bank' after the name of his father's
farm in Berwickshire.

> Well I remember the long drive all through a hot summer's day over thirty five miles
> of plains, only seeing a few trees once at The Frenchman's Inn (now Gressy). We
> were in a heavy double gig and the horse got very tired and Joseph six years old stuck
> holding to his pony till thirty miles were over and then he cried that his hips were
> to sore he could ride no more and he was squeezed in amongst us. It was very late
> before we reached our new house and as soon as Mattresses were put on the floor we
> children got on to them and hard work it was to get the little ones undressed, being
> nine of course I did not consider myself a child and helped the others.
>
> In the morning what did we see. A large garden well filled with fruit trees in full
> bearing, but the hot wind of the previous day had caused the fruit to drop off in
> large quantities. The house was made of a wooden frame work of Maple trees then
> covered with rough plaster, white washed on the outside and lined and papered
> inside and a back roof – only four rooms and two of them skillions, big roofs sloping
> to the outer wall and very hot and small, how we all slept I never can make out, for
> there were 7 children and Miss Odell the Governess . . .

Mack tells of the 'Bungip' about which they had heard from Aborigines. The
family went on a picnic to "the basins", two little lakes separated by a narrow
ridge of land:

The Natives would not bathe in those basins because they said "The Bungip was last seen there." Many people suppose "The Bungip" was an extinct animal which had been a terror to the Natives. They were asked to sketch it, but no two drawings bore any resemblance to each other; still the early settlers thought there might be a ferocious animal though they had not come across it and one morning it was currently reported that the monster had been seen by some Gentlemen on their way home from a convivial evening, and their account was after an encounter with a ferocious black animal and trying in vain to shoot it (they always carried guns in case of being attacked by the natives) it took refuge in a swamp filled with high rushes. One settler when he heard the tale laughed and said "I'm sure it was one of Mack's pigs" and so it turned out, for the footprints and hair showed plainly that one of the Boars of my Father's which had gone wild was the supposed Bungip. The natives were not supposed to be Cannibals but a Mr. Beattie and old Gentleman came upon a couple finishing their meal and asked where their child was and could get no satisfactory reply, they decamped and he raked the ashes and found some human bones!

Jane was the third of nine children. At the age of sixteen she was sent to a boarding school in Geelong in 1855 and 1856. The children in the family were:

educated principally by Governesses, many of whom were incompetent and who thought their duties only consisted in hearing our lessons and making us work at our sums till our tears washed out our figures. When 16, I went to a boarding school in Geelong built by Mrs Boyce and her daughters refined English ladies and had been educated in France. The first year was on the whole profitably spent, but at the end of the second upon being asked if I wished to remain another year or go home, my answer was that if I could not be sent to a school where there were more advanced pupils I would not leave, so now you must picture our household as consisting of our much loved parents and 9 children – All ages from Catherine about 25 to Albert about 5 years old. Catherine was then teaching Nelly and Frank, Joseph at boarding school and John and Albert not having regular lessons and for a few weeks there seemed no place for me for Nancy was housekeeper. I said I would like the schoolroom, so the children were handed over to me and for two years I taught them regularly, often far more regularly than they approved of, for they were very fond of riding and Father often wanted Frank the eldest boy out, but by saying if he took Frank he could have the others too for I would not teach the discontented ones, he soon left off asking him out.

The extracts below are from the letters of John and Margaret Anderson, Hamilton, Ontario, to Jean Lindsay at Rumbling Bridge, Kinross, in the 1850s. The family of which the correspondents formed a part were from Glenquaich in Perthshire; they had left at a time when it was impossible for the family to own land from which they could make a living. The landowner, the Marquis of Breadalbane, had begun to clear tenants from his land in the 1840s; thus emigration resulted from this pressure though it is not clear whether it was a 'forced evacuation'. Over time many people from the area moved to western Ontario, moving 'as a community' of interconnected families.

In February 1858, John and Margaret Anderson suffered the loss of their infant daughter Margaret, not yet two years old. The letter below indicates their distress at not having had any response to the communication of their sad news:

To her Friends in general. Hamilton, Cda, 7th June 1858.
Dear Brothers and Sisters
I have longed very much for an answer to our letter sent you in February you told me when I left Scotland that I would soon be like the rest of people that went to America write for a little and then give it up. but I am mistaken if we have not wrote two for one we have received if not more. but we well expected an answer to the one reffered to., perhaps you may not think of it. so many of you. so near to each other. although I am far distant from you all still for anything that I know I deserve the respect of a Sister. it is now within a very few days of 5 months since we wrote the letter refered to + we may say it is very little consolation from them that are nearest related to us especially on such an occasion.
I remain your Affect.
Sister Margaret Anderson

A letter the following year to their cousin Jean Lindsay at Rumbling Bridge, made practical requests for clothing and fabrics which were expensive or hard to acquire in Canada. Their landlord had offered to pick up the goods for the Andersons from Kinross on a visit to Scotland. In the event he failed to do so; a subsequent letter requested that the articles be shipped on to Canada.

5th September, 1859
Dear Cousin
. . . He [their landlord Wm Allan] says he will bring out anything we might think on. Mgt would feel very much obliged if you would get a few things for her as follows: 3 sewed collars, 1 babbit shirt, 1 pair black kid gloves, 2 black with aprons. Please get the silk and make them she says to get a piece of velvet ribbon for trimming them with and line them. The making is too much to ask but it is to save duty. She wants the gloves and collars good as they are expensive here and 1 pair of hand-sewed sleeves. Collars that can be got for 3/6 or 3/9 with you runs about 10/- here and very much worse at that. 1 coloured handkerchief for her neck, 2 coloured silk pocket handkerchiefs for John pretty stout and 1 black cloth cap. size 7 and an eighth. with cloth peak. Mr Blyth knows about the style and his head and mine are just the same size. ½ yard pure silk. Mgt also wants one French moriney – blue childs carrying dress. A short one embroidered with a cape. Also we want a highland dress for George. A forty second kilt black cloth jacket and vest. scarf purse bonnet and two pairs of hose to match. We were thinking the best way to get them was to go to R Robertson, Dumferline and what he has not got he would send to Glasgow for. Mgt thinks the best way is to get the carrying dress made and readied as to George's dress. D Saunders Jnr and him are both one age so there cannot be much difference in their size. So we think if you were to get his dress made to D S's measure it would

be just the thing, but be sure to get it made large for George is growing very fast. If you could find it convenient to take D Saunders to Dumfermline with you for to get the measure, we think Robertson's will have a good idea what tailor would make it best and send it up to you. We think that will be all . . .

John and Maggie Anderson

Margaret McDonald's letter described work on their farm in Australia, as well as giving family news.

---

### 2.6 Letter from Margaret McDonald from Wallaloo, Australia to her brother in Rosshire, 1884 [NLS, Acc. 7024]

Wallaloo, by Glenorchy
Jan(ry) 10th 1884

Dear Brother

It is a long time since I wrote to you last yet still it is not because I do not think of you and the land I love so well but you must forgive me as I will not be so long the next time. we are all well . . .

. . . We have Bella's block we have alltogether 1200 acres this has been a very good year for sheep as they shire well and there was a good price for the wool indeed it is the only thing that keeps up in price up in this part wheat is only worth three and four pence per bushel and best beef ten shillings per 100 pounds and potatoes from five shillings to ten per ton which will show you that living is very cheap in this country we sold to two hundred and seventy sheep at eight and ninepence and the 500 that were shorn at home averaged four and sixpence each for the wool. We have nearly finished harvesting here there is a great difference in the way it is done here from the way which it was done in Scotland we have a machine that cuts the corn and binds it at the same time with thin wire such as you use to snare hares with at home you no doubt heard of them before but this year we are doing it with a machine called a stripper as the crops are shorter this year than usual this machine only takes the head of and threshes it at the same time leaving the straw standing as soon as the heads are threshed the fall into a large box as soon as the box is full it is emptied on a cloth where it is winnowed it is a great deal cheaper as three men can harvest 300 acres one to work the stripper and two the winnower.

### Section 3: Travelling the Empire

As the extracts above, from the correspondence, journals, and published writings of women emigrants, show, many women travelled long distances as emigrants, many travelled within their new homelands, and some also made the journey home for visits or permanently as 'return migrants'. Communication of their observations of living conditions and working conditions, flora, fauna, and scenery was thus fairly commonplace though little appears to have been said in these sources about indigenous peoples in colonies of settlement. Only a few Scots women in the nineteenth century dedicated themselves to travel: among them Isabella Bird Bishop‡ (1831–1904), Constance Gordon-Cumming‡ (1837–1924) and, in the early twentieth century, Olive Macleod (1880–1936); and their writings indicate their perspectives on Empire and how Imperial rule facilitated their travels.[2] The extracts quoted here illustrate some of the capacities in which women travelled. Some recorded their impressions, for example, in diaries and private journals, while others wrote for a public readership. Some women, resident in British Imperial territories, also travelled as part of their work or accompanying husbands or family.

Little is known about Janet Schaw‡ (1737–1801) whose journal covers her travels in 1774–6: a voyage to Antigua, then to St Kitts, North Carolina, and return via Portugal. Her journal, edited by Evangeline Walker Adams and Charles McLean Andrews, was first published in 1923: the extract below quotes this edition. Adams and Andrews established that Schaw was born in Lauriston, then a suburb of Edinburgh, and was probably about thirty-five to forty years old at the time of her voyage. She was from an old Scottish family and a distant relative of Sir Walter Scott. Schaw's journal was reprinted by the University of Nebraska Press in 2005. The original manuscript is in the British Library.

### 3.1 Janet Schaw, *Journal of a Lady of Quality* (New Haven: Yale University Press, 1923) (74–5)

Description of arrival in Antigua.

I was already on deck to see the lead thrown, to sound our depths, the colour of the water has already begun to change to a lighter blue, and in a little time became quite green like that at Leith. You remember how much Ossian was criticised for calling the Sea blue and the stars green, but that is truly the appearance they have, when sufficiently distant from land. We soon had a pilot on board, who with his black assistants, brought us round the rocks at the utmost points of Antigua. The beauty of the Island rises every moment as we advance towards the bay; the first plantations we observed were very high and rocky, but as we came farther on, they appeared more improved, and when we got into the bay, which runs many miles up the Island, it is out of my power to paint the beauty and the Novelty of the scene. We had the Island on both sides of us, yet its beauties were different, the one was hills, dales and groves, and not a tree, plant or shrub I had ever seen before; the ground is vastly uneven, but not very high; the sugar canes cover the hills almost to the top, and bear a resemblance in colour at least to a rich field of green wheat; the hills are skirted by the Palmetto or Cabbage tree, which even from this distance makes a noble appearance. The houses are generally placed in the Valleys between the hills, and all front to the sea. We saw many fine ones. There were also some fine walks along the Shore shaded by different trees, of which I am yet ignorant. Will you not smile, if after this description, I add that its principal beauty to me is the resemblance it has to Scotland, yes, to Scotland, and not only to Scotland in general, but to the Highlands in particular. I found out a Dunkeld in one of these walks, nor do I think the birches there inferior in beauty to the myrtles here.

Letitia Hargrave‡ (née Mactavish) (1813–54) was granddaughter of the Chief of Clan Tavish and grew up in Argyllshire. In 1830, at the age of twenty-seven, she married James Hargrave, chief trader in charge of York Factory, of the Hudson Bay Company. She lived there for ten years, giving birth to five children. Her letters, edited by Margaret Arnett McLeod, were published by the Champlain Society in 1947. The volume provides a detailed account of the family backgrounds of Letitia and her husband, and of their life at York Factory of the Hudson Bay Company, and is available online at http://link.library.utoronto.ca/champlain/

### 3.2 Letters of Letitia Hargrave (65–6)

To Florence Mactavish [a younger sister]

York Factory 1st [to 5th ] Septr 1840

My dear Flora

I began and continued a sort of diary but in the hubbub of leaving the ship and my being so unwell that I c$^d$ do nothing Mr Hargrave and Marg$^t$ lost the sheet containing our adventures in Hud$^n$ Straits so that I must remember what I can. On first entering we were becalmed among the ice & lay 2 days off Savage islands. For 24 hours night & day we were beset w$^{th}$ Huskies. They were heard shouting for a least 2 hours & a ½ before they reached us w$^{ch}$ they did in light canoes with a hole in the middle. Each holds one man & a few tusks of ivory (walrus teeth) w$^{ch}$ they brought to traffic. There were 34 canoes – We moved so slowly that they kept with us all the time – 3 hours after their arrival the luggage boats came up manned by women & laden with children husky dogs images or dolls in imitation of themselves – There were several large boats holding the various families of the gents in the light ones. Almost every woman had a huge fat child in her hood[3] & when they saw anything in the sailors hands that they wanted they seized the babies, pulled off their one article of dress, shrieking *pilly tay* (give me) threw the weans who squalled like any white back into the hood. If they did not get quiet they put their breasts some how over their shoulders & continued their *pilly tay*. When a saw was shown them the whole fleet got into commotion & screamed *cutty swaback*. A gimblet, was *billy linga*. They w$^d$ give any thing for them but poor wretches except a few seal skins & the walrus teeth they had nothing worth trading – When they got any thing a broken pair of rusty scissors or horrid old iron off a barrel (the hoop) they rubbed their tongue over it. They use their boots as y$^u$ used to do y$^r$ wide sleeves that is put every thing into them, pot lids & darning needles. I gave one some needles he tried to stick them into his trowsers but always pricked his fingers, so after licking both finger & needles, he said *coonah* looking very knowing, & handed them over the ships side to his coonah (wife). They were evidently quite ignorant of the use of water & nothing more horrible than the old black dirt of the ladies can be imagined. They rub themselves all over with grease & from the hood always being dragged down by the child's weight their necks & shoulders are blackened by wind & weather. I got a doll & will see if it can get a place among the tongues.[4] The hood is on the head & the tail behind is too short, but the carriage & shoulders are the very thing & the shape of the face. They keep bawling *Chimoo Chimoo*, signifying good & aha when pleased w^ch indeed they always seemed. The men looked well each in his beautiful canoe but the women gathered together in the luggage canoes were hideous, the children like Johnnie McBride in feature & colour.

While the canoes were round us a shouting & yelling arose & off they all paddled towards a berg, where on looking thro' a glass an unfortunate seal was discovered. Their clamor stupefied the animal & he stood quietly till they harpooned him on w^ch he fell head over feet off the ice into the water. Any thing like the rapidity of their progress I never saw. All the mens canoes were there. They cut the seal up, eat what they wanted (they dont cook) & then divided the remains faithfully among them. When they returned to the ship each man had a lump of red seal behind him. Every moment they w^d put a hand back rub it over the store & lick the fat & blood off the paw with great satisfaction – We had great difficulty in getting rid of them, they followed & made such a noise & the smell they left was insufferable all about for days . . .

Another account of northern travel which is of much interest is the journal of Margaret Penny‡ (1812–91), recently published in W. Gillies Ross, *This Distant and Unsurveyed Country: A Woman's Winter at Baffin Island, 1857–1858* (Montreal and Kingston, London, Buffalo: McGill-Queen's University Press, 1997). Penny accompanied her sea captain husband, William, on a voyage to Baffin Island on the Aberdeen whaler, *Lady Franklin*. The *Aberdeen Journal* reported on her voyage, and the Aberdeen Arctic Company, owners of the ship, presented her with an ornate silver tea service on her return.

The extracts below are from the diary of Mrs Duncan, of Banff, who accompanied her sea captain husband 'Willie' on voyages to various destinations. In her diary Duncan discusses conditions on board ship, the type of cargoes carried, and social interactions in the various ports they put into. During her visit to Barbados in 1880, she demonstrated a lively interest in local women and fashions, and in the workings of the sugar industry.

### 3.3 Extracts from the Diary of Mrs Isabel Duncan [Aberdeen University Library, Special Collections, MS 2526.]

Friday, 19th March
The first view of Barbadoes was beautiful, at the dawn of the day. The land on the S east-side is all in cultivation the trees and fields of sugar cane also other crops, had each their shade of green, the Wind Mills and chimney stacks pointed out the different plantations and to judge by the number of huts visible on that side the population must be large.

On rounding the point to enter the harbour the number of ships almost frightened us from going in to seek a cargo. I am sure there were between forty and fifty. We came to anchor a little after 7 and at ten Willie went ashore. From the bay Bridgetown looks very well the dunes do extend almost round the bay and from the water's edge away back when the ground seems to rise up, but very little wood on the high land.

Monday 22nd March.

Busy at odds and ends in the forenoon. Afternoon went on shore; on landing we met Capt Duncan and the Master of another vessel a cab was got and we had a drive some distance out of town, round the garrison and race course. The darkie gals were very amusing, flirting with every one as they went along the street and so shy like when a young man was approaching. As to fashion I can only compare them to peacocks their dresses are sweeping behind them fully a yard while the front is only half way below the knee which shows off their ankles to advantage, they walk with a very straight back and their head in the air.

Thursday 25th March [description of visit to plantation]

The cab was in waiting so we set out at once a distance of about five miles. On the way we met waggons with hogs heads of sugar drawn by mules, six or seven on each waggon. Farther on we saw men cutting down the canes, women were tying them in bundles and carrying to the carts which were drawn by oxen. The island is covered I may say with wind mills some for driving the mills and some for pumping water on the estate there were two for pumping, the mill was driven by steam. The cane was crushed between heavy rollers and the juice ran down into a trough and on to tanks where it was heated and lime added to it to separate the refuse – then it was boiled and passed on from pan to pan (these were made of copper) and up into a place where it was strained and several other processes gone through. They made sugar of dif. qualities also syrup and molasses and lastly rum. The canes after the juice was extracted were spread out to dry and was the fuel for the engine which was a great saving of coals and also suited better. I was very interested in it all and enjoyed it much.

Described as 'the first lady traveller in South Central Africa', Jane Moir was married to Fred Moir who, with his brother John, was Director of the African Lakes Company, set up with the aim of developing commercial activities to replace slave trading around Lake Nyasa where several Scottish missions had been established. The Moirs were closely linked to the missions, and Jane's letters were published with the approval of the Free Church. It is likely that they were written with a public readership in mind. Her book contains an account of their journey from the northern end of Lake Nyasa (now Lake Malawi) to Lake Tanganyika and back. The letters are reprinted in Klaus Stierstorfer, *Women Writing Home, 1700–1920: Female Correspondence across the British Empire*, Vol. 1, *Africa* (London: Pickering and Chatto, 2006).

> 3.4  Jane F. Moir, *A Lady's Letters from Central Africa* (Glasgow: James Maclehose and Sons, 1891) (27–9, 51–2, 77–9)

Moir described the reaction of villagers on the Tanganyika plateau to their arrival:

22 June 1890

. . . the very primitive inhabitants come out of their stockaded village to stare at
the white people, and presently they hear that the second white man is a *woman!* a
fact which astonishes them very much, and the women and children now venture
near and gaze at the creature that is said to be a woman, but who to their eyes is so
little like one. The reason is that I wear a very loose belt, and have unfortunately
for the credit of Englishwomen here, a waist. This is what puzzles them. She has no
stomach; how can she be so thin if she is a woman? yet they say she is Chindevu's
wife, so English women must be like her. I explain that if the black women were
dressed in my clothes, they would be just the same, but it is no use, and I feel quite
disappointed with myself, and if it weren't for fear of sunstrokes and a few other
difficulties, I would very much like to dress in a big bath towel, and then probably I
would be much admired! As it is, Fred gets all the admiration; they think his beard
magnificent. Feeling so unworthy of my sex, I do not very much enjoy the staring
process, and at first was a good deal overcome by the terribly nude condition of the
people. The men are very much dressed in a small skin, and many simply have a bit
of bark string tied round the waist, and a few leaves slung on in front. The ladies
here wear a loose string of beads or shells round their bodies, and piece of bark cloth
or calico, if they have it, fastened to this in front, brought up between the limbs
and spread out behind. They have some strings of beads round their necks, and
glass bracelets, and anklets. Everyone without exception during this cold season is
frightfully dirty, and is covered with dust. How would you enjoy a crowd of these
ladies, some fat and young, some old and shrivelled, some with big babies, some
with little, all in the national costume, to come, and curiously look, and talk about
the white man and his queer looking wife!

When they reached Ujiji on Lake Tanganyika they were given hospitality by
Rumalisa, 'the chief Arab at Ujiji', where they observed aspects of the slave trade:

15 July 1890

There are many slaves in Ujiji, but they are kept out of sight as much as possible.
The misery of the few we saw in Rumalisa's, and others, chained at the houses of
several of the Arabs, made us feel keenly the wickedness of tearing these poor simple
people from their homes, and then selling and buying them like animals. One of
the regular articles of sale at the market every morning is Human Beings, and to
supply the demand, and also to provide carriers for their tons of ivory, such men as
Rumalisa keep large bands of lawless, ruthless soldiers, scouring the country, and
raiding all the peaceful and less powerful tribes. We saw one of these fierce armies
come in one day, gesticulating, shouting, and firing guns. It was so dangerous that
Rumalisa ordered the doors of his courtyard to be shut till they had fired off all their
guns, and it was safe to let them in. And these were his own men.

Having returned to the Lake Nyasa area they spent some time in the Wankonde
villages at north end of Lake Nyasa:

7 September 1890

I cannot tell you how lovely these Wankonde villages are. They extend for miles on
the higher parts of the plain, and it is most refreshing to leave the glare of the hot sun

and to walk along under the cool green shade of the endless banana groves in which the villages nestle. It is like walking through one vast palm house or winter garden, and the beautifully made cow houses, and huts, are like ornamental summer houses. There are also magnificent India-rubber trees, many of them equal to fair-sized Horse Chestnut trees at home, and you can fancy in this hot land how delightful the perfect shade they make is. In the Chief's principal villages there are always some very large trees – either Cotton or Missianguti; the last are immense, and the leaves are of a dark glossy green, in shape something like the Ash, only much bigger . . . And the people, of whom there are thousands, are almost, without exception, very handsome. Especially at Makyusa's, the men are magnificent, the larger proportion of them being over six feet high, and splendidly made.

Journalists Marie Imandt and Bessie Maxwell wrote for the publications of D. C. Thomson of Dundee. Imandt, born in 1860, was the daughter of Peter Imandt, a Prussian émigré and friend of Karl Marx. Educated at the Dundee High School, she was in 1880 among the first women to receive a Lady Literate in Arts from St Andrews University. Bessie Maxwell, born in 1871, also educated at Dundee High School, studied at University College, Dundee. In 1894 they were sent by D. C. Thomson on a tour round the world, articles about their trip being published regularly in the *Dundee Courier and Argus* and *Weekly News* in 1894 and early 1895.[5] The tour included France, Italy, Egypt, India, Singapore, Hong Kong, China, Japan, the United States and Canada. Publicised as a unique and innovative initiative, it was specifically part of their remit to write about the position of women in the countries they visited. The *Dundee Courier and Argus* is available online at the British Library Nineteenth Century Newspapers.

### 3.5 Marie Imandt and Bessie Maxwell, articles from *Dundee Courier and Argus* and *Weekly News*, 1894 and 1895

Calcutta Jute Workers
Titaghur Mill (Mr George Nairn) has also an excellent situation, and in its organisation shows considerable care for the workers and enterprise. I also visited Howrah Mill (Messrs Ernesthansen & Co), manager, Mr Donald. Here I noticed women employed in the selecting, carding, and warp winding departments. The employees here are – men, 2371, women, 771, and children, 565. At Ganges Jute Mill, the oldest in Calcutta (Messrs McNeil & Co), manager, Mr Alexander, I had a good deal of conversation with women workers . . . To my questions as to whether they liked the mill work the usual reply was that they had to make their own living, and could not do it in any other way. Some were widows, others were wives of the men working in the mill. Nearly every woman had the edges of her teeth quite black. This is caused by betel chewing, and at Ganges Mill I saw within the mill yard an ancient dame squatted on the ground with a variety of baskets spread before her. The women patronised her as they came from work, and I could not but appreciate the healthy nature of the food they were buying. These were little bundles of dahl and parched grain, sweet meats made of dahl and butter, with sugar rolled into

round balls and fried, also choupatti. She had a goodly stock of betel, the luxury that blackens the teeth, and makes the inside of the mouth red, but is otherwise inoffensive. At Barnagore branch,

### Mill at Balliaghatta

1500 people are employed, 300 of whom are women. Mr Byars, the manager here, told me that many of the workpeople are Musulmans, and very wild and trouble-some. The Bengali, on the other hand, are gentle and timid. I was told in most of the mills that strikes do occur at times, in which cases the workers band themselves firmly together, and are wild and difficult to manage . . .
[F Marie Imandt]

## *Dundee Courier and Argus,* 30 July 1894

Mining in India, Women as Miners
The statement that

### Women are Employed in the Mines

is likely to strengthen the indignant protests made at home against the employment of women as "beasts of burden." That women have to work all the world over is now a fact allowing no question. To those who work with head or hands at occupations light physically compared to the manual toil of field work or mines the condition of women in the East appears pitiable. One grows accustomed very quickly to the sight of the woman toiler, the headcarrier, the fieldworker, the miner, and then one begins to question whether after all our British ideas are like the Pope himself, infallible. One thinks of the barmaid whose conditions of labour are well known; of the 'slavey' in a large household, the only one; of the girl in the sweater's den; the clerk in a large cheap-jack establishment in a prosperous city; the girl who has to keep up appearances necessary according to European ideas on a pittance, and then one's faith in the infallibility of a Christian land's decrees on the conditions of woman and woman's labour totters.

. . .

. . . Women are employed to carry away the coal dust, and also to load the trolleys. The mine was quite clean and dry, the gallery and passages large, roomy, and high. There was no fire-damp to cause bad air, consequently the position of the women workers did not strike me as in way peculiarly hard compared to that of other women workers. Their appearance was much more healthy than that of the women in European sweaters' dens to whom I have already referred . . .
[F Marie Imandt]

In articles on Canada, women's work was discussed: for example, teachers, librar-ians, seamstresses, shop workers, and domestic servants. Discussion on domestic servants was accompanied by advice for would-be emigrants from Scotland.

*Weekly News,* 19 January 1895
As to women emigrating to Canada, I have made a very careful study of the condi-tion of domestic servants. The question is a very serious one, and the sending out

of Scotch girls wholesale is not its solution. "Keep your women at home," an old settler told me, "unless they are sent out under protected emigration. Some of the girls who are sent out are utterly unfitted for domestic service. What Scotch lady at home would employ them? A lady here is far less likely to hire such servants since she can so easily get a Chinaman." "The man in my kitchen is a gentleman," I was told in one of the settlements, as the Chinese servant led us home across the prairie with a lantern which he had considerately brought to the station for the master's benefit. I went into his kitchen next morning, and beheld a picture which one rarely finds under the reign of a Scotch general. The kitchen was absolutely and perfectly tidy. The range shone like a mirror. Ironing at a table in the centre of the kitchen, the Chinaman stood dressed in snowy, starched linen, his pigtail tied with scarlet. He smiled me a kind good morning, and gave me the recipe for some exquisite hot cakes he had served up for breakfast. By recognising in his servant a gentleman, my friend gave the whole key to

### The Present Domestic Battle

To say all servants are bad is to prate like a fool. There are many excellent servants, but these are wanted at home. They always find good places. The servants who spoil the market, who are driven to emigrate, are the lazy and careless, along with the incompetent . . .

. . .

. . . "Keep your ignorant, untrained Scotch lassies at home." They are serious words, and they were spoken seriously. Girls, before you dream of emigrating, be sure what work you mean to take up, and master it. If you wish to be servants, you have every opportunity of earning a comfortable livelihood, but you must go abroad as *trained* servants. Do not think mistresses in Canada will muddle along with you as so many do in Scotland, tolerating half-done work, slipshod rooms, general untidiness, and impertinence into the bargain. They will simply turn you adrift and engage Chinamen, or, where they can't get Chinamen, do the work themselves. A clever American woman will rather do her own work than have a lassie muddling along. If, however, the Scotch lassie is smart and knows how to do her work the mistress on the other side of the pond is quite ready to make it well worth her while to emigrate.

[F Marie Imandt]

Isabella Plumb, born in Norfolk, was a Church of Scotland missionary, working for many years in Sialkot, then in Northern India, now in Pakistan. Her papers contain notebooks and other material on her mission work, and on her travels. An enthusiastic traveller, she went on trips and walking tours in India, and on one occasion returned to Scotland on a 'tour round the world', via China, Canada and the United States. Her mission work included working in orphanages, teaching, and 'zenana' work. In 1909 she published a pamphlet of her walking tour, reprinted from the *Aberdeen Journal*, 16 March 1909. In this Plumb was described as Senior Missionary at Sialkot of the Aberdeen Auxiliary of the Church of Scotland Women's Association for Foreign Missions. The tour

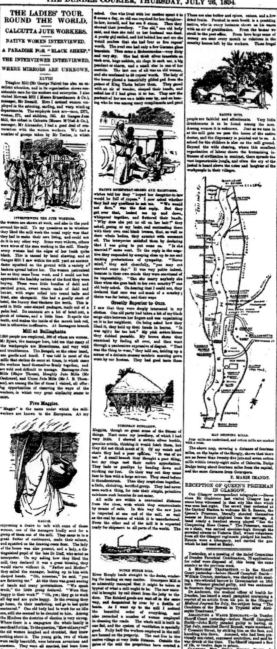

**Figure 8.2** 'The Ladies' Tour Round the World', *Dundee Courier*, Thursday, 26 July 1894. Courtesy of D. C. Thomson.

was undertaken in 1908 by Plumb, a 'lady friend', Dr Hutchison of the Chamba mission and Mr Carter, an honorary lay missionary, along with the 'coolies' who carried their tents and other equipment.

### 3.6  Isabella Plumb, *A Holiday Walking Tour in the Himalaya Mountains* (1909) [NLS, Acc. 12680/11] (4–5)

It took us three days to walk the 28 miles over the Sach Pass, 14,328 feet above sea level: we saw grand mountain torrents and lovely waterfalls. Our tents, travelling bedsteads, camp tables, and folding chairs, along with our personal baggage, were carried by coolies. On the first day, before dark, we reached Sibrundi, wet and cold; for it had rained heavily, and we were already at a height of 12,000 feet. There were no trees, for these do not grow above 11,500 feet. Next morning we resumed our climb up the mountain slopes, which were carpeted with gentians, primelias, buttercups, blue poppies, and other flowers of every hue. As we ascended higher, the colour of the flowers showed a deeper shade. On we went until we reached the top of the pass, which was covered with snow. Our attendants paid reverence to gods of stone on the summit; but on this occasion no sheep or goat was sacrificed as a thank-offering for bringing them to the top in safety. The descent was much more difficult that the ascent. There was no visible path – nothing but a wide expanse of snow: we stepped cautiously on the foot-prints of the coolies who went in front. A postman who overtook us helped me for a few yards; then his foot slipped, and he slid down the mountain side – fortunately, he was able to stop himself before reaching the rocks below. Five men had tried to cross this pass in the spring: two perished; the other three, after struggling on for five days without food, required to have part of their frost-bitten limbs cut off – an operation performed by the village blacksmith! We trudged on over snow bridges and glaciers, along narrow paths, and across mountain torrents, until we reached Donei. It was a lovely starlit night, and the row of trees above our camping-place looked like sentinels keeping guard over us.

Early next morning we proceeded first over snow and then through forests to Kilar. At Bindraban, where we halted for breakfast, two women came to have a look at us. A Pangi woman is warmly clad: a thick blanket – her only garment – is draped tastefully around her, and fastened with large brass pins. On her head is a small round cap; on her feet shoes of straw – usually a new pair every morning. We also took to straw shoes on dangerous roads, and found them safe and comfortable. The cliffs overhanging the river near Didh rise to a height of 1500 feet. We crossed this river by a wooden bridge, and climbed a steep hill on the other side, enjoying by the way delicious raspberries which grow on the hill side. At Kilar, a beautiful place encircled by huge mountains, we halted three days in the forest bungalow; cherries and English apples grow in the garden. Mr Carter exhibited his magic-lantern to a native audience, who were much interested. An ibex, only six months old and very timid, was brought to our bungalow for inspection.

## Section 4: Perspectives on Empire and colonial rule

Women's perspectives on Empire and colonial rule were perhaps most explicitly articulated within the context of support for foreign missions and the anti-slavery movement, illustrated respectively in Chapters 6 and 7. The extracts quoted below illustrate the perspectives of women who encountered Empire in a range of different ways, whether as long-term residents commenting on life in the Caribbean, India and Africa, or as critics of Imperial administration. The poem by Janet MacKenzie illustrates the response of women at home to the common experience of having a soldier son, fighting in Imperial territories.

Among Scots, slavery had its defenders as well as opponents, not surprising given the extent of Scots' Caribbean interests. Mrs Carmichael, in her description of Caribbean society, professed that she had not seen slaves maltreated. In the extracts below, she discusses frictions between white and slave society, giving her views on how slaves should be treated. Born Alison Charles Stewart to Dr Charles Stewart and Mary Erskine Stewart in the 1790s, in 1815 she married John Wilson Carmichael. She 'belonged to the upper end of the social spectrum of Scots in the Caribbean'.[6]

### 4.1 Mrs Carmichael, *Domestic Manners and Social Condition of the White, Coloured, and Negro Population of the West Indies* (London: Whittaker, Treacher and Co., 1833) (101, 105–7, 108)

I had now been about a month in Trinidad; and was already forced to admit, that the society of the Port of Spain was greatly superior to that of St. Vincent, and the style of entertainment, &c. very different. One cause of this was, the superiority of the servants; but let it be well understood that I speak of the town only, and not of the country.

. . .

. . . The old Spanish law, which had never been altered up to the period of my being in Trinidad, though it may perhaps now be changed, was a much milder code as regarded master and slave, than that of any English colony. It is but fair however to state, that though the laws of St. Vincent were not so mild, yet the inclination of the masters of slaves rendered it of little consequence to them, for the receiving of slave evidence under proper limitations was as practically followed up in St. Vincent, as if it had been the legal code of the island. In Trinidad there was even then, a positive law, that every slave upon paying his own price at a fair valuation, might if he chose immediately claim his freedom. Now this was an excellent law, because independently altogether of justice, it constituted an incitement to the slave to work with industry: that is, if he happened to have any wish for freedom, – a wish by the way, I never heard of in St. Vincent, unless by the term free, be understood *free time*, with all the allowances of a slave. The greatest boon that could be conferred on a St. Vincent slave, was to let him remain a slave with all his allowances; his grounds, house, clothing, &c., and have his *own time free*. Many good and attached negroes in St. Vincent had this favour bestowed on them; and they judged very wisely, for it enabled them to get rapidly rich, and at the same time in sickness or old age, they had a sure provision for themselves.

In Port of Spain, it may be advantageous for a domestic slave to free himself; because no servant in town can make so much money as if he were free, and either rented or possessed, in right of his wife (a slave) a piece of land. The return for the most trifling labour on land in Trinidad is so great, owing to the richness of the soil, that I know of no situation, free or slave, in town, that can bring the same income as the cultivation of vegetables and fruit. But when I was in Trinidad, it was customary (though I am not sure, but rather think it was not the law), that a slave might come to his master, and paying a certain part of his purchase money, and agreeing at a future period to pay the remainder, promise so many days in the week to serve his master, or at all events, so much time, until he had paid him all. But no sooner was this partial freedom secured, than the master was completely in their power, for there was no getting them to work the time promised to the master, – though they worked for themselves: and thus the master was cheated out of both the remaining work and money promised . . .

Many such instances of dishonesty came under my notice: nothing is more detrimental to the well-being of society than carelessness as to the performance of a promise; and as the negroes, generally speaking, are strict enough in exacting the performance of one in their favour, such conduct is not owing to ignorance, but to a deliberate want of honesty.

The extracts below come from Mrs Colin Mackenzie's *Six Years In India* published in 1857, a later edition of *The Mission, the Camp, and the Zenana* published around 1853. Mrs Mackenzie was born Helen Catharine Douglas, eldest daughter of Admiral John Erskine Douglas. She married Colin Mackenzie in 1843, returning with him to India, where he had served in the army since 1825. Both were devout evangelicals, joining the Free Church at the Disruption of 1843. The 1854 edition of her book is available online at: http://www.archive.org/details/lifeinmissionca00mackgoog

Following Mackenzie's original title, the extracts illustrate the themes of the mission, the camp, and the zenana.

4.2 Mrs Colin Mackenzie, *Six Years in India; Delhi: The City of the Great Mogul, with an account of The Various Tribes in Hindostan; Hindoos, Sikhs, Affghans, etc.* (London: Richard Bentley, New Burlington Street, 1857) (10, 112–13, 137)

*The mission*

Thursday, December 17th, 1846. – According to appointment, we drove to Dr. Duff's [Alexander Duff] house this morning, and he accompanied us to the Female Orphan School in connexion with the Free Church. Miss Laing has just moved into a new house, with a nice garden, and accommodation for one hundred pupils. As yet she has only thirty, besides one day scholar (a country-born girl), and a little Bengali child of three years old, who comes of her own free will. Most of the orphans are of Portuguese origin: they are all dressed according to the custom of their respective nations. Miss Laing is a very lady-like, attractive person, the daughter of a captain in the army, and had devoted herself to this good work from love to Him who said, "Feed my lambs." The children were all assembled in three classes, in a spacious apartment on the ground-floor, open on two sides to the outer air. Their copy-books were laid out for inspection, and, like those at the Jewish school, were remarkable for their neatness; there were no blots, no letters left out, no carelessness, like *some* copy-books at home . . .

Miss Laing showed us the house; it is very clean and simple; everything is done by the girls, who learn to wash, cook, and all kinds of household work . . . The only thing that can be done for them, as they grow up, is to marry them to Christians, as it impossible to send them to service in *any* family, on account of the heathen servants they would be obliged to mingle with. Some have been baptized in infancy; of course, none of the others are until they give evidence of conversion . . .

Miss Laing conducts morning and evening worship daily, and one of the missionaries preaches to them on the Sabbath; they are taught Bengali and English simultaneously, as at the College. Miss Laing told me that the average expense of each child, exclusive of house-rent (which is very high in Calcutta) and of the teachers' salaries, is three rupees, or six shillings a month! How many could subscribe this sum, and thus rescue an orphan from wild beasts, or from men who are even worse!

## The camp

September 30th, 1847. – A young Scotchwoman, wife of a bombardier, came to ask me if I could get a situation for her. She told us that coming up the country, the women and children were brought up in the river boats; and the voyage from Calcutta to Cawnpore was only fourteen days shorter than from Liverpool to Calcutta. They were sent up in June, the very middle of the hot season, in boats, as usual, pervious to the sun. The doctor (Macpherson by name) who was with them, took no charge of them whatever. Doctors seldom do give advice or warning to either the soldiers or their wives, thinking it of no use. The surgeon of a hussar regiment laughed at me for warning a ruddy young girl fresh from England, who was sitting bareheaded in the sun, saying, "We never give them any advice, it is of no use; we let them take their own way:" and of course numbers are sacrificed to their ignorance of the climate and its dangers. Many, doubtless, are obstinate, but not all. Money was given to these poor women for subsistence, but no one told them what food they would require, or what they ought to get; so that many of them lived on a little tea, without any milk or sugar, and thick, indigestible chapátis of wheat-flour and water. The consequence was that the deaths were frightfully numerous, five or six bodies of women and children being often buried by the river side in one morning; and yet no representation was made by their officers.

A poor soldier's wife is indeed to be pitied; she is often a young, inexperienced country girl: nobody cares for her, no one looks after her; her health is as likely to give way as any lady's in India; she is treated more like an animal than a woman, obliged to live day and night in barracks, in the same room with a crowd of rude, depraved men, married and single; probably her husband beats and kicks her; and when on board ship, she is worse off than a female convict. In India she is sent hither and thither at all seasons, and she may truly say, "No man careth for my soul," for hitherto, I have only seen two chaplains who can be considered as truly Christian men; undoubtedly there are others, but they are rari nantes &c.

### *The zenana*
Headed 'Funeral scene in a zenana', this probably took place in Delhi.

A respectable grey-bearded man showed us the way to the woman's apartments and garden, the other side of the house being occupied by the men. We found the garden full of women of all ranks, so that it was a gay rather than a mournful scene. Some of Shah Shujah's family were seated on a kind of terrace spread with carpets, where they invited us to sit; and after talking to them a little, they asked us to go within to see the nearer relations. Two of these, daughters of the poor old lady, seemed in real grief; it is not *etiquette* for them to speak, but they may be spoken to. One of them seemed as if she had wept until she could weep no more, and she occasionally groaned and rocked herself; we sat down by them and expressed our sympathy, but the other women showed no signs of feeling . . .

. . . There were several women there of great beauty, as fair as Europeans, with a very noble style of features and winning manners. There was also the first really beautiful Kashmirí I have seen, rather dark, but such eyes, nose and mouth! She looked like one of the most beautiful of the Greek Bacchante. They wanted us to stay to the feast, but this we could not do, as Mrs Newton was quite anxious to get home. Indeed, the noise and crowd were quite fatiguing; it was more like a fair than a funeral . . .

Following emancipation of slaves throughout the empire in 1838, the anti-slavery societies focused most of their attention on the campaign to abolish slavery in the United States of America. Developments in the Empire were, however, kept under scrutiny. The extract below illustrates the response of the Edinburgh Ladies' Emancipation Society to the imposition of martial law in Jamaica by Governor Eyre in response to the Morant Bay rebellion of 1865, and also their concern about developments in Sierra Leone.

### 4.3   Edinburgh Ladies' Emancipation Society, *Annual Report* (1867)

In regard to the future, these proceedings are very important; but many among us have grieved for the sufferers who have been deprived of their all by the Governor's hasty zeal, and we have been glad to find measures set on foot in several quarters for providing a Restitution Fund to assist in rebuilding the ruined dwellings, and otherwise restoring to the survivors some of the comforts torn from them by Martial Law . . . The best compensation it is in the power of their friends in this country to provide, is to send means of education, so that, under careful protection, these poor people may be able to expand the moral dignity of free citizens, and to understand contracts, regulations of wages, and other arrangements which materially affect them, and in which they have been so grievously imposed upon by the white race.

. . . The change of Government in Jamaica affords hope for the Colony, and we anxiously watch, trusting that the trials through which they have passed, may eventuate in beneficial results to the coloured population.

It is not in Jamaica alone that British Colonial subjects have to complain of class legislation. In Sierra Leone, where there is a population of nearly fifty thousand, of whom but a few hundred are white, the Governor, in Council, has passed an ordinance which . . . abolishes the right of trial by jury in civil actions, which has ever been looked upon as a great charter of social justice . . . That the body of coloured people, whom it principally affects, are sufficiently intelligent to understand the right in which they are in danger of being deprived, is evidenced by a spirited and well arranged "protest of the Africans against the ordinance to abolish trial by jury . . . "

Maria Hay Flyter Mitchell lived in India for many years with her missionary husband, the Reverend John Murray Mitchell. As noted in Chapter 6, she was an enthusiastic supporter of missionary work with women. She published several books on her life in India, including accounts of travels, domestic life and colonial society, visits to missions, and discussion of the position of women in India. The extract quoted below describes the retinue of servants required to run a household. How to manage servants, and relationships with ayahs, the Indian women who looked after European children, were also the subject of discussion by Flora Annie Steel‡ (1847–1929) and Grace Gardiner in *The Complete Indian Housekeeper and Cook* (1888).

4.4 Mrs Murray Mitchell, *In India: Sketches of Indian Life and Travel from Letters and Journals* (London, Edinburgh and New York: T. Nelson and Sons, 1876) (70–2)

The number of servants one requires is appalling. Indeed, servants and house-rent are the most formidable items in Indian expenditure; and you *must* have what is considered the proper number. It is not a matter of choice, but of necessity. The man who cleans the rooms won't touch a plate off which you have eaten, to be made Emperor of Hindustan. It would break his caste. The man who drives your horse won't groom him or cut the grass for him.

The list is pretty much as follows: – You must have the headman of whom I have spoken (the khansaman), who is responsible for all the others. He goes to bazaar and buys your food; another man (the cooly) carries it home; a third cooks it; a fourth (the khitmutgar) brings it to table, and waits on you while you eat it; and a fifth washes the plates. Then you must have a "bearer" to dust the furniture, and a "sweeper" to sweep the rooms. You must have a man to supply the house with water (the bheestee), and another (the dhobee) to take away your clothes and wash them. Then a durwan is necessary to keep your gate; and a gardener, or two if you cultivate flowers. The size of your stable must regulate the number of men required for it, as one man will not look after two horses. You must have a syce for each horse, and a coachman besides, if you own "a machine." Then if you have children, you must have ayahs corresponding with their number, and bearers as well. A durzee, or tailor, to counteract the mischief your dhobee does, who washes your clothes by thumping them on not always very smooth stones; and a peon, to go with chits, or notes, are certainly desirable, if not indispensable; besides the race of day and night punkah-walas, – who are quite indispensable in the hot season, – who have nothing else to do but pull your punkah when they choose to keep awake. As to *cheating*, a certain amount always goes on, and you must just give in to it if you want a quiet life . . .

The interview with Lady Muir, quoted below appeared in a supplement to *Woman at Home*, entitled 'Ladies of Edinburgh'. Born Elizabeth Huntly, daughter of James Wemyss, collector of Cawnpore, Lady Muir was the wife of Sir William Muir who, following a career as a colonial administrator, became Principal of Edinburgh University in 1885. From an aristocratic family, she married at seventeen, and spent much of her adult life in India. 'Ladies of Edinburgh' included interviews with Margaret Blaikie (wife of Professor Blaikie of New College), Mrs Montgomery (wife of the Dean of St Mary's Cathedral), Eliza Wigham, Louisa Stevenson, Flora Stevenson, and Mrs Wauchope (a daughter of the Muirs, married to Colonel Wauchope, then Commanding Officer of Edinburgh Castle).

### 4.5 Interview with Lady Muir by Sarah Tooley, from *Woman at Home* (Annie S. Swan's magazine) (1895)

. . .

ST: "Did you find the climate of India trying, Lady Muir?" I asked.
"Not at all. I lived for thirty-eight years in India, and had very good health. My husband did not get the long furloughs which are the fashion now, and we just took one month's holiday to the hills; and that was all. Nowadays, I am told, the ladies go up to the hills as early as March, and remain throughout the hot season."

"But you must surely have found it very trying, Lady Muir, to stay down during the hot weather?"

"I should have found it much more trying to go to the hills and leave my husband to frizzle and stew on the plains by himself with no one to attend to his comforts," quickly replied Lady Muir, and I gave up the argument, for her ladyship is an old campaigner, and has a supreme contempt for modern self-indulgence. When she was in India she adopted the habits of the country, rising at five o'clock in the morning and retiring not later than ten at night. All her household concerns were over by the *déjeûner* at half-past ten, and she could spend the rest of the day in reading and resting. "It is a great mistake," she said, "for ladies to take their European habits to India. When I hear of ladies who do not rise until nine o'clock in the morning, and remain up until long past midnight, I do not wonder that they cannot endure the climate of India, and are obliged to leave their husbands and run off to the hills on the first warm day in spring. I was in India for twenty years, and never went up to the hills except with my husband when he had his yearly leave."

. . .

"And you were in the Mutiny, of course, Lady Muir?"

"Yes, I went all through the Mutiny, and was at Agra when two battles were fought. I had five children with me, and when it was thought that there would be a night attack, I was obliged to take refuge with them in a rendezvous, guarded by British soldiers. There is a model of the Kandaham-Bagh in the civil lines at Agra, where the women and children went at night to sleep," said Lady Muir, pointing to the table on which it stood, under a glass shade. "There was a great disturbance caused," she continued, "through one of the Generals not allowing the native Christians to be sheltered in the fort, and good Bishop French said, 'If those 400 native women and children are not allowed inside the fort, then I and my people will remain outside too,' and they did for one night. This was at Gwalior. Bishop French was a wonderful man, and I always thought it was such a brave stand for him to make. Of course the General had to yield and admit the natives."

When I asked Lady Muir her views about the position of women in India, she spoke with pleasure of the advance in education now being made amongst them, and deplored the unhappy position in which the widows of India still are, although, as she explained, their treatment depends greatly on the members of their own family, and cases of extreme cruelty are not general . . .

The involvement of Scots in the armed forces was prominent in their experience of Empire in the nineteenth century. As the extracts from Mrs Colin MacKenzie and Lady Muir indicate, soldiers, particularly higher-ranking commanders, could be accompanied by wives and families. At home, the Highland soldier came to be celebrated as an iconic image of Imperial conquest, and returning troops were often welcomed by large crowds.[7] Many women at home, however, viewed with anxiety the dangers that the troops of Empire faced. The poem by Janet MacKenzie, below, expresses concern for her son serving with the Seaforth Highlanders in Egypt on his way to fight in the Boer War in South Africa.

4.6 Janet MacKenzie, Bean Choinnich MhicCoinnich, Sildinis, 'Amhran Jasper', in *Sgìre a' Bhradain, Bàrdachd bho Cheann a' Loch, Eilean Leòdhais, A collection of poems and verse from Kinloch, Isle of Lewis* (Stornoway: Comunn Eachdraidh Cheann a' Loch, 2010) (133)

1

Ille dhuinn, gur tu bu toigh leam
co-dhiù a theireadh càch e.
Ille dhuinn a dh'fhàg Diluain

's a dh'fhàg fo ghruaim do mhàthair.

1

Brown-haired boy, it's you I'm missing
at least that's what others would say,
my brown-haired boy who left on
Monday,
and left your mother miserable.

2

Siud far an robh na gillean sgoinneil de
Chlann Choinnich a bha iad.
Siud far an robh na gillean ciatach
bha deich cheud air march dhiubh.

3

Bha iad ann de gach seòrsa
Dòmhnallaich is MacAoidhean ann.
Sibh mar chaoraich am buaile
sibh cuartaich air ar bràighean.

4

Sibh mar chaoraich ann am faing
's na nàimhdean is iad làmh ribh.
Is òg leam chaidh thu seachad
fo bhratach na bàn-righinn.

5

Smaointean ort le cion a' bhùirn
's tu muigh air cùl an fhàsaich.
Smaointean ort bhith san leabaidh
nad shìneadh anns na blàran.

6

Smaointean ort fo chlaidheamh rùisgt'
's e siud a chrùb gu làr mi.
'S truagh nach robh mi air do chùl
leis a' bhùrn chaoidh nach tràghadh.

7

'S truagh nach robh mi air do bheulaibh
leis a' bhiadh nam làmhan.
'S nam biodh agam sgiathan peucaig
dhan an Èipheit gun snàmhainn.

8

Dheidhinn deas air a' Mhuir Ruadh
le gaoth tuath nam fhàbhar.
Dheidhinn gu gearasdan Cheiro
b' èibhinn leamsa an t-àite.

---

2

Over there is where those brave boys
from the Seaforth's were.
That's where those fine boys were,
a thousand of them on the march.

3

There were some of every sort,
MacDonalds and MacKays.
You were like sheep in a pen,
fenced in on our high ground.

4

You were like sheep in a fank,
with the enemy close at hand.
You seemed so young as you passed by
under the banner of the Queen.

5

I think of you now without water,
out in the wilds of the desert.
I think of you in bed,
lying out on the open ground.

6

I think of you under a drawn sword.
That is what bows me to the ground.
If only I could be there behind you,
with the water that never fails.

7

If only I could be there in front of you,
with the food in my hands.
If I had the wings of a peacock,
I would fly to Egypt.

8

I would go south over the Red Sea,
with the north wind in my favour.
I would go to the garrison at Cairo
and would be happy to be there.

---

To be a supporter of the Imperial mission did not necessarily imply uncritical support for Imperial administrations, as the extract below from Flora Annie Steel's‡ popular history of India indicates. She suggests that British interventions over the position of Indian women were instrumental in causing the uprising of 1857. Born Flora Annie Webster in England, Steel came from an Anglo-Indian family with Scottish roots. She married Henry William Steel, moving with him to India, and later serving as the first female inspector of schools on the Punjab Educational Board in the 1880s. She was a prolific author, including of novels, short stories and an autobiography, but is perhaps best known for *The Complete Indian Cook and Housekeeper* (1888) co-authored with Grace Gardiner. This handbook on how to live in India was a popular success, going through several editions.

> ## 4.7 Flora Annie Steel, *India Through the Ages: a popular and picturesque history of Hindustan* (London: George Routledge & Sons, Limited; New York: E. P. Dutton & Co., 1908) (345–7)

Chapter: 'Manners, Morals, and Missionaries A.D. 1850 to A.D. 1857

. . . The question of the annexation of Oude . . . is so often cited as one of the chief causes of the Great Mutiny of 1857, that it is best discussed among the many other reasons for resentment and rebellion which undoubtedly existed in India at this time. One of these was the change of manners in the ruling white-faced race.

In the old days of a good year's voyaging and sea-sickness round the Cape few women had been found to face it; and so the Englishmen in India had formed irregular connections with native women, often of very good birth. These connections, though, of course, contrary to our marriage laws, were not exactly immoral; they were, indeed, often as regular as the differing codes of Christianity, Hinduism, and Mahommedanism would allow. And, naturally, they greatly bridged over the gulf between the rulers and the ruled.

The short sea-passage changed all this. English ladies came out in crowds, and seeing themselves surrounded by native sister-subjects who thought differently to what they did on almost every conceivable social subject, held up holy hands of horror at everything they saw, oblivious, apparently, of the obvious fact, that if the native sister appeared a bogey to them, they also must have been a bogey to the native sister.

She, however, by her very seclusion, was prevented from airing her opinion. Not so the Englishwomen and young girls who began to come to live amongst those who were generally called the heathen. There is no more charitable and kindly soul than the average British matron, and in the days before '57 she was beyond measure romantic. This was the time when, escaping from the stern rule of papa and mama, who had been ready with bread and water for "miss" if she refused an eligible *parti*, the English girl looked on Love with a big L, as something only a trifle less divine than the God whom she worshipped. She was not, therefore, likely to find anything but militant pity and charity for a social system which began by ignoring love as synonymous with passion. Thus the Englishwoman was no factor for peace in the new order of things. Then the changes inaugurated by the inclusion of the "introduction of religious and moral improvement" as a licensable trade had borne much fruit. One has only to read missionary reports to find out how enormously organised effort to convert the people of India had increased since 1813, and still more from 1833. In the year 1840 Dr Duff's Christian college at Calcutta numbered over six hundred pupils, and in 1845 came the added interest to the cause of Missions brought by the great Evangelical movement, not only in the Church of England, but throughout all Europe. This wave of religiosity left no Christian sect untouched, and part of its result was the introduction into India of a race of Church-Militant officials, admirable in character, in work, who, despite their faithful performance of duties to Caesar which demanded absolute impartiality, could not divest themselves absolutely of their other duty (as they held it) to God; that is to say, to influence the natives for good – in other words, to Christianity . . .

Then, ever since the days of Lord William Bentinck, legislation had favoured the new faith. It will be remembered that he was mixed up with the mutiny at Vellore – a mutiny, if ever there was one, caused by abject fear of enforced conversion. His abolition of *suttee*, his tinkering with Indian law so as to free Hindu converts to Christianity from disabilities in succession (or as it has been put, "to free them from the trammels of their former superstitions and secure them in the full possession of Christian freedom"), had passed muster at the time, but as their effects became palpable, their interference in matters of custom and religion was resented. The very inauguration of female education was an offence, and as the years went on, bringing ever more and more missionary effort, and, above all, more support to that effort on the part of the ruling race, fear of wholesale conversion sprang up amongst the ignorant people, and was carefully fostered by the priests and preachers who had all to gain and nothing to lose by revolt.

And behind this lay slumbering a great resentment. Say what folk would, be the excuse what it might, the fact remained that the last hundred years had seen every Indian prince reduced to the position of a pensioner, his land annexed . . .

Kenya began to be settled by British colonists in the late nineteenth century; at the same time missions were established. Marion Stevenson, a minister's daughter from Forfar, financed herself from 1907 as a missionary in the Church of Scotland's mission at Kikuyu. Among other things, the mission attempted to challenge the practice of female genital mutilation, and to raise awareness of this issue at home; this was subsequently to involve the mission in political controversy. Stevenson's writings often allude to this practice. The extract below, however, describes her work itinerating to villages.

4.8 *Kikuyu News*, Church of Scotland Mission, British East Africa, No. 17, March 1910 (13–14)

'Village Work' by Miss Marion Stevenson.
*Saturday, 25th September*, 10.30 A.M. to 5 P.M. – *Muhori's*. Went down the hill past our own villages and saw a number of our people. Crossed the Nyungara river and up the opposite bank to Old Mogo's villages. All empty except for one very unpleasant old woman, who would not even show me the path. Missed it and went through a number of gardens, "greeting" the women. Two girls came to speak to me, but were at once called away. This is very frequent both in the gardens and villages. Before crossing the Nairobi river sat down to lunch. Six shepherd lads whom I know came running across to me; we talked, and I showed them Bible pictures. I

was going first to see Nyagicuhi, a woman who, at a service in Muhori's, had asked me to go to her village; so they convoyed me up the opposite bank. We found her, along with about thirty others, in Wawero's village preparing to take part in the "dance of the old women," which is danced when the sheep paid for a bride are driven into her owner's village. Some young women were there also, and the men's hut was full of drunk old men; indeed, some of the women had been drinking too. At once they wanted to see what was in my basket, and as the children here are still frightened of me, I had toys. This caused great excitement. Then the old head of the village came out to greet me, but he was so drunk that I told him I did not talk to drunk people, and he laughed and was led away by the others. I find I can do this quite without offence, and its saves me the tight corners I used sometimes to get into when drunk old men wished to be affable! Then the old women invited me to see the dance, and half a dozen began. It was so revolting, the posturings and gestures and the loathsome look on their faces, that I stopped them at once, saying I did not like Kikuyu dances. They then went into the men's hut where the main part of the "dancing" takes place. I talked to the younger women and the children, but some more drunk young men came and I thought it better to depart . . . The "work" of the day, you observe, was telling some Bible stories to six boys and the singing of a hymn, and this is a very typical day's work here.

## Select bibliography

Esther Breitenbach, *Empire and Scottish Society: the Impact of Foreign Missions at Home c.1780–c.1914* (Edinburgh: Edinburgh University Press, 2009).

T. M. Devine and John MacKenzie (eds), *Scotland and the British Empire* (Oxford: Oxford University Press, 2011).

Marjory Harper, *Emigration from North East Scotland* (Aberdeen: Aberdeen University Press, 1988).

Marjory Harper, *Adventurers and Exiles: The Great Scottish Exodus* (London: Profile Books, 2003).

Angela McCarthy, 'The Scottish Diaspora since 1815', in Devine and Wormald, *Oxford Handbook of Modern Scottish History* (Oxford: Oxford University Press, 2012), pp. 510–32.

Rosalind McClean, 'Reluctant Leavers? Scottish women and emigration in the mid nineteenth century', in Tom Brooking and Jennie Coleman (eds), *The Heather and the Fern: Scottish Migration and New Zealand Settlement* (Dunedin: University of Otago Press, 2003), pp. 103–16.

Karina Williamson, 'Mrs Carmichael: A Scotswoman in the West Indies, 1820–1826', *International Journal of Scottish Literature,* Issue 4 (2008), pp. 1–17.

## Notes

1. Dr Thomas Morland Hocken was a collector of cultural and ethnological artefacts and historical records concerning setttlement in New Zealand. His collection founded the Hocken Library, now part of the University of Otago.

2. Extracts from the works of some of these writers are included in Dorothy McMillan, *The Scotswoman at Home and Abroad* (Glasgow: Association for Scottish Library Studies, 1999).
3. A footnote by Macleod points out that Letitia was making a common mistake to say the naked baby was carried in its mother's hood – in fact, it was carried against its mother's naked back.
4. A footnote by Macleod notes that Hargrave sent a present of smoked buffalo tongues to Kilchrist House in Argyll every year.
5. Imandt and Maxwell's tour forms part of the display in the recently renovated McManus Galleries in Dundee. See also Susan Keracher, *Dundee's Two Intrepid Ladies: A Tour Round the World by D. C. Thomson's Female Journalists in 1894* (Dundee: Abertay Historical Society, 2012).
6. Karina Williamson, 'Mrs Carmichael: A Scotswoman in the West Indies, 1820– 1826', *International Journal of Scottish Literature,* Issue 4 (2008), pp. 1–17.
7. Edward Spiers, *The Scottish Soldier and Empire* (Edinburgh: Edinburgh University Press, 2006).

# Index

* denotes extract from primary source
**bold** denotes image